T0305231

Macroeconomics

Macroeconomics

The Development of Modern Methods for Policy Analysis

William Scarth

McMaster University, Canada

Edward Elgar
Cheltenham, UK • Northampton, MA, USA

Published by
Edward Elgar Publishing Limited
The Lypiatts
15 Lansdown Road
Cheltenham
Glos GL50 2JA
UK

Edward Elgar Publishing, Inc.
William Pratt House
9 Dewey Court
Northampton
Massachusetts 01060
USA

A catalogue record for this book
is available from the British Library

Library of Congress Control Number: 2013946808

ISBN 978 1 78195 387 7 (cased)
ISBN 978 1 78195 388 4 (paperback)
ISBN 978 1 78195 389 1 (eBook)

Typeset by Servis Filmsetting Ltd, Stockport, Cheshire
Printed and bound in Great Britain by T.J. International Ltd, Padstow

Contents in brief

Contents in full

Preface

Thirty-five years ago, Robert Lucas and Thomas Sargent argued that conventional macroeconomic methods were 'fatally flawed'. During the last five years, since the financial crisis in the United States and the recession throughout the Western world, the modern macroeconomics that Lucas and Sargent have championed has been roundly criticized, with Paul Krugman (2011) referring to this period of the subject's development as 'dark age macroeconomics'. Perhaps partly because of this level of controversy, macroeconomics has been a most exciting part of our discipline throughout this period. After all, it is stimulating to be involved in the initiation of new research agendas. But, while this activity is exciting for researchers in the field, it can be frustrating for students and their instructors. Journal articles by original researchers rarely represent the best pedagogic treatment of a subject, especially when the analysis becomes quite technical. Thus, a fundamental purpose of this book is to bridge the gap between intermediate macro texts and the more advanced analysis of graduate school.

But I have two other goals as well – to draw attention to the work of macroeconomists who have been trying to integrate two quite different schools of thought, and to highlight the work that can be, and has been, used to directly address policy debates. Concerning the integration of alternative paradigms, there have been two themes. On the one hand, there is the rigour and explicit micro-foundations provided by the New Classical approach, and, on the other hand, the concern with policy that stems from the Keynesian tradition of focusing on the possibility of market failure. The problem in the 1970s and 1980s was that the Classicals achieved their rigour by excluding market failure, while the Keynesians achieved their intended policy relevance by excluding explicit micro-foundations. So both schools of thought were limited in a fundamental way. This book draws attention to the analyses of macroeconomists who saw the merit in both traditions, and who were, therefore, developing models that could score well on both the criteria for judging model usefulness (consistency with empirical observation and consistency with constrained maximization principles). In many important ways, this drive toward integration has succeeded. Indeed, the integrated approach has acquired a title – the 'New Neoclassical Synthesis' – and it now occupies centre stage in the discipline. It is high time that an accessible book should focus on this accomplishment, and highlight both its historical development and its use in policy-making circles.

With the increasing use of mathematics in graduate school, virtually all undergraduate programmes now offer advanced theory courses, and it has become less appealing to use the same books at both levels. I have found it best to leave PhD students to be served by the excellent books that now exist for them, and to focus this book on the needs of senior undergraduate students and MA students in more applied programmes. With this emphasis, it is appropriate that the book stress policy application, not just the teaching of techniques. The tradition has been to assume that every student who enrols in a course at this level is so motivated that no effort is needed to demonstrate the applicability of the analysis. In contrast to this, I have found that, especially at the senior undergraduate level, each student's ability to master research methods is still very much dependent on her belief that this analysis is fundamentally 'relevant' for the issues that she talks about with non-economists. The book respects this need in every chapter. The New Neoclassical Synthesis permits a consistent comparison of the 'short-term pain' and the 'long-term gain' that are part of many policy initiatives.

Here is a brief introduction to the book's structure. Chapter 1 provides a concise summary (and extension) of intermediate-level macroeconomics, and it introduces students to both New Classical macroeconomics and Roger Farmer's (2013b) suggestions for reformulating the treatment of Keynes's ideas. The chapter ends with the identification of three shortcomings of intermediate-level modelling – the need for more explicit treatment of dynamics, expectations and micro-foundations. The next three chapters cover the analysis that has emerged to address each of these issues. Chapter 2 examines the first Neoclassical Synthesis – a system that involved the Classical model determining full equilibrium, and a Keynesian model of temporarily sticky prices determining the approach to that full equilibrium. Chapter 3 gives extensive discussion of the development of rational expectations, and Chapter 4 provides the dynamic optimization analysis that is necessary for models to have a more thorough micro base. The next three chapters cover models that are not so limited, since they incorporate model-consistent expectations and optimization underpinnings. Chapter 5 covers the first school of thought to stress the desirability of keeping these features central – real business cycle theory. Then, with temporary nominal rigidity added to a simplified New Classical model, Chapters 6 and 7 explain both the methods needed to analyse the New Neoclassical Synthesis, and the success we have had in applying this approach to a set of central policy issues. The book shifts to long-run issues for the final five chapters. Chapters 8 and

9 focus on theory and policy issues concerning the natural unemployment rate, while Chapters 10, 11 and 12 discuss both old and new growth theory. With the chapters on micro-foundations serving as the base for both the short-run and long-run analyses, roughly half of the book is devoted to each of short-run stabilization policy questions and long-run issues that relate to structural unemployment, income distribution and productivity growth.

I have tried to maintain the user-friendly exposition that has been appreciated both in my earlier book written for students at this level (Scarth, 2007) and in the several editions of the intermediate macroeconomics text (for Canadian students) that I have co-authored with Greg Mankiw (Mankiw and Scarth, 2011). I give equal treatment to explaining technical details and to exposing the essence of each result and controversy. Using basic mathematics throughout, the book introduces readers to the actual research methods of macroeconomics. But, in addition to explaining methods, it discusses the underlying logic at the intuitive level, and with an eye to both the historical development of the subject and the ability to apply the analysis to ongoing policy debates.

Concerning application, some of the highlighted topics are: the Lucas critique of standard methods for evaluating policy, credibility and dynamic consistency issues in policy design, the sustainability of rising debt levels and an evaluation of the austerity versus stimulation debate, the optimal inflation rate, the implications of alternative monetary policies for pursuing price stability (price-level versus inflation-rate targeting, fixed versus flexible exchange rates), how fiscal initiatives can substitute for monetary policy that may be constrained by the zero lower bound on nominal interest rates, tax reform (trickle-down controversies and whether second-best initial conditions can ease the trade-off between efficiency and equity objectives), theories of the natural unemployment rate and the possibility of multiple equilibria, alternative low-income support policies, and globalization (including the alleged threat to the scope for independent macro policy). Also, particular attention is paid to non-renewable resources, the ageing population, happiness economics, progressive expenditure taxes, how New Classical economists calculate 'wedges' to diagnose the causes of the recent recession, and why Keynesians stress both stability corridors and multiple equilibria in their approach.

Since economics is a learning-by-doing subject, both students and instructors may find it useful to consult the practice questions for each chapter that are available on the publisher's website: http://goo.gl/mej8LJ. There are now three questions for each chapter, and these will be updated and replaced periodically. In addition, when less technical articles and books appear that evaluate alternative approaches and branches of the literature – writings that are particularly helpful for providing overview and perspective – these references will be added to the recommended general readings section on the website. Comments on both the questions and suggestions for additional readings are most welcome: scarth@mcmaster.ca.

I have many debts to acknowledge. First, several instructors during my graduate training had a lasting and important impact on my work (David Laidler, Dick Lipsey, Michael Parkin and Tom Sargent). Second, the published work of, and most helpful discussions with, Peter Howitt, Ben McCallum and Steve Turnovsky have been instrumental in my development and contributions over the years. Third, I have benefited greatly from interaction with some impressive colleagues and graduate students: Roy Bailey, John Burbidge, Buqu Gao, Ben Heijdra, Ron Kneebone, Jean-Paul Lam, Lonnie Magee, Hamza Malik, Thomas Moutos, Tony Myatt, Siyam Rafique and John Smithin. It should, of course, be emphasized that none of these individuals can be held responsible for how I may have filtered their input.

As to the production of the book, Alan Sturmer, Alison Hornbeck and Jane Bayliss at Edward Elgar Publishing were most patient, efficient and helpful. But my greatest debt is to my wife, Kathy, whose unfailing love and support have been invaluable. Without this support I would have been unable to work at making the exciting developments in modern macroeconomics more accessible.

1

Keynes and the Classics

1.1 Introduction

Over 70 years have elapsed since the publication of Keynes's *The General Theory of Employment, Interest and Money* (1936), yet the controversies between his followers and those macroeconomists who favour a more Classical approach have remained active. One purpose of this book is to examine some of these controversies, to draw attention to developments that have led to a synthesis of important ideas from both traditions, and to illustrate in some detail how this integrated approach can inform policy debates.

At the policy level, the hallmarks of Keynesian analysis are that involuntary unemployment can exist and that, without government assistance, any adjustment of the system back to the 'natural' unemployment rate is likely to be slow and to involve cycles and overshoots. In its extreme form, the Keynesian view is that adjustment back to equilibrium simply does not take place without policy assistance. This view can be defended by maintaining either of the following positions: (1) the economy has multiple equilibria, only one of which involves 'full' employment; or (2) there is only one equilibrium, and it involves 'full' employment, but the economic system is unstable without the assistance of policy, so it cannot reach the 'full' employment equilibrium on its own.

We shall consider the issue of multiple equilibria in Chapter 9. In earlier chapters, we focus on the question of convergence to a full equilibrium. To simplify the exposition, we concentrate on stability versus outright instability, which is the extreme form of the issue. We interpret any tendency toward outright instability as analytical support for the more general proposition that adjustment between full equilibria is protracted.

In this first chapter, we examine alternative specifications of the labour market, such as perfectly flexible money wages (the textbook Classical model) and completely fixed money wages (the textbook Keynesian model), to clarify some of the causes of unemployment. We consider fixed goods prices as well (the model of generalized disequilibrium), and then we build on this background in later chapters. For example, in Chapter 2, we assume that nominal rigidities are only temporary, and we consider a dynamic analysis that has Classical properties in full equilibrium, but Keynesian features in the transitional periods on the way to full equilibrium. Almost 60 years ago, Paul Samuelson (1955) labelled this class of dynamic models the Neoclassical Synthesis. This synthesis remained the core of mainstream macroeconomics until the 1970s, when practitioners became increasingly dissatisfied with two dimensions of this work: the limited treatment of expectations and the incomplete formal micro-foundations. We devote the next two chapters to addressing these shortcomings.

In Chapter 3, we explore alternative ways of bringing expectations into the analysis. One of the interesting insights to emerge is that, even with the Classicals' most preferred specification for expectations, there is significant support for Keynes's prediction that an increased degree of price flexibility can *increase* the amount of cyclical unemployment that follows from a decrease in aggregate demand. In Chapter 4, we address the other major limitation of the analysis to that point – that formal micro-foundations have been missing. The inter-temporal optimization that is needed to overcome this shortcoming is explained in Chapter 4. Then, in Chapter 5, we examine the New Classical approach to business cycle analysis – the modern, more micro-based version of the market-clearing approach to macroeconomics, in which *no* appeal to sticky prices is involved. Then, in Chapters 6 and 7, we examine what has been called the 'New' Neoclassical Synthesis – a business cycle analysis that blends the microeconomic rigour of the New Classicals with the empirical applicability and a focus on certain market failures that have always been central features of the Keynesian tradition and the original Neoclassical Synthesis.

In the final five chapters of the book, the focus shifts from short-run stabilization issues to concerns about long-run living standards. In these chapters, we focus on structural unemployment and the challenge of raising productivity growth.

For the remainder of this introductory section, we discuss the two broad criteria economists have relied on when evaluating macro models. First, models are subjected to empirical tests, to see whether the predictions are consistent with actual experience. This criterion is fundamentally important. Unfortunately, however, it cannot be the only one for model selection, since empirical tests are often not definitive. Thus, while progress has been made in developing applied methods, macroeconomists have no choice but to put at least some weight on a second criterion for model evaluation.

Since the hypothesis of constrained maximization is at the core of our discipline, all modern macroeconomists agree that macro models should be evaluated as to their consistency with optimizing underpinnings. Without a microeconomic base, there is no well-defined basis for arguing that either an ongoing stabilization policy or an increase in the average growth rate improves welfare. Increasingly, Keynesians have realized that they must acknowledge this point. Further, the challenge posed by New Classicals has forced Keynesians to admit that it is utility and production functions that are independent of government policy; agents' decision rules do not necessarily remain invariant to shifts in policy. A specific microeconomic base is required to derive how private decision rules may be adjusted in the face of major changes in policy. Another advantage is that a specific microeconomic rationale imposes more structure on macro models, so the corresponding empirical work involves fewer 'free' parameters (parameters that are not constrained by theoretical considerations and can thus take on whatever value will maximize the fit of the model). It must be admitted that the empirical success of a model is compromised if the estimation involves many free parameters.

Despite these clear advantages of an explicit microeconomic base, those who typically stress these points – the New Classicals – have had to make some acknowledgements too. They have had to admit that, until recently, their models have been inconsistent with several important empirical regularities. As a result, many of them, like Keynesians, now allow for some temporary stickiness in nominal variables. Also, since the primary goal of this school of thought is to eliminate arbitrary assumptions, its followers should not downplay the significance of aggregation issues or of the non-uniqueness problem that often plagues the solution of their models. These issues have yet to be resolved in a satisfactory manner.

During the 1970s and 1980s, controversy between New Classicals and Keynesians was frustrating for students. Each group focused on the advantages of its own approach, and tended to ignore the legitimate criticisms offered by the 'other side'. The discipline was fragmented into two schools of thought that did not interact. In the 1990s, however, there began an increased willingness on the part of macroeconomists to combine the best features of the competing approaches so that now the subject is empirically applicable, has solid micro-foundations, and allows for market failure – so economic policy can finally be explored in a rigorous fashion. Students can now explore models that combine the rigour of the New Classicals with the policy concern that preoccupies Keynesians.

The purpose of any model is to provide answers to a series of if–then questions: if one assumes a specified change in the values of the exogenous variables (those determined outside of the model), what will happen to the set of endogenous variables (those determined within the model)? A high degree of simultaneity seems to exist among the main endogenous variables (for example, household behaviour makes consumption depend on income, while the goods market-clearing condition makes output (and therefore income) depend on consumption). To cope with this simultaneity, we define macro models in the form of systems of equations for which standard solution techniques (either algebraic or geometric) can be employed. A model comprises a set of structural equations, which are definitions, equilibrium conditions, or behavioural reaction functions assumed on behalf of agents. The textbook Classical model, the textbook Keynesian model, the 'more Keynesian' model of generalized disequilibrium and the 'new' Classical model (all summarized graphically in later sections of this chapter) are standard examples.

In constructing these models, macroeconomists have disciplined their selection of alternative behavioural rules by appealing to microeconomic models of households and firms. In other words, their basis for choosing structural equations is constrained maximization at the individual level, without much concern for problems of aggregation. To keep the analysis manageable, macroeconomists sometimes restrict attention to particular components of the macroeconomy, considered one at a time. They record the resulting decision rules (the consumption function, the investment function, the money-demand function, the Phillips curve and so on, which are the first-order conditions of the constrained maximizations) as a list of structural equations. This series of equations is then brought together for solving as a standard set of simultaneous equations in which the unknowns are the endogenous variables. In other words, the procedure has two stages:

- **Stage 1**: Derive the structural equations, which define the macro model, by presenting a set of (sometimes unconnected) constrained maximization exercises (that is, define and solve a set of microeconomic problems).
- **Stage 2**: Use the set of structural equations to derive the solution or reduced-form equations (in which each endogenous variable is related explicitly to nothing but exogenous variables and parameters) and perform the counterfactual exercises (for example, derivation of the policy multipliers).

Before 1970, macroeconomics developed in a fairly orderly way, following this two-stage approach. In recent decades, however, the discipline has seen some changes in basic approaches following from the fact that macro-economists have tried to consider ever more consistent and complicated theories of household and firm behaviour. That is, the specification of the constrained maximizations in stage 1 of the analysis has been made more general by allowing for such things as dynamics and the fact that agents must make decisions on the basis of expectations of the future.

This expansion has led to some conceptual and methodological complications. Many analysts now regard it as unappealing to derive any one component structural equation without reference at stage 1 to the properties of the overall system. For example, if agents' behaviour turns out to depend on expected inflation, it is tempting to model their forecast of inflation so that it is consistent with the actual inflation process, which is determined as one of the endogenous variables within the model. From a technical point of view, such an approach means that stages 1 and 2 must be considered *simultaneously*. It also means that the form of at least some of the structural equations, and therefore the overall structure of the model itself, depends on the assumed time paths of the exogenous variables. Thus, it may be a bad practice for economists to use an estimated model found suitable for one data period as a mechanism for predicting what would happen in another period under a different set of policy reactions. We shall consider this problem, which is referred to as the Lucas critique, in later chapters. Initially, however, we restrict attention to models whose structures are assumed to be independent of the behaviour of the exogenous variables. The textbook Keynesian and Classical models (covered in the remainder of this chapter) are examples of such models.

1.2 The textbook Classical model: the labour market with flexible wages

The Classical macro model is defined by the following equations:

$$Y = C[(1-k)Y] + I(r) + G \tag{1.1}$$

$$L(Y, r) = M/P \tag{1.2}$$

$$Y = F(N, K) \tag{1.3}$$

$$W = PF_N(N, K) \tag{1.4}$$

$$W(1-k) = PS(N) \tag{1.5}$$

Equations 1.1 and 1.2 are the *IS* and *LM* relationships; the symbols Y, C, I, G, M, P, k and r denote real output, household consumption, firms' investment spending, government program spending, the nominal money supply, the price of goods, the proportional income tax rate and the interest rate. Since we ignore expectations at this point, anticipated inflation is assumed to be zero, so there is no difference between the nominal and real interest rates. The standard assumptions concerning the behavioural equations (with partial derivatives indicated by subscripts) are: I_r, $I_r < 0$, $L_Y > 0$, $0 < k$, $C_{Yd} < 1$. The usual specification of government policy (that G, k and M are set exogenously) is also imposed. The aggregate demand for goods relationship follows from the *IS* and *LM* functions, as is explained below.

Equations 1.3, 1.4 and 1.5 are the production, labour demand and labour supply functions, where W, N and K stand for the nominal wage rate, the level of employment of labour and the capital stock. The assumptions we make about the production function are standard (that is, the marginal products are positive and diminishing): F_N, F_K, $F_{NK} = F_{KN} > 0$, F_{NN}, $F_{KK} < 0$. Equation 1.4 involves the assumption of profit maximization: firms hire workers up to the point that labour's marginal product equals the real wage. It is assumed that it is not optimal for firms to follow a similar optimal hiring rule for capital, since there are installation costs. The details of this constraint are explained in Chapter 4; here we simply follow convention and assume that firms invest more in new capital, the lower are borrowing costs. We allow for a positively sloped labour supply curve by assuming $S_N > 0$. Workers care about the after-tax real wage, $W(1 - k)/P$.

In the present system, the five equations determine five endogenous variables: Y, N, r, P and W. However, the system is not fully simultaneous. Equations 1.4 and 1.5 form a subset that can determine employment and the real wage $w = W/P$. If the real wage is eliminated by substitution, equations 1.4 and 1.5 become $F_N(N, K) = S(N)/(1 - k)$. Since k and K are given exogenously, N is determined by this one equation, which is the labour market equilibrium condition. This equilibrium value of employment can then be substituted into the production function, equation 1.3, to determine output. Thus, this model involves what is called the *Classical dichotomy*: the key real variables (output and employment) are determined solely on the basis of aggregate supply relationships (the factor market relations and the production function), while the demand considerations (the *IS* and *LM* curves) determine the other variables (r and P) residually.

The model can be pictured in terms of aggregate demand and supply curves (in price-output space), so the term 'supply-side economics' can be appreciated. The aggregate demand curve comes from equations 1.1 and 1.2. Figure 1.1 gives the graphic derivation. The aggregate demand curve in the lower panel represents all those combinations of price and output that satisfy the demands for goods and assets. To check that this aggregate demand curve is negatively sloped, we take the total differential of the *IS* and *LM* equations, set the exogenous variable changes to zero, and solve for (dP/dY) after eliminating (dr) by substitution. The result is:

Slope of the aggregate demand curve = (rise/run in *P-Y* space):

$$dP/dY = -[L_Y L_r + L_r(1 - C_{Yd}(1-k))]/[I_r M/P^2] < 0 \qquad (1.6)$$

Figure 1.1 Derivation of the aggregate demand curve

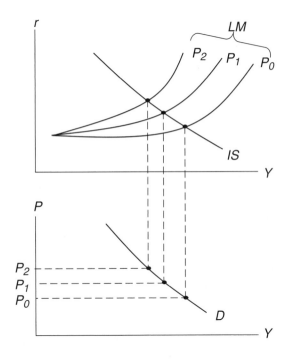

The aggregate supply curve is vertical, since *P* does not even enter the equation (any value of *P*, along with the labour market-clearing level of *Y*, satisfies these supply conditions). The summary picture, with shift variables listed in parentheses after the label for each curve, is shown in Figure 1.2. The key policy implication is that the standard monetary and fiscal policy variables, *G* and *M*, involve price effects only. For example, complete 'crowding out' follows increases in government spending (that is, output is not affected). The reason is that higher prices shrink the real value of the money supply so that interest rates are pushed up and pre-existing private investment expenditures are reduced. Nevertheless, tax policy has a role to play in this model. A tax cut shifts both the supply and the demand curves to the right. Thus, output and employment must increase, although price may go up or down. Blinder (1973) formally derives the (dP/dk) multiplier and, considering plausible parameter values, argues that it is negative. 'Supply-side' economists are those who favour applying this 'textbook Classical model' to actual policy making (as was done in the United States in the 1980s, when the more specific label 'Reaganomics' was used).

Figure 1.2 Aggregate demand and supply curves

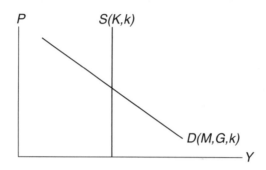

From a graphic point of view, the 'Classical dichotomy' feature of this model follows from the fact that it has a vertical aggregate supply curve. But the position of this vertical line can be shifted by tax policy. A policy of balanced-budget reduction in the size of government makes some macroeconomic sense here. Cuts in G and k may largely cancel each other in terms of affecting the position of the demand curve, but the lower tax rate stimulates labour supply, and so shifts the aggregate supply curve for goods to the right. Workers are willing to offer their services at a lower before-tax wage rate, so profit-maximizing firms are willing to hire more workers. Thus, according to this model, *both* higher output and lower prices can follow tax cuts.

This model also suggests that significantly reduced prices can be assured (without reduced output rates) if the money supply is reduced. Such a policy shifts the aggregate demand curve to the left but does not move the vertical aggregate supply curve. In the early 1980s, several Western countries tried a policy package of tax cuts along with decreased money supply growth; the motive for this policy package was, to a large extent, the belief that the Classical macro model has some short-run policy relevance. Such policies are controversial, however, because a number of analysts believe that the model ignores some key questions. Is the real-world supply curve approximately vertical in the short run? Are labour supply elasticities large enough to lead to a significant shift in aggregate supply? A number of economists doubt that these conditions are satisfied. Another key issue is the effect on macroeconomic performance that the growing government debt that accompanies this combination policy might have. After all, a decreased reliance on both taxation and money issue as methods of government finance, at the same time, may trap the government into an ever-increasing debt problem. The textbook Classical model abstracts from this consideration (as do the other standard models that we review in this introductory chapter). An explicit treatment of government debt is considered later in this book (in Chapter 7). At this point we simply report that a negative verdict on the possibility of tax cuts paying for themselves has emerged (in addition, see Mankiw and Weinzierl, 2006).

Before leaving the textbook Classical model, we summarize a graphic exposition that highlights both the goods market and the labour market. In Figure 1.3, consider that the economy starts at point A. Then a decrease in government spending occurs. The initial effect is a leftward shift of the IS curve (and therefore in the aggregate demand curve). At the initial price level, aggregate

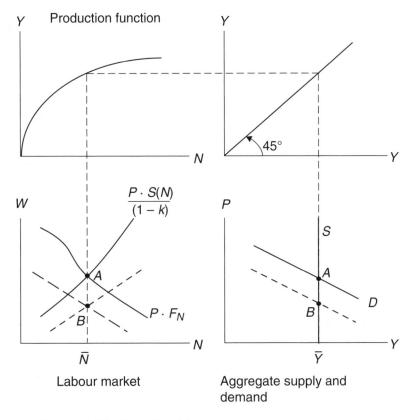

Figure 1.3 The Classical model

supply exceeds aggregate demand. The result is a fall in the price level, and this (in turn) causes two shifts in the labour market quadrant of Figure 1.3: (1) labour demand shifts down (because of the decrease in the marginal revenue product of labour); and (2) labour supply shifts down by the same proportionate amount as the decrease in the price level (because of workers' decreased money-wage claims). Both workers and firms care about real wages; had we drawn the labour market with the real wage on the vertical axis, neither the first nor the second shift would occur. These shifts occur because we must 'correct' for having drawn the labour demand and supply curves with reference to the nominal wage. The final observation point for the economy is B in both bottom panels of Figure 1.3. The economy avoids ever having a recession in actual output and employment, since the shock is fully absorbed by the falling wages and prices. These fixed levels of output and employment are often referred as the economy's 'natural rates' (denoted here by $\overline{Y}$ and $\overline{N}$).

Many economists find this model unappealing; they think they do observe recessions in response to drops in aggregate demand. Indeed, many have interpreted both the 1930s and the recent recession in 2008 as having been caused by drops in demand. What changes are required in the Classical model to make the system consistent with the existence of recessions and unemployment? We consider the New Classicals' response to this question in section 1.5 of this chapter. But, before that, we focus on the traditional Keynesian responses. Keynes considered: (1) money-wage rigidity; (2) a model of generalized disequilibrium involving both money-wage and price rigidity; and (3) expectations effects that could destabilize the economy. The first and second points can be discussed in a static framework and so are analysed in the next section of this introductory chapter. The third point requires a dynamic analysis, which will be undertaken in Chapters 2 and 3.

1.3 The textbook Keynesian model: the labour market with money-wage rigidity

Contracts, explicit or implicit, often fix money wages for a period of time. In Chapter 8, we shall consider some of the considerations that might motivate these contracts. For the present, however, we simply presume the existence of fixed money-wage contracts and we explore their macroeconomic implications.

On the assumption that money wages are fixed by contracts for the entire relevant short run, W is now taken as an exogenous variable stuck at value $\overline{W}$. Some further change in the model is required, however, since otherwise we would now have five equations in four unknowns – Y, N, r and P.

Since the money wage does not clear the labour market in this case, we must distinguish actual employment, labour demand and labour supply, which are all equal only in equilibrium. The standard assumption in disequilibrium analyses is to assume that firms have the 'right to manage' the size of their labour force during the period after which the wage has been set. This means that labour demand is always satisfied, and that the five endogenous variables are now Y, r, P, N, N^S, where the latter variable is desired labour supply. Since this variable occurs nowhere in the model except in equation 1.5, that equation solves residually for N^S. Actual employment is determined by the intersection of the labour demand curve and the given money-wage line.

Figure 1.4 is a graphic representation of the results of a decrease in government spending. As before, we start from the observation point A and assume a decrease in government spending that moves the aggregate demand curve to the left. The resulting excess supply of goods causes price to decrease, with the same shifts in the labour demand and the labour supply curves as were discussed above. The observation point becomes B in both panels of Figure 1.4. The unemployment rate, which was zero, is now BD/CD. Unemployment has two components: lay-offs, AB, plus increased participation in the labour force, AD.

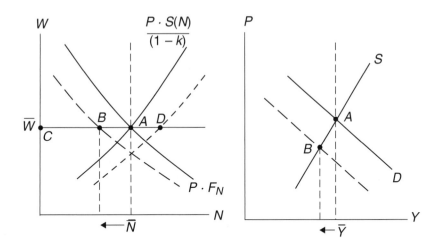

Figure 1.4 Fixed money wages and excess labour supply

The short-run aggregate supply curve in the Keynesian model is positively sloped, and this is why the model does not display the Classical dichotomy results (that is, why demand shocks have real effects). The reader can verify that the aggregate supply curve's slope is positive, by taking the total differential of the key equations (1.3 and 1.4) while imposing the assumptions that wages and the capital stock are fixed in the short run (that is, by setting $d\overline{W} = dK = 0$). After eliminating the change in employment by substitution, the result is the expression for the slope of the aggregate supply curve:

$$dP/dY = -PF_{NN}/F_N^2 > 0. \qquad (1.7)$$

The entire position of this short-run aggregate supply curve is shifted up and in to the left if there is an increase in the wage rate (in symbols, an increase in $\overline{W}$). A similar change in any input price has the same effect. Thus, for an oil-using economy, an increase in the price of oil causes stagflation – a simultaneous increase in both unemployment and inflation.

Additional considerations can be modelled on the demand side of the labour market as well. For example, if we assume that there is monopolistic competition, the marginal-cost-equals-marginal-revenue condition becomes slightly more complicated. Marginal cost still equals W/F_N, but marginal revenue becomes equal to $[1 - 1/(n\varepsilon)]P$ where n and ε are the number of firms in the industry (economy) and the elasticity of the demand curve for the industry's (whole economy's) output. In this case, the number of firms becomes a shift influence for the position of the demand curve for labour. If the number of firms rises in good times and falls in bad times, the corresponding shifts in the position of the labour demand curve (and therefore in the position of the goods supply curve) generate a series of booms and recessions. And real wages will rise during the booms and fall during the recessions (that is, the real wage will move pro-cyclically). But this imperfect-competition extension of the standard textbook Keynesian model is rarely considered. As a result, the following summary is what has become conventional wisdom.

Unemployment occurs in the Keynesian model because of wage rigidity. This can be reduced by *any* of the following policies: increasing government spending, increasing the money supply or reducing the money wage (think of an exogenous decrease in wages accomplished by policy as the static equivalent of a wage guidelines policy). These policy propositions can be proved by verifying that $dN/dG, dN/dM > 0$ and that $dN/d\overline{W} < 0$. Using more everyday language, the properties of the perfect-competition version of the rigid money-wage model are:

1. Unemployment can exist only because the wage is 'too high'.
2. Unemployment can be lowered only if the level of real incomes of those already employed (the real wage) is reduced.
3. The level of the real wage must correlate inversely with the level of employment (that is, it must move contra-cyclically).

Intermediate textbooks call this model the Keynesian system. However, many economists who regard themselves as Keynesians have a difficult time accepting these three propositions. They know that Keynes argued, in Chapter 19 of *The General Theory*, that large wage cuts might have only worsened the Depression of the 1930s. They feel that unemployment stems from some kind of market failure, so it should be possible to help unemployed workers without hurting those already employed. Finally, they have observed that there is no strong contra-cyclical movement to the real wage; indeed, it often increases slightly when employment increases (see Solon et al., 1994 and Huang et al., 2004).

1.4 Generalized disequilibrium: money-wage and price rigidity

These inconsistencies between Keynesian beliefs on the one hand and the properties of the textbook (perfect competition version of the) Keynesian model on the other suggest that Keynesian economists must have developed other models that involve more fundamental departures from the Classical system. One of these developments is the generalization of the notion of disequilibrium to apply beyond the labour market, a concept pioneered by Barro and Grossman (1971) and Malinvaud (1977).

If the price level is rigid in the short run, the aggregate supply curve is horizontal. There are two ways in which this specification can be defended. One becomes evident when we focus on slope expression (equation 1.7). This expression equals zero if $F_{NN} = 0$. To put the point verbally, the marginal product of labour is constant if labour and capital must be combined in fixed proportions. This set of assumptions – rigid money wages and fixed-coefficient technology – is often appealed to in defending fixed-price models. (Note that these models are the opposite of supply-side economics, since, with a horizontal supply curve, output is completely demand-determined, not supply-determined.)

Another defence for price rigidity is simply the existence of long-term contracts fixing the money price of goods as well as the money price of factors. To use this interpretation, however, we must re-derive the equations in the macro model that relate to firms, since, if the goods market is not clearing, it may no longer be sensible for firms to set marginal revenue equal to marginal cost. This situation is evident in Figure 1.5, which shows a perfectly competitive firm facing a sales constraint. If there were no sales constraint, the firm would operate at point A, with marginal revenue (which equals price) equal to marginal cost. Since marginal cost $= \overline{W}(dN/dY) = \overline{W}/F_N$, this is the assumption we have made throughout our analysis of Keynesian models up to this point. But, if the market price is fixed for a time (at $\bar{P}$) and aggregate demand falls so that all firms face a sales constraint (sales fixed at $\tilde{Y}$), the firm will operate at point B. The marginal revenue schedule now has two components: $\bar{P}B$ and $\tilde{Y}D$ in Figure 1.5. Thus, marginal revenue and marginal cost diverge by amount BC.

Figure 1.5 A competitive firm facing a sales constraint

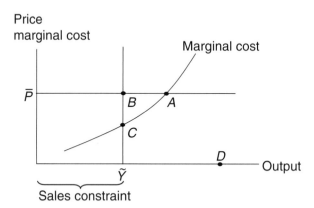

We derive formally the factor demand equations in Chapter 4 – both those relevant for the textbook Classical and textbook Keynesian models (where there is no sales constraint), and those relevant for this generalized disequilibrium version of Keynesian economics. Here, we simply assert the results that are obtained in the sticky-goods-price case. First, the labour demand curve becomes a vertical line (in wage-employment space). The corresponding equation is simply the production function – inverted and solved for N – which stipulates that labour demand is whatever solves the production function after the historically determined value for the capital stock and the sales-constrained value for output have been substituted in. The revised investment function follows immediately from cost minimization. Firms should invest more in capital whenever the excess of capital's marginal product over labour's marginal product is bigger than the excess of capital's rental price over labour's rental price. Using δ to denote capital's depreciation rate, the investment function that is derived in Chapter 4 is:

$$I = a[(F_K(W/P))/(F_N(r + \delta)) - 1]. \qquad (1.8)$$

The model now has two key differences from what we labelled the textbook Keynesian model. First, labour demand is now independent of the real wage, so any reduction in the real wage does not help in raising employment. Second, the real wage is now a shift variable for the IS curve, and therefore for the aggregate demand curve for goods, so nominal wage cuts can decrease aggregate demand and thereby lower employment. (This second point is explained more fully below.) These properties can be verified formally by noting that the model becomes simply equations 1.1 to 1.3 but with W and P exogenous and with the revised investment function replacing $I(r)$. The three endogenous variables are Y, r and N, with N solved residually by equation 1.3.

The model is presented graphically in Figure 1.6. The initial observation point is A in both the goods and labour markets. Assume a decrease in government expenditure. The demand for goods curve moves left so firms can only sell $\tilde{Y}$; the labour demand curve becomes the $\tilde{N}$ line, and the observation point moves to point B in both diagrams. Unemployment clearly exists. Can it be eliminated? Increases in M or G would shift the demand for goods back, so these policies would still work. But what about a wage cut? If the $\overline{W}$ line shifts down, all that happens is that income is redistributed from labour to capitalists (as shown by the shaded rectangle). If capitalists have a smaller marginal propensity to consume than workers, the demand for goods shifts further to the left, leading to further declines in real output and employment. The demand for goods shifts to the left in any event, however, since, given the modified investment function (equation 1.8), the lower wage reduces investment. Thus, wage cuts actually make unemployment worse.

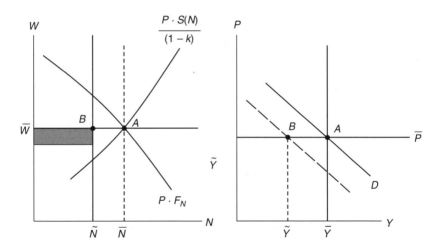

Figure 1.6 The effects of falling demand with fixed wages and prices

Some Keynesians find this generalized disequilibrium model appealing, since it supports the proposition that activist aggregate demand policy can still successfully cure recessions while wage cuts cannot. Thus the unemployed can be helped without taking from workers who are already employed (that is, without having to lower the real wage). However, the prediction that wage cuts lead to lower employment requires the assumption that prices do not fall as wages do. In Figure 1.6, the reader can verify that, if *both* the given wage and price lines shift down (so that the real wage remains constant), output and employment must increase. The falling price allows point *B* to shift down the dashed aggregate demand curve for goods, so the sales-constrained level of output rises (sales become less constrained). Further, with a less binding sales constraint, the position of the vertical labour demand curve shifts to the right.

Many economists are not comfortable with the assumption that goods prices are *more* sticky than money wages. This discomfort forces them to downplay the significance of the prediction that wage cuts could worsen a recession, at least as shown in generalized disequilibrium models of the sort just summarized. As a result, other implications of sticky prices are sometimes stressed. One concerns the accumulation of inventories that must occur when firms are surprised by an emerging sales constraint. In the standard models, firms simply accept this build-up and never attempt to work inventories back down to some target level. Macro models focusing on inventory fluctuations were very popular many years ago (for example, Metzler, 1941). Space limitations preclude our reviewing these analyses, but the reader is encouraged to consult Blinder (1981). Suffice it to say here that macroeconomic stability is problematic when firms try to work off large inventory holdings, since periods of excess supply must be followed by periods of excess demand. As a result, it is difficult to avoid overshoots when inventories are explicitly modelled. Readers wishing to pursue the disequilibrium literature more generally should consult Stoneman (1979) and especially Backhouse and Boianovsky (2013).

It may have occurred to readers that more Keynesian results would emerge from this analysis if the aggregate demand curve were not negatively sloped. For example, if it were vertical, a falling goods price would never remove the initial sales constraint. And, if the demand curve were positively sloped, falling prices would make the sales constraint ever more binding. Is there any reason to believe that such non-standard versions of the aggregate demand curve warrant serious consideration? Keynes would have answered 'yes', since he stressed a phenomenon which he called a 'liquidity trap'. This special case of our general model can be considered by letting the interest sensitivity of money demand become very large: $L_r \rightarrow -\infty$. By checking the slope expression for the aggregate demand curve (equation 1.6 above), the reader can verify that this situation involves the aggregate demand curve becoming ever steeper and becoming vertical. In this case, falling wages and prices *cannot* eliminate the recession. And this situation can be expected to emerge if interest rates become so low that expected capital losses on assets other than money are deemed a certainty. This is precisely what Keynes thought was relevant in the 1930s, and what others have thought was relevant in Japan in the 1990s and in the United States after the 2008 recession – all periods when the short-term nominal interest rate became zero.

More Classically minded economists have always dismissed the relevance of the liquidity trap, since they have noted that the vertical-demand-curve feature does not emerge when the textbook model is extended in a simple way. Following Pigou (1943), they have allowed the household consumption–savings decision to depend on the quantity of liquid assets available, not just on the level of disposable income – by making the consumption function $C[(1 - k)Y, M/P]$. With this second term in the consumption function, known as the Pigou effect, the aggregate demand curve remains negatively sloped, since falling prices raise the real value of household money hold-ings and so they stimulate spending directly, *even if* there is a liquidity trap. However, according to Tobin's (1975) interpretation, the Pigou effect has been paid far too much attention. Tobin prefers to stress I. Fisher's (1933) debt-deflation analysis. Tobin notes that the nation's money supply is mostly people's deposits in banks, and that almost all of these deposits are matched on the banks' balance sheets by other people's loans. A falling price of goods raises both the real value of lenders' assets and the real value of borrowers' liabilities. The overall effect on aggregate demand depends on the propensi-ties to consume of the two groups. Given that borrowers take out loans to spend, they must have higher spending propensities than lenders. Indeed, people who can afford to be lenders are thought to operate according to the permanent income hypothesis, adjusting their saving to insulate their current consumption from cyclical outcomes. So Fisher stressed that the effect of falling prices on borrowers would have to be the dominant consideration. With their debts rising in real terms as prices fall, they have to reduce their spending. Overall, then, the aggregate demand curve is positively sloped in periods when the liquidity trap is relevant.

We can use this insight to provide a simplified explanation of recent work by Farmer (2010, 2013a, 2013b). Farmer argues against the disequilibrium tra-dition in Keynesian analysis, since he thinks that sticky wages and prices are not the essence of Keynes at all. Farmer believes that the Classical demand for explicit micro-foundations must be respected, but he advocates a version of those foundations that can lead to multiple equilibria. In this approach, the essence of Keynes is that an exogenous change in 'confidence' can shift the economy from one equilibrium to another, and no appeal to sticky prices or irrationality is needed to defend how this outcome can emerge. Farmer generates the multiple-equilibria feature from a particular search-theoretic interpretation of the labour market (which we explain in Chapters 8 and 9). But we can illustrate the essence of his approach more simply by appealing to Solow's (1979) simplest version of efficiency-wage theory. As explained in Chapter 8, when worker productivity depends positively on the real wage workers receive, and when firms face a sales constraint, cost-minimizing firms find it in their interest to keep the real wage constant (even if the level of that sales constraint changes, and even if nominal wages and prices are falling).

We now combine this efficiency-wage theory of the labour market with Farmer's suggestion that we take nominal *GDP* as exogenously depending on people's confidence (what Keynes referred to as 'animal spirits'). In price-output space, the exogenous nominal *GDP* locus is a negatively sloped rectangular hyperbola. A drop in confidence shifts this locus toward the origin in the graph. If a positively sloped aggregate demand curve closes the model, the flexible-price equilibrium point shifts in the south-west direction: we observe falling prices and falling output. And people's expectations are fulfilled, so there is no inconsistency with the initial assumption that caused the shift. Flexible wages and prices do not move the economy away from this new outcome point unless they reverse animal spirits, but there is no reason for this expectational effect to emerge – given the logical structure of the model. While this is a very simplified version of Farmer's work, it is sufficient to make readers aware of the fact that there are important strands of Keynesian analysis that both reject the traditional Keynesian emphasis on disequilibrium and accept the modern dictum that macroeconomics involve explicit micro-foundations.

1.5   The New Classical model

Previous sections of this chapter have summarized the traditional macro models, the ones that are labelled Classical and Keynesian in intermediate-level texts. In recent decades, the term 'new' has been introduced to indicate that modern Classical and Keynesian macroeconomists have extended these traditional analyses. We examine this work in later chapters (Chapter 5 in the case of New Classicals and Chapter 8 in the case of New Keynesians). But it is useful to put these developments into a simple aggregate supply and demand context at this stage, and that is why we considered the work of both the generalized disequilibrium theorists and Farmer in the preceding section. The present section turns to a brief summary of the New Classical approach (again, in terms of basic aggregate supply and demand curves). As above, the goal at this stage is to allow readers to appreciate how the new work compares to the more traditional intermediate-level discussions.

New Classicals have extended the micro-foundations of their models to allow for inter-temporal decision making. One key dimension is the household labour–leisure choice. When optimizing, individuals consider not just whether to work or take leisure now, but also whether to work now or in the future. This choice is made by comparing the current real wage with the expected present value of the future real wage. The value of the real interest rate affects this calculation: a higher interest rate lowers the discounted value of future work and so stimulates labour supply today. This means that the entire position of the present period's labour supply curve, and therefore of the goods supply curve (which remains a vertical line, since wages and prices are still assumed to be fully flexible), depends on the interest rate. As a result, in the algebraic derivation of the current aggregate supply curve of goods, the *IS* relationship is used to eliminate the interest rate. The implication is that any of the standard shift influences for *IS* move the aggregate supply curve, not the aggregate demand curve, in this model. Actually, the standard *IS* relationship is replaced by one that is developed from a dynamic optimization base, but that modification need not concern us at this stage.

Following the thought experiment that we have considered in earlier sections of this chapter, consider a decrease in autonomous spending (G) as an example event that allows us to appreciate some of the properties of this New Classical framework. The first thing to consider is the effect on the interest rate and, for this, Classicals focus on the loanable funds market (with savings and investment as the supply and demand schedules respectively). Savings is output not consumed, so lower government spending on consumption goods increases national savings. With the supply curve for loanable funds shifting to the right, a lower interest rate emerges. With a higher discounted value for future work, households postpone supplying labour until this higher reward can be had, so they work less today. The result of this leftward shift in today's labour supply function is lower employment, so in the goods market graph the vertical aggregate supply curve shifts to the left. Real *GDP* falls, and the real wage rises, just as these variables move – for different reasons – in the traditional Keynesian models.

With the *IS* relationship now a part of the supply side of the goods market, what lies behind the aggregate demand function in price-output space? The answer: the *LM* relationship. For illustration, let us consider the simplest version of that relationship – the monetarist special case in which the interest sensitivity of money demand is zero and the income elasticity is unity. This 'quantity-theory' special case implies that the transactions velocity of money, V, is a constant, so the equation of the aggregate demand curve is $PY = MV$. In price-output space, this is a rectangular hyperbola which shifts closer or farther from the origin as MV falls or rises. The position of this locus is not affected by variations in autonomous spending. So the fall in G that we discussed in the previous paragraph moves the supply curve, not the demand curve, to the left. The New Classical model predicts the same as the Keynesian models do for output (a lower value for real output) but the opposite prediction for the price level (that price rises).

There are other differences in the models' predictions. For example, the Keynesian models suggest that the reduction in employment can be interpreted as lay-offs, so that the resulting unemployment can be thought of as involuntary. In the New Classical model, on the other hand, the reduction in employment must be interpreted as voluntary quits, since with continuous clearing in the labour market there is never any unemployment. Put another way, the Keynesian models predict variation in the unemployment rate, while the New Classical model predicts variation in the participation rate. But for the most basic Classical dichotomy question – can variations in the demand for goods cause variations in real economic activity – the New Classical model answers 'yes', and in this way it departs from the traditional Classical model. We pursue the New Classical research agenda more fully in Chapter 5.

1.6   Conclusions

In this chapter we have reviewed Keynesian and Classical interpretations of the goods and labour markets. Some economists, known as post-Keynesians, would argue that our analysis has been far too Classically focused, since they feel that what is traditionally called Keynesian – New or otherwise – misses much of the essence of Keynes. One post-Keynesian concern is that the traditional tools of aggregate supply and demand involve inherent logical inconsistencies. For a recent debate of these allegations, see Grieve (2010), Moseley (2010) and Scarth (2010a). Another post-Keynesian concern is that mainstream analysis treats uncertainty in a way that Keynes argued was silly. Keynes followed Knight's (1921) suggestion that risk and uncertainty were fundamentally different. Risky outcomes can be dealt with by assuming a stable probability distribution of outcomes, but some events occur so infrequently that the relevant actuarial information is not available. According to post-Keynesians, such truly uncertain outcomes simply cannot be modelled formally. Yet one more issue raised by post-Keynesians is that a truly central concept within mainstream macroeconomics – the aggregate production function – cannot be defended. We assess this allegation in Chapter 4, but beyond that we leave the concerns of the post-Keynesians to one side. Given our objective of providing a concise text that focuses on what is usually highlighted in a one-semester course, we cannot afford to consider post-Keynesian analysis further in this book. Instead, we direct readers to Wolfson (1994), and focus on the New Classical and New Keynesian revivals, and the synthesis of these approaches that has emerged, in our later chapters.

Among other things, in this chapter we have established that – as long as we ignore New Keynesian developments that focus on market failures (such as asymmetric information that leads to the payment of real wages above market clearing levels) – unemployment can exist only in the presence of some stickiness in money wages. Appreciation of this fact naturally leads to a question: should we advocate increased wage and price flexibility? We proceed with further macroeconomic analysis of this and related questions in Chapter 2, while we postpone our investigation of the microeconomic models of sticky wages and prices, market failures and multiple equilibria until later chapters.

2

The first Neoclassical Synthesis

2.1   Introduction

The traditional (that is, pre-New Classical) analysis of economic cycles involved a compact structure that included the textbook Classical and Keynesian models as special cases. This simple – yet encompassing – framework was achieved by dropping any explicit treatment of the labour market (and the production function). Instead, a single summary relationship of the supply side of the goods market was specified. That one function was an expectations-augmented Phillips curve – a relationship that imposes temporary rigidity for goods prices in the short run, but Classical dichotomy (natural-rate) features in full equilibrium. This simple, but complete, model of simultaneous fluctuations in real output and inflation consisted of two equations: a Phillips curve (the supply-side specification) and a summary of *IS–LM* theory – a simple reduced-form aggregate demand function. The purpose of this chapter is to review the properties of this standard dynamic model.

2.2   A simple dynamic model: Keynesian short-run features and a Classical full equilibrium

As just noted, traditional dynamic analysis combined a simple aggregate demand function and a Phillips curve, and expectations were ignored. The aggregate demand function was a summary of the *IS–LM* system. To proceed in a specific manner, we assume the following linear relationships:

$$y = -\alpha r + \beta g, \qquad \text{the } IS \text{ function, and}$$

$$m - p = \gamma y - \Omega r, \qquad \text{the } LM \text{ relationship.}$$

Here y, g, m and p denote the natural logarithms of real output, autonomous expenditure (sometimes assumed to be government spending), the nominal money supply, and the price level; r is the level (not the logarithm) of the interest rate, and, since (for the present) we assume that expectations of inflation are zero, r is both the real and the nominal interest rate. The Greek letters are positive slope parameters.

These *IS* and *LM* relationships can be combined to yield the aggregate demand function (by eliminating the interest rate via simple substitution). The result is:

$$y = \theta(m - p) + \xi g \qquad (2.1)$$

where

$$\theta = \alpha/(\alpha\gamma + \Omega)$$

$$\xi = \beta\Omega/(\alpha\gamma + \Omega).$$

This aggregate demand function is combined with a standard dynamic supply function (a Phillips curve) in which the 'core' inflation rate is assumed to be zero.

$$\dot{p} = \phi(y - \bar{y}) + \pi. \qquad (2.2)$$

The new notation, $\bar{y}$ and π, denote the natural rate of output (the value that emerges in the textbook Classical model, and a value we take as an exogenous variable in the present chapter) and the core inflation rate. Since p is the logarithm of the price level, its absolute time change equals the percentage change in the price level. Thus, $\dot{p}$ is the inflation rate. Initially, the core inflation rate is assumed to be zero. Later on in the chapter, we explore two other assumptions: that the core inflation rate is assumed to equal the full-equilibrium inflation rate, and that the core inflation rate adjusts through time according to the adaptive expectations hypothesis. Since we assume a constant natural rate of output, the full-equilibrium inflation rate is simply equal to the rate of monetary expansion: $\pi = \dot{m}$. If we assume the rate of monetary expansion to be zero, there is no difference between the first two definitions of the core inflation rate.

The full-equilibrium properties of this system are: $y = \bar{y}$, $\dot{p} = \pi = \dot{m}$ and $\bar{r} = (\beta g - \bar{y})/\alpha$, so (as already noted) macroeconomists talk in terms of the 'natural' output rate, the 'natural' interest rate, and the proposition that there is no lasting inflation–output trade-off. Milton Friedman (1963) went so far as to claim that inflation is 'always and everywhere' a monetary phenomenon, but this assertion is supported by the model only if prices are completely flexible (that is, if parameter φ approaches infinity). In general, the model involves simultaneous fluctuations in real output and inflation, bringing predictions such as: disinflation must involve a temporary recession. Such properties imply that Friedman's claim is accurate only when comparing full long-run equilibria. Nevertheless, the presumption that the model's full equilibrium is, in fact, reached as time proceeds should not be viewed as terribly controversial, since it turns out that this model's stability condition can be violated in only rather limited circumstances.

Keynes's approach to macroeconomics involved the concern that convergence to a Classical full equilibrium should *not* be presumed. Indeed, Keynes argued that a central task for macroeconomists is to identify those circumstances when convergence is unlikely, so that policy can be designed to ensure that real economies do not get into these circumstances. So, while this traditional model involves sticky prices in the short run (and from this vantage point, at least, it is appealing to Keynesians), the fact that – when expectations are ignored – it rejects the possibility of instability as rather unlikely makes it offensive to Keynesians. How has this model been altered to avoid this offensive feature? The answer is: by letting expected inflation depend on actual inflation, and by allowing these expectations to have demand-side effects. Thus far, we have limited the effects of anticipated inflation to the wage-/price-setting process (by allowing the core, or full-equilibrium, inflation rate to enter the Phillips curve). As an extension, we can allow the nominal and the real interest rates to differ by people's expectations concerning inflation in the short run. But, before we introduce this distinction, we discuss stability in this initial, more basic, model.

Mathematically, we can focus on the question of convergence to full equilibrium by taking the time derivative of the aggregate demand equation, assuming that autonomous spending and the money supply are not changing in an ongoing fashion (setting $\dot{g} = \dot{m} = 0$), and substituting out $\dot{p}$ by using the Phillips curve (with $\pi = 0$). The result is:

$$\dot{y} = -s(y - \bar{y}) \tag{2.3}$$

where s is the stability coefficient: $s = \phi\theta$. For the convergence of actual real output to the natural rate, we require that y rise when it is 'too low' and that y fall when it is 'too high'. These outcomes are consistent with equation 2.3 only if parameter s is positive. Thus, the model's stability condition is $s > 0$. Since summary parameter θ is defined as $\theta = \alpha/(\alpha\gamma + \Omega)$, we see that, in general, instability is impossible. The only problem that can develop is if the aggregate demand curve is not negatively sloped. It can be vertical if θ is zero, and this (in turn) is possible if the economy gets into what Keynes called a 'liquidity trap'. If the nominal interest rate approaches its lower bound of zero, the demand for money becomes limited only by agents' wealth, and the interest elasticity of money demand approaches infinity ($\Omega \rightarrow \infty$). This situation is sufficient to make both θ and s equal to zero. In short, the system does not converge to full employment in this case. Observing that interest rates were essentially zero in the United States during the 1930s, and in Japan during the 1990s, many analysts have argued that the economy's self-correction mechanism broke down in these cases. We certainly did observe very protracted recessions during these episodes (even the Great Depression in the 1930s case), so it may well be appropriate to interpret these periods in this manner. Many recent papers have returned to the zero lower bound on the nominal interest rate issue, since it has seemed most relevant to many Western economies following the financial crisis and recession of 2008. Some of the early papers in this regard are Svensson (2003), Bernanke and Reinhart (2004), Eggertsson and Woodford (2004) and Coenen et al. (2006).

Figure 2.1 illustrates the convergence to full equilibrium in the 'normal' (non-liquidity-trap) case. The long-run aggregate supply curve is vertical at the natural rate of output – reflecting the fact that, in full equilibrium, this model coincides with the textbook Classical system. But the Keynesian feature is that the price level is predetermined at each point in time, so the instantaneous, short-run aggregate supply curve is horizontal at that height. Normally, the aggregate demand curve is negatively sloped (and the shift variables are the nominal money supply and the level of autonomous spending). We consider a once-for-all drop in exogenous spending. The aggregate demand curve shifts to the left, and the economy moves from point A to B instantly. Output is completely demand-determined in the instantaneous

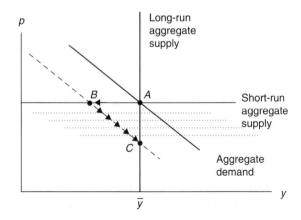

Figure 2.1 Short-run and long-run equilibria

short run. But then, as time begins to pass, prices begin to fall, and the short-run supply curve moves down to reflect this fact. The economy traces along the B-to-C time path as output comes back up to the natural rate (as point C is reached). The recession is only temporary. But this benign conclusion does not emerge if the aggregate demand curve is very steep (or vertical). If it is very steep, and it moves significantly to the left, then the price level will fall to zero before the economy gets back to the natural output rate. Keynesian economists argue that we should not downplay this non-convergence-to-full-employment possibility. More Classically minded economists are comfortable interpreting this possibility as just a remotely relevant pathology. In the next section of this chapter, we see how allowing inflationary expectations to play a role in this model makes instability a much more realistic possibility. This is why Keynesian economists always stress expectations.

2.3   The correspondence principle

We now extend our simple dynamic aggregate supply and demand model by allowing inflationary and deflationary expectations to affect aggregate demand. We continue to assume descriptive behavioural equations, leaving the consideration of formal micro-foundations until Chapter 4. We now distinguish real and nominal interest rates. The former are involved in the IS relationship, since we assume that households and firms realize that it is the real interest rate that represents the true cost of postponing consumption and borrowing. But it is the nominal interest rate that belongs in the LM equation, as long as we assume that people's portfolio choice is between non-indexed 'bonds' (which involve a real return of $r = i - \dot{p}$) and money (which involves a real return of $-\dot{p}$). The real yield differential is, therefore, i – the nominal interest rate. Notice that, to avoid having to specify a relationship between actual and expected inflation, we have simply assumed that they are equal. We consider alternative specifications later in this chapter and in Chapter 3. In any event, when the nominal interest rate is eliminated by substitution, the IS–LM summary is:

$$y = \theta(m - p) + \psi \dot{p} + \xi g. \qquad (2.1a)$$

Two of the summary aggregate demand parameters have already been defined earlier in the chapter. The coefficient on the new term is:

$$\psi = \alpha \Omega / (\alpha \gamma + \Omega).$$

At the intuitive level, the basic rationale for this term is straightforward: aggregate demand is higher if expected (equals actual) inflation rises, since people want to 'beat the price increases' by purchasing the items now. Similarly, aggregate demand is lower if people expect deflation, since in this case they want to postpone purchases so that they can benefit from the expected lower prices in the future. Thus, while current aggregate demand depends inversely on the current price of goods, it depends positively on the expected future price of goods.

On the supply side, as long as we assume (as above) that the natural output rate is constant, we know that the core (full-equilibrium) inflation rate is the money growth rate, so the aggregate supply relationship can remain as specified earlier. The model now consists of equations 2.1a and 2.2.

We are interested in determining how this simple economy reacts to shocks such as a once-for-all drop in autonomous spending. What determines how real output is affected in the short run? Under what conditions will the economy's self-correction mechanism work (that is, under what conditions will the short-run effect – a recession – be temporary and automatically eliminated)? Was Keynes right when he argued that it is a 'good' thing that prices are sticky? That is, is the magnitude or duration of the recession made worse if the short-run Phillips curve is steeper (if coefficient ϕ is larger)? It is to these questions that we now turn.

The effect of a change in autonomous expenditure on output is calculated by substituting equation 2.2 into equation 2.1a to eliminate the inflation rate. Further, we simplify by setting $\pi = \dot{m} = 0$. The resulting at-a-point-in-time reduced form for output is:

$$y = [1/(1 - \phi\psi)][\theta(m - p) - \psi\phi\bar{y} + \xi g] \qquad (2.4)$$

Taking the derivative with respect to g, we have the impact effect:

$$dy/dg = \xi/(1 - \phi\psi),$$

which is positive only if the denominator is positive. Thus, the model supports the proposition that a drop in demand causes a recession only if the denominator is positive.

It may seem surprising that – in such a simple model as this one – our basic assumptions about the signs of the parameters are not sufficient to determine the sign of this most basic policy multiplier. If we cannot 'solve' this problem in such a simple setting, we will surely be plagued with sign ambiguities in essentially all macro models that are more complicated than this one.

Macroeconomists have responded to this problem in three ways. First, on the basis of empirical work, theorists have become more confident in making *quantitative* assumptions about the model's parameters, not just *qualitative* (or sign) assumptions. But, given the controversy that surrounds most econometric work, this strategy has somewhat limited appeal. The second approach is to provide more explicit micro-foundations for the model's behavioural equations. By having a more specific theory behind these relationships, we have more restrictions on the admissible magnitudes for these structural coefficients. While this approach limits the model's sign ambiguity problems, as we shall see in Chapter 3, it does not fully eliminate them. Thus, some reliance must remain on what Paul Samuelson (1947) called the *correspondence principle* many years ago. He assumed that the least controversial additional assumption that can be made concerning the model's parameters (other than their signs) is to assume that – given infinite time – the system will eventually converge to its full equilibrium. After all, most economists presume that we eventually get to equilibrium. To exploit this belief, Samuelson's recommendation was to derive the system's *dynamic* stability condition, and then to use that condition as a restriction to help sign the *corresponding* comparative *static* multipliers. Since macroeconomists are assuming eventual convergence implicitly, Samuelson felt that nothing more of substance is being assumed when that presumption is made more explicit to sign policy multipliers. This has been standard procedure in the profession for 75 years, and we will apply the correspondence principle in our analysis here. But, before doing so, we note that some macroeconomists regard the use of the correspondence principle as suspect.

The dissenters can see that there is a partial analogy between macroeconomists using the correspondence principle and microeconomists focusing on second-order conditions. Microeconomists use the second-order conditions to resolve sign ambiguities in their analyses – which are based on agents obeying the first-order conditions. There is no controversy in this case, because the second-order conditions are an integral part of the model, and analysts are simply making implicit assumptions explicit. But the analogy between second-order conditions in micro and dynamic stability conditions in macro breaks down, since, in most macro models, analysts have the freedom to specify more than one set of assumptions for the model's dynamics. Thus, there is an element of arbitrariness in macro applications of the correspondence principle that is not present when microeconomists rely on second-order conditions for additional restrictions. One of the purposes of providing explicit micro-foundations for macroeconomics is to discipline macro model builders so that they have less opportunity for making what others might regard as arbitrary assumptions.

A more fundamental problem with the correspondence principle is that some economists (for example, Keynes) are not prepared to assume stability. Indeed, some of them can be viewed as arguing that this issue should be the fundamental focus of research (see Tobin 1975, 1977; and Hahn and Solow, 1986). According to this approach, we should compare the stability conditions under alternative policy regimes, to see whether or not a particular policy is a built-in stabilizer. Policy regimes that lead to likely instability should be avoided. Thus, even though the stability conditions are not presumed to hold by all analysts, all economists must know how to derive these conditions. Thus, we now consider the stability condition for our aggregate supply and demand model.

The stability of the economy is assessed by taking the time derivative of equation 2.4 and using equation 2.2 to, once again, eliminate the inflation rate. In this derivation, we assume that there are no further (ongoing) changes in autonomous spending and that the natural rate is constant $(\dot{g} = \dot{\bar{y}} = 0)$. As in the simpler model which suppressed the distinction between real and nominal interest rates, the result is $\dot{y} = -s(y - \bar{y})$, but now the expression for the stability parameter is:

$$s = \theta\phi/(1 - \phi\psi).$$

As before, stability requires that s be positive; in this case, we require $\psi\phi < 1$. Applying the correspondence principle, we see that this restriction is sufficient to guarantee that the expenditure multiplier has its conventional sign. This restriction is the familiar requirement that the income sensitivity of total spending not be 'too large'. In this case, the income sensitivity comes indirectly through the dependence of aggregate demand on the expected rate of inflation, and through the dependence of inflation on the output gap.

2.4   Can increased price flexibility be destabilizing?

We are now in a position to assess whether increased price flexibility leads to more desirable responses to aggregate demand shocks. There are both 'good news' and 'bad news' aspects to an increase in the size of parameter ϕ. The good news is that the economy's speed of adjustment back to full equilibrium (following all shocks) is higher (since the speed coefficient, s, rises with ϕ). There are two dimensions to the 'bad' news. First, the size of the initial recession is larger; second, the likelihood of outright instability is increased. In terms of this standard model, it appears that Keynes expected the 'bad' news effects to outweigh the 'good' news effect. Should we agree?

Before proceeding, we should consider simple intuition. How is it possible that more flexible prices can enlarge a recession? The logic of this result runs as follows. Given that aggregate demand depends on both autonomous expenditure and inflationary expectations, which are perfectly anticipated, a decrease in autonomous expenditure has both a direct and an indirect effect. The direct effect leads to lower output. The indirect effect follows from the fact that agents realize that the fall-off in output will reduce inflation; other things being equal, this deflation raises the real interest rate, so firms reduce the investment component of aggregate demand. With increased price flexibility, this secondary effect is larger than it would be otherwise. So the Keynesian proposition that increased price flexibility has this 'bad' aspect is supported by this analysis which stresses expectations effects.

The other 'bad' aspect of higher price flexibility is that it can make the economy unstable. Some would argue that there is some support for Keynes on this question as well. It is widely presumed that we have had longer-term wage contracts since the Second World War, and this is captured in our model by a smaller value for coefficient ϕ. Except for the financial breakdown in 2008, many believe that Western economies have displayed less volatility since the Second World War. As a result, there would seem to be some evidence to support Keynes. However, C. Romer (1986) has noted that – over time – there have been important changes concerning how we measure GDP. When GDP for recent years is measured in the same way as we were constrained to measure this aggregate in pre-Second World War days, we find that the economy has not been less volatile. Thus, the jury is still out on this question. Nevertheless, we can pursue Keynes's conjecture more fully if we presume stability, and calculate the cumulative output loss following a once-for-all drop in demand.

As noted already, increased price flexibility is not all 'bad' in this model. As long as the economy remains stable, we know that the speed with which the temporary recession is eliminated is proportional to the stability and speed parameter s. We have already seen that increased price flexibility must raise s and so speed up the elimination of output disturbances.

Assuming eventual convergence, the solid line in Figure 2.2 shows the output time path following a once-for-all reduction in autonomous spending. The dashed line indicates how output responds when parameter ϕ is a larger coefficient (on the assumption that the system remains stable). The size of the initial recession is bigger, but that larger recession is eliminated more quickly. The output time path is closer to the natural output line in the latter part of the adjustment period (when prices are more

Figure 2.2
Implications of
increased price
flexibility

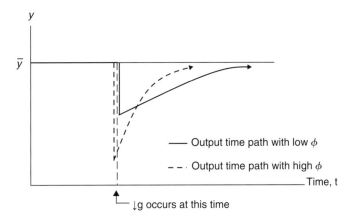

flexible), and Classicals often argue that this may be the more important consideration.

One calculation that supports the Classicals' interpretation is the total undiscounted output loss that follows a permanent decrease in aggregate demand. From a geometric point of view, this measure is the area between the output time path and the natural rate line in Figure 2.2. It can be calculated as $\int -(y - \bar{y})\, dt$, which, as Buiter and Miller (1982) show, equals the initial output loss (the impact multiplier) divided by the speed of adjustment. Thus, in this case, the cumulative output loss is $\xi/\theta\phi$. According to this method of weighting the 'bad' short-run effect and the 'good' longer-run effect of a larger parameter ϕ, then, an increased degree of price flexibility is deemed desirable. Of course, supporters of Keynes can argue that what matters is a *discounted* cumulative output loss calculation – not what we have just calculated. Once the short run is given more weight than the longer run, it is immediately apparent from Figure 2.2 that the undesirable aspects of an increased degree of price flexibility could dominate. Overall, this analysis provides at least partial analytical support for the Keynesian proposition that increased price flexibility may not help the built-in stability properties of the economy. But this partial support is limited. While the details are not presented here, it is relatively straightforward to calculate the discounted overall output loss. For plausible values for the model's parameters, the annual discount rate must be assumed to be as high as 65 per cent for the model to support Keynes. On the other hand, related analyses, for example De Long and Summers (1986) and Bhattarai, Eggersston and Schoenle (2012), find support for Keynes's concern.

Whichever way it is resolved, this issue is particularly important, since many policy analysts advocate that governments use taxes and/or subsidies to stimulate private firms and their workers to adopt such arrangements as profit sharing and shorter wage contracts. One motive for encouraging these institutional changes is a desire to increase wage flexibility (which would indirectly bring increased price flexibility), and the proponents of these policies simply presume that their adoption would be 'good'.

The opposite presumption seems to be involved at central banks, such as the Bank of Canada. Analysts there have noted that one of the 'beneficial' aspects of our reaching approximate price stability during the last quarter-century is that average contract length has increased. With low inflation, people are prepared to sign long-term wage contracts. While this means lower industrial-dispute and negotiation costs, it also means that the size of parameter ϕ is now smaller. This development is 'good' for macroeconomic stability only if Keynes was right. It appears that the Bank of Canada is comfortable siding with Keynes on this issue.

Before leaving this section, we investigate what things make the economy's stability condition more or less likely to be satisfied. We derived above that convergence to full equilibrium occurs only if $\phi\psi < 1$. To assess the plausibility of this condition being met, we focus on the detailed determinants of the reduced-form aggregate demand parameters given earlier. Using these interpretations, the stability condition can be re-expressed as:

$$1 + (\alpha\gamma/\Omega) > (\alpha\phi).$$

We consider this convergence condition in two separate situations: an ongoing inflation, such as that of the 1970s, and a deep depression, such as that of the 1930s. In a period of inflation, the equilibrium nominal interest rate is high and the interest elasticity of money demand is very low. This situation can be imposed in the stability condition by letting parameter Ω approach zero, and the result is that the stability condition *must* be satisfied. The opposite case involves extremely low interest rates (as were observed throughout the world in the deep depression of the 1930s, in Japan during its prolonged recession of the 1990s, and throughout much of the Western world in recent years). As the nominal interest rate approaches zero, many macroeconomists believe that the interest elasticity of money demand, parameter Ω, approaches infinity. As noted above, this 'liquidity-trap' situation can make it very difficult for the stability condition to be satisfied.

So, under monetary aggregate targeting at least, the efficacy of the economy's self-correction mechanism very much depends on the interest elasticity of money demand. The intuition behind this fact is straightforward. Lower prices have two effects on aggregate demand. Falling *actual* prices stimulate demand and (other things equal) help end a recession. But *expectations* of falling prices raise real interest rates, and (other things equal) dampen demand and thereby worsen a recession. The stabilizing effect of falling actual prices works through its expansionary effect on the real money supply, while the destabilizing effect of expected deflation works through lower interest rates and the associated increase in money demand. If real money demand increases more than real money supply, the initial shortfall in the demand for goods is increased. A liquidity trap maximizes the chance that the money-demand effect is stronger – making the economy unstable.

We conclude that this simple dynamic model represents a compact system that allows for Keynes's worry that wage and price decreases can worsen a deep recession through expectational effects. At the same time, however, it is important to realize that the model does not suggest that instability *must* always occur. Indeed, macroeconomists can appeal to this one simplified model, and consistently argue that government intervention was justified in the 1930s (to avoid instability or at least protracted adjustment problems) but was not required in the 1970s (to avoid hyperinflation). Since any scientist wants a single, simple model to 'explain' a host of diverse situations, it is easy to see why variants of this model represented mainstream macroeconomics for many years.

Some macroeconomists such as Leijonhufvud (1973) interpret the economy as having a stable 'corridor'. The term 'corridor' has been used to capture the notion that the economic system may well be stable in the face of small disturbances that do not push the level of activity outside its normal range of operation (the corridor). But that fact still leaves open the possibility that large shocks can push the economy out of the stable range. For example, as long as shocks are fairly small, we do not get into a liquidity trap. But sometimes a shock is big enough to make this extreme outcome relevant, and the economy is pushed out of the stable corridor. This appears to be a reasonable characterization of the Great Depression in the 1930s. At that time, individuals became convinced that bankruptcies would be prevalent. As a result, they developed an extraordinary preference for cash, and the corresponding liquidity trap destroyed the applicability of the self-correcting mechanism. It is important for Keynesians that instability does *not always* occur, so that Keynesian concerns cannot be dismissed by simply observing that there have been many episodes which have not involved macroeconomic breakdown. Leijonhufvud (1973) and Howitt (1978) have argued that models that do not permit a corridor feature of this sort cannot claim to truly represent Keynes's ideas. While this discussion of corridors has been instructive, it has not been completely rigorous. After all, formal modelling of corridors would require *non-linear* relationships, and our basic model in this chapter has involved linear relationships. It is also dated, since central banks no longer target monetary aggregates. We address this particular deficiency in the next section of this chapter.

2.5 Monetary policy as a substitute for price flexibility

Throughout the previous section of this chapter, we have reasoned as if government policy could choose the degree of price flexibility. While some countries have institutional structures that might permit this, for many others policy options are less direct. The government can only affect price flexibility indirectly, through such measures as tax incentives that might stimulate the use of profit-sharing arrangements. The question which naturally arises is whether monetary policy – an instrument over which the government has much more direct control – can be used as a substitute for price flexibility. Keynes believed that monetary policy could be used in this way. Even Milton Friedman (1953) agreed; his advocacy of flexible exchange rates was based on the presumption that this monetary policy could substitute for flexible wages and prices.

To investigate this issue formally we examine nominal income targeting – a monetary policy advocated by many economists and *The Economist* magazine in recent years. Letting $z = p + y$ denote the logarithm of nominal *GDP*, we can specify the following monetary policy reaction function:

$$m = \bar{m} - \chi(p + y - \bar{z}) \tag{2.5}$$

where the bars denote (constant) target values and parameter χ defines alternative policies: $\chi \to 0$ implies a constant money supply (what we have been assuming in the previous section); $\chi \to \infty$ implies pegging nominal income. Since the target variables are constant, the equilibrium inflation rate is zero for both of these monetary policies. This policy reaction function can be combined with equations 2.1a and 2.2. Using the methods already described, the reader can verify that the impact autonomous spending multiplier is:

$$dy/dg = \xi/(1 - \phi\psi + \theta\chi),$$

the stability and the adjustment speed parameter is:

$$s = \theta\phi(1 + \chi)/(1 - \phi\psi + \theta\chi),$$

and the cumulative output loss is $\xi/(\theta\phi(1 + \chi))$. These results imply that nominal income targeting (an increase in parameter χ) reduces the size of the impact effect which follows an aggregate demand shock, and it has an ambiguous effect on the speed with which this temporary output deviation is eliminated. These effects are not quite the same as we obtained for an increase in price flexibility, but the net effect on the undiscounted cumulative output outcome is similar. The overall output effect is made smaller by nominal income targeting. In this sense, then, a more active attempt to target nominal income *can* substitute for an attempt to vary the degree of wage/price flexibility.

As noted in the previous section, readers may regard even this extended analysis of monetary policy as somewhat dated, since central banks no longer set policy in terms of focusing on monetary aggregates. Instead, they adjust interest rates with a view to targeting price stability directly. Their research branches investigate whether their interest rate reaction function should focus on the deviation of the *inflation rate* from target (the current practice) or on the deviation of the price *level* from target. This alternative policy is preferable, since it precludes long-run drift in the cost of living, but it may not impart as much short-run built-in stability to the economy. We investigate this question in Chapter 6 (section 6.5). Here we simply assume price-level targeting on the part of an interest-rate-setting central bank. We use the analysis to consider an alternative assumption concerning inflationary expectations for two reasons. First, this alternative hypothesis was very popular at the time of the initial Neoclassical Synthesis. Second, this analysis allows us to extend our exposition of how the dynamic properties of models can be derived. The revised model involves the *IS* relationship, the relationship between the nominal and real interest rates, the central bank's nominal-interest-rate-setting rule, the Phillips curve, and the specification of adaptive expectations:

$$(y - \bar{y}) = -\alpha(r - \bar{r})$$

$$i = r + \pi$$

$$i = \bar{r} + \tau p$$

$$\dot{p} = \phi(y - \bar{y}) + \pi$$

$$\dot{\pi} = \lambda(\dot{p} - \pi)$$

We proceed by eliminating the two interest rates from the first three equations and unexpected inflation from the final two equations:

$$(y - \bar{y}) = -\alpha\tau p + \alpha\pi$$

$$\dot{\pi} = \lambda\phi(y - \bar{y})$$

Next, we take the time derivative of the first of these results, then eliminate the price change and expected inflation terms, and then take the time derivative one more time. The result is:

$$\ddot{y} = \alpha\phi(\lambda - \tau)\dot{y} - \alpha\tau\lambda\phi(y - \bar{y}) \qquad (2.6)$$

We analyse equation 2.6 by positing a trial solution and using the undetermined coefficient solution procedure.

It is worth a brief aside to explain this procedure – to clarify that it is likely to be more familiar to economics students than they realize. Consider the familiar example of compound interest. The basic relationship (the economic model) of compound interest is $x_t = (1 + r)x_{t-1}$, where r is the interest rate and x the accumulated value of wealth. We know that the solution equation for this dynamic process is $x_t = (1 + r)^t x_0$, where x_0 is the initial amount that is invested. Let us pretend that we do not know that this is the answer. To derive this solution equation, we simply posit a trial solution of the form $x_t = \mu^t A$, where the arbitrary parameters, μ and A, are yet to be determined. Substituting the trial solution into the model, we have: $\mu^t A = (1 + r)\mu^{t-1}A$ or $\mu = (1 + r)$. Similarly, substituting $t = 0$ into the trial solution, we have $A = x_0$. As a result, the initially arbitrary reduced form coefficients, μ and A, are now determined as functions of the economically meaningful parameters, r and x_0.

We use this same procedure for our macro model here. The general form for the solution of any second-order differential equation such as equation 2.6 can be written as:

$$y = \bar{y} + A_1 e^{\delta_1 t} + A_2 e^{\delta_2 t}$$

where t denotes time, the As are determined by initial conditions that disturb y away from its full-equilibrium value, and the δs are the eigenvalues. If full equilibrium is to be reached, so that any output deviation is eliminated, the time-dependent terms in this solution must eventually vanish. This requires that both the δs be negative. The expressions for the δs can be determined by substituting $y = \bar{y} + Ae^{\delta t}$ and the first and second time derivatives of this equation into the model (equation 2.6). The result is:

$$\delta^2 - \alpha\phi(\lambda - \tau)\delta + \alpha\tau\phi\lambda = 0$$

which implies that the two eigenvalues are:

$$\delta = [1/2][\alpha\phi(\lambda - \tau) \pm \sqrt{(\alpha\phi(\lambda - \tau))^2 - 4\alpha\tau\phi\lambda}]$$

The necessary and sufficient condition for both eigenvalues to be negative – that is, for the economy to be stable – is $\tau > \lambda$. This condition cannot be met when the zero lower bound on nominal interest rates is binding, since, in this case, the central bank cannot lower the interest rate, and it is as if its aggressiveness parameter τ is zero. The economy is not generally unstable, but this problem develops even before τ falls to zero.

The material in this section has had two purposes: to explain how macro models that involve two dynamic forces (not just one) can be analysed, and to establish that the stability 'corridor' concept remains of central relevance in such a more complicated setting. Of course, to be considered important in a fully modern environment we would need several further additions to the model (in addition to more dynamic forces and an up-to-date specification of monetary policy). All the behavioural equations in the model would need to be based explicitly on dynamic optimization, and there would have to be at least two different groups of households. This is precisely the setting that Eggertsson and Krugman (2012) have explored. In their model, one group of households base their current consumption decision on their optimal inter-temporal plan. For this group to increase consumption the interest rate must be lower. The other household group have a higher rate of time preference, so these individuals consume as much as they can. As a result, their consumption is given by the excess of their current income over their debt service obligations. When a financial sector shock occurs that forces this second group to lower their debt, they have no option but to lower their consumption. If the interest rate can fall enough to induce the other group to increase their consumption by an equivalent amount, there is no adjustment problem for the overall economy. But, if the required fall in the interest rate is that it become negative, then there is a recession and there is no automatic tendency for the system to return to full equilibrium. Thus, big deleveraging shocks cause problems and call for traditional Keynesian remedies, even though small shocks do not. Once again, the stability 'corridor' concept is a most helpful interpretation – whether or not the macro model embraces the modern demands of micro-foundational rigour.

2.6   Conclusions

The bulk of the analysis in this chapter has focused on a simple model that summarizes mainstream macroeconomics before the rational-expectations and New Classical 'revolutions'. This version of macroeconomics is called the Neoclassical Synthesis, since it combines important elements of both Classical and Keynesian traditions. It involves both the long-run equilibrium defined by the static textbook Classical model, and the temporary nominal stickiness feature that is the hallmark of the textbook Keynesian model (as the mechanism whereby the system departs from its full equilibrium in the short run). We have used this model to explain the correspondence principle, to examine how several monetary policies might be used to make up for the fact that prices are not more flexible, to establish whether more flexible prices are desirable or not, and to appreciate the concept of a stability 'corridor' – the proposition that we can expect macroeconomic stability in the face of 'small' shocks but perhaps not in the face of large disturbances.

We have learned how important it is to add expectations to a macro model. Initially, expectations was an issue stressed by Keynesians, since it represents a mechanism that makes convergence to full equilibrium less assured. But, more recently, macroeconomists of all persuasions highlight expectations in their analysis. This is because stabilization policy is now modelled as an ongoing operation, not an isolated one-time event, and analysts are drawn to models in which agents are fully aware of what the government has been, and will be, doing. Thus, as far as stabilization policy analysis is concerned, there has been a convergence of views in the sense that all modern analysis focuses on model-consistent expectations (as we did by equating actual and expected inflation in this chapter).

We extend our appreciation of these issues in the next two chapters, by exploring more fully alternative treatments of expectations in Chapter 3 and by providing more explicit micro-foundations for the synthesis model in Chapter 4. Once the rational-expectations (Chapter 3) and the New Classical (Chapter 5) revolutions have been explored, we will be in a position to consider an updated version of the synthesis model – the so-called 'New Neoclassical Synthesis' – in Chapters 6 and 7.

3

Model-consistent expectations

3.1 Introduction

As noted in Chapter 1, early work in macroeconomics involved a bold simplifying assumption – that economic agents have static expectations concerning the model's endogenous variables. This assumption facilitated the separation of the 'stage 1' and 'stage 2' analyses. The unappealing thing about this approach is that individuals are always surprised by the fact that these variables change. By 1970, macro theorists had come to regard it as unappealing to model households and firm managers as schizophrenic individuals. On the one hand, we assumed that individuals took great pains to pursue a detailed plan when deciding how much to consume and how to operate their firms (focusing on points of tangency between indifference maps and constraints). However, in that traditional approach, we assumed that these same individuals were quite content to just presume that many important variables that affect their decisions will never change. Why is it appealing to assume that individuals are content to be so consistently wrong on this score, while they are so careful making detailed plans in other dimensions of their decision making? And why should economists be content to build models which explain the time paths of these variables and yet involve individuals who apparently do not believe in the relevance of these models (since they do not use them to help them forecast what will happen)?

In fact, modern macroeconomists have become quite dissatisfied with this procedure that had been traditional, and they now limit their attention to models containing individuals whose expectations are consistent with the model itself. This is the rational-expectations approach (which is also called the perfect-foresight approach, if stochastic disturbances are not involved).

As far as the historical development of the subject is concerned, we can identify four approaches to modelling expectations:

- **Static expectations**. Individuals are always surprised by any changes, and so they make systematic forecast errors. This early approach had the advantage of simplicity (so that model solutions could be derived more easily) but it had the disadvantage that we assumed irrational agents. After all, when errors are *systematic*, it should be straightforward to do better.

- **Adaptive expectations**. Individuals forecast each endogenous variable by assuming that the future value will be a weighted average of past values for that variable – with the weights summing to unity and getting smaller as ever earlier time periods are considered. This hypothesis was proposed by Cagan in 1956, and it was made popular by Friedman (1957), since it played a central role in his permanent-income theory of consumption. This approach had the advantage that it did not complicate solution procedures too much, and it involved *long-run consistency* (in the sense that forecasters eventually 'get it right'). For example, consider a situation in which inflation doubles. Under adaptive expectations, expected inflation eventually doubles. However, all during the (infinite) time it takes for forecasters to reach this final adjustment, they underpredict inflation. In other words, this hypothesis still involves systematic forecast errors, so it does not involve *short-run consistency*.

- **Perfect foresight**. Individuals are assumed to be so adept at revising their forecasts in the light of new information concerning the economy's evolution that they never make any forecast errors. Economists (and other scientists) often find it useful to 'bracket the truth' by considering polar cases. For example, economists focus on the extremes of perfect competition and pure monopoly – knowing that most real-world firms find themselves in industries that are in between these two extremes. Nevertheless, since formal analysis of these intermediate cases is difficult, we learn a lot by understanding the polar cases. The hypothesis of perfect foresight has some appeal, since it is the opposite polar case to static expectations. This hypothesis was involved in our treatment of the first Neoclassical Synthesis analysis in Chapter 2. Many economists find it appealing to adopt a hypothesis that is between the polar-case extremes of perfect foresight and static expectations, and in a sense that is what adaptive expectations is. After all, perfect foresight coincides with adaptive expectations if the *very* recent past gets *all* the weight in the weighted average, and static expectations coincides with adaptive expectations if the infinitely distant past gets all the weight. But the adaptive-expectations approach – with some weight given to all time horizons – is still an unappealing way to achieve a compromise, since it involves systematic forecast error. In addition, there is no reason for agents to limit their attention to just past values of the variable that they are trying to forecast. Why wouldn't they use their knowledge of macroeconomics when forecasting? For example, suppose individuals were told that the central bank will double the money supply next year. Most people would raise their expectations of inflation when presented with this policy announcement. But people following the adaptive-expectations approach would make no such change in their forecast, because the announcement concerning the future cannot change *pre-existing* outcomes (and the latter are the only items that appear in a backward-looking forecasting rule).

- **Rational expectations**. Like adaptive expectations, this hypothesis is an attempt to have an analysis that is between perfect foresight and static expectations. It is used in models that involve the economy being hit with a series of stochastic shocks, so agents cannot know everything. But the agents in the model understand the probability distributions that are generating the shocks, so they can form expectations in a purposeful manner. Under the rational-expectations hypothesis, each agent's subjective expectation for the value of each endogenous variable is the same as what we can calculate as the mathematical expectation for that variable – as we formally solve the model. Thus, agents make forecast errors (so this hypothesis is more 'realistic' than perfect foresight), but those errors are not systematic. Perhaps a better name for this hypothesis is model-consistent expectations. In any event, most modern macroeconomists find rational expectations a very appealing approach.

As noted above, the perfect-foresight and rational-expectations hypotheses coincide if the variance of the stochastic shocks shrinks to zero. Since the policy implications of two models that differ only in this dimension are often the same, macroeconomists often rely on perfect-foresight analyses – despite the fact that this approach 'sounds' more 'unrealistic'.

We proceed through a series of analyses in this chapter. First, we introduce a stochastic disturbance term in an otherwise familiar macro model, by reconsidering the basic model of Chapter 2 when it is defined in a discrete-time specification. It turns out that – since stochastic differential equations are very difficult to analyse and since stochastic difference equations are much simpler – macroeconomists switch to discrete-time specifications when they want to stress incomplete information. We consider three aspects of uncertainty: situations in which economic agents have incomplete information concerning exogenous variables, situations in which agents (and the stabilization policy authorities) have incomplete knowledge concerning the model's slope parameters, and situations in which the functional forms of important macroeconomic relationships are not known with certainty.

Finally, in later sections of the chapter, we move on to adaptive and rational-expectations analyses.

3.2 Uncertainty in traditional macroeconomics

In Chapter 2, we focused on the economy's response to a single *one-time* shock, and the resulting time path – a one-time departure of output from its natural rate, and then a monotonic return to full equilibrium. But we are also interested in analysing *ongoing* cycles and ongoing *stochastic* shocks. One focus of this chapter is to outline how these analyses can be accomplished. We begin this chapter by reconsidering the static-expectations model of Chapter 2 – this time specified in discrete time, with a central bank that cannot perfectly control the size of the nation's money supply at each point in time.

Ignoring the autonomous spending variable and assuming a zero core inflation rate for simplicity, the model can be defined by the following equations:

$$y_t = \theta(m_t - p_t) \qquad \text{aggregate demand}$$

$$(m_t - m_{t-1}) = -\chi(y_{t-1} - \bar{y}) + u_t \qquad \text{monetary policy}$$

$$p_t - p_{t-1} = \phi(y_{t-1} - \bar{y}) = \phi\hat{y}_{t-1}. \qquad \text{Phillips curve}$$

The 'hat' denotes the output gap. The monetary policy reaction function involves the money growth rate adjusting to the most recent observation on the output gap (if χ is positive, not zero). Otherwise the money growth rate is a random variable, since we assume that u is a standard 'error' term, with expected value of zero, no serial correlation, and a constant variance. Among other things, the model can be used to assess whether 'leaning against the wind' is a good policy (as Keynesians have always recommended) or whether (as Milton Friedman has long advocated) a 'hands-off' policy is better. We can evaluate this 'rules versus discretionary policy' debate by analysing whether a zero value for parameter χ leads to a smaller value for output variance (the variable the central bank is assumed to care about, given the policy reaction function) or whether a positive value for parameter χ delivers the smaller variance. But we postpone this policy analysis for the moment, by imposing $\chi = 0$. By taking the first difference of the demand function, and substituting in both the policy reaction function and the Phillips curve, we have:

$$\hat{y}_t = v\hat{y}_{t-1} + \theta u_t. \tag{3.1}$$

where $\upsilon = (1 - \theta\phi)$. Aside from the ongoing error term, there are (in general) four possible time paths that can follow from a first-order difference equation of this sort (as shown in Figure 3.1, where we label the diagram by referring to the corresponding real output, not the percentage output gap). We observe explosion if $\upsilon > 1$, asymptotic approach to full equilibrium if $0 < \upsilon < 1$, damped oscillations if $-1 < \upsilon < 0$, and explosive cycles if $\upsilon < -1$. The standard way of using the model to 'explain' business cycles is to assume that $0 < \upsilon < 1$, and that the stochastic disturbance term keeps the economy from ever settling down to full equilibrium. With these assumptions, the model predicts *ongoing* volatility.

Figure 3.1 Possible time paths for output

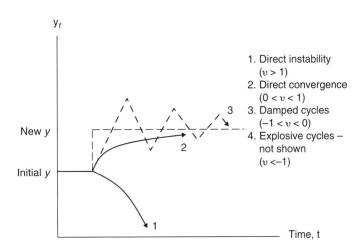

1. Direct instability
   ($\upsilon > 1$)
2. Direct convergence
   ($0 < \upsilon < 1$)
3. Damped cycles
   ($-1 < \upsilon < 0$)
4. Explosive cycles –
   not shown
   ($\upsilon < -1$)

It is useful to compare the stability conditions for continuous-time and discrete-time macro models. In the former, we saw that overshoots were not possible, so the stability condition is just a *qualitative* restriction (that the *sign* of parameter *s* be appropriate). But, in discrete time, overshoots of the full equilibrium are possible, so the stability condition involves a *quantitative* restriction on the model's parameters (that the absolute value of υ be less than unity). To maximize the generality of their analyses, macro theorists prefer to restrict their assumptions to qualitative, not quantitative, presumptions. This fact clarifies why much of modern macro theory is specified in continuous time. But, as noted above, if stochastic considerations are to form the focus of the analysis, we must put up with the more restrictive stability conditions of discrete-time analysis, since stochastic differential equations are beyond the technical abilities of many analysts.

Now let us re-introduce ongoing policy, by considering the possibility of $\chi > 0$. In this case, $\upsilon = (1 - \theta(\phi + \chi))$. Is an increase in χ a 'good' thing?

The answer appears to depend on whether v is positive or negative *before* the interventionist policy is introduced. If it is positive, interventionist policy makes parameter v smaller, and this is desirable since it either eliminates explosive behaviour or speeds up the asymptotic approach path to full equilibrium (if v were initially a positive fraction). But making χ positive could make v *become* negative, and so the well-intentioned stabilization policy could *create* cycles in economic activity that did not exist without policy. In this case, interventionist policy is not recommended. Further, if v were already a negative fraction, policy could make v go beyond the minus one value, so that policy would have caused damped cycles to be replaced by explosive cycles. These possibilities support Friedman's concern that even well-intentioned policy can be quite undesirable.

Another way of summarizing this possibility is by focusing on the asymptotic variance of the output gap, and therefore of output, y. To derive this expression, we take the expectations operator, E, through equation 3.1, using the assumption that – entering each period – the expected value of each error term is zero. The result (for output) is:

$$E(y_t) = vE(y_{t-1}).$$

When this relationship is subtracted from equation 3.1, and the outcome is squared, we have:

$$[y_t - E(y_t)]^2 = v^2[y_{t-1} - E(y_{t-1})]^2 + \theta^2 u_t^2 + 2\theta v u_t[y_{t-1} - E(y_{t-1})]. \tag{3.2}$$

The variance of y is now calculated by taking the expectations operator through equation 3.2. The result is:

$$\sigma_y^2 = [\theta^2/(1 - v^2)]\sigma_u^2. \tag{3.3}$$

It is important to clarify the information set upon which this expectation is based. We discuss two extreme assumptions. The first is that expectations are based on $(t - 1)$ period information. If so, $E_{t-1}(y_{t-1}) = y_{t-1}$ in equation 3.2 and so $\sigma_y^2 = \theta^2 \sigma_u^2$. But this assumption is not appealing if we wish to consider the effects on the economy of a whole series of stochastic shocks buffeting the system through time (at any moment, the shocks from many periods continue to have some effect). To capture this *ongoing* uncertainty in the variance calculation, we need to assume that expectations for period t are based on information from period $(t-j)$, where j is much larger than one. The convention is to calculate the *asymptotic variance* by letting j approach infinity. In this case, both $E\,[\,y_t - E(y_t)\,]^2$ and $E\,[\,y_{t-1} - E(y_{t-1})\,]^2$ equal σ_y^2, so equation 3.2 leads to 3.3.

Another way of explaining the calculation of asymptotic variance helps us appreciate this result and why it is important. The asymptotic variance captures the ongoing effect on output of an entire series of short-run disturbances. It can be calculated by evaluating:

$$E[y_{t+n} - E(y_{t+n})\,]^2.$$

An expression for y_{t+n} can be had by recursive substitution:

$$y_{t+1} = vy_t + \theta u_{t+1}$$

$$y_{t+1} = v(vy_{t-1} + \theta u_t) + \theta u_{t+1}$$

$$y_{t+1} = v^2 y_{t-1} + \theta (u_{t+1} + vu_t)$$

Following this pattern, we have:

$$y_{t+n} = v^{n+1} y_{t-1} + \theta z$$

where

$$z = u_{t+n} + vu_{t+n-1} + \ldots + v^n u_t.$$

As long as v is a fraction and n approaches infinity, we have $E(y_{t+n}) = 0$, and

$$\sigma_y^2 = \theta^2 (1 + v^2 + v^4 + \ldots)\sigma_u^2 = \theta^2 \sigma_u^2 / (1 - v^2).$$

Since an increase in the degree of policy intervention can magnify the coefficient that connects the variance of national output to the variance of the temporary shock process, it can reduce the degree to which the economy is insulated from a series of ongoing disturbances. We conclude that, when stochastic considerations are combined with time lags, it is difficult to define what institutional arrangements provide the economy with a 'built-in stabilizer'.

We can summarize as follows. The relevant coefficient for evaluating built-in stability in the face of a *series* of *temporary shocks* is $1/(1 - v^2)$, not the deterministic full-equilibrium multiplier that is familiar from intermediate macroeconomics, $1/(1 - v)$. This latter expression is relevant only for summarizing the effects of a *one-time permanent* shock. The coefficient that relates the variances is the only one that refers to the extent to which random shocks cumulate through the system. In the case of our demonstration model, we see that a more Keynesian policy (a less hands-off Friedman-like monetary policy) *must* lower $1/(1 - \upsilon)$ whether υ is positive or negative, but such a policy *may raise or lower* the more relevant reduced-form coefficient $1/(1 - \upsilon^2)$. A more Keynesian policy decreases this coefficient if υ is positive, but increases it if υ is negative. This result threatens the standard idea that an interventionist central bank can do better than one that follows Friedman's hands-off dictum. This conclusion is interesting in itself because the question of stabilization policy is important. But there is also a more general message. Simple intuition can be misleading when both time lags and the consideration of uncertainty are involved. There appears to be no substitute for an explicit treatment of these factors.

We now consider uncertainty in two different ways. First, we refer to Brainard's (1967) more general analysis, which allows both the intercept and the slope parameters to be uncertain. Second, we examine the implications of the policy maker being uncertain about the functional form of a structural equation.

Brainard was the first to analyse a stochastic macro model in which the policy maker did not know the structural parameters with certainty. Brainard considered a stabilization policy authority that tries to minimize the expected deviation of output from its target value, $E(Y - \bar{Y})^2$, subject to the fact that output, Y, is related to the policy instrument G by a simple macro model: $Y = aG + u$. Both a and u are stochastic variables with expected values equal to $\bar{a}$ and 0, with constant variances equal to σ_ε^2 and σ_u^2, and with no serial correlation or cross-correlation.

After substitution of the constraints into the objective function, we have:

$$E((\bar{a} + \varepsilon)G + u - \bar{Y})^2 = \bar{a}^2 G^2 + G^2 \sigma_\varepsilon^2 + \sigma_u^2 + \bar{Y}^2 - 2\bar{a}G\bar{Y}.$$

Differentiating this objective function with respect to the decision variable, G, we have the optimizing rule, and the optimal value for the policy variable that emerges is:

$$G^* = \bar{a}\bar{Y}/(\bar{a}^2 + \sigma_\varepsilon^2).$$

It is instructive to consider the limiting cases. If the policy multiplier coefficient is known with certainty ($\sigma_\varepsilon^2 = 0$), then the optimal value for the policy variable is the target value for output divided by the multiplier. But as uncertainty about the multiplier rises (that is, as the variance of ε approaches infinity) G should be set at zero. For intermediate values of the variance, it is best to set the policy instrument at a value that is somewhere between the 'certainty equivalent' optimum and the 'do nothing' value.

This formal analysis of uncertainty supports Friedman's long-standing argument that policy makers should attempt less when they are unsure of the connection between policy and the economy's performance. In this sense, then, the analysis supports 'rules' over 'discretion'. There have been a number of extensions of this analysis in recent years. For example, Basu et al. (1990) apply this method to a situation in which a policy adviser is unsure about whether her advice will be followed. Others (Brock et al., 2003; Majundar and Mukand, 2004; Favero and Milani, 2005; and Wieland, 2006) explore why it may be optimal for the authority to depart temporarily from what would otherwise be the optimal stabilization policy, just so it can learn more about the structure of the system and so be less burdened with uncertainty in the future.

There is an alternative to modelling uncertainty in a stochastic framework. Uncertainty can take the form of the policy maker not knowing the curvature involved in a particular structural relationship. To establish the implications of this form of uncertainty, we now compare two models that are exactly the same except for the fact that the precise degree of curvature in one relationship, the Phillips curve, is not known. The first model is defined by the following three equations:

$$y_t = \theta(m_t - p_t) \qquad \text{aggregate demand}$$

$$m_t = \bar{m} - \chi(p_t - \bar{p}) \qquad \text{monetary policy}$$

$$p_t - p_{t-1} = \phi(y_{t-1} - \bar{y}) \qquad \text{Phillips curve}$$

This system is quite similar to the model we have discussed thus far in this chapter. Indeed, the aggregate demand and Phillips curve relationships are exactly the same. The policy reaction function is more up to date in the present specification, with the central bank adjusting its monetary aggregate with a view to hitting a price-level, not an output, target. For simplicity, we assume that the value of the level of all variables with bars above them is unity (so the associated logarithms – the lower-case variables appearing in this system – are zero). The solution equation for the output gap then is:

$$y_t = \upsilon y_{t-1}$$

where $\upsilon = 1 - \phi\theta(1 + \chi)$. As was the case with our earlier analysis, this model reduces to a first-order linear difference equation. Convergence to full equilibrium occurs if υ is a fraction. The model cannot predict an ongoing cycle of constant amplitude. Is a policy of price-level targeting recommended? Not necessarily: an increase in parameter χ can make υ exceed unity, so more aggressive price-level targeting can be destabilizing. But this policy can never change the fact that output gravitates to its natural rate value (unity) as long as instability is avoided. We now show that this property is lost if the curvature involved in the Phillips curve is altered just slightly. Indeed, the classical dichotomy is lost in this case.

These assertions can be defended by replacing the Phillips curve in this simple model with the following:

$$p_t - p_{t-1} = \phi(Y_{t-1} - 1).$$

This one change leads to a reduced form for output that is slightly different:

$$y_t - y_{t-1} = -\phi\theta(1 + \chi)(Y_{t-1} - 1).$$

Since the left-hand side of this equation can be approximated by $((Y_t - Y_{t-1})/Y_{t-1})$, and since we can define $X_t = ((\beta - 1)/\beta)Y_t$, where $\beta = 1 + \phi\theta(1 + \chi)$, this reduced form can be re-expressed as:

$$X_{t+1} = \beta X_t(1 - X_t). \tag{3.4}$$

This reduced form is a first-order *non-linear* difference equation; it is the simple logistic function involved in basic chaos theory. One purpose of this section of the chapter is to relate standard stabilization policy analysis to the chaos literature in a simple and clear fashion. We will see that the average rate of output observed in the long run (a real variable) is affected by the policy reaction coefficient (that is, by monetary policy).

Despite its simplicity, equation 3.4 is consistent with many different time paths for output, as is summarized in Table 3.1. Two of the possible dynamic patterns are shown in Figure 3.2. The general shape of equation 3.4 that is shown in both parts of the figure can be verified by noting that both the

Table 3.1 Possible time paths in a non-linear model

Range for β	Nature of time path
0<β≤1	X must approach 0
1<β<3	X must approach (β−1)/β so Y approaches 1
3≤β<3.449	X follows a 2-period limit cycle
3.449≤β<3.549	X follows a 4-period limit cycle
3.549≤β<3.57	X follows even-numbered-period limit cycles of ever greater number (8, 16, 32 . . .)
3.57≤β≤4.0	X is subject to chaotic fluctuations
β>4.0	X must approach negative infinity

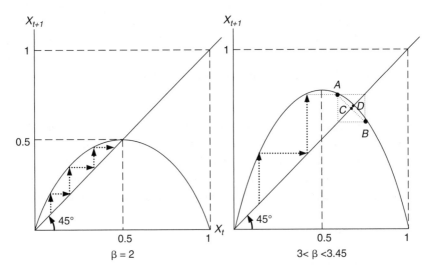

Figure 3.2 Convergence and cycles in a non-linear model

values 0 and 1 for current X imply that next period's X is zero, and that the slope of the relationship decreases as current X rises (and is zero when current X is 0.5).

The dashed lines in Figure 3.2 indicate the time sequence. Convergence to the natural rate (which involves X equal to 0.5 and Y equal to 1) occurs with the 'low' value for β, but a limit cycle (one that maintains a constant amplitude forever) occurs with the 'high' value for β. In the right-hand panel of Figure 3.2, 'full equilibrium' involves the economy shifting back and forth between points A and D (every other period) forever. The average level of economic activity is represented by point C. Since point D corresponds to the natural rate of output, point C involves an average activity level for the economy that is below the natural rate. Thus, with a non-linear reduced-form relationship, it is possible that output remains below the natural rate (on average) even in the long run.

This analysis is a deterministic variant of Lipsey's (1960) non-linear aggregation hypothesis. The interesting features of this variant are that stochastic elements are not required to generate a cycle that maintains its amplitude as time passes, and that it is variations in *monetary* policy that can make these permanent output effects important.

In this model, a more aggressive attempt to target the price level (a larger value for parameter χ) can lower the average rate of output. Since uncertainty concerning the appropriate functional form for one of the model's structural equations is what leads to the possibility that something as basic as the classical dichotomy can break down (even in a natural-rate setting), it must be admitted that the standard practice of linear approximations in macroeconomics is a definite limitation.

One final point worth explaining is how Figure 3.2 is altered when the macro-economy is chaotic. Chaotic cycles occur with larger values for β than are assumed for Figure 3.2, since a higher β makes the reduced-form relationship pictured in Figure 3.2 more non-linear. (The end points are unaltered, but the height of the hump is increased.) Chaotic cycles involve an 'observation box' like that formed by points *A* and *B* in Figure 3.2, but with the location and size of the box moving around the plane forever, with no regular pattern ever emerging.

There are three reasons for integrating basic macro analysis and chaos theory. First, we can appreciate that ongoing changes in exogenous variables do *not* need to be assumed to explain business cycles. Second, we can see that intuitively appealing policies can *create* cycles (both regular ones and chaotic ones), so, once again, built-in 'stabilizers' can be destabilizing. Finally, we can appreciate that the entire nature of the full equilibrium for *real* variables – whether it involves asymptotic approach to the natural rate or a limit cycle which averages out to an output level that is less than the natural rate (to take just two of the possibilities) – can depend on the *short-run* targeting strategy for implementing *monetary* policy. Keynesians have become particularly excited about this implication of non-linearity, since it implies that they need not follow what has been the convention – conceding the full-equilibrium properties of macro models to the Classicals, and limiting the Keynesian contribution to a discussion of approach paths. With non-linearities, the short- and long-run properties of models cannot be so readily separated.

Two useful surveys of work on non-linear dynamics are Mullineux and Peng (1993) and Rosser (1990). It has proved difficult for econometricians to distinguish between the traditional view of business cycles (linear systems with stochastic shocks maintaining the amplitude of cycles that would otherwise dampen out) and this alternative view (endogenous deterministic cycles in a non-linear system that never die down). Despite this inability to reject the relevance of the non-linear approach, it has not become too popular. Mainstream macroeconomists have limited their attention to linear stochastic systems, as we do for the remainder of the chapter.

3.3   Adaptive expectations

Real-world business cycles are not the two-period sawtooth cycles that we see in Figure 3.1; they are more irregular. But, if mainstream analysis does not rely on exogenous variables following cyclical time paths (and it does not), and if it simplifies by ignoring non-linearities (and it does), how does the mainstream approach generate realistic-looking cycles in the model's endogenous variables? The answer is by extending the order of the dynamics involved in a linear model, say by complicating the model to the point that the reduced-form for output deviations is a *second-order* (or higher) linear difference equation. One way of doing this is by allowing for adaptive expectations. Other ways are discussed in Chapter 5, where we explore New Classical macroeconomics.

Ignoring all policy variables and error terms for simplicity, the revised demand and supply functions are:

$$y_t = -\theta p_t + \psi \pi_t$$

$$p_t - p_{t-1} = \phi(y_{t-1} - \bar{y}) + \pi_{t-1},$$

where π stands for expected inflation. As explained in Chapter 2, the revised demand function comes from distinguishing the nominal from the real interest rate. The revised Phillips curve involves the assumption that the 'core' inflation rate is the adaptively formed expected inflation rate. The adaptive-expectations hypothesis is defined by the following equation:

$$\pi_t - \pi_{t-1} = \lambda(p_t - p_{t-1} - \pi_{t-1}).$$

This hypothesis is often called the error-learning model, since it specifies that the change in the agents' forecast is equal to a fraction of the previous forecast error (as long as parameter λ is assumed to be a positive fraction).

An alternative interpretation of this hypothesis can be seen if it is rewritten for several time periods:

$$\pi_t = (1 - \lambda)\pi_{t-1} + \lambda\Delta p_t,$$

$$\pi_{t-1} = (1 - \lambda)\pi_{t-2} + \lambda\Delta p_{t-1}, \ldots$$

so that successive substitution leads to:

$$\pi_t = \lambda[\Delta p_t + (1 - \lambda)\Delta p_{t-1} + (1 - \lambda)^2\Delta p_{t-2} + \ldots]$$

This last formulation of the hypothesis states that π is a weighted average of past actual values, with less weight given to the more distant past. The weights decline geometrically. Both the error-adjustment interpretation and the weighted-average interpretation suggest a certain plausibility for the adaptive-expectations hypothesis, as does its long-run consistency property (discussed in section 3.1). Thus, it is not surprising that this hypothesis was the mainstream way of modelling expectations in macroeconomics from the mid-1950s to the mid-1970s.

The three equations of this simple model can be combined to yield a second-order difference equation ($\hat{y}_t$ as a function of both $\hat{y}_{t-1}$ and $\hat{y}_{t-2}$). In particular, we proceed through the following steps. We begin by first-differencing the demand function, and using the Phillips curve and the adaptive-expectations equations to eliminate the change in the price level and the change in expectations (respectively). The result is:

$$\hat{y}_t = (1 + \phi(\psi\lambda - \theta))\hat{y}_{t-1} - \theta\pi_{t-1}.$$

This relationship itself is first-differenced, and the resulting $(\pi_{t-1} - \pi_{t-2})$ term is eliminated by combining lagged versions of the Phillips curve and the expectations equations: $(\pi_{t-1} - \pi_{t-2}) = \lambda\phi\hat{y}_{t-2}$. The result is:

$$\hat{y}_t = v_1\hat{y}_{t-1} + v_2\hat{y}_{t-2}$$

where $v_1 = 2 + \phi(\psi\lambda - \theta)$ and $v_2 = -(1 + \phi\lambda(\theta + \psi)) - \phi\theta)$. As in the first-order linear difference equation case, there are four possible time paths (as is explained in all standard mathematics-for-economists texts, such as Chiang, 1984, p. 576). The only difference is that, in this case, the cycles involve damped and explosive sine curves, not two-period sawtooth cycles. With slope parameter values that lead to damped cycles, and exogenous disturbances to keep those cycles from ever dying down, we have the standard approach to business cycles.

It turns out that the condition for cycles to occur is that $v_1^2 < 4v_2$ and the stability conditions are: $v_2 < 1$, $v_1 + v_2 + 1 > 0$, and $v_1 - v_2 < 1$. It is left for the reader to verify that the bigger is the role that adaptive expectations play in the system (that is, the bigger is parameter λ), the more likely it is for the system to display cycles and for the system to display instability. It is for this reason that Keynesian economists have emphasized expectations. And, as we discovered in Chapter 2, similar conclusions emerge when a model-consistent form of expectations (perfect foresight) is assumed, instead of adaptive expectations.

While the adaptive-expectations hypothesis has some appealing features, it has an unappealing one as well. It makes little sense to analyse the effectiveness of any government policy that is intended to improve agents' economic welfare if that analysis does not permit those agents to understand both the environment they live in and the effect of the ongoing policy intervention within that environment. Our modelling has allowed for all these considerations only in the perfect-foresight case – not in the adaptive-expectations case.

A less 'unrealistic' version of model-consistent expectations (compared to perfect foresight) is the 'rational-expectations' hypothesis. According to this hypothesis, agents make forecast errors, but (since they are aware of the probability distributions that generate the random shocks that hit the macro economy) they make their forecasts of the endogenous variables as if they were calculating the best forecast possible from the formal model. Thus, forecast errors occur, but they are not systematic. The remaining sections of the chapter explain how we can analyse models of this sort and what some of the policy implications are.

3.4   Rational expectations: basic analysis

The basic idea behind rational expectations can be explained in an extremely basic setting – the simple fixed-price, fixed-interest-rate income–expenditure model that students encounter in their introductory economics course. That model can be defined by the following relationships:

$$Y_t = C_t + G$$

$$C_t = cY_t^e$$

and one of

$$Y_t^e = Y_{t-1}$$

$$Y_t^e = E_{t-1}(Y_t)$$

The first two equations define goods market clearing, and that private demand is proportional to agents' expectations concerning what income they will receive that period. The remaining equations define two hypotheses concerning how those income expectations may be formed. The former can be thought of as either static expectations (the forecast for today is equal to what was actually observed yesterday) or a degenerate version of adaptive expectations (with the entire weight in the weighted average put on the most recent past). The second hypothesis is rational expectations. According to this hypothesis, agents' subjective forecast is the same as we can calculate by evaluating the mathematical expectation of actual current income (as determined in the model).

In the static-expectations case, the at-a-point-in-time solution equation for current *GDP* is:

$$Y_t = cY_{t-1} + G.$$

Consider a once-for-all increase in autonomous spending, *G*. The solution equation for *Y* indicates that *GDP* rises by the same amount as the increase in *G* in that very period. Then, *Y* keeps rising by smaller and smaller amounts each period, with the overall increase in output (given infinite time) being:

$$Y = (1/(1-c))G.$$

In the rational-expectations case, the same substitution of the second and third equations into the first results in:

$$Y_t = cE_{t-1}(Y_t) + G.$$

This is not a solution equation for actual output, *Y*, since there are still two endogenous variables (*Y* and its expectation) in this one equation. We need a second equation – one for the forecast of *Y*. This can be had by taking the expectations operator through this 'almost reduced form'. The result is:

$$E_{t-1}(Y_t) = G/(1-c).$$

When this expression is substituted back into the almost reduced form, we end with the full reduced form (solution equation) for actual output:

$$Y_t = (1/(1 - c))G.$$

By comparing the two solution equations (for static expectations and for rational expectations), we can determine how the model's properties are affected by embracing this model-consistent forecasts hypothesis. We see that the impact effect of a once-for-all increase in autonomous spending is bigger in the rational-expectations case. Indeed, the impact effect on Y is now equal to the eventual effect. With forward-looking agents, it makes sense that there not be a gradual increase in income. In this case, agents correctly see that this higher income is coming. They raise their consumption immediately as a result, and this (in turn), since output is demand-determined in this model, makes overall income rise immediately. In short, what used to be called the model's long-run properties become the model's short-run properties (when agents have rational expectations). Worded in this general fashion, this summary applies to all rational-expectations models.

We now explore the properties of a slightly more complicated rational-expectations model. The system we now consider is similar to that in the previous section in that it involves descriptive aggregate demand and supply functions. But there are several extensions here. For one thing, we allow for variable prices and interest rates. Also, we focus on monetary (not fiscal) policy. Initially, we continue to suppress any distinction between nominal and real interest rates. The initial model is defined by the following four equations:

$$y_t = \alpha - \psi r_t + v_t \tag{3.5}$$

$$p_t - p_{t-1} = \phi y_t + p_t^e - p_{t-1} + u_t \tag{3.6}$$

$$r_t = \bar{r} + \gamma(p_t^e - 0) \tag{3.7}$$

$$p_t^e = E_{t-1}(p_t) \tag{3.8}$$

Here y and p stand for the natural logs of real output and the price level. Both the natural rate of output and the central bank's target for the price level are unity, so the logs of these variables are zero (and $\bar{Y} = \alpha - \psi \bar{r} = 0$); v and u are stochastic shocks – drawn from distributions that involve zero means, constant variances and no serial correlation, and r is the interest rate, not its logarithm.

Equation 3.5 is a standard (descriptive) *IS* relationship, which is also the aggregate demand function, since the central bank sets the interest rate. Since we focus exclusively on monetary policy in this discussion, fiscal variables are constant (and embedded in the intercept). Equation 3.6 summarizes the supply side of the goods market. It is a standard expectations-augmented Phillips curve. Equation 3.7 is the central bank's reaction function. The bank raises (lowers) the interest rate above (below) its long-run average value whenever the bank's forecast for the (log of the) price level is above (below) target. There is no need to specify an *LM* equation, since its only function is to determine what value the bank had to adjust the money supply to (in order for the public's demand for money function to be satisfied at this interest rate). Since the money supply enters none of the other equations of the model, we can afford to ignore this consideration.

Equation 3.8 defines rational expectations; it specifies that the agents' subjective expectation for price is equal to what we (as model manipulators) can calculate as the mathematical expectation of price. The time subscript for the expectations operator denotes that agents know all values for the stochastic shocks up to and including the previous period (time period $t - 1$). Agents (and the central banker) must forecast the current shock – at the end of the previous period before it is revealed – on the basis of all past information. Agents know the exact structure of the economy (the form of all equations and all slope coefficients). The only thing they do not know is what the current and all future values of the additive error terms are.

To solve the model, we first eliminate the interest rate and the expected price variables by simple substitution. The results are:

$$y_t = -\psi\gamma E_{t-1}(p_t) + v_t \tag{3.9}$$

$$p_t = \phi y_t + E_{t-1}(p_t) + u_t \tag{3.10}$$

Taking the expectations operator through these two equations, we realize that the expected value for both p and y is zero. Substituting this value for the expected price level back into equations 3.9 and 3.10, we end with very simple reduced forms:

$$y_t = v_t$$

$$p_t = \phi y_t + u_t$$

These reduced forms lead to the following volatility expressions:

$$\text{var}(y) = \sigma_v^2$$

$$\text{var}(p) = \phi^2\sigma_v^2 + \sigma_u^2$$

Since neither variance is a function of the policy maker's parameter, γ, monetary policy is irrelevant. This makes sense; after all, the central bank must set its instrument variable (the interest rate) before the current shocks are known – just as the private agents must commit to setting their nominal variables before the current shocks are known. There is nothing that the central bank can do for the private agents that they cannot do for themselves.

We can remove this 'policy irrelevance' result by changing the model in at least two ways. For one thing, we could have some of the private agents constrained to set their nominal variables more than one period in advance. For another, we could let the central bank wait until the current shocks are known before the interest rate is set. In either case, the central bank would be able to do more than can agents on their own, so monetary policy should matter. We choose the second alternative here, and consider multi-period private sector nominal contracts in Chapter 6. We verify that policy irrelevance is a very model-specific result by changing equation 3.7 to the following:

$$r_t = \bar{r} + \gamma(p_t - 0) \tag{3.7a}$$

and re-deriving the output and price variances. It is left for the reader to duplicate the earlier steps, and to verify that the revised solutions are:

$$y_t = (\psi\gamma u_t + v_t)/(1 + \psi\gamma\phi)$$

$$p_t = \phi y_t + u_t$$

These results imply that a more aggressive price-level targeting policy (a bigger value for parameter γ) is desirable, since it makes demand shocks have a smaller effect on real output, but it is undesirable since it makes supply shocks have a larger effect on real output. So the monetary authority faces a *permanent volatility* trade-off, even though it does *not* face a *permanent* trade-off between the average *level* of real output and inflation (or the price level).

These results make sense at the intuitive level. The natural-rate feature (the Classical dichotomy) is a built-in feature of the Phillips curve specification, so it is not surprising that there is no lasting trade-off between inflation and the level of real activity. But this does not mean that central bankers should ignore the effect of their policies on real variables. Even within the class of policies that deliver long-run price stability within a natural-rate model, there is a basis for preferring one specific monetary policy rule to another, since there are *lasting* differences in the *volatility* of real activity about its natural-rate value.

When a negative demand shock hits, the aggregate demand curve shifts left. If the *short-run* aggregate supply curve is positively sloped, price falls. An aggressive price-targeting central bank reacts vigorously to reverse this effect – by shifting aggregate demand back to the right. Since the exogenous shock and the policy variable both affect the same curve (demand, not supply), the central bank cannot help but limit output volatility as it pursues price stability. But things are different when the shock is on the supply side. If the aggregate supply curve shifts left, there is pressure for the price level to rise and for real activity to fall. To limit the rise in price, the central bank must shift the demand curve to the left. The problem is that this policy accentuates the output fall, and so there is a volatility trade-off. The fact that we can appreciate these outcomes so easily at the intuitive level makes it seem as though there is no need to work things out formally. But such a conclusion is not warranted, as we will see in the next section – where we consider a more complicated model. In such settings, it is much more difficult to sort things out without the precision that accompanies a formal solution.

3.5   Rational expectations: extended analysis

We now consider a more complicated model – one that involves today's expectation of tomorrow's outcomes, not yesterday's expectation of today's outcomes, and one that, as a result, requires a more involved solution procedure known as the undetermined coefficient solution method. The following model is fully consistent with the micro-foundations that modern macroeconomists insist upon, and readers will be able to verify this when they read Chapter 4. For the remainder of this chapter, however, we simply take this model as 'to be defended later'. The model involves a proper distinction between nominal and real interest rates, and *IS* and Phillips curve equations that are based on inter-temporal optimization. To simplify slightly, we set the demand shock to zero in all time periods. The revised *IS*, supply, and policy-reaction functions are:

$$y_t = E_t(y_{t+1}) - (i_t - (E_t(p_{t+1}) - p_t)) \tag{3.11}$$

$$i_t = \lambda(p_t - p_{t-1}) \tag{3.12a}$$

$$p_t + y_t = 0 \tag{3.12b}$$

$$p_t - p_{t-1} = E_t(p_{t+1}) - p_t + \phi y_t + u_t \tag{3.13}$$

Equation 3.11 is the expectations-augmented *IS* relationship: current demand depends inversely on the expected real interest rate and positively on households' expected future level of income. Equations 3.12a and 13.12b represent two possible monetary policies. In the first, the central bank adjusts the nominal interest rate with a view to achieving an inflation target of zero (raising – or lowering – the interest rate whenever inflation exceeds – or falls short of – the target inflation rate of zero). Parameter λ is the central bank's aggressiveness coefficient. In the second alternative specification for central bank policy, the bank is very aggressive and it pegs nominal *GDP* (as stipulated in equation 3.12b). In this case, this relationship replaces the *IS* equation in the model's solution, since all the latter is needed for is to (residually) determine what interest rate was needed at each point in time to meet the nominal *GDP* target. Finally, equation 3.13 is the Phillips relationship that emerges when agents are forward-looking.

We begin by considering nominal *GDP* targeting. Combining equations 3.12b and 3.13 by eliminating the real-output variable, we have:

$$p_t = [1/(2 + \phi)] [p_{t-1} + E_t (p_{t+1}) + u_t] \qquad (3.14)$$

If we try to use this equation updated by one period to get an expression for the expectation of the future price (a term that needs to be eliminated by substitution on the right-hand side) we will have to embark on a never-ending series of future-period substitutions. To avoid this infinite set of steps, we need to assume, and make use of, a trial version of the model's solution equation. This is known as the undetermined coefficient solution method, and we introduced the reader to this solution method in section 2.5. Here, since there is only one predetermined variable in the model (the previous period's price) and one exogenous variable (the error term), there can only be these two terms in the solution equation for the price level. Thus, we assume the following trial solution:

$$p_t = ap_{t-1} + bu_t$$

We use the undetermined coefficient solution procedure to determine how the reduced-form coefficients (the Arabic letters *a* and *b*) depend on the underlying structural parameter that has economic meaning (the Greek letter ϕ). We now write the trial solution one period forward in time, and take the expectations operator (dated at *t*) through. When the result is substituted into equation 3.14, we have:

$$p_t = [1/(2 + \phi - a)][p_{t-1} + u_t].$$

For model consistency both solution equations (the assumed trial solution and the equation just given) must be identical, and this will be true if and only if:

$$a = b = 1/(2 + \phi - a).$$

The first of these identifying restrictions is a quadratic equation that solves for a:

$$a^2 - (2 + \phi)a + 1 = 0$$

$$a = [1/2][(2 + \phi) \pm \sqrt{(2 + \phi)^2 - 4}]$$

There are two mathematically admissible values for reduced-form parameter a, but only one is economically admissible if we reject (on correspondence principle grounds) the positive square-root value, since it implies instability ($a > 1$). By expanding the term within the square root, the reader can immediately verify that both a values are real, and that the one involving the negative square root must be a positive fraction. So that value is selected (for both a and b) for further analysis. The expression for output volatility follows directly from the trial solution and the nominal GDP target equation:

$$\sigma_y^2 = [b^2/(1 - a^2)]\sigma_u^2.$$

An illustrative value for this volatility expression can be had if a representative value for the Phillips curve slope parameter is inserted. Walsh (2003a, p. 576) has used 0.2 as an estimate of the slope of the short-run (annual) Phillips curve, so for our illustrative calculation here we follow his lead and take $\phi = 0.2$. With these representative values, we find:

$$\sigma_y^2 = 0.70\sigma_u^2$$

We now compare this result to what emerges when the central bank behaves less aggressively and targets the inflation rate rather than nominal GDP. Using $\pi_t = p_t - p_{t-1}$ to define the inflation rate, the model can be rewritten as:

$$y_t = E_t(y_{t+1}) - (i_t - (E_t(\pi_{t+1}))) \tag{3.11a}$$

$$i_t = \lambda\pi_t \tag{3.12c}$$

$$\pi_t = E_t(\pi_{t+1}) + \phi y_t + u_t \tag{3.13a}$$

In this case, it is convenient to proceed in two stages; first we ignore the error term (and therefore drop the expectations operator) to consider the dynamic features of this system. It can be summarized in a single equation by using equation 3.12c to eliminate the interest rate, and by substituting equation 3.11a into the forward first difference of equation 3.13a to eliminate output. The result is:

$$\pi_{t+2} - (2 + \phi)\pi_{t+1} + (1 + \phi\lambda)\pi_t = 0.$$

This dynamic system involves two eigenvalues, and if either of them is less than one in absolute value then there is an infinity of stable solutions since – while the price level is a sticky-at-a-point-in-time variable – the inflation rate is not. Macroeconomists strive to avoid multiple-stable-solutions outcomes, since such outcomes imply that, as analysts, we can give no definitive answer regarding the behaviour of the economy. Walsh (2003a, p. 246) has referred to these undesirable outcomes as involving sunspot equilibria. The convention, then, is to assume that the policy maker must make such outcomes impossible. In this case, the two eigenvalues are:

$$[1/2][(2 + \phi) \pm \sqrt{(2 + \phi)^2 - 4(1 + \phi\lambda)}]$$

The reader can verify that the term within the square root can be re-expressed as $\phi(\phi - 4(\lambda - 1))$ and that $\lambda > 1$ is necessary and sufficient to ensure that this expression is less than ϕ^2, and so to ensure that even the smaller of the eigenvalues exceeds unity. Imposing $\lambda > 1$ is known as the Taylor principle, since Taylor (1993) was the first to emphasize that an inflation-targeting central bank needs to respond more than one for one when adjusting the interest rate in response to inflation developments – so that the economy has a unique, non-sunspot, solution. With both dynamic forces involving instability in this case, but with forward-looking agents able to set initial conditions to make both these dynamic forces non-operative, the system degenerates to one that involves no dynamics at all. As a result, the rational expectation for the future (log of) output and inflation values is zero. Substituting in these expectations, the expression for output volatility follows immediately:

$$\sigma_y^2 = [(1 + (1 + \lambda)\phi)/(1 + \lambda)]^2\sigma_u^2.$$

For illustration, inserting the same value for the Phillips curve slope as above, and Taylor's recommendation for the central bank ($\lambda = 1.5$), we have $\sigma_y^2 = 0.27\sigma_u^2$. While the primary purpose of this section has been to explain the solution procedures that are required in dynamic rational-expectations models that are based on forward-looking agents, we have obtained some advice for monetary policy as an additional dividend. It is that, according to this simplified but mainstream model, if the goal is to limit output volatility, a policy of inflation targeting that embraces the Taylor principle is recommended over a policy of aggressive nominal *GDP* targeting.

Related analyses have compared inflation targeting to price-level targeting (instead of nominal *GDP* targeting). For example, Svensson (1999) finds that price-level targeting provides both lower price and output volatility, and he refers to this outcome as a 'free lunch' – progress made with respect to two goals, with this achieved by adjusting just one policy instrument. Walsh (2003b) has shown that this desirable outcome is much less likely to emerge when the model involves a Phillips curve which allows past inflation, not just expected future inflation, to play a role. We return to this issue in Chapter 6, where we provide additional perspective on 'free lunch' possibilities.

A more complete analysis would consider both real output and inflation volatility, since the policy analysis should remain true to the micro-foundations of the model. For internal consistency, alternative policies should be ranked according to the utility function of the agents that populate the model economy. That is, if the government is to be benevolent and not paternalistic, our normative analysis should be based on the representative agent's utility function. Woodford (2003a) and Walsh (2003a, pp. 550–55) explain how maximizing that utility function can be approximated by minimizing a discounted quadratic loss function involving real-output and inflation deviations. In the analysis above, we have arbitrarily focused on just output volatility, and only on the asymptotic variance of real output. There were two reasons for this: to simplify the exposition and to focus primarily on positive, not normative, considerations as we explained the actual solution procedures involved with rational-expectations models.

Before closing, it is worth reflecting further on the practice of rejecting unstable solutions as economically inadmissible. We noted in Chapter 2 that this presumption is often 'justified' on the basis of the correspondence principle. However, if the policy that is being examined has never been tried, it is not clear how the fact that instability has not been observed in the past (when other policies were in place) can be relevant. An alternative line of argument involves justifying the presumption of stability by arguing that only this assumption is consistent with the first-order conditions of the underlying optimizations being satisfied. But since this solution ambiguity exists at the *overall market* level – not at the level of an *individual* decision maker – it is not clear what leads *decentralized* individuals to focus on only the stable solution. In any event, in some cases, both solutions involve stability. In this case, Taylor (1977) has suggested that the solution that involves the minimum variance be selected, and the other rejected. However, since some models involve a volatility trade-off (as we discovered in the last section of this chapter, and as was initially emphasized in Taylor, 1979a), it is not clear which endogenous variable the minimum variance criterion should be applied to. McCallum (1983) has suggested that analysts should avoid this non-uniqueness problem by including in the trial solutions only the minimal set of state variables that is warranted by considering the structure of the basic model. The idea is that only 'fundamentals' should matter. However, when selecting our trial solution above we followed this advice, and we have still obtained two solutions. So, all things considered, it must be admitted that there has been no fully satisfactory solution of the non-uniqueness problem in rational-expectations models.

Readers who wish to pursue the non-uniqueness issue could consult McCallum (2003) and the critical commentary on this paper offered by Woodford (2003b). Another development in this literature focuses on which of the multiple equilibria agents converge to, if they start with incomplete information and have to gradually acquire what we have assumed they have from the outset – rational expectations. The idea is that only equilibria agents can get to via gradual learning should be deemed admissible. Two references for this literature are Honkapohja and Mitra (2004) and Giannitsarou (2005). A general survey on the non-uniqueness problem in monetary policy models is available in Driskill (2006). Despite the incompleteness in the methodology for dealing with multiple equilibria, modern macroeconomists regularly proceed by simply rejecting the unstable outcomes.

3.6   Conclusions

This chapter has surveyed alternative approaches to modelling uncertainty and business cycles. A primary focus has been on the alternative treatments of expectations that have featured in the development of modern macroeconomics. Initially, expectations was an issue stressed by Keynesians, since it represents a mechanism that makes convergence to full equilibrium less assured. But, more recently, macroeconomists of all persuasions highlight expectations in their analysis. This is because stabilization policy is now modelled as an ongoing operation, not an isolated one-time event, and analysts restrict their attention to models in which agents are fully aware of what the government has been, and will be, doing. Thus, as far as stabilization policy analysis is concerned, there has been a convergence of views in two senses. First, all modern analysis focuses on model-consistent expectations. A central task for this chapter has been to equip readers to be able to execute the required derivations. The second dimension of convergence among macroeconomists – whether they come from either New Classical or more traditional Keynesian traditions – is that they all emphasize micro-foundations. Without starting from a specification of utility and a well-identified source of market failure, there is no way we can argue that one policy is 'better' than another. Understanding these micro-foundations is our task for the next chapter.

The analyses covered in the latter sections of this chapter are examples of current research in macroeconomics. Unfortunately, space constraints force us to exclude many interesting studies. For example, further work on the theory of monetary policy has focused on more general objective functions for the central bank. Instead of assuming that the bank restricts its attention to hitting a price-level target in just the current period, for example, a vast literature considers central banks with an objective function involving both current and future values of several macroeconomic outcomes. A central consideration in this literature is a *credibility* issue. Since current outcomes depend on agents' expectations of the future, it can be tempting for the central bank to promise a particular future policy (to get favourable expectations effects at the present time) and then to deliver a different monetary policy once the future arrives (since agents cannot then go back and change their earlier expectations). Walsh (2003a, chap. 11) surveys this literature, and we cover some of it in Chapter 7.

Other interesting work enriches the theory of rational expectations. In one strand of the literature, agents are assumed to know some, but not all, of the current endogenous variable values, when forecasts of the other variables are being made. For example, when forecasting this period's real *GDP*, we usually know more than just the lagged values of all variables. We know a couple of current variable values, for example for the interest rate and the exchange rate (which are reported in the news media every day, and which are never revised). We do not know enough to figure out the current values for *all* the current 'error terms', but we can make somewhat better forecasts than we assumed agents could make in our analysis above. Minford and Peel (2002) provide a good summary of this class of rational-expectations models.

As already noted, another interesting line of investigation involves agents who have to use least-squares forecasting techniques to *learn* about a change in the economy's structure. In these models, agents' forecasts gradually converge to the version of rational expectations that we have assumed from the outset, and examined, in this chapter. While the level of technical difficulty rises quite dramatically as these extensions are pursued, they represent important developments. One reason for this importance is the fact that some empirical work has been 'unkind' to the basic version of rational expectations that we have considered here. One awkward bit of evidence for the rational-expectations hypothesis is that surveyed series on expectations differ from the associated actual series in *systematic* ways.

Another source of tension follows from sectoral econometric studies, such as estimated consumption functions. For example, when Friedman (1957) tested his permanent-income theory of consumption, he tested that hypothesis and an additional one – that permanent income is related to actual measured income according to the adaptive-expectations scheme – simultaneously. This *package* of hypotheses was not rejected by the data. Rational-expectations theorists have criticized Friedman's work on the grounds that the adaptive-expectations part of the package gave him a 'free' parameter. Since there was no restriction based on the theory for the coefficient of expectation revision to be anything other than a positive fraction, Friedman's computer was free to pick a value for that parameter that maximized the goodness of fit of the overall package of hypotheses. When Friedman's critics re-estimate the permanent-income theory of consumption – as a package with rational expectations instead – they find much less support. It can be argued that these later studies (for example, Sargent, 1978) have gone too far in replacing the free-parameter problem with a very restrictive assumption concerning the rest of the economy. Since rational expectations has to be implemented as a *full-model* proposition, the consumption function cannot be estimated without specifying the entire rest of the macro model. Since this is done in a boldly simplified way in any study that is focusing on just one relationship (for example, the consumption function), imposing the associated cross-equation restrictions can essentially destroy any chance that the original theory might have had to get a 'passing grade'. In other words, as it is often applied, empirical work that combines inter-temporal optimization by one group of agents, an over-simplified specification of the rest of the economy, and rational expectations may involve too few – not too many – free parameters.

Carroll's (2001) concern goes even further. He generates fictitious data from sets of simulations involving hypothetical consumers who behave exactly according to the theory (the strict permanent-income hypothesis plus rational expectations). He finds that fictitious researchers who use this data still reject the theory. So there is certainly more research to do on how to test both our inter-temporal models and the hypothesis of rational expectations.

Beyond acquiring an initial awareness of these challenges, it is hoped that readers have acquired two things by studying this chapter: an ability to solve and interpret basic rational-expectations models, and a sense of perspective concerning this literature.

We end this chapter by summarizing the prerequisites for any analysis of stabilization policy to be deemed acceptable by modern macroeconomists – whether their background is Classical or Keynesian. These features are: consistent with inter-temporal optimization, allowing for some short-run nominal stickiness, and involving model-consistent expectations. In addition to these features, if the analysis is to be used to directly inform actual policy debates, it has to be highly aggregative and fairly simple (that is, involve a limited number of equations). The framework that appears to satisfy all these prerequisites has been called the New Neoclassical Synthesis. We considered a slightly simplified version of this framework in section 3.5 in this chapter. In the next chapter, we discuss the micro-foundations of this framework. Then, in Chapters 5 and 6, we explore in a much more complete manner the development of this new synthesis.

4

The micro-foundations of modern macroeconomics

4.1   Introduction

The traditional analysis that was reviewed in previous chapters involved some appeal to micro-foundations. For example, in the textbook Classical model (in Chapter 1), it is customary to refer to a static theory of household utility maximization to rationalize the household labour supply function. (We assumed that households maximize a utility function containing two arguments – after-tax real income and leisure – subject to a simple budget constraint: that income equals the after-tax real wage times the amount of time worked.) Also, we assumed that firms maximize their profits, and this was the rationale behind the standard optimal hiring rule for labour – that workers be hired until the marginal product of labour is pushed down to the rental cost of labour (the wage). But we did not assume a similar optimal hiring rule for the other factor input – capital. This different treatment is explained later in the present chapter, in section 4.4. But first we consider the micro basis for the equations of a standard macro model that summarize the behaviour of households. And even before that, in the next section of the chapter, we motivate what lies behind the drive for more explicit micro-foundations in modern macroeconomics.

4.2   The Lucas critique and related controversies

Before the early 1970s, virtually all macro policy analyses were inconsistent with the principles of microeconomics. The households and firms that operated within the macro model followed the same decision rules no matter how their environment was altered by changes in policy regime. Economics is often defined as the subject that explores the implications of constrained maximization. But this description did not apply to traditional macroeconomics. Since this was forcefully first pointed out by Nobel laureate Robert Lucas in 1976, and since macroeconomists have been working hard to avoid this criticism ever since, we begin this chapter by explaining what has become known as the 'Lucas critique' of more traditional macro-economics. The material in this section provides a compact summary of Lucas's argument – with an explicit applied example that documents actual policy by the Bank of Canada. We rely on a simple theory behind the Phillips curve. A fuller (inter-temporal) version of this theory of sticky prices is available in McCallum (1980) and Mussa (1981). Here, for simplicity, we consider just a one-period optimization.

Firms (price setters) are assumed to minimize the following cost function:

$$\text{cost} = \gamma(p_t - x)^2 + (1 - \gamma)(p_t - p_{t-1})^2$$

The first term can be understood by assuming that the firm's average cost curve is U-shaped – indicating that there is an optimal scale of plant. Firms incur higher costs whenever output is either above or below this level. With monopolistic competition, there is a slightly downward-sloping demand curve for the firm's product, so there is a particular value for the (log of the) price, x, that generates sales just equal to that optimal size of plant. A value for price above or below that value means that the firm is producing either less than or more than that lowest-cost level of output. The first term in the cost function captures this outcome. The fact that the gap between the current and the optimal value for price is squared reflects the fact that this is the simplest functional form that imposes the fact that any gap – positive or negative – raises the firm's costs. If there were no other cost, firms would simply set price equal to x in all time periods. But, according to this cost function, there *is* another consideration – it costs firms something just to change prices. These costs could be printing up a new catalogue or distributing the information to customers. In the literature, these costs are called 'menu' costs. This term is squared as well – for the same reason – to make it the case that firms incur the menu costs whether they are raising or lowering prices. The weights in the cost function, γ and $(1 - \gamma)$ indicate the relative importance of the cost of being away from long-run equilibrium and the costs of moving to close this gap. Given that it costs the firm both to move and to not move, it will not strike the reader as surprising that optimal behaviour involves partial or gradual adjustment.

To verify this, we differentiate this objective function with respect to the choice variable, p_t, and set this to zero. After a bit of manipulation, we get:

$$(p_t - p_{t-1}) = -\gamma(p_{t-1} - x)$$

which we rewrite in continuous time as:

$$\dot{p} = -\gamma(p - x).$$

This relationship would look like a traditional short-run Phillips curve if the $(p - x)$ gap were replaced with a term involving the output gap: $y - \bar{y}$. Thus, we now outline the simplest possible way in which this link can be made. We assume the quantity theory of money, $MV = PY$, with velocity assumed to be a constant equal to unity, and a simple monetary policy reaction function in which the money supply is set above (below) its long-run average value whenever the price level is below (above) its target value. In logarithmic form, these relationships can be written as:

$$m = p + y$$

$$m = x - \chi(p - x)$$

Parameter χ indicates the central bank's aggressiveness in pursuing price stability. Milton Friedman's (1959) advice was that the central bank should be confident that price stability would emerge on average as long as the money supply remained constant. He thought that trying to do more than that would simply add confusion for households and firms, so he advocated χ equal to zero. Modern central banks have rejected this advice and have opted for a positive χ, indeed a value that exceeds unity. The Bank of Canada shifted from following Friedman's advice to opting for a significantly higher χ at just about the same time that it pursued disinflation in the early 1980s. This section of the chapter assesses the importance of this development.

When the two latest equations are combined, we have:

$$(p - x) = -(1/(1 + \chi))y. \tag{4.1}$$

It is the case that output equals its natural rate when p equals x, so the full-equilibrium version of this relationship is $0 = -(1(1 + \chi))\bar{y}$. Subtracting this relationship from equation 4.1, we acquire the desired linkage between the price gap and the output gap:

$$(p - x) = -(1/(1 + \chi))(y - \bar{y})$$

We now substitute this relationship into the first-order condition that we derived from the firm's optimization, $\dot{p} = -\gamma(p - x)$, and we get the traditional Phillips curve:

$$\dot{p} = \phi(y - \bar{y}), \tag{4.2}$$

but *only if* parameter φ is *not* interpreted as 'primitive'. Instead, given this micro-foundation, this parameter must be interpreted as $φ = γ/(1 + χ)$. Since γ is a technology (primitive) parameter, while χ is not (indeed, we are *defining* different monetary policy regimes in terms of different values for this parameter), the summary slope of the short-run Phillips curve parameter, φ, *must* be non-primitive. The bottom line: once formal micro-foundations for the short-run Phillips curve are supplied, we see that the slope of this relationship depends on changes in monetary policy regime. Indeed, when the Bank of Canada switched to its high-χ regime, and pursued a policy of disinflation at essentially the same time, it should have expected that the Phillips curve that was then relevant for Canada would have a flatter slope than the estimations of the Phillips curve that came from historical data when the Bank had a low χ value indicated. Thus, it should not have been surprised when its pre-disinflation simulations (involving the previously estimated steeper short-run Phillips curve) gave a prediction that was far too optimistic. Had the Bank respected the Lucas critique it would not have taken χ as 'primitive' and it would not have been surprised by the large and prolonged recession that accompanied the disinflation. We conclude that the Lucas critique is both logically appealing and – as this historical episode illustrates – quantitatively important.

Standard practice in applied economics (in all fields – not just macroeconomics) involves estimating a model and then using those estimated coefficients to simulate what would happen if policy were different. The Lucas critique is the warning that it may not make sense to assume that those estimated coefficients would be the same if an alternative policy regime were in place. The only way we can respond to this warning is to have some theory behind each of the model's equations. We can then derive how (if at all) the coefficients depend on the policy regime. The derivation of the short-run Phillips curve that has just been presented illustrates two things. First, the Lucas critique does apply to the Phillips curve – its slope *is a policy-dependent* coefficient. Second, the derivation illustrates how we can react constructively to the Lucas critique. Just because the slope coefficient depends on policy, it does not mean that legitimate counterfactual experiments cannot proceed. The value of micro-foundations is evident. They do not just expose the non-primitive nature of the Phillips curve slope; they also outline precisely how to adjust that parameter to conduct theoretically defensible simulations of alternative policy rules.

An additional illustration of how the answers to policy questions change when the micro-foundations are respected can be had by reconsidering the results that were reported in Chapter 2. In that analysis, which involved essentially exactly this model but without the micro underpinnings, we determined that the speed of adjustment between full equilibria (parameter s in $\dot{y} = -s(y - \bar{y})$) could be derived in a straightforward fashion. Following that analysis here (by taking the time derivative of equation 4.1, assuming $\dot{x} = 0$, and substituting the result into equation 4.2), we have $s = \phi(1 + \chi)$. As a result, without considering micro underpinnings, we conclude that more aggressive policy increases the economy's adjustment speed back to full equilibrium following disturbances. But, according to the Lucas critique, we should take account of the micro basis of the Phillips curve, and substitute out the policy-dependent Phillips curve slope parameter (by using the $\phi = \gamma/(1 + \chi)$. result) *before* conducting the policy analysis. When this is done, the expression for the adjustment speed parameter becomes $s = \gamma$. This result has dramatically different policy implications. It says that monetary policy has *no* effect on the economy's adjustment speed. So respecting the Lucas critique does not just affect the smaller details of policy analysis; it can change the analysis in fundamental ways.

Is the Lucas critique actually important in the real world? Our discussion above, focusing on the fact that the estimated slope of the short-run Phillips curve has fallen dramatically as data from periods when central banks have moved toward direct price-level targeting is involved in the estimations, suggests that it is important. Similarly, the invention of substitutes for *M1* immediately after central banks limited *M1* growth as they embraced monetarism in the 1980s is additional evidence that agents re-optimize when the policy regime changes. But some authors (such as Rudebusch, 2005) have noted that the empirical evidence concerning less bold changes in policy does not support the conclusion of structural breaks in the estimated reduced forms of macro models. Perhaps it is results such as these, along with the level of mathematics that is required to pursue explicit micro-foundations in an inter-temporal setting, that have led a number of policy makers to ignore the Lucas critique. Our analysis suggests that this may be a dangerous decision.

There is another consideration that has kept some macroeconomists from working toward a more elaborate microeconomic base for conventional macro models. This problem is aggregation – an issue which was not addressed in the Phillips curve analysis just given. The conclusion which emerges from the aggregation literature is that the conditions required for consistent aggregation are so rigid that constrained maximization at the *individual* level may have *very few* macroeconomic implications – that is, *essentially no* useful insights for *aggregative* analysis. This presents a problem, since the only way to address the Lucas critique is to use optimizing underpinnings to go 'behind demand and supply curves' (Sargent, 1982) and to treat only the ultimate taste and technology parameters as primitive (policy-invariant). If aggregation issues prevent these individual optimizations from imposing any restrictions on macroeconomic relationships, the Lucas critique cannot be faced. Yet only a few commentators (for example, Geweke, 1985) have explicitly illustrated and emphasized that ignoring aggregation issues can be as important as ignoring the Lucas critique.

Thus, we are on the horns of a dilemma. Economists should ignore neither aggregation problems nor optimizing underpinnings. Yet the current convention is, in essence, to ignore aggregation issues by building macro models involving no differences between any individuals – the so-called representative-agent model. The only justification for this approach is an empirical one – that the predictions of the macro models, which are based on such a representative agent, are not rejected by the data. Thus macro-economists have reacted to this dilemma in a pragmatic way. Since aggregate models seem consistent with the macroeconomic 'facts', then, no matter how restrictive the aggregation requirements seem, not too much seems to be lost by assuming that the economy operates as if these restrictions are appropriate. Some macroeconomists find this pragmatic approach unconvincing, and they draw attention to inherent logical difficulties within the representative-agent methodology (see Kirman, 1992; and Hartley, 1997).

In Chapters 10 and 12, we make use of an overlapping generations macro model that involves *both* appealing optimization underpinnings *and* explicit aggregation across cohorts of different ages. Indeed, we introduce readers to this model that generalizes the single everlasting representative-agent framework later in the present chapter. The overlapping generations model certainly respects the Lucas critique without ignoring the aggregation challenge. Nevertheless, since much of the modern macro literature that we need to survey in this book follows the representative-agent convention, we focus on this simpler model as well.

Nevertheless, we would be remiss if we did not acknowledge that, even before optimization is considered, one of the central building blocks of modern macro – the aggregate production function – is regarded as an unacceptable construct to some economists. More than half a century ago, aggregation issues were debated within a discussion that centred on how economists can measure – even in principle – the overall quantity of capital. Since there are all kinds of different machines, and since we cannot add 'apples and oranges', we must – as with the *GDP* – add up machines in dollar terms. But, to do this, we need the prices of each capital good. According to the marginal productivity theory of factor prices, these values get determined by intersecting the supply of capital with its marginal productivity schedule. It seems that we need the quantity measures to determine the prices, and vice versa. The economists who first raised this issue taught at Cambridge University in the UK. They focused most of their attention on a phenomenon referred to as factor-intensity reversals. They demonstrated that there was not a unique mapping between the factor price ratio (the interest rate/wage ratio) and the level of capital intensity selected by firms. Neoclassical theory involved just such a relationship: the lower the interest rate/wage ratio, the more capital-intensive production is. Since the most obvious home of the Neoclassical approach at the time was MIT in Cambridge, Massachusetts – given Solow's (1956) revival of growth theory and his estimation of an aggregate production function – this debate on capital theory was referred to as the battle between the two Cambridges.

Cambridge, Massachusetts responded by relying on Friedman's 'positive economics' methodology. Solow (and colleagues) acknowledged that there was a theoretical problem – that factor intensity reversals could happen. But, they argued, this problem may not occur often enough to matter in aggregate data. The 'proof of the pudding is in the eating' was the retort; if an empirically estimated aggregate production function appears to fit the data, then the practical relevance of the capital controversy can be viewed as low. If we get acceptable summary statistics, and if we find that the function, once fitted, has partial derivatives with respect to each factor that closely mimic observed factor prices, it would seem fair to conclude that the problem raised by Solow's counterparts in England is simply not important from an empirical relevance point of view. Since these outcomes are precisely what Solow found in his empirical estimation, this 'right in theory – but irrelevant in practice' evaluation of the capital controversy is what has stuck. This literature seems to have died off (except among a lively group known as the post-Keynesians, who are regularly ignored by mainstream economists). Such a reaction – among 'practical' people – would seem justified if it were not for a much neglected study undertaken by one of Solow's mainstream colleagues at MIT – Franklin Fisher (see his 2005 summary of this literature).

Fisher set up some fictitious theoretical economies in which – by deliberate construction – 'we know with certainty that an aggregate production function is a poor description of the actual technology'. Fisher then took the data that emerged from these calibrated models, and pretended that he was a researcher in Solow's mould. The fictitious researchers all concluded that the Cobb–Douglas production function is a good description of the data. These simulations would seem to indicate that the 'proof of the pudding is in the eating' approach is unappealing after all. It would seem that most economists have ignored this study – written more than 40 years ago – and, as a result, the pride exuded by modern analysts in their apparent respecting of the Lucas critique is not well founded. After all, if even the basic constructs of modern macro are suspect, the micro-foundations have to be viewed as incomplete.

How is it that Fisher's results emerged as they did? The following analysis provides a partial answer. We begin with the national-income identity: $Y = wL + rK$. We get per-capita values by dividing through by L: $y = w + rK$, where y and k denote per-capita output and capital. Take the time derivative of this last equation, divide both sides by y, and simplify by defining capital's share of output as $s = rk/y$. The result is:

$$\dot{y}/y = (1-s)(\dot{w}/w) + s((\dot{r}/r) + (\dot{k}/k)).$$

We next ask: what will this manipulation of an identity imply if we insert the proposition that labour's and capital's shares of national income stay constant over time? We ask this simply because we have observed such constancy over many decades. Taking the time derivative of the definition of s, and setting the change in s equal to zero, we get:

$$\dot{y}/y = \dot{r}/r + \dot{k}/k.$$

Combining the last two equations, we learn that the growth rate for wages and for *GDP* must be the same. Roughly speaking, this is what we observe in all market-oriented economies, so we denote this common growth rate in living standards by n. Finally, the other fact that emerges from economic history is that there has been no long-run trend in real interest rates (so $\dot{r}$ has been zero). Substituting these 'facts' into the dynamic version of the income identity, we have:

$$\dot{y}/y = ((1-s)n) + s(\dot{k}/k).$$

Integrating this equation, we end with $y = Ak^s$ where $A = ae^{(1-s)n}$. This is the equation of a Cobb–Douglas production function with neutral technological progress occurring at rate n. It would seem that the good fits that people, including Fisher, get when estimating Cobb–Douglas production functions are consistent with at least two interpretations: (1) there is an aggregate production function (that is Cobb–Douglas); or (2) there is not an aggregate production function, but there exist social pressures to keep factor shares roughly constant, as the economy grows, so it *appears* that there is an aggregate production function.

It is difficult to avoid the conclusion that there is no empirical basis for selecting interpretation 1. Instead, our selection is based on our desire to abide by Lucas's decree – that we start all economic analyses with the only things that can be taken as policy-invariant (primitive) in our discipline – tastes and technology. It was one thing for Solow to use an aggregate production function on the grounds that it may be an adequate characterization of aggregate outcomes; it is quite another to use this relationship in an analysis that emphasizes its respecting of the Lucas critique (and its attempted consistency with underlying microeconomic principles) but ignores observational equivalence issues. Perhaps a little more mutual tolerance between the generations of macroeconomists is warranted. After all, in the words of one of this author's mentors (David Laidler), 'ad hocery is in the eye of the beholder'.

Similar challenges exist for the tastes part of the taste and technology fundamentals of our subject. Behavioural economics is the branch of our discipline that explores the fact that psychologists' experiments have cast doubt on some of the traditional specifications of the household utility function, for example exponential discounting. But consideration of these controversies takes us well beyond the scope of this book. As a result, we now turn to a discussion of the conventional analysis of the micro-foundations behind the relationships describing household behaviour in modern macro policy analyses.

4.3 Household behaviour

The standard (descriptive) *IS* relationship involves households that are liquidity-constrained; current consumption is limited by current income. In fact, many households can borrow and lend, so current consumption can exceed current income for many periods (as long as the household is solvent – in the sense that the present value of its debts can be covered by the present value of its assets). Many young families borrow as they purchase a home and then use future income to cover both the purchase price and the interest on the mortgage. Households do this because they are impatient; other things equal, they get higher utility if consumption of any item can occur sooner rather than later. The following model captures this behaviour.

Assume that the household utility function is:

$$utility = \sum_{i=0}^{\infty}(1/(1+\rho))^i \ln C_i$$

Here i is the index of time periods, ρ is the rate of time preference (the higher is ρ, the more impatient people are), and the logarithmic form for the utility function at each point in time is consistent with two propositions – that a certain minimum amount of consumption (defined to be one unit) is needed to live (to receive any positive amount of utility) and that (beyond that one unit) there is diminishing marginal utility of consumption.

The household maximizes this utility function subject to the constraint that the present value of the entire stream of consumption be no more than the present value of its disposable income. As readers will have learned in basic micro theory, to achieve utility maximization, the household must arrange its affairs so that the ratio of the marginal utilities of any two items is equal to the ratio of the prices of those two items. In this case, the two items are the levels of consumption in any two adjacent time periods. If the price of buying one unit of consumption today is unity, then the price of one unit of consumption deferred for one period is less than unity, since the household's funds can be invested at the real rate of interest for one period. Thus, the price of one-period-deferred consumption is $(1/(1+r))$. With this insight, and the knowledge that marginal utility for a logarithmic utility function is the inverse of consumption, we can write the condition for utility maximization as:

$$(MU_i/MU_{i-1}) = ((\text{price of } C \text{ in period } i)/(\text{price of } C \text{ in period } i-1))$$

$$[(1/(1+\rho))^i(1/C_i)]/[(1/(1+\rho))^{i-1}(1/C_{i-1})] = 1/(1+r)$$

$$C_i = [(1+r)/(1+\rho)]C_{i-1}$$

By subtracting lagged consumption from both sides of this last representation of the household's decision rule, and by noting that $(1+\rho)$ is approximately equal to unity (a reasonable value for the annual rate of time preference is something like 0.04), the consumption function can be simplified further:

$$\Delta C = (r - \rho)C.$$

Re-expressing this relationship in a continuous-time format, we have:

$$\dot{C} = (r - \rho)C.$$

We now show how this lifetime-wealth-based consumption function – which is consistent with inter-temporal optimization – is just another way of thinking about Friedman's (1957) model of permanent income. According to Friedman, consumption is proportional to broadly defined wealth – the sum of non-human assets, A, and human wealth, H:

$$C = \rho(A + H).$$

The factor of proportionality is the rate of time preference. To see that this is the same theory as the one just derived, we need to know how both human and non-human wealth change over time. In the case of non-human wealth, the specification is familiar. If each individual's level of employment is one unit, she acquires assets when the sum of her wage income, w, and interest income, rA, exceeds current consumption:

$$\dot{A} = w + rA - C.$$

Human wealth is the present value of all future after-tax wage income. Since intuition is more straightforward in a discrete-time specification, initially we write human wealth as:

$$H_i = [w_i/(1+r)] + [w_{i+1}/(1+r)^2] + \ldots$$

Writing this relationship forward one period in time, we have:

$$H_{i+1} = [w_{i+1}/(1+r)] + [w_{i+2}/(1+r)^2] + \ldots$$

Multiplying this last equation through by $(1/(1+r))$, and subtracting the result from the H_i equation, we have:

$$H_{i+1} - H_i = rH_i - w_i, \text{ or}$$

$$\Delta H = rH - w.$$

In a continuous-time specification, then, Friedman's model can be summarized by the following three relationships:

$$C = \rho(A + H)$$

$$\dot{A} = w + rA - C$$

$$\dot{H} = rH - w$$

By taking the time derivative of the first relationship, and substituting the other two equations into the result, we have:

$$\dot{C} = (r - \rho)C.$$

This derivation proves that the permanent-income hypothesis and the inter-temporal optimization theory are equivalent. As a result, the inter-temporal utility-maximization approach is supported by the extensive empirical work that has established the profession's confidence in the applicability of the permanent-income model, and Friedman's approach gains from this equivalence as well, since it is now seen as more consistent with formal optimization than had been previously thought.

Before proceeding with some extensions to this basic framework, it is useful to indicate how the consumption function can be derived more formally. We do so in two stages – first with time treated as a discrete variable, and second with time treated as a continuous variable. Households are assumed to maximize:

$$utility = \sum_{i=0}^{\infty} (1/(1+\rho))^i \ln C_i$$

subject to:

$$C_i + (A_{i+1} - A_i) = rA_i + w_i.$$

After eliminating consumption by substitution, differentiating with respect to the ith period value of A, and setting to zero, we have:

$$C_i = [(1+r)/(1+\rho)]C_{i-1}$$

as derived less formally above.

The same result can be derived in a continuous-time setting if the calculus of variations is used. This is how Ramsey (1928) originally cast this analysis. In this case, the specification is that households maximize:

$$\int_0^{\infty} \ln C e^{-\rho t} dt$$

subject to:

$$C = rA + w - \dot{A}.$$

Since many readers will not have been taught how to deal with a situation in which the objective function is an integral and the constraint is a differential equation, a simple 'cook book' rule is given here. Whenever readers confront this situation, they should write down what is known as the Hamiltonian. In this case it is:

$$\Delta = e^{-\rho t} \ln[rA + w - \dot{A}].$$

Optimal behaviour then follows from:

$$\Delta_A - \dot{\Delta}_{\dot{A}} = 0,$$

where subscripts stand for partial derivatives. It is left for the reader to verify that, in this case, following this procedure leads to exactly what was derived earlier:

$$\dot{C} = (r - \rho)C.$$

Since the reader already knew the answer in this case, he or she can feel reassured that the 'cook book' method for dealing with continuous-time specifications does 'work'.

To have more intuition about this model of household behaviour, consider Figure 4.1. For simplicity, the diagram refers to a planning horizon with only two periods: the present (measured on the horizontal axis) and the future (measured on the vertical axis), and taxes on interest income are ignored. The household's endowment point is A. Since the household can borrow and lend at rate r, the maximum amount of consumption in each of the two periods is marked on both axes. The line joining these two points (which has a slope equal to $-(1 + r)$) is the inter-temporal budget constraint, and the household chooses the point on this boundary of its feasible set that allows it to reach the highest indifference curve (point B).

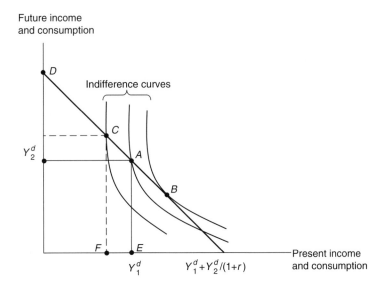

Figure 4.1 Ricardian equivalence

What happens if the government raises taxes today to retire some government bonds? Since this operation just amounts to the government substituting current for future taxes (with the present value of the household's tax liabilities staying constant), all that happens is that the endowment point shifts in a north-west direction along a fixed budget constraint to a point such as C. The household simply borrows more, and remains consuming according to point B. Thus, the Ramsey model involves what is known as 'Ricardian equivalence' – the proposition that the size of the outstanding government debt is irrelevant.

Some OECD governments have taken great pride as they have been working down their debt-to-GDP ratios. In a similar vein, policy analysts have regularly referred to other governments with rising debt-to-GDP ratios as irresponsible. It is clear that these governments and commentators do not believe in Ricardian equivalence. Perhaps this is because they know that some 'real-world' individuals are liquidity-constrained – that is, they cannot borrow. We can focus on this situation in Figure 4.1, by realizing that such an individual faces a budget constraint given by DAE. Such an individual would be at point A – a corner solution – initially. Then, after an increase in current taxes (which retires some bonds and, therefore, cuts future taxes), the budget constraint becomes DCF. The individual moves to point C. Since current consumption is affected by the quantity of bonds outstanding, Ricardian equivalence does not apply.

Allowing for liquidity constraints is just one way to eliminate the Ricardian equivalence property. Another consideration is that people may discount the future, since they expect to die. The Ramsey model assumes that the decision-making agent lives forever. If agents are infinitely lived dynasties (households that have children), this assumption may be quite appropriate. Nevertheless, some households have no children, so we should consider the case in which agents do not live forever. The model has been extended (by Blanchard, 1985b) by assuming that each individual faces a constant probability of death, p. With this assumption, life expectancy is $(1/p)$ and (as derived in Blanchard and Fischer, 1989, chap. 3) the aggregate consumption function becomes:

$$C = (\rho + p)(A + H).$$

Aggregation across individual agents of different ages (to obtain the aggregate consumption function from the first-order condition derived at the individual level) is messy. Nevertheless, it is feasible – given the assumption that life expectancy is independent of age. Not surprisingly, individuals who expect to die consume a bigger proportion of their broadly defined wealth. Saving is less appealing when there is a larger probability that the individual will not live to enjoy the spoils. The overall rate of time preference becomes $(\rho + p)$ – the sum of the individual's rate of impatience and her probability of death. As in the simpler set-up, the consumption function can be re-expressed as a consumption-change relationship. The time derivative of the permanent-income representation is taken, and the aggregate version of the accumulation identities for both human and non-human wealth are substituted in. In this case, these identities are:

$$\dot{A} = w + (r + p)A - C - pA$$

$$\dot{H} = (r + p)H - w.$$

The new terms in the wealth-accumulation identities stem from the fact that people realize that the present value of their future wage income is smaller when death is a possibility. The most convenient way to think of the arrangements for non-human wealth is that there is a competitive annuity industry in the economy. It provides each individual with annuity income on her holdings of A throughout her lifetime, and in exchange the individual bequeaths her non-human wealth to the annuity company when she dies. Since a new person is born to replace each one that dies (so that the overall population size is constant), in aggregate, both these payments to and from the annuity companies are pA each period. When these identities are substituted into the level version of the aggregate consumption function, the result is:

$$\dot{C} = (r - \rho)C - p(p + \rho)A.$$

This consumption function collapses to Ramsey's when the death probability is zero. Since government bonds are part of non-human wealth (variable A), empirical workers have utilized this formulation to test Ricardian equivalence (the proposition that $p = 0$). In pooled time-series cross-section regressions with future consumption regressed on current consumption and non-human wealth, empirical researchers are able to reject the null hypothesis that the A variable's coefficient is zero. We respect these empirical results when using an overlapping generations analysis to evaluate deficit and debt reduction, and the implications of an ageing population, in Chapters 10 and 12, by allowing for $p > 0$ in those analyses. However, since the New Neoclassical Synthesis approach to stabilization policy analysis simplifies by setting $p = 0$, we follow this convention as we report on that literature in Chapters 6 and 7.

Thus far, our theory of households has been simplified by assuming exogenous labour supply. If households can vary the quantity of leisure they can consume, inter-temporal optimization leads to the derivation of both the consumption function and a labour supply function. With endogenous leisure, both current goods consumption and leisure turn out to depend on permanent income. As far as labour income is concerned, permanent income depends on both the current wage rate and the present (discounted) value of the future wage rate. Thus, current labour supply depends positively on both the current wage and the interest rate, and negatively on the future wage. This aspect of the inter-temporal model of household behaviour plays a central part in New Classical macroeconomics (Chapter 5) – the first generation of fully micro-based macro models. Also, the theory behind the 'new' Phillips curve (which forms an integral part of the New Neoclassical Synthesis) relies very much on this same labour supply function. To have a micro base for the new synthesis that is internally consistent, we want the labour supply function to emerge from the same theory of the household that lies behind the consumption function. Thus, for several reasons, we must now extend that earlier analysis to allow for a labour–leisure (labour supply) choice.

As noted, for simplicity and to be able to report the New Neoclassical Synthesis literature as it is, we revert to the everlasting family-dynasty version of the theory of the household, for this extension. These household dynasties live forever, and they choose a saving plan that is designed to smooth consumption over time. Here we assume that households maximize the discounted value of a utility function that is a positive function of consumption *and* a negative function of labour supplied:

$$\int_0^\infty [\ln C - (1/(1 + \varepsilon))N^{1+\varepsilon}]e^{-\rho t}dt$$

N is employment, and parameter ε turns out to be the inverse of the wage elasticity of labour supply. The constraint is the standard accumulation identity for non-human wealth – that asset accumulation equals total income minus consumption:

$$C = rA + (W/P)N - \dot{A}.$$

The Hamiltonian for this problem is:

$$\Delta = e^{-\rho t}[\ln C - (N^{1+\varepsilon}/(1+\varepsilon)) + \lambda(rA + (W/P)N - C - \dot{A})],$$

where λ is a Lagrange multiplier. By following the method explained above, readers can verify that households must follow the two rules specified below (which are the consumption and labour supply functions) if they, in fact, maximize utility:

$$\dot{C}/C = r - \rho \text{ and}$$

$$N = (W/PC)^{1/\varepsilon}.$$

We use the labour supply function in the derivation of the Phillips curve in section 4.5. In this section of the chapter, we focus on the *IS* relationship. If, for simplicity, we ignore investment and government spending, we know that $C = Y$. Using lower-case letters to denote logarithms (for all variables except the interest rate) and using $\bar{r}$ to represent the rate of time preference, the consumption function can be re-expressed as $\dot{y} = (r - \bar{r})$.

Except for adding an autonomous component of expenditure, this completes the derivation of the 'new' *IS* relationship. To add a component of demand that is independent of interest rates we take a logarithmic approximation of the economy's resource constraint $(Y = C + G)$: $y = \bar{y} + \alpha c + (1 - \alpha)g$, where α is the full-equilibrium ratio of interest-sensitive consumption to output; we end with the following slightly more general micro-based *IS* relationship:

$$\dot{y} = \alpha(r - \bar{r}) + (1 - \alpha)\dot{g}.$$

The final term is eliminated (by setting $\alpha = 1$) when analysts are not focusing on fiscal policy. We consider the policy implications of this 'new' *IS* relationship in Chapters 6 and 7.

Space limitations preclude our discussing other dimensions of the theory behind the 'new' *IS* relationship, but we can, at least, mention a couple. Some theorists (such as McCallum, 2001) add a transaction cost term in the household's budget constraint, and specify that these trading costs are lowered when households maintain a high money/consumption ratio. This set-up leads to a standard demand for money function emerging from the optimization and for the 'new' *IS* relationship to contain a real money balance term. These complications are not usually involved in modern policy analysis, however, since calibrated versions of this more complete model involving plausible parameter values have shown that the properties of the model are almost completely unaffected by ignoring the Pigou effect in the *IS* relationship. As a result, at least before the financial crisis in 2008, analysts were not defensive about the fact that money does not appear in modern analyses of monetary policy.

Some extensions of the basic approach involve households having two assets for placing their saving – government bonds and equities issued by private firms. With the extra risk involved in the latter, the stock yield involves an 'equity premium'. Given the restrictions of the formal model, however, the size of the equity premium is strictly related to the parameters of the house-hold utility function. Researchers have had a big challenge (which has yet to be addressed in a satisfactory manner), since the large equity premium in the data is quite inconsistent with standard specifications of the household utility function. Some progress has been made in addressing this challenge by allowing for differences among households. If one group is highly dependent on wage income, which is quite volatile over the business cycle, and if this group reacts by refusing to bear additional risk through the buying of stocks, the other group receives a premium as compensation for having to hold most of the equities. While we do not consider this literature directly in this book, at various points we do embrace heterogeneity among households. In some later sections, we consider households of different age, and models involving a subset of households living hand to mouth – consuming all their disposable income in each period. Mankiw (2000) and Carroll (2001) present empiri-cal work that leads them to strongly approve this embracing of heterogeneity.

Up until recently, the drive to meet the Lucas critique has led many macro-economists to resist this call to move away from the simpler representative-agent analysis. As already noted, meeting Lucas's challenge requires that there be clear macro implications that follow from the micro underpinnings, and this connection is broken if more than limited allowance for heteroge-neity is considered. So addressing Lucas's challenge has often meant ignor-ing heterogeneity to ensure that aggregation problems cannot develop. For many macroeconomists, it has only been since the financial crisis that this consideration has become dominated by the desire to bring a more fully specified financial sector into the standard model. And this requires that there be two groups – borrowers and lenders – so much modelling involving this form of heterogeneity has emerged in recent years.

4.4   Firms' behaviour: factor demands

The consumption function is not the only behavioural relationship that is embedded within the *IS* function. The investment function is an integral part of the *IS–LM* system as well, so (to have a micro base for this relationship) we consider the inter-temporal theory of the firm in this section. Since firm managers may not know the time preference rate of the firm owners, the best thing that managers can do for their owners (who consume according to the permanent-income hypothesis) is to deliver a flow of income that has the maximum present value. Thus, firms are assumed to maximize the present value of net revenues:

$$\int e^{-rt}[F(N, K) - wN - I - bI^2]dt$$

subject to the standard accumulation identity for the capital stock: $I = \dot{K} + \delta K$. Here δ is capital's depreciation rate. The final term in the objective function captures the 'adjustment costs'. It is assumed that – to turn consumer goods into installed new machines – some output is used up in the installation process. The quadratic functional form is the simplest that can ensure that the installation costs for capital rise more than in proportion to the amount of investment being undertaken. This assumption is needed if investment is to adjust gradually to changing conditions, and it is necessary for the production-possibility frontier (between consumption and capital goods) to be the standard bowed-out shape.

The Hamiltonian for this optimization is:

$$\Delta = e^{-rt}[F(N, K) - wN - I - bI^2 + q(I - \dot{K} - \delta K)],$$

where q is a Lagrange multiplier that denotes the value to the firm of a slight relaxation of the constraint – that is, the value of a bit more capital. Thus, q is the relative price of capital goods in terms of consumption goods (and, if equity markets function in an informed manner, q also equals the value of equities). By using the 'cook book' rule (applying it for N, K and I), the reader can verify that the following rules must be followed for the firm to maximize its affairs:

$$F_N = w$$

$$I = a(q - 1) \quad a = 1/2b$$

$$r = F_k/q - \delta + \dot{q}/q$$

The first rule is familiar; it stipulates that firms must hire labour each period up to the point that its marginal product has been driven down to its rental cost (the real wage). The second rule is intuitive; it states that firms should invest in acquiring more capital whenever it is worth more than consumption goods (alternatively, whenever the stock market values capital at more than its purchase price). The third equation states that individuals should be content to own capital when its overall return equals what is available on alternative assets (interest rate r). The overall return is composed of a 'dividend' plus a 'capital gain'. When measured as a percentage of the amount invested, the former term is the gross earnings (capital's marginal product divided by the purchase price of capital) minus the depreciation rate. The final term on the right-hand side measures the capital gain. In our specification of the firms' investment function in Chapter 1 (which was embedded within the basic IS relationship), we assumed static expectations ($\dot{q} = 0$). In Chapter 6 we are more general; we examine what insights are missed by assuming static expectations. But, to simplify the exposition concerning installation costs for the remainder of this section, we assume static expectations.

It is useful to focus on the implications of this theory of the firm for the several models that were discussed in Chapter 1. In the textbook Classical and Keynesian models, firms were assumed to have investment and labour demand functions just like those that we have derived here. As a result, we can now appreciate that the implicit assumption behind these models is that firms maximize profits. That is, they pick factor inputs according to cost minimization, *and* they can *simultaneously* adjust employment and output to whatever values they want. With no installation costs for labour, the standard marginal-product-equals-wage condition applies. But, with adjustment costs for capital, a gap between the marginal product of capital and its rental cost (the interest rate plus capital's rate of depreciation) exists in the short run. The optimal investment function is:

$$I = a[(F_K/(r + \delta)) - 1].$$

This relationship states that investment is proportional to the gap between capital's marginal product and its rental cost. Since capital's marginal product is positively related to the employment of labour, this result 'justifies' assuming that investment depends positively on output and negatively on the rate of interest. (This is standard in traditional IS–LM theory, although sometimes, as in Chapter 1, analysts simplify by excluding the income argument.)

If firms encounter a sales constraint (that is, if they pick factor inputs with the goal of achieving cost minimization *without* being able to simultaneously adjust employment and output to whatever values they want), the optimal investment function is:

$$I = a[(F_K(W/P))/(F_N(r + \delta)) - 1].$$

Readers can verify this by re-specifying the Hamiltonian to:

$$\Delta = e^{-rt}[F(N, K) - wN - I - bI^2 + q(I - \dot{K} - \delta K) + \lambda(\tilde{Y} - F(N,K))],$$

where $\tilde{Y}$ and λ represent the sales-constrained level of output and the Lagrangian multiplier attached to that constraint. The revised investment function emerges after λ is eliminated by substitution – using the first-order conditions for labour. Some of the implications of this revision in the investment function were explained in our analysis of the extended Keynesian model of generalized disequilibrium in Chapter 1.

Returning to a setting with no sales constraints, it is worth drawing attention to the fact that the investment function that is consistent with profit maximization can be written in several different ways. We have already seen that it can be written as $I = a(q - 1)$ and $I = a[(F_K/(r + \delta)) - 1]$. A third option is also possible. Let K^* denote the optimal holding of capital in full equilibrium. In a no-growth setting, investment in full equilibrium is just for replacement purposes, so we have $I = \delta K^*$. When this equation is combined with the accumulation identity for capital, $I = \dot{K} + \delta K$, we have $\dot{K} = \delta(K^* - K)$. This way of summarizing optimal behaviour says that firms should follow a partial-adjustment rule when setting *net* investment. Net investment should equal a constant fraction of the gap between the actual and the desired capital stocks. Empirical workers have made this assumption for many years. The contribution of the formal micro-foundations is that we can appreciate that the partial-adjustment coefficient should not be treated as a 'free' parameter (using Lucas's terminology). For the theory to receive empirical support, we must find that the estimated partial-adjustment coefficient must equal the depreciation rate.

It was mentioned above that we could interpret the Lagrange multiplier, q, as the value of stocks. In fact, it can also be interpreted as the slope of the nation's production-possibilities curve as well. We defend both interpretations now. In a well-functioning stock market, the value of equities equals the present value of the income derived from owning capital. If capital is held into the indefinite future, its per-period earnings will be national output, $PF(N, K)$, minus the wage bill, WN. To obtain the present value of this flow, it is discounted by the sum of the real interest rate and the depreciation rate. (Not only must the future be discounted to calculate present value, but also the capital stock must be maintained.) Assuming constant returns to scale, we have $F(N, K) = F_K K + F_N N$. Using this fact and $PF_N = W$, the market value of equities can be re-expressed in nominal terms as $PF_K K/(r + \delta)$. We can define q as the ratio of the market's valuation of capital to its actual purchase price, PK. This means $q = F_K/(r + \delta)$. This is most appealing. When shares can be sold for such a price that capital can increase at the same rate as the ownership of the company is being diluted, and there are some additional funds left over, the existing owners should approve expansion. This was the intuition behind the Keynes (1936) and Tobin (1969) approach to the investment function. It is reassuring to know that we can embrace a model of investment that is consistent with both this Keynesian intuition and formal inter-temporal optimization.

Without adjustment costs, there is no difference between consumption goods and investment goods. In that case, the economy's production-possibilities curve (drawn in C–I space) is a straight (negatively sloped) 45-degree line. But, with adjustment costs, this is not the case. Ignoring government spending for a simplified exposition, the amount of goods that are available for consumption is given by $C = F(N, K) - I - bI^2$. The slope of the production-possibilities curve is had by taking the total differential of this definition, while imposing the condition that factor supplies are constant $(dN = dK = 0)$. The result is $dC = -qdI$, since we know from our earlier derivations that $q = 1 + 2bI$. Thus, Tobin's valuation ratio can also be interpreted as the relative price of investment goods in terms of consumption goods. As long as macro theorists specify the resource constraint to include the installation-cost term, the production-possibilities curve has its normal bowed-out shape, and the model involves a consistent aggregation of the two kinds of goods (even though it appears as simple as a one-sector model).

Other versions of the firms' investment function emerge if we specify alternative installation-cost functions. For example, with an installation-cost specification that normalizes for the size of the firm (such as bI^2/K or bI^2/Y), we get slightly different investment functions: $I/K = a(q - 1)$ and $I/Y = a(q - 1)$. In this last specification, since the installation process involves labour, there is also an important revision in the labour demand function: $F_N(1 + b(I/Y)^2) = W/P$. With this specification, the separation of demand and supply-side fiscal policy instruments is blurred. Anything, such as program spending, that can affect interest rates and therefore investment is a policy variable that causes a shift in the position of the labour demand function. (With higher interest rates, fewer workers are needed for installing capital (at any real wage).) Since the labour market is what lies behind the aggregate supply curve for goods, G is a policy variable that shifts the position of *both* the demand and supply curves for goods. While some New Keynesian economists (such as Stiglitz, 1992) use models of equity rationing to give their model this very feature, space constraints limit our ability to pursue further these models involving interdependent aggregate supply and demand curves.

Finally, before closing this section, it is worth noting what would happen if there were no adjustment costs. In this case, parameter b would be set to zero, and the first-order conditions imply that q would always equal one, and that $F_K = r + \delta$ would hold at all times. In such a world, capital and labour would be treated in a symmetric fashion. Both factors could be adjusted costlessly at each point in time, so that – even for capital – marginal product would equal rental cost. There would be no well-defined investment function in such a world, since firms would always have the optimal amount of capital. As a result, firms would passively invest whatever households saved. We examine macro models with this feature, when we discuss economic growth in Chapters 10–12. But all models that focus on short-run fluctuations (that is, *both* Classical and Keynesian models of short-run cycles) allow for adjustment costs.

4.5 Firms' behaviour: setting prices

The purpose of this section is to explore the micro-foundations of what has come to be called the 'new' Phillips curve. This relationship now forms an integral part of both New Classical macroeconomics and the New Neoclassical Synthesis. The particular micro model of sticky prices that is favoured in the literature is Calvo's (1983), so we explore that analysis here.

A full treatment would be very complicated. We would need to derive the firms' factor demand functions (labour demand and investment) *and* the firms' optimal price-setting strategy *simultaneously* – within one very general inter-temporal optimization. This is rarely attempted in the literature. Instead, it is assumed that there are two separate groups of firms. The first produces an 'intermediate' product, and it is these firms that demand labour and capital. The second group of firms buys the intermediate product and (without incurring any costs, but subject to a constraint on how often selling prices can be changed) sells it as final goods. This two-stage procedure is an ad hoc simplification that is intended to 'justify' our not integrating the optimal factor demands problem with the optimal price-setting problem. Even with this separation, a full treatment of the price-setting problem is more complicated than what is presented here. The fuller treatment involves product differentiation across firms. Strictly speaking, this is necessary, since each individual firm must have some monopoly power to have a price-setting decision. To ease exposition, however, the present discussion suppresses the formal treatment of monopolistic competition. By comparing this analysis to

King (2000) and Goodfriend (2004), the reader can verify that the 'bottom line' is unaffected by our following the many authors who take this short cut.

Prices are sticky. Specifically, a proportion, θ, of firms cannot change their price each period. One way of thinking about the environment is to assume that all firms face a constant probability of being able to change price. That probability is $(1 - \theta)$, so the average duration of each price is $(1/\theta)$. Then, if p denotes the index of all prices ruling at each point in time and z denotes what is set by those who do adjust their price at each point in time, we have:

$$p_t = \theta p_{t-1} + (1 - \theta) z_t.$$

The objective function for each firm is to minimize a quadratic cost function – the discounted present value of the deviations between (the logarithms of) its price and its nominal marginal cost, mc. The discount factor is $(1/(1+\rho))$, and the cost function is:

$$\sum_{j=0}^{\infty} (1/(1+\rho))^j \theta^j E_t (p_t - mc_{t+j})^2$$

It is shown in the following paragraphs that the first-order condition for this problem can be approximated by the following equation (if the discount factor is set to unity):

$$(p_t - p_{t-1}) = (p_{t+1} - p_t)^e + \mu(mc_t - p_t),$$

where the e superscript denotes expectations. Assuming perfect foresight and switching to a continuous-time specification, we can write:

$$\dot{p} = -\mu(mc - p).$$

To appreciate how we can reach these outcomes, we must first motivate the initial objective function and then outline the derivation. Firms discount the future for two reasons: the normal rate of time preference applies, and (as time proceeds) there is an ever smaller probability that they are stuck with a fixed price. Using $\chi = 1/(1 + \rho)$ as the discount factor, the cost function for the ith firm that was introduced above can be simplified to:

$$\sum_{j=0}^{\infty} \chi^j \theta^j E_t (p_{it} - mc_{t+j})^2$$

$$= \sum_{j=0}^{\infty} \chi^j \theta^j E_t (p_{it}^2 + mc_{t+j}^2 - 2 p_{it} mc_{t+j}).$$

We differentiate this objective function with respect to the firm's choice variable, p_{it}, and obtain:

$$p_{ij} \sum_{j=0}^{\infty} \chi^j \theta^j = \sum_{j=0}^{\infty} \chi^j \theta^j E_t(mc_{t+j}), \text{ so}$$

$$p_{ij} = (1 - \theta\chi) \sum_{j=0}^{\infty} \chi^j \theta^j E_t(mc_{t+j}).$$

We assume that a symmetric equilibrium holds in each period, so that $p_{it} = z_t$ for all firms. To summarize the derivation thus far, we have:

$$p_t = \theta p_{t-1} + (1 - \theta)z_t. \tag{4.3}$$

$$z_t = (1 - \theta\chi) \sum_{j=0}^{\infty} \chi^j \theta^j E_t(mc_{t+j}). \tag{4.4}$$

We simplify equation 4.4 as follows:

$$z_t = (1 - \theta\chi)mc_t + (1 - \theta\chi)\theta\chi E_t(mc_{t+1}) + (1 - \theta\chi)\theta^2\chi^2 E_t(mc_{t+2}) + \ldots$$

$$z_t = (1 - \theta\chi)mc_t + (1 - \theta\chi)\theta\chi \sum_{j=0}^{\infty} \theta^j \chi^j E_t(mc_{t+j+1})$$

$$z_t = (1 - \theta\chi)mc_t + (1 - \theta\chi)\theta\chi E_t(z_{t+1}) \tag{4.5}$$

The next steps in the derivation are as follows. First, write equation 4.3 forward one period in time. Second, take the expectations operator, E_t, through the result. Third, substitute the result into equation 4.5 and then that result into equation 4.3. Finally, simplify what remains, using the definition of the inflation rate: $\pi_t = p_t - p_{t-1}$. We end with:

$$\pi_t = \chi E_t(\pi_{t+1}) + [(1 - \theta)(1 - \theta\chi)/\theta]rmc_t \tag{4.6}$$

where rmc stands for (the logarithm of) each firm's real marginal cost: $rmc_t = mc_t - p_t$. Thus:

$$\pi_t = \chi E_t(\pi_{t+1}) + \mu(rmc_t)$$

where $\mu = ((1 - \theta)(1 - \theta\chi))/\theta$. We approximate this relationship below by setting the discount factor, χ, equal to unity.

The final step in the derivation involves replacing the real marginal-cost term with the output gap. This substitution can be explained as follows. We start with the definitions of nominal marginal cost, total product, and the marginal product of labour, assuming that the production function is Cobb–Douglas:

$$MC = dTC/dY = d(WN)/dY = W(dN/dY) = W/MPL$$

$$Y = N^\sigma$$

$$MPL = \sigma Y/N$$

We combine these relationships with the household labour supply function (which was derived above, and which has been modified by replacing C with Y): $N = (W/PY)^{1/\varepsilon}$. After eliminating MPL, N and W by substitution, we have $(MC/P) = Y^\Omega/\sigma$, where $\Omega = (1 + \varepsilon)/\sigma$. Rewriting this in logarithms, we have:

$$(mc - p) = \Omega y - \ln \sigma.$$

We pick units so that, in full equilibrium, price equals marginal cost equals unity. This implies that firms have monopolistic power only when they are out of long-run equilibrium, and it implies that the logarithm of both price and marginal cost is zero. Thus, the full-equilibrium version of this last equation is:

$$(\overline{mc} - \overline{p}) = \Omega \overline{y} - \ln \sigma.$$

Subtracting this last relationship from the previous one, we end with:

$$(mc - p) = \Omega(y - \overline{y}).$$

When this relationship is combined with either the discrete-time or the continuous-time relationships derived above:

$$(p_t - p_{t-1}) = (p_{t+1} - p_t)^e + \mu(mc_t - p_t), \text{ or } \dot{p} = -\mu(mc_t - p_t),$$

the final result is the 'new' Phillips curve:

$$(p_t - p_{t-1}) = (p_{t+1} - p_t)^e + \phi(y - \overline{y}), \text{ or } \dot{p} = -\phi(y - \overline{Y}),$$

where $\phi = \mu\Omega$. This completes the standard derivation of the closed-economy version of the 'new' micro-based Phillips curve.

This 'new' Phillips curve is often called the 'New Keynesian' Phillips curve. Thus far, I have not embraced this label, since one of the central messages of Keynes is that he believed that involuntary unemployment exists. But, as our derivation clarifies, this new price-change relationship assumes that individuals are *always* on their labour supply curve, so there is never any unemployment at all. Several authors (for example, Ravenna and Walsh, 2008; Blanchard and Galí, 2010; and Galí, 2011) have begun to address this issue by adding search frictions to the specification of the labour market that is appended to Calvo's (1983) price-setting model. An alternative is to focus on another of the several analyses of the labour market that lead to unemployment that we explore in Chapter 8. One of those other theories is Solow's (1979) efficiency-wage theory. According to that model, all observations in the labour market are on the labour demand, not supply, curve, and (abstracting from long-run productivity growth) the real wage is constant. For simplicity, then, we can rely on that analysis to provide a more Keynesian derivation of the new Phillips curve. In this case, all that is needed is that we appeal to efficiency-wage theory to motivate the assumption that the real wage is constant. Thus, we assume a constant real wage rather than use the household labour supply relationship to substitute out the real wage, as we connect the real marginal cost gap to the output gap. With this interpretation, then, we are more justified in referring to this dynamic supply relationship as a 'New Keynesian' Phillips curve.

4.6   Conclusions

The hallmarks of modern macroeconomics are model-consistent expectations, and micro-based, not simply descriptive, behavioural reaction functions on the part of private agents. Chapter 3 contained the analysis that is needed to allow readers to solve macro systems involving model-consistent expectations, and the present chapter contains the analysis that is required to permit readers to understand the inter-temporal optimization that lies behind modern macro models.

The remaining task is to develop an understanding of how the policy implications of the 'new' macro models differ from those of the more traditional descriptive models. We took a first pass at exploring this question in Chapter 3 (section 3.5). The reader is now in a position to appreciate and verify that the system examined there is 'new', since it involves both the 'new' *IS* and Phillips curve relationships, and it involves rational expectations. We now want to pursue this set of issues in more detail, and to do so we proceed in two stages. First, we explore the work of the first group of macroeconomists to take explicit micro-foundations seriously – the New Classicals who assume completely flexible prices – in the next chapter. Then, we consider the sticky-price extension in Chapter 6. With or without sticky prices, these systems are referred to as DSGE (standing for dynamic stochastic general equilibrium) models. Sometimes the sticky-price version is referred to as the New Keynesian macro model, or the 'New Neoclassical Synthesis'. De Vroey and Duarte (2013) argue that the new synthesis label is inappropriate. But, whatever the label, this compact structure now represents mainstream macroeconomics, and that is why we study its properties in some detail in Chapters 6 and 7.

Before moving on to exploring the properties of this mainstream approach to modelling cycles in the next three chapters, we offer some final thoughts on perspective. Several authors have commented on the progress made in macroeconomics in recent decades. Blanchard's (2009) verdict is 'enormous progress and substantial convergence', Woodford (2009) notes that we are 'now widely agreed that macroeconomic analysis should employ models with coherent intertemporal general-equilibrium foundations', and Chari et al. (2009) echo these evaluations: 'modern macroeconomists, whether new Keynesian or Neoclassical, are all alike, at least in the sense that we use the same methodology, work with similar models, agree on which . . . shocks are needed for models to fit the data, and agree on broad principles for policy'. But why is this the case, when the verdict of the critics, such as Howitt (2012), concerning the approach's empirical limitations is so accurate? Howitt notes that the aggregate Euler equation derived from household utility maximization 'does a bad job, on multiple dimensions, of fitting the data', and that the Calvo model of price setting, even when broadened to the 'hybrid' version (discussed in Chapter 6) in an attempt to reflect the data better, is quite inconsistent with micro-based empirical studies.

Three comments can be made to partially answer this question. First, to be useful, *any* model has to involve serious simplification, and so it will have to be wrong on some dimensions. This fact of life must be accepted, and this implies that simulations with calibrated versions of the model could perhaps be viewed as doing theory via numerical methods. A further implication of this response is that there is no justification for intolerance regarding colleagues who work at developing alternative analyses. Second, simulation studies (such as Cogley and Yagihashi, 2010) have shown that – even when a standard DSGE model is constructed with a central specification error – it gives a reasonable approximation to the answer that emerges from the true model (to standard policy questions). Third, some macroeconomists would simply disagree with the convergence-of-views assessment. For example, Shiller (2010) calls for a rejection of model-consistent expectations, while Solow and Touffut (2012) emphasize the fact that the focus on individual optimization means that important system-wide features that were highlighted in earlier versions of macroeconomics – such as coordination failures and externalities – are left out. Finally, Leijonhufvud (2009) is critical of the fact that the linear approximations involved in the new synthesis analysis preclude two considerations that he regards as fundamentally important: multiple equilibria and the possibility of the economy getting outside a stability corridor.

In the end, Howitt (2012) is surely right when he notes that it is impossible to avoid subjective judgements when we have to compare two or more specification errors. All specification errors contribute toward the unreliability of a theory, and how can we know whether failing to impose oversimplified micro optimizations or ignoring heterogeneity, aggregation, coordination frictions and monetary institutions is the greater sin? Howitt sees no alternative to putting at least some weight on the common-sense believability of the model's narrative. Regarding the specific theory behind the mainstream DSGE framework that we have summarized in this chapter, he concludes that 'it would be hard to find many intelligent observers that were capable of understanding the models, without having been socialized by professional training, who would really be convinced by the stories told by the model's developers'. The purpose of this chapter has been to explain these narratives to ensure that readers are duly 'socialized'. It is hoped that readers both have acquired the ability to be active participants in conducting modern macro analyses and have developed perspective on the current state of the discipline.

5

The challenge of New Classical macroeconomics

5.1 Introduction

Our analysis thus far may have left the impression that all macroeconomists feel comfortable with models which 'explain' short-run business cycles by appealing to some form of nominal rigidity. This may be true as far as macro policy makers are concerned, but this has not been a good description of the view of many macro theorists. These theorists are concerned that (until relatively recently) the profession has not been very successful in providing micro-foundations for nominal rigidity. Even those who have pioneered the 'new synthesis' of Keynesian and Classical approaches (for example, King, 2000) have expressed concern that some of its underlying assumptions concerning sticky prices can be regarded as 'heroic'.

The response of New Keynesian academics is to work at developing more convincing models of 'menu' costs (the costs of changing nominal prices), and to elaborate how other features, such as real rigidities and strategic complementarities, make the basing of business cycle theory on seemingly small menu costs appealing after all (see Chapter 8, section 8.5). But there has been another reaction – on the part of New Classicals. Their reaction to the proposition that menu costs 'seem' too small to explain business cycles is to investigate whether cycles can be explained *without any reference to nominal rigidities at all*. They have been remarkably successful in demonstrating that this is possible. Further, some revolutionary conclusions have been derived from this 'equilibrium' approach to cycles. Perhaps the most central result is that the estimated benefit to society of completely eliminating business cycles may be trivial! This chapter explains this so-called real business cycle approach, and how it leads to this strong verdict regarding stabilization policy.

5.2   The original real business cycle model

The unifying theme in New Classical work is 'equilibrium' analysis. Markets always clear; agents make intelligent, forward-looking plans; and expectations are rational. By adopting this framework, New Classicals can rely on the existing general equilibrium analysis provided by microeconomists over more than a century. New Classicals feel that, when Keynesians focus on sticky prices and disequilibria, they lose the ability to benefit from this long intellectual heritage. New Classicals see this as a big price to pay to make macroeconomics 'relevant'. This view becomes particularly firm when the New Classicals feel that they may have demonstrated that the equilibrium approach may be just as relevant – even for explaining short-run cycles. One purpose of this chapter is to permit the reader to form an independent decision on whether this claim of the New Classicals can be sustained.

According to standard intermediate textbooks, Keynesian analysis explains the business cycle by assuming rigid money wages. Demand shocks push the price level up in booms and down in recessions. This set of outcomes makes the real wage rise in recessions and fall in booms, and the resulting variations in employment follow from the fact that firms slide back and forth along a given labour demand curve. Thus, the model predicts that the real wage moves contra-cyclically (and this is not observed), and, because the labour market is not clearing, it makes the labour supply curve irrelevant for determining the level of employment.

New Classicals prefer to assume that wages are flexible and that the labour market always clears. To their critics, a model which assumes no involuntary unemployment is an 'obviously' bad idea. But if this is so, say the New Classicals, it should be easy to reject their theory. While the approach has encountered some difficulties when comparing its predictions to the data, it has turned out to be much more difficult to reject this modelling strategy than had been first anticipated by Keynesians.

New Classicals explain business cycles by referring to real shocks (shifts in technology), so the approach is called real business cycle analysis. The basic idea is that workers make a choice concerning the best time to work. If something happens to make working today more valuable (such as an increase in today's wage compared to tomorrow's), workers make an inter-temporal substitution; they work more today and take a longer-than-usual holiday tomorrow. Similarly, an increase in interest rates lowers the present value of future wages, and so leads individuals to work more today.

If there is a positive technology shock today, the higher marginal product of labour implies a shift to the right of the labour demand curve. Similarly, a negative development in the technology field next period shifts the labour demand curve back to the left. Thus, according to this view, business cycles are interpreted as *shifts in the position of* the labour demand curve, not *movements along* a fixed labour demand curve. Cycles trace out the points along the labour supply curve, and it is the reaction of the suppliers of labour which is central. Since the observation point in a graph of the labour market is never off the labour supply curve, any unemployment that occurs in the low-activity period must be interpreted as voluntary. Critics of the New Classical view are uncomfortable with this interpretation of unemployment.

It should be noted that the New Classical model cannot explain both a wide fluctuation in employment and a very mild fluctuation in real wages over the cycle unless the wage elasticity of labour supply is very large. Micro panel data suggest, however, that this elasticity is quite small. Before addressing the several methods that New Classicals have used to try to get around this problem, we explain the basic approach in more specific terms, by reviewing Hansen and Wright's (1992) version of the real business cycle model. It is defined by the following equations:

$$utility = E\sum_{t=0}^{\infty} (1/(1 + \rho))^t [\ln C_t + \beta \ln L_t] \tag{5.1}$$

$$L_t + N_t = 1 \tag{5.2}$$

$$Y_t = e^{\bar{z}_t} K_t^\alpha N_t^{(1-\alpha)} \tag{5.3}$$

$$\bar{z}_t = \bar{z}t + z_t \tag{5.4}$$

$$z_t = \phi z_{t-1} + v_t \tag{5.5}$$

$$K_{t+1} = (1 - \delta)K_t + I_t \tag{5.6}$$

$$Y_t = C_t + I_t \tag{5.7}$$

Equation 5.1 is the household utility function; E, ρ, C and L denote expectations, the rate of time preference, consumption and leisure. Equation 5.2 is the time constraint (N is employment). Formal utility maximization is used to derive consumption and labour supply functions. Equations 5.3, 5.4 and 5.5 define the production function and the one stochastic variable in the system – the technology shock, z. An ongoing trend is involved, and the stochastic part is a normally distributed error term with zero mean and constant variance, and ϕ is the coefficient of serial correlation in this exogenous process. Formal profit maximization is used to derive the demands for capital and labour. Finally, equations 5.6 and 5.7 define the accumulation of the capital stock (δ is its depreciation rate and I is gross investment), and the economy's resource constraint. New Classicals refer to the capital stock accumulation identity as a 'propagation' or 'persistence-generation' mechanism. Like the Keynesian assumption of staggered overlapping wage or price contracts, this mechanism imparts persistence to the system's dynamics, and this gives the model a serious chance to fit the facts.

While it has now become common practice for practitioners to estimate simple aggregative models like this one, New Classicals initially preferred to pick plausible values for the few parameters and then to use the model to generate data (by simulation). They compared the moments of the time series that were generated by stochastic simulations from the calibrated model to the moments of the various time series from a real (usually the US) economy. If the model's data 'looked like' the real-world data, researchers concluded that this simple approach had been vindicated. Of course, to avoid this exercise being circular, analysts must choose the parameter values on the basis of empirical considerations that are *not* econometric papers involving aggregate time-series data.

Hansen and Wright (1992) report quarterly simulations with the following chosen parameter values. The rate of time preference is set at 0.01 per quarter, which implies 4 per cent on an annual basis. We have learned that (with infinitely lived agents) this parameter should be the same as the average risk-free real interest rate, so 4 per cent is a plausible value. Utility function parameter β is chosen so that the average proportion of discretionary time spent working is one-third – a value consistent with time-use studies. The production function exponent α is set at 0.36, a very plausible value for capital's share of output in the United States (as observed in the national accounts). A similar reference justifies that 10 per cent of the capital wears out annually (so δ = 0.025). Finally, the technology shock process was calibrated by assuming a standard deviation for the error term of 0.007 and a serial correlation coefficient of 0.95. These values were borrowed from one of the original contributions in this field (Kydland and Prescott, 1982), which in turn obtained these values by estimating the combination of equations 5.3 to 5.5 with time-series data for the United States. By estimating the Cobb–Douglas production function with data for Y, N and K only, the estimated residuals – the so-called 'Solow residuals' – can be taken as data for z. Thus, except for the parameters which define this error process, all coefficient values are chosen from sources other than the time series that the modellers are trying to replicate. Nevertheless, since the coefficients for equation 5.5 were chosen so that the time-series properties of *GDP* would be simulated well, we cannot count that feature of the results as a victory.

But there is an achievement nonetheless, since other important stylized facts of the business cycle are well illustrated by the 'data' that is generated from this very simple structure. For example, the simulations show that consumption is less variable than income and that investment is more volatile than income. This outcome follows from the assumption of diminishing marginal utility of consumption. If a positive technology shock occurs today, people can achieve higher utility by spreading out this benefit over time. So they increase consumption by less than their income has increased initially, and, as a result, some of the new output goes into capital accumulation. Since this additional capital makes labour more productive in the future, even a one-time technology shock has an impact for a number of periods into the future. It is impressive that these very simple calibrated models can mimic the actual *magnitude* of investment's higher volatility relative to consumption – and this has been accomplished without researchers allowing themselves the luxury of introducing 'free' parameters.

Despite these encouraging results, however, this model does not generate the wide variations in employment and the very low variability in real wages (which we observe in real data) without an implausibly high value for the wage elasticity of labour supply (an unacceptable value for parameter β). Thus, in the next section of the chapter, we consider a number of extensions to the basic New Classical model that have been offered as mechanisms that can make the 'data' that is generated from the calibrated models more representative of the actual co-movements in real wages and employment.

5.3 Extending and using the real business cycle model

The first extension we consider is an alteration in the utility function. The one given in equation 5.1 embodies the assumption that the marginal utility of leisure in one period is not affected by the amount of leisure enjoyed in other periods. When that function is changed so that this separability is removed, it makes agents more willing to substitute their leisure across time and so respond more dramatically to wage changes. Keynesians regard this extension as ad hoc. They say that the Classicals are introducing 'free' parameters (as the Classicals accuse the Keynesians of doing when they assume arbitrary elements of nominal rigidity) just to make the model fit. If the whole point of the New Classical approach is to have a simple and standard market-clearing model that fits the facts, then such an adjustment made after it was found to be necessary indicates failure to some Keynesians. In any event, the modern approach to adapting the utility function (central to much recent New Classical work) is to specify that today's utility depends on both today's level of consumption and today's level of habits. Habits evolve over time according to the following relationship:

$$h_{t+1} - h_t = \lambda(c_t - h_t)$$

This relationship is an additional persistence-generation mechanism that helps both calibrated and estimated models match real-world data (see, for example, Bouakez et al., 2005). But, since the habit-adjustment process is *identical* to the adaptive-expectations formula, critics argue that New Classicals cannot simultaneously argue that rational expectations is fundamentally more appealing than adaptive expectations and that this extension to the standard utility function is not ad hoc. New Classicals ignore such criticism. Since our subject starts from a specification of tastes and technology, *every* assumption about such matters is necessarily 'arbitrary', and it seems to demonstrate a misunderstanding of the bounds of our discipline to call any such assumption 'ad hoc'. On the other hand, since the hypothesis of adaptive expectations concerns the relationship between actual and forecasted values of *endogenous* variables, not exogenous items such as the definition of tastes, it is legitimately viewed as an arbitrary (ad hoc) specification.

It is not useful for us to get bogged down in methodological dispute. At the practical level, two considerations are worth mentioning. First, since it is difficult to find any non-time-series-econometrics evidence to use as a basis for choosing an 'appropriate' value for the habit-persistence parameter, λ, it has been difficult for practitioners to avoid some proliferation of the free-parameter problem as they implement this extension. The second point worth noting is that this generalization of the utility function does not adequately repair the real wage–employment correlations, so other changes to the basic model have become quite prevalent in the literature as well. It is to some of these other modifications that we now turn.

One such extension is indivisible labour. Some New Classical models make working an all-or-nothing choice for labour suppliers. At the macro level, then, variation in employment comes from changes in the number of people working, not from variations in average hours per worker. This means that the macro correlations are not pinned down by needing to be consistent with evidence from micro studies of the hours supplied by each individual (which show a very small elasticity). For more detail, see Hansen (1985) and Rogerson (1988).

Another extension focuses on non-market activity. Statistical agencies in OECD countries have estimated that, on average, households produce items for their own consumption equal in value to about one-third of measured GDP. Thus, 'home' production is a very significant amount of real economic activity. Benhabib et al. (1991) have shown that, when the real business cycle model involves this additional margin of adjustment, its real wage–employment correlations are much more realistic. The basic idea is that the amount of leisure consumed can remain quite stable over the cycle – even while measured employment in the market sector of the economy is changing quite dramatically – when households have the additional option of working at home (doing chores which they would otherwise have paid others to do).

Other New Classicals, for example Christiano and Eichenbaum (1992) and McGrattan (1994), have introduced variations in government spending. This work involves adding an additional (demand) shock (in addition to technology shocks) to the model; for example:

$$G_t = (1 - \gamma)\overline{G} + \gamma G_{t-1} + u_t \tag{5.8}$$

is added to the system, and the market clearing condition is changed to:

$$Y_t = C_t + I_t + G_t \tag{5.7a}$$

When representative values for the additional persistence-generating parameter γ and for the variance of this additional error term are included in the simulations, the resulting real wage–employment correlations look much more realistic. It is straightforward to understand why. Increases in government spending raise interest rates, and higher interest rates decrease the present value of working in the future. With the relative return of working in the current period thereby increased, the current-period labour supply curve shifts to the right. With these supply-side shifts in the model, some of the variations in employment are explained by shifts along a given labour demand curve. With this additional source of employment fluctuation, the magnitude of the technology shocks does not need to be as great for the calibrated model to generate realistic changes in employment. In addition, with both labour supply and demand curves shifting back and forth, wide employment variations can easily occur with very modest changes in the real wage. That is, as long as the labour supply curve shifts back and forth enough, its steepness is no longer a concern. Needless to say, while Keynesians view the transmission mechanism quite differently, they are delighted to see the alternative school of thought relying on autonomous expenditure variations – a central concept in traditional Keynesian models – to improve the new model's predictions.

As we noted in section 1.5, the New Classical model can be depicted in terms of aggregate demand and supply curves in price-output space. That picture appears just as in Figure 1.1 (in Chapter 1), but the list of shift influences for the aggregate demand and supply curves is different from what variables cause shifts in the textbook version of the classical framework. For simplicity, in the present discussion, we assume static expectations, so no separate expected future consumption and expected future wage rates need to be considered. But, when the labour supply and demand equations are combined (to eliminate the real wage by substitution), we are left with a relationship that stipulates output as a positive function of the interest rate. We can use the *IS* relationship to replace the interest rate. The resulting summary of the labour demand, labour supply, production function and *IS* relationships is a vertical line in *P-Y* space, with government spending and tax rates – in addition to the technology shock – as shift influences.

The real business cycle model allows no role for the money supply, so – to have the model determine nominal prices – we must add some sort of *LM* relationship to the system. Initially, to avoid having to re-specify the household's optimization, this relationship was assumed to be the quantity theory of money relationship $(L(Y) = M/P)$ – justified as a specification of the nation's trading transactions *technology*. This relationship *is* the economy's aggregate demand function, and the nominal money supply is the only shift influence. Thus, the New Classical model still exhibits the classical dichotomy as far as monetary policy is concerned. But fiscal policy – even a change in programme spending – has a supply-side effect, so it has real-output effects. Readers are encouraged to draw the appropriate aggregate demand and supply diagram to compare the effects on output and the price level of variations in autonomous expenditure across several models. Since the traditional Keynesian model involves the prediction that the price level rises during business cycle booms, while this New Classical model has the property that the price level falls during booms, various researchers (for example, Cover and Pecorino, 2004) have tried to exploit this difference in prediction to be able to discriminate between these alternative approaches to interpreting cycles.

Care must be exercised when pursuing this strategy, however, since there is no reason to restrict our attention to an *LM* relationship that does not involve the interest rate. As we see in section 5.4 below, it is not difficult to extend the household optimization part of the New Classical model to derive such a more general *LM* relationship from first principles. When this more general specification is involved in the model, the *IS* function is needed to eliminate the interest rate both from the labour market relationships (to obtain the aggregate supply of goods function) and from the *LM* relationship (to obtain the aggregate demand for goods function). As a result, changes in autonomous spending shift the position of both the aggregate supply and demand curves, and the model no longer predicts that the price level must move contra-cyclically.

And nor is it necessarily the case that a dynamic version of the traditional macro model predicts that the price level moves pro-cyclically. To appreciate this, consider the following very simple specification involving a Phillips curve in which the current inflation rate equals the lagged inflation rate plus an output gap term. In continuous time, this means that the acceleration in inflation is given by $\ddot{p} = \phi(y - \bar{y})$. Add to this an aggregate demand specification that nominal *GDP* moves cyclically due to a sine-curve time path followed by an exogenous demand-side variable x: $p + y = x$ and $x = \bar{x} + \beta \sin(t)$. We assume that $\bar{x} = \bar{y} = 0$; we take the first and second time derivatives of the demand equation, and then eliminate the acceleration in inflation in the Phillips curve. The result is: $\ddot{y} + \phi(y - \bar{y}) = \ddot{x}$. We can determine how real output and price vary over the cycle by using the undetermined coefficient solution procedure. Following Chiang (1984, p.472) the trial solution for output in this case can be written as $y = \bar{y} + B[\cos(t)] + C[\sin(t)]$. After taking the second time derivative of both this trial solution and the x equation, and substituting into the summary of the model, we have:

$$\phi(B\cos(t) + C\sin(t)) - B\cos(t) - C\sin(t) = -\beta\sin(t).$$

The resulting coefficient-identifying restrictions are $B = 0$ and $C = \beta/(1 - \phi)$. Given the available empirical work, we take ϕ to be a fraction, and so assume C to be positive. This implies, not surprisingly, that the cycle in real output mirrors the cycle in the autonomous demand shock. We can examine the cycle in the price level by assuming a second trial solution: $p = \bar{p} + A\sin(t)$. The second time derivative of this trial solution is $\ddot{p} = -A\sin(t)$. Substituting both this relationship and the solution for the output gap into the Phillips curve equation, we have $-A\sin(t) = (\phi\beta/(1 - \phi))\sin(t)$. We conclude that A must be negative, so that the deviations of the price level are contra-cyclical in this standard pre-New Classical model. Therefore, just because we find this contra-cyclical time path in the data (which we often do), we should not conclude that this finding supports the New Classical model.

Other extensions to the basic New Classical model can be understood within the same labour supply and demand framework that we have discussed above. Any mechanism which causes the labour demand curve to shift over the cycle decreases the burden that has to be borne by technology shocks, and any mechanism which causes the labour supply curve to shift accomplishes the same thing – while at the same time decreasing the variability of real wages over the cycle. The variability of price mark-ups over the cycle is an example of a demand-shift mechanism, and households shifting between market-oriented employment and home production are an example of a supply-shift mechanism. Regarding the former, we know that the mark-up of price over marginal cost falls during booms because of the entry of new firms. This fact causes the labour demand curve to shift to the right during booms. Devereux et al. (1993) have shown how this mechanism can operate within a real business cycle model involving imperfect competition.

There are still other reasons for the labour demand curve to move in a way that adds persistence to employment variations. Some authors (such as Christiano and Eichenbaum, 1992) introduce a payment lag. If firms have to pay their wage bill one period before receiving their sales revenue, the labour demand function becomes $F_N = (W/P)(1 + r)$, so variations in the interest rate shift the position of the labour demand curve. Further, firms may encounter adjustment costs when hiring or firing labour, and learning-by-doing may be an important phenomenon (see Cooper and Johri, 2002). In the latter case, tomorrow's labour productivity is high if today's employment level is high. Simulations have shown that the consistency between the output of calibrated equilibrium models and real-world time series is increased when persistence-generation mechanisms such as these are added. It can be challenging to discriminate between some of these mechanisms. For example, there is a strong similarity between the habits extension and the learning-by-doing extension. But, despite this, Bouakez and Kano (2006) conclude that the habits approach fits the facts better.

As mentioned above, it is interesting to note the convergence involved with parts of New Keynesian and New Classical work. Keynesians have been taking expectations and micro-foundations more seriously to improve the logical consistency of their systems, while Classicals are embracing such things as autonomous expenditure variation, imperfect competition and payment lags to improve the empirical success of their models. Despite this convergence, however, there is still a noticeable difference in emphasis.

Classical models have the property that the observed fluctuations in employment have been *chosen* by agents, so there is no obvious role for government to reduce output variation below what agents have already determined to be optimal. This presumption of social optimality is inappropriate, however, if markets fail for any reason (such as externalities, moral hazard or imperfect competition).

Hansen and Wright (1992) have shown that, when all of these extensions are combined, a simple aggregative model can generate data that reflects fairly well the main features of the real-world real wage–employment correlations after all. But still the model does not fit the facts well enough, so even pioneers of this approach (for example, Goodfriend and King, 1997) have called for the New Neoclassical Synthesis in which temporarily sticky prices are added to the real business cycle model. We consider this synthesis in some detail in Chapter 6.

It may seem surprising that New Classicals have embraced the hallmark of Keynesian analysis – sticky prices. Why has this happened? Perhaps because there is one fact that appears to support the relevance of nominal rigidities – the well-documented correlation between changes in the *nominal* money supply and variations in *real* output. Either this is evidence in favour of nominal rigidities or it is evidence that the central bank always accommodates – increasing the money supply whenever more is wanted (during an upswing) and withdrawing money whenever it is needed less (during a recession). In response to this reverse causation argument, C.D. Romer and Romer (1989) have consulted the minutes of the Federal Reserve's committee meetings to establish seven clear episodes during which contractionary monetary policy was adopted as an unquestionably exogenous and discretionary development. The real effects that have accompanied these major shifts in policy simply cannot be put down to accommodative behaviour on the part of the central bank. Further evidence is offered in C.D. Romer and Romer (2004), and further support is provided by Ireland's (2003) econometric results. This evidence – especially that which is derived from independent evidence of the central bank's deliberations – removes the uncertainty that remains when only statistical causality tests are performed. One final consideration is that real and nominal exchange rates are very highly correlated. Many economists argue that there appears to be no way to account for this fact other than by embracing short-run nominal rigidities.

Keynesians welcome this convergence of research approaches, yet (at the conceptual level) they remain concerned about the lack of market failure involved in the classical tradition. Also, they have some empirical concerns, and a few of these are summarized in the next few paragraphs.

The real business cycle approach is based on the notion of inter-temporal substitution of labour supply. However, micro studies of household behaviour suggest that leisure and the consumption of goods are complements, not substitutes (as assumed in New Classical theory). Another awkward fact is that, in the United States at least, only 15 per cent of actual labour market separations are quits. The rest of separations are lay-offs. In addition, the data on quits indicates that they are higher in booms. The real business cycle model predicts that all separations are quits and that they are higher in recessions. Finally, it is a fact that a high proportion of unemployment involves individuals who have been out of work for a long time – an outcome that does not seem consistent with the assumption of random separations.

Other interpretation disputes stem from the fact that it is impossible to observe the technology shocks directly. In Solow's (1957) original work, the residual accounted for 48 per cent of the variation in the output growth rate. Later work, which was able to measure inputs more carefully, avoid some aggregation problems, and allow for a variable utilization rate for both labour and capital, pushed the residual's contribution down dramatically. It is no wonder that New Classicals can explain a lot with the original Solow residuals; they contain a lot more than technology shocks. Incidentally, many analysts find it reassuring that the residuals are now perceived to be much smaller. Surely, if there are both positive and negative technology shocks, disturbances at the individual firm or industry level would largely 'cancel out' each other, so that, in the aggregate, there would not be large losses in technological knowledge. Possibly it would be better if New Classicals interpreted real shocks more broadly, and included such things as variations in the relative price of raw materials, as well as technology shocks, in what they consider as supply-side disturbances.

Quite apart from all these specific details, and even the general question of the relative magnitude of the real-wage and employment correlations, some economists regard the inter-temporal substitution model as outrageous. In its simplest terms, it suggests that the Great Depression of the 1930s was the result of agents anticipating the Second World War and deciding to withhold their labour services for a decade until that high labour demand period arrived. Summers (1986) remarks that, even if workers took such a prolonged voluntary holiday during the 1930s, how can the same strategic behaviour be posited for the machines that were also unemployed?

Given these problems, why does real business cycle theory appeal to many of the best young minds of the profession? Blinder (1987) attributes the attraction to 'Lucas's keen intellect and profound influence', but it also comes from the theory's firm basis in microeconomic principles and its ability to match significant features of real-world business cycles. Rebelo (2005) provides a clear and balanced assessment of both the successes and some of the challenges that remain for the research agenda of real business cycle theorists. It is likely that both this ongoing willingness to address these challenges, and the shift of the New Classicals from calibration to estimation have strengthened the appeal of this approach to young researchers. Finally, perhaps another consideration is that this school of thought's insistence on starting from a specification of utility makes it possible for straightforward normative (not just positive) analysis to be conducted. Since the theory is so explicitly grounded in a competitive framework with optimizing agents who encounter no market failure problems, the output and employment calculations are not just 'fairly realistic'; they can be viewed as optimal responses to the exogenous technology shocks that hit a particular economy.

Using this interpretation, economists have a basis for calculating the welfare gains from stabilization policy. Lucas (1987) has used data on the volatility of consumption over the cycle and an assumed degree of curvature in the utility of consumption function that appears to fit some facts to calculate how much business cycles lower utility. He concludes that 'eliminating aggregate consumption variability entirely would ... be the equivalent in utility terms of an increase in average consumption of something like one or two tenths of a percentage point'. Lucas's conclusion has been influential; it is one of the reasons macroeconomists shifted their emphasis away from stabilization policy concerns and toward long-run growth theory (covered in Chapters 10–12) until the financial crisis and major recession in 2008.

With a view to explaining the recent development of a synthesis involving both Classical and Keynesian ideas, it is interesting to interpret the early simulations produced by real business cycle theorists as an updated version of Adelman and Adelman (1959). These authors performed a similar stochastic simulation experiment with a small econometric model; their intention was to show that a standard Keynesian model (with just a few numerical parameters) could mimic the actual US data. Since both groups (Old Keynesians and New Classicals) have established that their models are consistent with significant parts of actual business cycle data (and therefore should be taken seriously), how can any one of them argue that its preferred approach should have priority in the profession's research agenda (for this reason alone)? Even New Keynesians, for example Ambler and Phaneuf (1992), have shown that an updating of the original Adelman and Adelman study gives the same support to the New Keynesian approach. Now that all groups have proved that their approach has passed this basic test – to be taken seriously as one of the legitimate and contending schools of thought – it seems that either some additional criterion for choosing among the different approaches is required or a synthesis of the New Classical and sticky-price approaches should be embraced. Indeed, as we explore in the next chapter, this synthesis has been just what has developed.

Before ending this chapter and moving on to the synthesis model, we do three things. First, in the remainder of this section, we explain how the basic real business cycle model has been used to develop a diagnostic procedure for determining the causes of the recent recession. Second, in section 5.4, we use a particular version of New Classical theory to illustrate how this school of thought can be used to contribute to policy debates. In particular, we show how it facilitates an estimation of the long-term benefits of adopting a low-inflation policy. Third, in section 5.5, we pursue Lucas's proposition that the value of stabilization policy is trivial.

The severe 2008 recession in the United States has stimulated much research in modern macroeconomics. Since financial sector breakdowns seem to be central features of the recession, and since there had been little analysis of intermediaries in the New Classical literature, it was deemed that this disconnect must be addressed. As a result, the Bernanke and Gertler (1989) analysis of information asymmetry between lenders and borrowers that was originally incorporated within the standard real business cycle model by Carlstrom and Fuerst (1997) has been extended. The analysis rationalizes a positive relationship between a firm's debt-to-net-worth ratio and its borrowing costs. The more leveraged the firm is, the more the lenders are exposed to losses. As a result, the general issue – that lenders know less about the firm's prospects than the borrowing firm does itself – becomes an ever bigger concern for the lender. When a negative real shock hits, the firm's net worth falls, and this deterioration in the firm's balance sheet means that the firm faces higher borrowing costs and increased loan rationing. The result is that firms must cut back their investment in capital and labour demand. These secondary contractionary effects, which emerge via financial intermediaries, accentuate the original negative real shock. This additional propagation mechanism is called the financial accelerator. Bernanke et al. (1999) have introduced it into New Neoclassical Synthesis models as well.

While applauding this introduction of asymmetric information into modern macroeconomics, Ohanian (2009) has argued that we still do not know why the balance-sheet deterioration problem seems to have affected the labour market more than the capital market, in the United States, during and following the recession. The remainder of this section outlines why Ohanian argues that there remain fundamental gaps in our understanding.

Ohanian focuses on a simplified and stripped-down version of the real business cycle model, just like the one discussed in section 5.2. The Cobb–Douglas production function is calibrated with a labour's share of two-thirds, the logarithmic utility function is calibrated so that working time is one-third of the time endowment, the rate of time preference (the annual interest rate) is 4 per cent, capital's depreciation rate is 7 per cent, and the productivity growth rate is 2 per cent. The model then implies three (calibrated) relationships: the production function; the time-allocation rule (that the marginal rate of substitution between consumption and leisure be equal to the marginal product of labour – the real wage); and the consumption-allocation rule (that the shadow price of today's consumption in terms of tomorrow's consumption be the interest rate). Ohanian feeds actual data into these three relationships to determine three 'wedges' – the amount by which the relationships are *not* satisfied. He interprets these wedges as the productivity deviation, the labour deviation and the capital deviation. He also refers to the latter two as implicit taxes on labour and capital. By assessing which wedges are big and small, Ohanian has a diagnostic tool for shedding some light on the underlying causes of the recession.

The three main findings of Ohanian's analysis are: (1) there are no large capital deviations for any of the G7 countries during any of the post-war recessionary periods; (2) the recessions in the non-US G7 countries, and all US recessions except that in 2008, involve large productivity deviations; and (3) the 2008 US recession involves a large labour deviation. Why is the recent US experience so different? If the balance-sheet deterioration issue was so much more important in the US, why did it matter a lot for labour and essentially not at all for capital? And why did the recession persist well after the financial sector was stabilized? The lack of answers to these questions leads Ohanian to an alternative interpretation of the recession, compared to the 'financial explanation'. He considers a 'policy explanation', following Mulligan (2010) and earlier work that has attributed 60 per cent of the Great Depression in the 1930s to the increase in monopoly and cartel arrangements that took place during that period. Ohanian indicates that it may be increases in the minimum wage and in the implicit income tax that was created by changes in mortgage regulations in the United States that explain why (as his diagnostic indicates) the value of leisure has been so much lower than the real wage in recent years in the United States.

Of course, Keynesians can take a different reaction. They can rationalize the excess of the going real wage over the height of the labour supply curve by thinking of Figure 1.6 (in Chapter 1). That is, this 'wedge' is not something unexpected within the Keynesian paradigm. Similarly, Keynesians do not interpret the production function 'wedge' as necessarily a productivity deviation. Since Ohanian makes no distinction between the amount of capital in existence and the fraction of that total that is utilized, Keynesians interpret the production function residual as including both productivity shocks and variations in capital utilization. According to this view, the recession could make it rational for firms to cut capital's utilization rate, and this would be picked up and labelled by Ohanian as a productivity wedge. Since Keynesians have alternative interpretations, they regard Ohanian's diagnostic tool as potentially misleading. Keynesians have always thought they could rationalize the fact that the real-wage/employment observations appear to be off people's labour supply curve. But they still need to address the question that has been raised by Ohanian: why is it only in the United States and recently that this outcome emerges in Ohanian's exercise? At a general level, then, even if readers find unconvincing the proposition that unintended effects of government labour market policy represent the key culprit in the recent American recession, all can agree with Ohanian's call for more research directed particularly at understanding how labour markets function. We pursue this issue in Chapters 8 and 9.

5.4   Optimal inflation policy

To justify a zero-inflation target, many analysts make the following argument. Since inflation is a tax on the holders of money, and since taxes create a loss of consumer surplus known as an 'excess burden', that tax (inflation) should be eliminated. The problem with this argument is that, if one tax is eliminated, the government must raise another tax (and that other tax creates an excess burden of its own). Recognizing this, the standard approach in public finance is to recommend the 'inverse elasticity rule' for setting taxes. Since excess burdens are bigger when taxes cause large substitution effects, the efficiency criterion for judging taxes stipulates that the largest tax rates should apply to the items that have the smallest price elasticities of demand. Since the interest rate is the (opportunity) cost of holding money, and since the estimated interest elasticity of money demand is very small, the inverse elasticity rule can be used to defend a relatively large tax on money. In other words, it supports choosing an inflation rate that is (perhaps well) above zero.

The full-equilibrium benefits of low inflation are independent of the complexities of the transition path that the economy takes to reach the long run (such as those caused by nominal rigidities). As a result, all analysts agree that a basic version of the New Classical model is the appropriate vehicle to use for estimating the benefits of that policy. It is true that a model with nominal rigidities is needed to assess the short-term costs of reducing inflation, and that is why we use such a model for addressing this issue in Chapter 7. But here, since our focus is on the long-term benefits of low inflation, we use an example of New Classical work that highlights money – Mansoorian and Mohsin (2004).

Households maximize a standard utility function. As usual, instantaneous utility is a weighted average of leisure and consumption $(\alpha \ln(1-N) + (1-\alpha)\ln C)$, and there is a constant rate of time preference, ρ. The budget constraint is:

$$C = wN + rK + \tau - \pi m - \dot{A}.$$

Consumption is the sum of wage and rental income, plus the transfer payments received from the government, τ, minus the inflation tax incurred by holding real money balances and minus asset accumulation. Since $A = K + m$ and $i = r + \pi$, we can re-express the constraint as $C = wN + rA + \tau - im - \dot{A}$. Households do not focus on the fact that their individual transfer payment may depend on how much inflation tax the government collects from them – individually. That is, they do not see the aggregate government budget constraint (given below) as applying at the individual level. However, there is an additional complication that confronts households. This novel feature is the 'cash-in-advance' constraint: each period's consumption cannot exceed the start-of-period money holdings. Since the rate of return on bonds dominates that on money, individuals satisfy the financing constraint as an equality: $C = m$. Thus, we replace the m term in the constraint with C. Finally, for simplicity, capital does not depreciate, and, since there is no growth or government programme spending, investment is zero in full equilibrium, and so (in full equilibrium) total output and C are identical. Firms have a Cobb–Douglas production function (with capital's exponent being θ), and they hire labour and capital so that marginal products equal rental costs. The full-equilibrium version of the model is described by the following equations:

$$r = \rho$$

$$(N/(1 - N)) = (1 - \alpha)(1 - \theta)/(\alpha(1 + r + \pi))$$

$$C = K^\theta N^{1-\theta}$$

$$\theta C/K = r$$

The first equation is the Ramsey consumption function when consumption growth is zero (which follows from the household differentiating utility with respect to variable C). The second equation is what emerges when the labour supply function (which follows from the household differentiating utility with respect to variable N) is equated with the firms' labour demand function. The third equation is the production function, and the fourth is the other relationship that follows from profit maximization – that capital is hired to the point that its marginal product equals the interest rate. The final three equations can be used to determine how consumption, employment and the capital stock respond to different inflation rates. As noted, the government budget constraint is:

$$\tau = \pi C.$$

This equation states that lump-sum transfer payments, τ, are paid to individuals, and in aggregate these transfers are financed by the inflation tax.

With τ endogenous, cutting inflation is unambiguously 'good'. Lower inflation eliminates a tax that distorts the household saving decision, and no other distortion is introduced by the government having to levy some other tax to acquire the missing revenue. Consumption, employment, output and the capital stock all increase by the same percentage when the inflation rate is reduced. Specifically:

$$(dC/C) = -((1-N)/(1+r+\pi))\,d\pi.$$

Mansoorian and Mohsin (2004) calibrate the model with standard real business cycle assumptions: $\alpha = 0.64$, $\rho = 0.042$, $\theta = 0.30$, and they assume an initial inflation rate of zero: $\pi = 0$. These assumptions allow them to evaluate the inflation multiplier. The result is that creating inflation of 2 per cent lowers steady-state consumption by 1.37 per cent. This outcome is an annual annuity. With no growth and a discount rate of 0.042, the present value of this annual loss in consumption is $0.0137/0.042 = 32$ per cent of one year's level of consumption. Most analysts regard this magnitude as quite large. The policy implication is that even a 2 per cent inflation rate should not be tolerated.

While we do not use a formal model to derive an estimate of the transitional costs of lowering the inflation rate in this chapter, it is worth pointing out what the magnitude of these costs turns out to be. Experience has shown (see Ball, 1994) that we suffer an increase in the *GDP* gap of about 2 percentage points for about 3.5 years to lower the inflation rate by 2 percentage points. This means that we lose approximately 7 percentage points of one year's *GDP* to lower steady-state inflation by this amount. The benefit–cost analysis says that the present value of the benefits exceeds this present cost (32 per cent exceeds 7 per cent), so disinflation is supported.

This is the standard defence for targeting zero inflation. It is an application of the Neoclassical Synthesis. The long-run benefits of lower inflation are estimated by appealing to our theory of the natural rate (New Classical macroeconomics). The short-run costs are estimated by appealing to a more Keynesian model of temporary deviations from that natural rate that stem from temporary nominal rigidities (our Chapters 2 and 3 model if microfoundations are not stressed, our Chapter 6 model if they are). In diagrammatic terms, the reasoning is illustrated in Figure 5.1, where we continue to abstract from any ongoing growth. New Classical analysis is used to estimate the shift up in the potential *GDP* line that accompanies disinflation, and the short-run synthesis model (in which potential *GDP* is exogenous) is used to calculate the temporary drop (and then later recovery) in actual *GDP*.

Figure 5.1
Implications of lower inflation

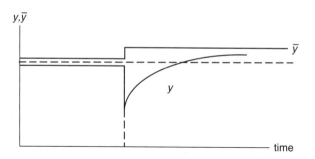

One unappealing aspect of this estimate of the long-term benefits of low inflation is that it involves the assumption that the monetary authority can dictate to the fiscal policy maker (and insist that the latter must cut transfer payments in the face of disinflation). How is the analysis affected if we assume that this is not possible? To explore this question, we add a tax on wage income. Assuming (as we have already) that the wage equals the marginal product of labour, we re-express the government budget constraint as:

$$\tau = \pi C + t((1 - \theta)C/N)N.$$

There is one change in the household budget constraint, since it must now stipulate that households receive only the after-tax wage. This results in only one change; the third equation in our list of the model's relationships becomes:

$$(N/(1-N))=(1-\alpha)(1-\theta)(1-t)/(\alpha(1+r+\pi)).$$

It is left for the reader to re-derive the effect on consumption of a change in the inflation rate, with t being the endogenous policy instrument instead of τ. It is more difficult for disinflation to be supported in this case, since one distortion (the wage tax) is replacing another (the inflation tax). Indeed, in this case, a wage tax rate that is less than one-half is a sufficient though not necessary condition, for the 'benefit' of lower inflation to be *negative*! So, for *any* reasonable calibration, disinflation forces the fiscal authority to rely more heavily on a *more* distortionary revenue source than the inflation tax. Similar results in more elaborate calibrated models are reported in Cooley and Hansen (1991). It would therefore appear that the public-finance approach (which in this case is simplified by using a New Classical model with no ongoing growth) does *not* lead to a solid underpinning for a zero inflation target.

A somewhat more reliable argument for choosing a very low inflation rate (perhaps zero) as 'best' concerns the effect of inflation on savings in a growth context. Most tax systems are not fully indexed for inflation. To appreciate why this is important, suppose you have a $100 bond that gives you a nominal return of 10 per cent. Suppose that inflation is 5 per cent and that the interest rate on your bond would be 5 per cent if inflation were zero. At the end of the year, the financial institution sends you a tax form indicating that you received $10 of interest earnings, and the government taxes you on the entire $10. In fact, however, only $5 of the $10 is interest earnings. The other $5 is compensation for the fact that the principal value of your investment has shrunk with inflation. An interest income tax system should tax only interest income, not the saver's depreciation expenses. An indexed tax system would do just this. Non-indexed tax systems make inflation amount to the same thing as a raising of the interest-income tax rate. Thus, inflation reduces the incentive to save, so that individuals living in the future inherit either a smaller capital stock (with which to work) or a larger foreign debt to service, or both. According to this analysis, then, to avoid a lowering of future living standards, we should pursue a 'zero' inflation target. We evaluate this line of argument more fully in Chapters 10–12. At this point, we simply assert what will be derived and explained there. If there are no 'second-best' problems, growth theory supports the removal of all taxes on saving (such as inflation when the tax system is not indexed). But, if there are second-best problems, this policy is not necessarily supported. Again, the case for zero inflation is far from complete.

5.5   Harberger triangles versus Okun's gap

Thus far, much of this book has focused on explanations of the business cycle and an evaluation of stabilization policy. It has been implicit that there would be significant gains for society if the business cycle could be eliminated. The standard defence for this presumption can be given by referring to Figure 5.2 (where we now allow for ongoing growth by drawing the (log of the) *GDP* time paths with a positive slope).

Figure 5.2 Output gaps

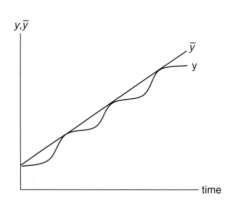

Without business cycles, actual output, y, would coincide with the natural rate, $\bar{y}$, and both series would follow a smooth growth path such as the straight line labelled $\bar{y}$ in Figure 5.2. But, because we observe business cycles, the actual output time path is cyclical – as is the wavy line labelled y in the figure. Traditionally, Keynesians equated the natural rate with potential *GDP*, and Figure 5.2 reflects this interpretation by having the actual and natural rates coinciding only at the peak of each cycle. Okun (1962) measured the area between the two time paths for the United States for a several-decades-long period of time, and, since the average recession involved a loss of several per cent of national output, the sum of the so-called Okun gaps was taken to represent a very large loss in material welfare. The pay-off to be derived from a successful stabilization policy seemed immense.

Before explaining how the New Classicals have taken issue with this analysis, it is useful to note how the likely pay-off that can follow from successful microeconomic policy was estimated back when Okun was writing. As an example, consider a reduction in the income tax rate, which (since it applies to interest income) distorts the consumption–savings decision. In section 4.3, we derived the consumption function that follows from inter-temporal optimization on the part of an infinitely lived agent who is not liquidity-constrained; the decision rule is:

$$\dot{C}/C = r(1 - t) - \rho,$$

where $C, r, \rho,$ and t denote consumption, the real interest rate, the rate of time preference, and an income tax rate that does not exempt interest income (as we assumed in the previous section).

Traditional applied microeconomic analysis involved focusing on full equilibrium without growth (that is, on the $r(1 - t) = \rho$ relationship) and combining this supply of savings function with the full-equilibrium demand for capital ($F_K = r + \delta$, where $F(K, N) = Y$ is the production function and δ is the depreciation rate for capital). Assuming a fixed quantity of labour employed, a Cobb–Douglas function, $Y = K^\theta N^{1-\theta}$, and that the rates of time preference and capital depreciation are independent of tax policy, these relationships imply:

$$(dY/Y) = [\theta rt/((r + \delta)(\theta - 1)(1 - t))](dt/t).$$

With representative parameter values ($t = 0.3, \theta = 0.36, r = 0.03, \delta = 0.1$), a 10 per cent reduction in taxes ($dt/t = -0.1$) involves an increase in national output of just one-half of 1 per cent. This *once-for-all* gain in material welfare is just one-tenth the size of what Okun estimated to be the benefit of avoiding *one* recession. Since the analysis of micro distortions was often presented geometrically as a consumer surplus triangle by public finance specialists such as Harberger, Tobin (1977, p. 468) concluded that 'it takes a heap of Harberger triangles to fill an Okun's gap'. Thus, traditional Keynesians have felt confident that stabilization policy was more important than microeconomic policy.

There has been a major change in thinking on these issues in more recent years. For one thing, analysts no longer feel comfortable with equating the natural rate of output and potential *GDP*. A strict interpretation of real business cycle theory involves the presumption that there is *no difference between the actual and the natural rate of output*. There are simply variations in *the* level of output that are caused by stochastic elements in the production process. Some take a slightly less doctrinaire view of the New Classical approach. According to this view, there are differences between the natural and the actual output rates, and the natural rate is what can be sustained on an average basis. The economy operates below this level during downturns and above this level during booms. Thus, a proper drawing of Figure 5.2 involves shifting the smooth natural-rate line down so that it cuts through the midpoint of each up and down portion of the actual output time path. Using such a revised graph to calculate the total Okun's gap over a period of years gives a very different answer. Output losses are still incurred during recessions, but these losses are approximately made up for by the output gains during booms. A perfect stabilization policy would eliminate both the output losses and the output gains. Thus, it is possible that, on balance, the net benefit of (even a perfectly successful) stabilization policy is close to zero.

Even if gains and losses did cancel out, there would still be some benefit to individuals as long as they are risk averse. That is, two income streams with the same present value are not evaluated as equal in utility terms if one income stream involves volatility. Figure 5.3 illustrates this issue. It shows that, with risk aversion, an individual refuses a fair bet – for example, she refuses to pay $100 for the right to play a game in which there is a 50–50 chance of receiving either $150 or $50. The expected value of the game is $100, but – given the uncertainty – the utility that can be derived from this expected value is not as big as what is enjoyed when the $100 is certain. Thus, an individual with diminishing marginal utility is willing to give up an amount of utility equal to distance *DB* to eliminate the variability in her income stream. If the degree of risk aversion is very slight, the utility of income function is almost linear, then distance *DB* is very tiny. This is the reasoning that Lucas (1987) used in arriving at his estimate of the value of stabilization policy. Using a time-separable utility function with a constant coefficient of relative risk aversion (for which empirical demand systems yield an estimate), Lucas was able to quantify the benefits of eliminating variability, and, as already noted, he concluded that they were trivial.

Keynesians have made three points in reacting to Lucas. The first concerns whether there is market failure. According to New Classicals, unemploy-

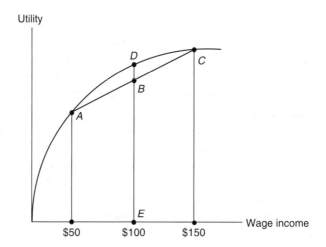

Figure 5.3
Diminishing marginal
utility and risk aversion

ment is voluntary, so when output is low it is because the value of leisure is high. What is so bad about an 'output loss' if it is just another phrase meaning a 'leisure gain'? But Keynesians think that a significant component of unemployment is involuntary, since it stems from some market failure such as asymmetric information, adverse selection, or externalities in the trading process. (We examine these possibilities in Chapter 8.) According to this view, smoothing is not the only result to follow from stabilization policy. Indeed, just the commitment to attempt stabilization may be sufficient to shift the economy to a Pareto-superior equilibrium in models that involve both market failure and multiple equilibria. Thus, stabilization policy can affect the mean, not just the variance, of income. In terms of Figure 5.2, stabilization policy can both reduce the wiggles in the y line *and* shift up its intercept in the $\bar{y}$ line. Lucas's calculations simply assume that this second effect is not possible.

A second point concerns the distribution of the gains and losses over the business cycle. A relatively small proportion of the population bears most of the variability, so these individuals are sliding back and forth around a much wider arc of their utility function (than Lucas assumed). Even staying within Lucas's framework and numerical values, Pemberton (1995) has shown that this distributional consideration can raise the estimated benefit of stabilization policy by a factor of eight. An even bigger revision is called for if a different utility function is used. Pemberton notes that many experimental studies have cast fundamental doubt on the expected utility approach. Indeed, the equity-premium puzzle implies that we cannot have confidence in utility functions like the one Lucas used. When some of the alternatives are used to rework Lucas's calculations, it turns out that business cycles do involve significant welfare implications.

Thus far, our discussion of the relative size of Okun's gap and Harberger triangles has ignored two things: what are the effects of tax changes *before* full equilibrium is reached, and what are the effects (if any) on the economy's average rate of growth? These issues can be clarified with reference to Figure 5.4. As we have seen, a cut in the interest-income tax stimulates savings. As a result, current consumption must drop, as shown by the step down in the solid-line time path in the left-hand panel of Figure 5.4. Individuals must suffer this lower standard of living for a time, before the increase in the stock of capital (made possible by the higher saving) takes place. Our illustrative calculations have estimated the long-term gain (the step up in the dashed line in the left-hand panel of the figure) but not this short-term pain. Thus, the comparison of Okun gaps and Harberger triangles is not complete without a dynamic analysis of tax policy (which is provided in Chapters 10–12). But we must also note that a tax policy which stimulates savings may not just cause a once-for-all increase in the *level* of living standards. It may raise the ongoing *growth rate* of consumption, as shown in the right-hand panel of Figure 5.4. There is still a period of short-term pain in this case, but the effect on the present value of all future consumption can be much more dramatic. Whether tax policy can have any effect on the long-run average growth *rate* has been much debated in recent years, and this debate is covered in Chapters 11–12. But, if it can, we would have to conclude that the size of Harberger triangles may be far bigger than earlier analysts had thought.

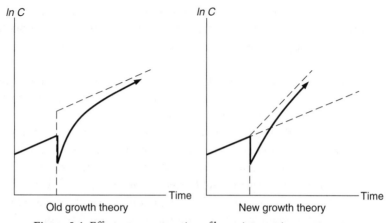

Figure 5.4 Effects on consumption of lower interest-income taxes

Does this mean that Lucas is right after all – that microeconomic policy initiatives are more important than stabilization policy? Not necessarily. As Fatas (2000), Barlevy (2004) and Blackburn and Pelloni (2005) have shown, there is a negative correlation between the variance of output growth and its mean value. It seems that a more volatile business cycle is not conducive to investment, and so it contributes to a smaller long-run growth rate than would otherwise occur. Thus, endogenous growth analysis raises the size of *both* Harberger triangles and Okun gaps.

It seems that a prudent reaction to the Okun gap versus Harberger triangle debate is to take the view that the profession should allocate some of its resources to investigating both stabilization policy and long-term growth policy (eliminating distortions). As we shall see in later chapters, the *same* analytical tools are needed to pursue both tasks.

5.6   Conclusions

Real business cycle theorists have convinced all modern macroeconomists of the value of explicit micro-foundations, and as a result they have made modern work much more rigorous than what preceded their challenge to that earlier literature. And, now that many New Classicals have acknowledged that some form of nominal rigidity needs to be part of their model, we have a convergence of views. Over the last several years, a particular version of nominal rigidity (Calvo, 1983) – which involves micro-foundations – has been added to the New Classical approach. The resulting 'New Neoclassical Synthesis' model (a real business cycle system with temporarily sticky prices) is quite similar to what New Keynesians had been developing independently. Indeed, when some other key features of New Keynesian work (for example, *real* wage rigidity stemming from incomplete information – discussed in Chapter 8) are added to the real business cycle framework, the empirical applicability of the synthesis approach is enhanced even more. It is to these developments that we turn our attention in the next two chapters – before shifting our focus to long-term growth theory.

6

The New Neoclassical Synthesis

6.1 Introduction

In this chapter, we analyse what has been called the 'New Neoclassical Synthesis' in macroeconomics. As noted in earlier chapters, this approach attempts to combine the best of two earlier schools of thought. First, it is consistent with the empirical 'fact of life' that prices are sticky in the short run (the Keynesian tradition). Second, it is based on the presumption that the Lucas critique must be respected. That is, it is in keeping with the demands of the New Classicals; both the temporary price stickiness and the determinants of the demand for goods must be based on a clearly specified inter-temporal optimization.

This synthesis involves the basic (infinitely lived representative agent) version of the inter-temporal theory of the household (derived in Chapter 4, section 4.3) to re-specify the *IS* relationship, and the similar theory of the firm (derived in Chapter 4, section 4.5) as a basis for a re-specified Phillips curve. The traditional (or 'old') *IS* relationship involves the *level* of aggregate demand (output) depending inversely on the interest rate, and the traditional Phillips curve involves the *level* of the inflation rate depending positively on the output gap. When we derived the micro-based *IS* and Phillips curve relationships in Chapter 4, they appeared rather different. With forward-looking households and firms, expected future output entered the 'new' *IS* relationship, and expected future inflation featured in the 'new' Phillips curve equation. We investigated one aspect of monetary policy in a model involving these 'new' relationships in a rational-expectations setting in Chapter 3 (section 3.5). Since that analysis was rather messy, in this chapter (at least until the penultimate section) we simplify in three ways. First, we ignore stochastic shocks, so that rational expectations becomes the same thing as perfect foresight. Second, we use a continuous-time specification, so that a geometric approach – phase diagrams – can be used instead of algebra. As a result, as we discovered in the previous chapter, the 'new' *IS* relationship involves the *change* in aggregate demand depending positively on the interest rate, and the 'new' Phillips curve involves the *change* in the inflation rate depending inversely on the output gap: $\dot{y} = (r - \bar{r})$ and $\ddot{p} = -\phi(y - \bar{y})$. The third simplification that we rely on for most of the chapter is that we consider only one aspect of the new model at a time – initially, the new *IS* relationship with a traditional Phillips curve, and then a new Phillips curve with a traditional *IS* relationship. In each case, we wish to explore how (if at all) these changes in the model's specification affect the answer to a standard stabilization policy question: what happens to output when the central bank embarks on a disinflation policy?

6.2 Phase diagram methodology

Chapter 2 focused on the first Neoclassical Synthesis – a model that combined traditional *IS* and Phillips curve relationships that were descriptive, not based on formal inter-temporal optimization. In somewhat modified notation, when a monetary policy reaction function is added, that system can be defined by equations 6.1 to 6.3:

$$(y - \bar{y}) = -\psi(r - \bar{r}) \tag{6.1}$$

$$\dot{p} = \phi(y - \bar{y}) + \dot{x} \tag{6.2}$$

$$r + \dot{p} = \bar{r} + \dot{x} + \lambda(p - x) \tag{6.3}$$

The first equation (the aggregate demand function) states that output falls below its full-equilibrium value when the real interest rate rises above its full-equilibrium value. The second equation (the dynamic aggregate supply function) states that inflation exceeds the authority's target inflation rate whenever the actual rate of output exceeds the natural rate. The third equation states that the central bank raises the nominal interest rate above its full-equilibrium value whenever the price level exceeds the bank's target value for the price level, x. The slope parameters (the three Greek letters) are all positive.

We focus on a contractionary monetary policy; the central bank lowers its target value for the price level in a once-for-all, previously unexpected fashion. Further, we assume that – both before and after this change – the bank did maintain, and will then revert to maintaining, a constant value for that target variable (x). If we were to graph this exogenous variable – the level of x as a function of time – it would appear as a horizontal line that drops down in a one-time step fashion at a particular point in time. At that very instant, the slope of the graph is undefined, but both before and after that point in time the slope, $\dot{x}$, is zero.

We are interested in knowing what the time graphs for real output and the price level are in the face of this one-time contractionary monetary policy. We learned how to answer this question in Chapter 2. We were able to rewrite the model as a single linear differential equation in one variable, and from that compact version of the system we could derive both the impact effect on real output, and the nature of the time paths after the policy change had occurred. Specifically, we learned that (as long as the system is stable) there is a temporary recession (which is biggest at the very instant that the target price level is cut). The output time path then starts rising asymptotically back up to the unaffected natural-rate line, and the temporary recession is gradually eliminated (see Figure 2.2 in Chapter 2). There is no jump in the price level; the Keynesian element of the synthesis is that the price level is a sticky variable. But, while it cannot 'jump' at a point in time, it can adjust gradually through time. In this case, it gradually falls to (asymptotically approaches) the new lower value of x. These properties represent the base for comparison in the present chapter. We want to know if the output and price-level time paths follow these same general patterns in a series of modified models.

The first modified model is defined by equations 6.1a, 6.2 and 6.3. The only change is that the traditional IS relationship is replaced by the 'new' IS function:

$$\dot{y} = (r - \bar{r}) \tag{6.1a}$$

To analyse this system, we are unable to use the methods of Chapter 2. This is because, with a second differential equation in the system, we cannot reduce it down to anything simpler than a set of *two* first-order linear differential equations. The purpose of this section is to explain how this system can be analysed – first graphically (in what is known as a phase diagram) and then more formally.

The first step in deriving the phase diagram is to reduce the system to just two differential equations that contain only the two endogenous variables that we most want to focus on. In this case, since we wish to highlight the output and price-level effects, we use the policy reaction function to eliminate the interest rate in the new IS function (after having used the Phillips curve to eliminate the inflation rate from the central bank's reaction function). The result is:

$$\dot{y} = \lambda(p-x) - \phi(y-\bar{y}) \tag{6.4}$$

Equations 6.2 and 6.4 represent the compact version of the model. These relationships contain no endogenous variables other than the two we are focusing on (y and p) and also the time rates of change of no endogenous variables other than these same two. This is exactly the format we need if we are to draw a phase diagram with y and p on the two axes. It is customary to put the 'jump' variable – in this case, y – on the vertical axis, and the sticky-at-a-point-in-time variable – in this case, p – on the horizontal axis. We now explain how to use equations 6.2 and 6.4 to derive the phase diagram.

The goal is to draw two 'no-motion' lines in a y–p space graph. The $\dot{p} = 0$ locus is all combinations of y and p values that involve p not changing through time. The $\dot{y} = 0$ locus is all combinations of y and p values that involve y not changing through time. The model's full equilibrium involves neither variable changing, so – graphically – full equilibrium is determined by the intersection of the two no-motion loci. Only that one point involves no motion in both variables. To draw each no-motion locus, we must determine its three properties: What is the slope of the locus? What precise motion occurs when the economy is observed at a point that is not on this line? And how does this locus shift (if at all) when each exogenous variable is changed? We now proceed to answer all three questions for both no-motion loci.

The properties of the $\dot{p} = 0$ locus can be determined from the $\dot{p}$ relationship – equation 6.2. When $\dot{p} = 0$, this relationship reduces to $y = \bar{y}$, and this fact is graphed as the horizontal line in Figure 6.1, labelled $\dot{p} = 0$. So we have already answered question one; the slope of the $\dot{p} = 0$ locus is zero. What motion takes place when the economy is at a point off this line? The best way to answer this question is to assume that we are at such a point, say point A in Figure 6.1, and then determine what equation 6.2 implies about point A. At A, actual output exceeds the natural rate, and (according to equation 6.2) $\dot{p}$ must be positive at point A as a result. This is just a mathematical way of saying that 'p is rising', so we draw in a horizontal line pointing to the right in this upper region of the diagram to show this rising price level. It may seem tempting to put an upward pointing arrow in the graph, since we are talking about 'rising' prices. But we must remember that we are graphing p on the horizontal axis, so a rising value means an arrow pointing east, not north. Similar reasoning leads to our inserting a western-pointing arrow below the ($\dot{p} = 0$) locus. We have now summarized what is happening (with respect to the price level, at least) at every point in the plane; p is rising when it is observed at values above the line, falling when observed at points below the line, and not moving at all when observed at points on the line. The third (and final) question of interest concerning the ($\dot{p} = 0$) locus is: does this line shift when the central bank lowers the value of x – its price-level target? Since this exogenous variable does not appear in equation 6.2, the answer is simply 'no'; this policy does not shift the position of this no-motion locus. We now proceed to ask and answer these same three questions for the ($\dot{y} = 0$) locus.

Figure 6.1 The properties of the $\dot{p} = 0$ locus

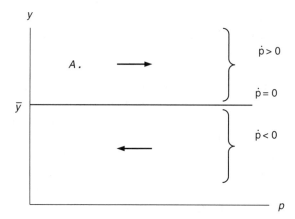

The properties of the ($\dot{y} = 0$) locus follow from equation 6.4. To determine the slope of this no-motion locus, we substitute in the definition of no motion ($\dot{y} = 0$), and solve for the variable that we are measuring on the vertical axis in our phase diagram, y:

$$y = (\lambda/\phi)p + [\bar{y} - (\lambda/\phi)x]$$

The slope expression in this equation is the coefficient on the variable that is being measured on the horizontal axis. Since this coefficient is $(\lambda/\phi) > 0$, we know that the ($\dot{y} = 0$) locus is positively sloped. The intercept is the term in square brackets. Within this term, the coefficient of x is $-(\lambda/\phi) < 0$, so we know that the reduction in x must increase the vertical intercept of the ($\dot{y} = 0$) locus. Thus, we know that the contractionary monetary policy moves the positively sloped ($\dot{y} = 0$) locus up on the page. To answer the remaining question – what motion is involved when the economy is observed at a point that is not on this locus? – we must revert to equation 6.4, which does not involve our having imposed ($\dot{y} = 0$). From equation 6.4, we see that $\partial\dot{y}/\partial y = -\phi < 0$, which means that the time change in y goes from zero to a negative value as we move to a point off the line and above the line. Thus, we label all points above the line as involving $\dot{y} < 0$, and this is what justifies the arrows pointing south in this region of Figure 6.2. Similarly, we label all points below the line as involving $\dot{y} > 0$, and, as a result, we insert a

Figure 6.2 The properties of the $\dot{y} = 0$ locus

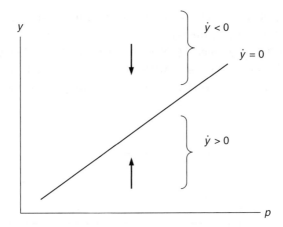

northern-pointing arrow – indicating this rising y motion for all observation points below the line in Figure 6.2.

There is an alternative way to realize that these are the appropriate arrows of motion, and this is by considering points that are to the right or left of the line, instead of above or below the line. To proceed in this way, we derive $\partial \dot{y}/\partial p = \lambda > 0$ from equation 6.4. This sign means that the time change in y goes from zero to a positive value as we move off the line to the right. Thus, we label all points in this region as having the property $(\dot{y} > 0)$, and we show this with the arrow that is pointing north. When deriving a phase diagram, we can select either a vertical-displacement thought experiment or a horizontal-displacement from the line thought experiment – whichever appears to involve the simpler algebra.

We are now ready to put both no-motion lines – with their corresponding arrows that indicate what changes occur when the economy is observed at points off these lines – in the same graph. This is done in Figure 6.3. Point E is full equilibrium, since it is the only point in the plane that involves no motion for either endogenous variable. The two loci divide the rest of the plane into four regions, and the combined forces that operate at all these other points are shown. These forces show that the system has both convergent and divergent tendencies. If the economy is ever observed at points in the north-east or the south-west regions of Figure 6.3, for example, the system diverges from full equilibrium, and we conclude that the system is unstable. This same conclusion is warranted for many points in the north-west and south-east regions of Figure 6.3. Readers can verify this by selecting an arbitrary 'starting' point in one of these regions and tracing the economy's possible time path. If that time path misses point E, the trajectory enters either the north-east or the south-west region, and instability is assured once again. But, since trajectories that start in the north-west and the south-east regions might just hit (and therefore end at) point *E*, stability is possible. The dotted negatively sloped line – labelled the saddle path in Figure 6.3 – shows this possible stable path. So, if this economy is ever observed on the saddle path, there will be convergence to full equilibrium.

Figure 6.3 Combining the $\dot{y} = 0$ locus and the $\dot{p} = 0$ locus

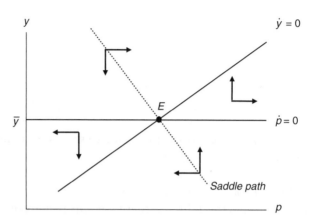

At this point, the outcome seems quite arbitrary; the system may or may not involve stability. To resolve this problem, we apply the correspondence principle. We observe, in the real world, that the instability prediction seems not to apply. Thus, if we are to relate the model to this reality, we must reject the unstable outcomes as mathematically possible, but inadmissible on empirical applicability grounds. Hence, we simply assume that the economy manages to get on the saddle path. This is possible, since history does not pin down a value for one of the two endogenous variables. The price level *is* predetermined at each point in time, but the level of output has been assumed to be a variable that is free to 'jump' at a point in time. These assumptions reflect the Keynesian feature of the synthesis model in the (instantaneous) short run. Even though prices are flexible as time passes, the quantity of output can change faster than its price in the short run. We can summarize this given-history constraint that operates on the price level, but not on output, by adding an 'initial conditions constraint' line in the phase diagram. This is done in Figure 6.4.

There are four loci in Figure 6.4. The intersection of two – the $(\dot{y} = 0)$ and the $(\dot{p} = 0)$ lines – determines the full equilibrium of the system (the long-run outcome – point *E*). The intersection of the other two lines – the saddle path that cuts through the long-run equilibrium point and the pre-existing initial conditions constraint – determines the short-run outcome (point *A*). The saddle path is the line we *need to jump* on to if outright instability (which is presumed to be impossible on empirical grounds) is to be avoided, and

Figure 6.4 Jumping on the saddle path

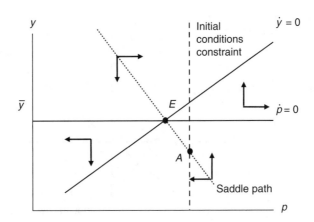

the initial conditions line is what we *can jump* along. The intersection (point A) is the only point in the plane that is both feasible (given the historically determined starting price level) and desirable. While this methodology offers no discussion of a decentralized mechanism that would help individual agents coordinate to find point A, it assumes – on the basis of instability not being observed – that agents somehow achieve this starting point. While this seems somewhat arbitrary, it must be realized that *some* additional assumption is needed to complete the model. After all, the two-equation system involves three endogenous items: $\dot{p}, y$ and $\dot{y}$. With y being a jump variable, both its level and its time derivative are determined within the model. So an additional restriction is needed to close the model, and this additional restriction is that the system always jumps on to the relevant saddle path the moment some previously unexpected event takes place. Any other assumption renders the system unstable and therefore unable to be related to the (presumed to be stable) real world.

It is easier to appreciate how the model works by actually following through a specific event. We do just this by referring to Figure 6.5. The economy starts in full equilibrium at point A – the intersection of the initial no-motion loci. Then a once-for-all, previously unexpected drop in x occurs, as the central bank performs this unanticipated monetary contraction. We have determined that this event shifts the $(\dot{y} = 0)$ line up to the left – to what is shown as the dashed line in Figure 6.5. The new full-equilibrium point is C, but the economy cannot jump immediately to this point, because the price level is predetermined at a point in time. The initial conditions line (always a vertical line if we follow the convention of graphing the jump variable on the vertical axis) is the vertical line going through the initial equilibrium point A. Since y is a jump variable, the economy can move – instantaneously – to any point on this line. To determine which point, we draw in the saddle path

Figure 6.5 Dynamic adjustment following a reduction in x

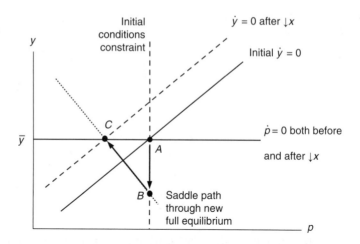

going through the *new* full-equilibrium point C. The intersection of this line with the initial conditions line determines the immediate jump point – B.

The full solution is now summarized. The observation point jumps immediately from A to B; then it travels gradually through time thereafter, from B to C. So the contractionary monetary policy involves a temporary recession, and that recession gets ever smaller thereafter as real output asymptotically returns to the natural rate. This is the same outcome that emerged in the first Neoclassical Synthesis model (Chapter 2), yet we have a new, not an old, IS relationship in the present system. This similarity in results is 'good news'. Since many policy makers were educated several decades ago – before the new synthesis with its more thorough micro-foundations was developed – some find it difficult to shift to a new paradigm. It appears that this may not be a serious problem. The new synthesis analysis indicates that at least this one aspect of the earlier policy analysis is robust. (This is not true for all policies, but at least it is for some initiatives.)

Before analysing related models with the phase diagram methodology, it is worth noting how a more formal approach can yield slightly more precise predictions. In other words, it is useful to be able to calculate impact and adjustment-speed effects in models of this sort formally, rather than simply illustrating them geometrically. The remainder of this section is devoted to explaining how this can be done.

As with all differential equations, the form of the solutions (for the system defined by equations 6.2 and 6.4) is:

$$p_t = x + z_1 e^{\delta_1 t} + z_2 e^{\delta_2 t} \quad \text{and} \quad y_t = \bar{y} + z_3 e^{\delta_3 t} + z_4 e^{\delta_4 t} \qquad (6.5)$$

where the δs are the characteristic roots (eigenvalues), and the zs are determined by initial conditions. Since we are restricting attention to saddle path outcomes, we know that one characteristic root must be positive and the other negative. Let us assume $\delta_2 > 0$ and $\delta_1 < 0$. By presuming a jump to the saddle path, the unstable root is being precluded from having influence, so $z_2 = z_4 = 0$ is imposed as an initial condition. With a linear system, the equation of the saddle path must be linear as well:

$$(y_t - \bar{y}) = \gamma(p_t - x) \tag{6.6}$$

where γ is the slope of the saddle path. It is immediately clear that equations 6.5 and 6.6 are consistent with each other only if $z_3 = \gamma z_1$. Thus, once on the saddle path, all motion is defined by:

$$p_t = x + z_1 e^{\delta_1 t} \quad \text{and} \quad y_t = \bar{y} + \gamma z_1 e^{\delta_1 t} \tag{6.7}$$

We substitute equations 6.7, and their time derivatives, into equations 6.2 and 6.4 and obtain:

$$\delta_1 = \phi\gamma \quad \text{and} \quad (\delta_1 + \phi)\gamma = \lambda \tag{6.8}$$

These two equations can be solved for the stable root and the slope of the saddle path. The absolute value of the stable root defines the speed of adjustment, while the slope of the saddle path is used to calculate impact multipliers. For example, the impact effect on real output of the unanticipated reduction in the target price level follows from the saddle path equation 6.6:

$$(dy/dx) = (d\bar{y}/dx) + \gamma[(dp/dx) - 1]$$

This result states that the impact effect on y is a weighted average involving the full-equilibrium effect on y (which we know, in this model, is zero), and the impact effect on p (which is also zero in this model). Thus, the impact effect on real output simplifies to $-\gamma$, the speed of adjustment is $-\delta_1$, and the cumulative output loss is the former divided by the latter. Using equations 6.8, this cumulative output loss expression – which, for contractionary monetary policy, is usually called the sacrifice ratio – can be simplified to $(1/\phi)$.

It is left for the reader to verify (using the methods of Chapter 2) that, when the new *IS* relationship that is involved in this model is replaced by the old *IS* function, the sacrifice ratio involved with this contractionary monetary policy is *exactly* the same. This fact adds to the assurance noted earlier that the old and new synthesis models can have – but do not always have – quite similar policy implications.

6.3 Stabilization policy analysis with a 'new' Phillips curve

The analysis in the previous section involved a model with a new *IS* function and an old Phillips curve. In this section, we consider a model with the opposite dimension of novelty – one with an old *IS* function and a new Phillips curve. Thus, the model in this section is defined by equations 6.1, 6.3 and 6.2a, where the revised equation is:

$$\ddot{p} = -\phi(y - \bar{y}) \tag{6.2a}$$

In this case, it is most convenient to draw a phase diagram in π-p space, where π is the inflation rate. We put π on the vertical axis (since it is a jump variable) and p on the horizontal axis. The definition of π:

$$\dot{p} = (\pi - 0)$$

is the equation we use to derive the properties of the $(\dot{p} = 0)$ locus. It is a horizontal line – drawn at the point where $\pi = 0$ on the vertical axis in Figure 6.6. There are rightward-pointing arrows above this line and leftward-pointing arrows below this line, indicating the forces of motion when the economy's observation point is not on this line. Since x does not enter this equation, this locus is not shifted when the central bank cuts its target price level.

To obtain the equation that is needed to determine the properties of the $(\dot{\pi} = 0)$ locus, we substitute equation 6.3 into equation 6.1 to eliminate the

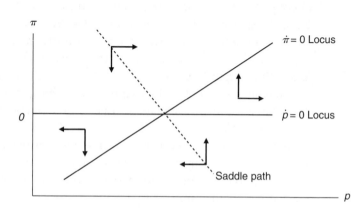

Figure 6.6 Properties of the $\dot{\pi} = 0$ locus and the $\dot{p} = 0$ locus

interest rate, and then substitute the result into equation 6.2a to eliminate the output gap. After noting that $\dot{p} = \dot{\pi}$, the result is:

$$\dot{\pi} = \phi\psi\lambda(p - x) - \psi\phi\pi \qquad (6.9)$$

This equation has exactly the same format as equation 6.4, with π playing the role in equation 6.9 that y plays in equation 6.4. This means that the $(\dot{\pi} = 0)$ locus in the present model has all the same properties that the $(\dot{y} = 0)$ locus had in the model of the previous section (it is positively sloped, there are downward-pointing arrows of motion above the locus, and the position shifts left when x is cut). Thus, the entire policy discussion proceeds in Figure 6.6 as an exact analogy to that which accompanied Figure 6.5. To save space, we leave it to the reader to review this discussion if necessary. We simply close this particular analysis with a short discussion that links the impact effect on π to the impact effect on y. Equations 6.1 and 6.3 combine to yield:

$$(y - \bar{y}) = -\psi\lambda(p - x) + \psi\pi$$

The phase diagram (Figure 6.5) proves that π falls when x falls. Given this outcome, and the fact that p cannot jump, this last equation implies that y must jump down. Thus, the predictions of this new Phillips curve model align with those of the new *IS* curve model (of section 6.2) and of the first synthesis model (of Chapter 2): there is a temporary recession that immediately begins shrinking as time passes beyond the impact period. We conclude, as in section 6.2, that the predicted effects of monetary policy are not specific to any one of these models.

6.4 Some precursors of the new synthesis

In this section, we outline a series of further alternative specifications for the aggregate demand (*IS*) and supply (Phillips curve) relationships. This survey allows readers to appreciate that versions of the new synthesis were present in the literature before the 'New Neoclassical' label became widespread. The first variation is based on the fact that the new *IS* function involves a fundamental limitation. The only component of aggregate demand is consumption spending by households. As a sensitivity test, we now consider a model that involves the opposite extreme specification – that aggregate demand is driven totally by firms' investment spending. As has been our practice in earlier sections of this chapter, we compare this new specification to the original synthesis model. Thus, we specify this investment-oriented demand model by a set of four equations: the same old Phillips curve and central bank reaction functions as used already (equations 6.2 and 6.3) along with the following set of two equations to replace equation 6.1:

$$(y - \bar{y}) = \alpha(q - 1) \tag{6.1b}$$

$$r = \bar{r} + \beta(y - \bar{y}) + \dot{q} \tag{6.1c}$$

These equations were explained in our derivation of firms' investment behaviour in Chapter 4 (section 4.4). The first relationship states that aggregate demand depends positively on Tobin's stock market valuation ratio, q, and the second relationship states that the overall yield on stocks is the sum of a dividend (the first two terms in equation 6.1c) and a capital gain (the final term). In long-run equilibrium, the dividend is the 'natural' real rate of interest; with cycles in the short run, dividends are higher in booms than they are in recessions. Since these relationships follow from dynamic optimization (as explained in Chapter 4), the analysis that we now explain can be thought of as both a precursor to the new synthesis and an integral part of that synthesis – one which involves a firms-oriented, as opposed to a households-oriented, version of a new *IS* relationship.

To achieve a more compact version of this model, we proceed with the following steps. Substitute equation 6.2 into equation 6.3 to eliminate the inflation rate; substitute the result into equation 6.1c to eliminate the interest rate; take the time derivative of equation 6.1b and use the result to eliminate the change in the stock price from equation 6.1c. We end with:

$$\dot{y} = \alpha\lambda(p - x) - \alpha(\phi + \beta)(y - \bar{y}) \tag{6.10}$$

The solution proceeds by drawing a phase diagram based on equations 6.2 and 6.10. As before, a straightforward comparison of this set of two equations to equations 6.2 and 6.4 indicates that the phase diagram is exactly as drawn in Figure 6.5. Thus, as long as we confine our attention to unanticipated monetary policy, there is no need to repeat the analysis. However, since much can be learned by considering *anticipated* policy initiatives, we proceed with this new use of the same phase diagram.

Initially the economy is as pictured in Figure 6.7 – at point A, the intersection of the original no-motion loci. While the variable that is calibrated and labelled on the vertical axis is national output, at some points in the following discussion we interpret movements up and down in the graph as increases and decreases in the stock market. This is permissible since, given equation 6.1b, y and q move one for one together. Assume that – starting from point

A – the central bank cuts its target for the price level. As usual, the $(\dot{y} = 0)$ locus shifts left, point D appears as the new full-equilibrium outcome point, and the saddle path drawn through point D becomes relevant. If this monetary policy were unanticipated, the economy would jump to the point of intersection between this saddle path and the initial conditions line. Stock prices would drop as soon as individuals realized that a temporary recession had been created and – since this hurts profits and dividends – it is not rational to pay as much for stocks as had been previously the case. The stock market gradually recovers – as does the economy.

Figure 6.7 Anticipated monetary policy

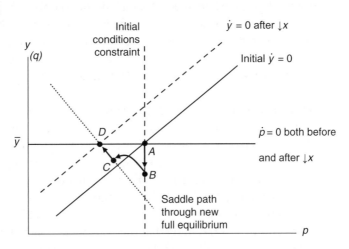

How does this scenario differ when the monetary contraction is pre-announced? For example, suppose the central bank states that, in exactly one year's time, it will cut the target price level. Forward-looking investors know that this will cause a drop in the stock market, and to avoid these anticipated capital losses they sell stocks at the very moment that the future policy is announced. Each individual is trying to sell her shares before anyone else does, to (at least in principle) avoid any capital loss. But everyone is just as smart as everyone else, so this one-sided pressure in the stock market to sell causes a drop in stock prices immediately. Since the monetary policy has not yet been implemented, however, there is no reason for stock prices to fall as much as they do in the unanticipated policy case. Thus, stock prices (and the level of GDP) fall by some intermediate amount – say to point B in Figure 6.7 – the moment the policy is announced.

What happens during the one-year time interval between the announcement of the policy and its implementation? First, since the observation point of the economy is not on either of its no-motion loci, all endogenous variables – real output, stock prices and goods prices – will start to change. By locating point B in Figure 6.3, readers will see that the joint force for motion is in the north-west direction. As a result, the economy tracks along in this fashion until the observation point crosses the ($\dot{y} = 0$) locus in Figure 6.7. Then, because Figure 6.3 involves south-west motion in this region, the economy's time path bends down as it approaches point C in Figure 6.7. With reference to the original full equilibrium (point A) the economy is following an unstable trajectory. But, if agents have perfect foresight (as we are assuming), they will have chosen the location of point B so that the policy is implemented just as point C is reached. At that very moment, the saddle path through point D becomes relevant, and the economy begins to track along it from C to D, after the one-year time interval has expired. To summarize: the economy moves instantly from A to B upon announcement of the policy; it moves gradually from B to C between announcement and implementation, and then gradually from C to D after implementation.

Of course, in reality, agents do not have perfect foresight. Thus, it can turn out that the economy is not at point C the moment the policy is implemented. In this case, the economy continues to follow an unstable trajectory until people realize that the stock market is departing by an ever-widening amount from the 'fundamental' determinants of stock values. At this point there is a 'correction' in the stock market. If the correction is in the downward direction, analysts refer to the 'bubble' bursting. By assuming perfect foresight, we are assuming that there are never any bubbles in asset markets. This is not fully realistic, and it means we may miss an extra wiggle or two in the actual time path. Nevertheless, to maintain precision, it is customary to abstract from such bubbles. An implication of doing so is that the implementation of the policy is not 'news'. Everyone knows from the announcement that it will be implemented, so its effect must be already fully capitalized into stock values. This is why the assumption of perfect foresight forces us to ignore bubbles.

This analysis suggests that we should exercise caution when running Granger causality tests. These tests establish causality between two time series by defining the causing influence as the item that happens first. In this situation, the stock market is observed to cycle – first a drop, then a rise, then another drop and a final rise. GDP follows the same sequence. The money supply follows a very different time path. It shows no action at all while q and y go through their first down-then-up-then-down motion. After that, the money supply falls (this is what the central bank does to raise interest rates) when the policy is implemented, and immediately both the stock market and GDP rise. Time-series evidence would appear to be totally against the monetarist view – that monetary policy is a fundamental determinant of variations in the stock market and economic activity. The time-series evidence would appear to support the Keynesian view that the 'animal spirits' of investors (as evidenced by the swings of optimism and pessimism in the stock market) drive the business cycle. But this interpretation of the evidence is entirely wrong. We know that in this model – by construction – monetary policy has caused everything. Clearly, if forward-looking behaviour is important, the validity of standard causality tests is threatened.

It is worth pointing out that there are other ways of bringing forward-looking behaviour and asset markets into macroeconomics. One branch of literature has distinguished long- and short-term interest rates. For this discussion, we define r to stand for the short-term interest rate – the one that is determined in the monetary policy reaction function. We use R to denote the long-term interest rate – the one that firms care about if they use bonds, not stocks, to finance real investment. In this setting, another equation is needed to close the macro model – a term-structure relationship that pins down the arbitrage equilibrium that would satisfy forward-looking investors. Letting the price of long-term bonds be $q = 1/R$, we can derive that arbitrage condition. Investors have two options: they can hold a short-term bond to maturity (and earn r) or they can hold a long-term bond for that same short period (and earn $R + \dot{q}/q$). There is a capital gain (or loss) term in the yield of a long-term bond over a short period, since the bond does not mature within that holding period. Risk-neutral investors are not in equilibrium if the two bonds have different yields. Imposing that equality, we have the term-structure equation we need to close the model: $\dot{R}/R = R - r$. The full system involves equations 6.2 and 6.3, along with:

$$(y - \bar{y}) = -\psi(R - \bar{R})$$

$$\dot{R} = \bar{R}(R - r).$$

The first of these relationships appears to be an old *IS* curve. The second is a linear approximation of the arbitrage condition just derived ($\bar{R} = \bar{r}$ is the full-equilibrium value of the interest rate). It is left for the reader to analyse this model with a phase diagram. Before proceeding, however, it is worth noting that this specification of aggregate demand essentially nests what we have been referring to as the 'old' and 'new' *IS* relationships. To appreciate this fact, take the time derivative of the second-last equation; use the last equation to eliminate the time derivative of R, and the original version of the second-last to substitute out the level of R. The result is:

$$\dot{y} = \bar{R}[\psi(r - \bar{r}) + (y - \bar{y})]$$

There are three terms in this general specification; the last two are involved in the 'old' *IS* function, while the first two are involved in the 'new' *IS* function. It is interesting that models involving this quite general relationship were being analysed for a number of years before the designation 'New Neoclassical Synthesis' was formally introduced in the literature (for example, see Blanchard, 1981).

Another analysis that involves forward-looking agents and asset prices within the demand side of the model is Dornbusch's (1976) model of over-shooting exchange rates. The open-economy equivalent of the 'old' *IS–LM* system is the Mundell–Fleming model (Fleming, 1962; Mundell, 1963). Dornbusch extended this framework to allow for exchange-rate expectations and perfect foresight. His goal was to make the model more consistent with what had previously been regarded as surprising volatility in exchange rates. Dornbusch's model involved the prediction that the exchange rate adjusts more in the short run than it does in full equilibrium – in response to a change in monetary policy. The following system is a version of Dornbusch's model.

The small open-economy model involves equations 6.2 and 6.3, along with:

$$(y - \bar{y}) = -\psi(r - \bar{r}) + \theta(e - p)$$

$$r + \dot{p} = \bar{r} + \dot{e}$$

The first of these open-economy equations is an old *IS* relationship; in addition to the usual interest rate determinant of aggregate demand, there is a terms-of-trade effect stemming from the net export component of spending; e is the nominal exchange rate – the (logarithm of the) value of foreign currency. The other new relationship defines interest arbitrage: the domestic interest rate equals the foreign interest rate (and we have assumed zero inflation in the rest of the world) plus the (actual equals expected) depreciation of the domestic currency. The properties of this model can be determined via a phase diagram. The compact version of the system (needed to derive the phase diagram) is achieved as follows. Combine the interest arbitrage relationship and equation 6.3 to yield $\dot{e} = \lambda(p - x)$. Combine the open-economy *IS* function with equations 6.2 and 6.3 to yield $(1 - \psi\phi)(y - \bar{y}) = -\psi\lambda(p - x) + \theta(e - p)$. Finally, take the time derivative of this last relationship, and substitute in the second-last equation. The final result is:

$$\dot{y} = (1/(1 - \psi\phi)) [\lambda\theta(p - x) - (\theta + \psi\lambda)\phi(y - \bar{y})] \qquad (6.11)$$

The phase diagram can be constructed from equations 6.2 and 6.11. As we have encountered several times already, the form of equation 6.11 is the same as that of equation 6.4, so the phase diagram analysis is very similar to what was presented in detail in section 6.2. For this reason, we leave it for interested readers to complete this specific open-economy analysis. We encourage readers to examine an unanticipated increase in the foreign interest rate. It turns out that the exchange rate changes more in the short run than it does in the long run. The intuition is that, with another endogenous variable (the price of goods) being sticky in the short run, that variable cannot change as much initially as it will later on. To compensate, the non-sticky variable (the asset price) over-adjusts initially. Since the differential adjustment speeds for these two variables is part of the 'fundamentals' that define this model, it is not appropriate to interpret the volatility of the exchange rate as 'excess' or inconsistent with rational expectations.

Before moving on, we do note that equation 6.11 can be re-expressed, using equation 6.3, as a relationship that involves just three variables: $\dot{y}$, $(r - \bar{r})$ and $(y - \bar{y})$. Just as we concluded with the interest rate term-structure model, then, Dornbusch's system appears to be a forerunner of the 'old' versus 'new' IS curve debate, since this last relationship nests both versions.

The final study that we include in this brief survey of work that is related to the New Neoclassical Synthesis is Taylor's (1979b) model of multi-period overlapping wage contracts (specified in change form, not in levels as was the case in the most widely used version of Taylor's work). This specification yields a model that is similar to one that involves Calvo's (1983) specification of the new Phillips curve, yet it relies on a descriptive, not a micro-based, definition of sticky wages. (For a more detailed comparison of the Taylor and Calvo versions of the Phillips curve, see Dixon and Kara, 2006.)

Let w_t denote the log of all wages contracted in period t; let τ be the proportion of contracts that are of one-period duration; let $\tau(1 - \tau)$ be the proportion of contracts that are of two-period duration; and so on. These definitions imply that p_t, the log of the overall wage index, is:

$$p_t = \tau[w_t + (1 - \tau)w_{t-1} + (1 - \tau)^2 w_{t-2} + \ldots]$$

Writing this equation lagged once, multiplying the result through by $(1 - \tau)$, and then subtracting the result from the original yields:

$$p_t - p_{t-1} = \Omega(w_t - p_t)$$

where $\Omega = \tau/(1-\tau)$. With constant returns to scale technology, units can be chosen so that the marginal product of labour is unity; thus p stands for both the wage index and the price level. Each contracted w is set with a view to the expected (equals actual) price that will obtain in the various periods in the future, and to the state of market pressure in all future periods (with the weight given to each period in the future depending on the number of contracts that will run for two, three or more periods). Thus, we have:

$$w_t = \tau[p_t + (1-\tau)p_{t+1} + (1-\tau)^2 p_{t+2} + \ldots] + \phi\tau[y_t + (1-\tau)y_{t+1} + \ldots]$$

since we define the (log of the) natural rate to be zero. Writing this last equation forward one period, multiplying the result by $(1-\tau)$, and subtracting this last equation from that result, we have:

$$w_{t+1} - w_t = \Omega(w_t - p_t - \phi y_t)$$

Continuous-time versions of these price- and wage-change relationships can be written as:

$$\dot{p} = \Omega(w - p) \text{ and}$$

$$\dot{w} = \Omega(w - p - \phi y).$$

The full model consists of these two relationships and equations 6.1 and 6.3. In continuous time, the length of one period is just an instant; thus, y, r and w are jump variables, while p is predetermined at each instant. Defining $v = w - p$ as an additional jump variable, we can re-express the system (using the by-now-familiar steps) as:

$$\dot{v} = \Omega\psi\phi[\lambda(p-x) - \Omega v]$$

$$\dot{p} = \Omega v$$

The first of these equations that define the compact system has the very same form as equation 6.9. The second is analogous to the definition of π in section 6.3. This symmetry implies that this descriptive model of overlapping wage contracts and the micro-based model of optimal price adjustment have the same macro properties.

6.5 An integrated analysis: a 'new' *IS* curve *and* a 'new' Phillips curve

Thus far, this chapter has proceeded in a piecemeal fashion; we have ana-lysed models with *either* a new *IS* function *or* a new Phillips curve, but not with both new relationships. If we combine both new features in the same system, it involves a first-order differential equation, $\dot{y} = (r - \bar{r})$, a second-order differential equation, $\ddot{p} = -\phi(y - \bar{y})$, and one static relationship – the central bank interest-rate-setting equation. If we arrange this system in the same format that we have followed in earlier sections of this chapter, we would have to deal with a system involving *three* first-order differential equations. Graphic analysis would then require a three-dimensional phase diagram involving two jump variables and one sticky variable. Such a graphic analysis is too cumbersome to pursue. We could use an extended version of the mathematical approach that was explained in the final paragraphs of section 6.2, but pursuing this more technical approach has been rejected as beyond the intended level of this book. Even if readers did invest in master-ing this more advanced mathematical analysis, the model would still have important limitations. In particular, we would be limited to considering one-time changes in the exogenous variables, and would be unable to consider *ongoing* (stochastic) changes.

Our other option is to switch to a discrete-time specification. We have already taken this approach when we examined the full new synthesis model with rational-expectations methods in Chapter 3 (section 3.5). But we have yet to use this methodology to compare the two monetary policies that central banks have been most debating in recent years: price-level targeting versus inflation-rate targeting. To increase the reader's familiarity with this method of analysis, we examine this topical policy issue here by focusing on the following new *IS* and Phillips curve relationships:

$$y_t = E_t(y_{t+1}) - [i_t - (E_t(p_{t+1}) - p_t)] + v_t \tag{6.12}$$

$$p_t - p_{t-1} = \phi y_t + (E_t(p_{t+1}) - p_t) \tag{6.13}$$

To simplify slightly, we limit our attention to a demand shock. The notation is standard; i denotes the nominal interest rate.

In the first instance, we assume price-level targeting on the part of the central bank. The bank's target is unity, so it tries to keep the logarithm of price at zero. To do this, the bank sets the nominal interest rate (i) each period (on the basis of ($t-1$) information) so that $E_{t-1}(p_t) = 0$. The implications can be seen by taking the expectations operator through the *IS* equation, solving the result for the interest rate, and imposing the central bank's goal (both in the resulting interest-rate-setting equation and throughout the model). This involves our simulating how the central bank determines what value of the interest would be needed to deliver a value for *GDP* that will ensure (at least expectationally) that its target for the price level is met.

We now perform the steps that were outlined in the last paragraph, so that we can explicitly derive the interest-rate-setting equation. First we take the $E_{t-1}(.)$ operator through equation 6.12, second we set $E_{t-1}(p_t) = E_{t-1}(v_t) = 0$, and finally (since the central bank sets the current interest rate equal to the value that it expects will deliver its goal) we set $i_t = E_{t-1}(i_t)$. The result is:

$$i_t = - E_{t-1}(y_t - y_{t+1}).$$

When this relationship is substituted back into the *IS* function, and the Phillips curve is simplified slightly, we have the model in the following revised form:

$$y_t = [E_t(y_{t+1}) - E_{t-1}(y_{t+1})] + E_{t-1}(y_t) - p_t + v_t \quad (6.12a)$$

$$p_t = (1/2)p_{t-1} + (\phi/2)y_t \quad (6.13a)$$

We now proceed with solving the model, using trial solutions and the undetermined coefficient method that was explained in Chapter 3. Since there is only one predetermined variable in the model (the previous period's price) and one exogenous variable (the demand shock), there can only be these two terms in the solution equations for real output and the price level. Thus, we assume the following trial solutions:

$$y_t = ap_{t-1} + bv_t \quad (6.14)$$

$$p_t = cp_{t-1} + dv_t \quad (6.15)$$

We use the undetermined coefficient solution procedure to determine how the reduced-form coefficients $(a, b, c$ and $d)$ depend on the underlying structural parameter that has economic meaning (ϕ).

We now substitute the trial solutions into equations 6.12a and 6.13a. First, after substituting equation 6.14 into equation 6.13a, we have:

$$p_t = ((1 + a\phi)/2) p_{t-1} + (b\phi/2) v_t \quad (6.16)$$

Equations 6.16 and 6.15 are the same if and only if:

$$c = ((1 + a\phi)/2)$$

and

$$d = (b\phi/2)$$

We need two more identifying restrictions. These are obtained by using the trial solutions to get expressions for all terms on the right-hand side of equation 6.12a except the error term. Once these are substituted in and the result is compared to equation 6.14, the remaining two identifying restrictions emerge:

$$c(a - 1) = 0$$

$$b = 1 + (a - 1)d$$

The four identifying restrictions are now solved explicitly for a, b, c and d; so the reduced forms contain only the primitive parameter ϕ. One of the identifying restrictions is a quadratic equation, so there are two sets of reduced-form parameter values. But one of these can be rejected, since it involves the stability condition (the absolute value of c being less than unity) being violated. The expressions for price and output volatility (the asymptotic variance for each variable) follow directly from the trial solutions:

$$\sigma_p^2 = [d^2/(1 - c^2)]\sigma_v^2 \tag{6.17}$$

$$\sigma_y^2 = a^2\sigma_p^2 + b^2\sigma_v^2 \tag{6.18}$$

Empirically relevant values for the volatility expressions can be had if a representative parameter value for parameter ϕ is inserted. Walsh (2003a, p. 576) has used 0.2 as an estimate of the slope of the short-run (annual) Phillips curve, so we recommend following his lead by assuming $\phi = 0.2$. It is left for readers to insert this value into the variance expressions and then to compare the numerical variance values to what we derive below.

We compare the outcomes just derived to what occurs if the central bank pursues an inflation-rate target. In this case, all the steps in the solution procedure are repeated, but with $E_{t-1}(p_t) - p_{t-1} = 0$, not $E_{t-1}(p_t) = 0$. Once again, there are two solutions, but it is left for the reader to follow the steps already outlined, and to verify that – if lower output and price variances are desired – this second policy of inflation-rate targeting is dominated by price-level targeting.

The intuition behind this result can be appreciated by considering an exogenous event that raises the price level. With inflation-rate targeting, such a 'bygone' outcome is simply accepted, since the central bank's only obligation is to resist future inflation. But with price-level targeting, future inflation has to be less than zero for a time to eliminate this past inflationary outcome. That is, only under price-level targeting is a policy-induced recession called for. So price-level targeting seems 'bad' from the point of view of limiting output volatility. The reason that this consideration may not be the dominant one, however, is that the avoidance of any long-term price-level drift (which is the central feature of price-level targeting) has a stabilizing effect on expectations. And, for the model we have examined, it appears that the former (destabilizing) effect of price-level targeting is slightly outweighed by the latter (stabilizing) effect.

Svensson (1999) has referred to this favourable outcome as a 'free lunch' – progress made with respect to *two* goals (avoiding long-run drift in the price level and enjoying lower output volatility in the short run), with just *one* policy instrument being adjusted. Walsh (2003b) has shown that this desirable outcome is much less likely to emerge when the model involves a Phillips curve which allows past inflation, not just expected future inflation, to play a role. Walsh considers an extension of the basic new synthesis model (which we have relied on above) that has come to be called the 'hybrid' model to reassess the relative magnitude of the stabilizing and destabilizing effects of price-level targeting.

It is important that we consider a reformulation of the new Phillips curve. This is because the strict version of this relationship makes a prediction that is clearly refuted by empirical observation. Recall that the strict version is $\ddot{p} = -\phi(y - \bar{y})$. Consider what this equation implies during a period of disinflation – a period when the inflation rate is falling (that is, when $\dot{p}$ is negative). This Phillips curve predicts that the output gap must be positive in such situations; that is, we must enjoy a boom – not a recession – during disinflations. This is clearly not what we have observed. Thus, while the new Phillips curve is appealing on micro-foundations grounds, it is less so on empirical applicability grounds. To improve the applicability without losing much on the optimization-underpinnings front, macroeconomists have allowed past inflation, not just future inflation, to play a role in the new Phillips curve. This extension avoids the counterfactual prediction concerning booms during disinflations. Jackson (2005) has shown that a substantial degree of such a 'backward-looking' element is needed in this regard. Since hybrid versions of the Phillips curve provide this feature, we consider them now. For the remainder of this section, we explain what is meant by both the hybrid Phillips curve and the hybrid *IS* relationships. And, since up to this point in the chapter we have focused on monetary policy and ignored fiscal policy, we add government spending to the extension of the Chapter 4 micro-foundations. We end the chapter with a brief evaluation of this more general version of the new synthesis.

Before focusing on hybrid considerations, we note that it should be straightforward for readers to rework the Chapter 4 analysis with an exogenous component of aggregate demand, g. With this extension, the resource constraint becomes $y = \alpha c + (1 - \alpha)g$, the new *IS* function becomes $\dot{y} = \alpha(r - \bar{r}) + (1 - \alpha)\dot{g}$ and the 'new' Phillips curve becomes $\dot{p} = -\phi(y - \bar{y}) + \beta(g - \bar{g})$; $(1 - \alpha)$ is the full-equilibrium ratio of autonomous spending to total output (that is, $\alpha = \bar{C}/\bar{Y}$, $Y = C + G$, $\phi = 2(1 - \theta)^2/\theta + \beta$, $\beta = [(1 - \theta)^2(1 - \alpha)]/(\theta\alpha)$, and θ is the proportion of firms that cannot change their price each period.

The hybrid version of the new *IS* and Phillips curve relationships are weighted averages involving both the new forward-looking specification and a backward-looking component. The latter is included by appealing to the notion of decision-making costs. It is assumed that there is a proportion of agents who find it too expensive to engage in inter-temporal optimization. In an attempt to approximate what the other optimizing agents are doing, the rule-of-thumb agents simply mimic the behaviour of other agents with a one-period lag.

For example, on the supply side (using π to denote the inflation rate and writing relationships in discrete time), the optimizers set prices according to:

$$\pi_t = \pi_{t+1} + \phi(y_t - \bar{y}) - \beta(g_t - \bar{g}),$$

while the rule-of-thumb agents set prices according to:

$$\pi_t = \pi_{t-1}$$

A hybrid Phillips relationship can be had by giving each of these component equations a weight of one-half in an overall equation for π. After doing just that, and replacing first differences with time derivatives to return to continuous time, we have the hybrid Phillips curve:

$$\ddot{p} = -\phi(y - \bar{y}) + \beta(g - \bar{g}) \tag{6.19}$$

Several authors (Galí and Gertler, 1999; Estralla and Fuhrer, 2002; H. Jensen, 2002; Amato and Laubach, 2003; Smets and Wouters, 2003; Walsh, 2003b; Christiano et al., 2005) have derived versions of a hybrid that are equivalent to equation 6.19 but which involve a more elaborate derivation. Some lead to the proposition that the coefficient on the output gap should be bigger in the hybrid environment than it is in the simpler Calvo setting, while others lead to the opposite prediction. At least one, Jensen, supports exactly equation 6.19. There is a mixed empirical verdict on alternative versions of the new hybrid Phillips curve. Galí et al. (2005) argue that most of the weight should be assigned to the forward-looking component, while the results of Rudd and Whelan (2005) lead to the opposite conclusion. Roberts's (2006) empirical findings support our 50–50 specification. Rudd and Whelan (2006) are quite negative on the general empirical success of the hybrid models, while Mehra (2004) reaches a more positive conclusion. Mankiw and Reis (2002) argue that a 'sticky information' approach is more appealing than any of the sticky-price models, and their approach is followed up in Ball et al. (2005) and Andrés et al. (2005). Given our inability to establish a clear preference for any one of these hybrid price-change relationships, it seems advisable to use the intermediate specification that equation 6.19 represents, with wide sensitivity testing on its slope parameters when reporting calibrated results derived from the model.

We now explain a representative specification of a hybrid *IS* relationship. The log-linear approximation of the resource constraint is common to both the forward-looking and backward-looking components:

$$y_t = \alpha c_t + (1 - \alpha) g_t$$

The optimizers follow the Ramsey rule:

$$c_t = c_{t+1} - (r_t - \bar{r}),$$

and the rule-of-thumb agents mimic what other agents did in the previous period:

$$c_t = c_{t-1}$$

Giving a one-half weight to each of these two decision rules, and replacing first differences with time derivatives as we switch to continuous time, we arrive at the hybrid *IS* curve:

$$\ddot{y} = \alpha(r - \bar{r}) + (1 - \alpha)\ddot{g} \tag{6.20}$$

As with the hybrid relationship on the supply side, the differences between several authors' particular models – concerning the size of the slope parameters, not the form of the equation – suggest that researchers should allow for a fairly wide set of sensitivity tests when reporting numerical simulation results.

We do not use the hybrid equations here. Readers are referred to Walsh (2003b) for the revised inflation-rate-versus-price-level targeting analysis, which shows that the free lunch that is supposed to accompany a switch from inflation-rate targeting to price-level targeting seems to disappear in this hybrid setting. Since empirical studies give stronger support for the hybrid relationships, it seems advisable that we put more weight on this result than on the free-lunch proposition that requires the original new synthesis model – with no backward-looking behaviour involved – for analytical support.

Before ending this chapter, we briefly discuss several general issues concerning the new synthesis model. First, it may strike readers as odd that the modern analysis of monetary policy makes no reference whatsoever to the money supply. McCallum (2001) has addressed this concern. He allows money to play a role in reducing transactions costs (in a manner that is more general than the strict cash-in-advance specification that we considered in Chapter 5, section 5.4). When the household's optimization is worked out in this setting, a money demand function emerges as one of the items that is derived along with the consumption function. The *IS* relationship contains real money balances as one of its terms, and this creates an additional channel through which the interest rate can affect spending. Using estimates of the interest elasticity of money demand, McCallum calibrates the model and concludes that being more complete along these lines makes only a trivial difference to the model's properties and policy implications. Others who have investigated this issue are Soderstrom (2002) and Nelson (2003).

Some researchers have raised the issue that there is more than one channel for the monetary policy transmission mechanism. As noted in Chapter 5, higher interest rates can have a cost-increasing effect, not just a demand-reducing effect. This can be important. A number of studies that are based on the standard hybrid new synthesis model show that nominal *GDP* targeting can dominate inflation-rate targeting (for example, see Kim and Henderson, 2005). Malik (2004) and Ravenna and Walsh (2006) have shown that these policy implications can be affected when there is a direct effect of interest rates in the new Phillips curve.

Finally, readers may be surprised by the following feature of the new synthesis framework. Much attention is paid to the proposition that the analysis starts from a clear specification of the agents' utility function. Then, when policies are evaluated with the model, analysis seems to revert to the 'old' habit of ranking the outcomes according to which policy delivers the smallest deviations of output and the price level from their full-equilibrium values. Shouldn't an analysis that is based on an explicit utility function (involving consumption and leisure as arguments) use that very same utility function to evaluate alternative policies? Indeed, this is the only approach that could claim to have internal consistency. It is reassuring, therefore, that Woodford (2003a) has derived how the standard policy maker's objective function – involving price and output deviations – can be explicitly derived as an approximation that follows directly from the private agents' utility function that underpins the analysis.

6.6   Conclusions

When the New Classical revolution began in the 1970s, strong statements were made concerning 'old-fashioned' macroeconomics. For example, Lucas and Sargent (1979) referred to that work as 'fatally flawed', and King (1993) argued that the *IS–LM–*Phillips analysis (the first Neoclassical Synthesis) was a 'hazardous base on which to . . . undertake policy advice'. But, as Mankiw (1992) has noted, that analysis has been 'reincarnated' (*not* 'resurrected' – since the 'new' *IS–LM–*Phillips analysis certainly involves important differences in its structure from its predecessor), and we are left with a framework that is now widely embraced as a base for undertaking policy advice. It is 'good news' that this analytical framework involves roughly the same level of aggregation and abstraction as the older analysis, since this facilitates communication between actual policy makers (who were brought up in the older tradition) and modern analysts. In short, there is reason for much more optimism than there was 40 years ago.

This is not to say that there is no controversy remaining. Indeed, some macroeconomists still actively debate the relative merits of the 'old' and 'new' specifications of the *IS* and Phillips curve relationships. This is because, as noted above, the 'old' relationships appear to be much more consistent with real-world data, despite the fact that the 'new' relationships are more consistent with at least one specific version of microeconomics. It is frustrating to have to choose between the two criteria for evaluating macro models – consistency with the facts and consistency with optimization theory. It is for this reason that many researchers are focused on developing the hybrid models that share some of the features of both the 'old' and 'new' approaches.

One purpose of this chapter has been to make the reader aware of these developments, and to thereby impart some perspective. But since we wished to limit the technical demands on the reader, for the most part, we limited the analysis to a set of 'partially new' models. We have found that some of the properties of these models are very similar. This is fortunate. It means that policy makers do not have to wait until all the controversies within modern macroeconomics are settled before taking an initiative. But the answers to some questions are model-specific. For example, the question as to whether the central bank should target the inflation rate or the price level receives different answers as we vary the model.

The main methodological tool that is used in this chapter is the phase diagram. We will use this tool in later chapters as well. One of the most interesting things that has emerged from our use of phase diagrams is that the impact of government policies can be very different – depending on whether private agents do or do not anticipate that policy. This sensitivity can sometimes make it very difficult for macroeconomists to test their models empirically. Despite these limitations, we use the modern analysis to shed some light on central stabilization policy challenges in the next chapter.

7

Stabilization policy controversies

7.1 Introduction

This is the second of a pair of chapters on the New Neoclassical Synthesis approach to macroeconomic policy questions. The first chapter in this sequence (Chapter 6) was concerned mostly with deriving the necessary methods of analysis. This preparation makes possible the focus in this chapter, where we apply the new approach to four central issues in stabilization policy. We begin by considering three questions that focus on the imposition of constraints on monetary policy. The first involves a self-imposed constraint: should the monetary authority reduce its own future freedom of action by pre-committing to a specified course of action? In section 7.2 we review the literature which shows that, despite losing the advantage of flexibility, the central bank can deliver better outcomes when commitment removes a dynamic consistency problem in policy making and stabilizes expectations.

We move from the general issue of dynamic consistency to specific questions in sections 7.3 and 7.4, where we focus on two specific constraints that are sometimes imposed on monetary policy. Often, based on political considerations such as the desire to make it more difficult to engage in future internal conflicts in the case of Europe, countries opt for currency union. This, and the related policy of fixing the exchange rate by maintaining a currency board, is a severe constraint on monetary policy; these policy decisions make independent monetary policy impossible. We consider whether this policy is recommended in section 7.3, by examining whether a flexible exchange-rate policy leads to a higher degree of built-in stability. Other constraints on monetary policy are imposed by nature, not political decisions. For example, since individuals always have the option of holding cash for a zero nominal return, there is a zero lower bound on nominal interest rates. This constraint makes it difficult for central banks to stimulate demand, when all they can do is to try to lower future interest rates, not the current rate. We consider this constraint on monetary policy, and the scope for relying on fiscal policy instead, in section 7.4.

Section 7.5 is devoted to a constraint on fiscal, not monetary, policy. The basic Keynesian message is that rigid budget-balance rules should be rejected, and that the fiscal authority should run deficits during recessions and surpluses during booms. This policy is intended to enhance built-in stability without having the government debt accumulate, as an ever-growing proportion of the *GDP*, over the longer term. But there is a vicious-circle possibility concerning bond-financed fiscal deficits. Meeting today's deficit by issuing commitments to make even more interest payments in the future can lead to a 'temporary' deficit turning into an ever-rising permanent one. We address this issue of long-run feasibility in section 7.5. But, for the Keynesian advice to be followed, it must be both feasible and desirable. Thus, in section 7.5, we ask what leads to more built-in stability: a budget balance that varies over the cycle (deficits during recessions and surpluses during booms) or a budget balance that is independent of variations in economic activity (which is imposed if the country adopts a balanced-budget rule, such as that embodied in Europe's former Stability Pact, or that imposed on many state governments in America). We now proceed with each of these analyses in turn.

7.2 Commitment and dynamic consistency in monetary policy

Perhaps the central question in monetary policy is: why should the central bank target a zero (or perhaps some low) rate of inflation? We analysed this question in Chapter 5 (section 5.4). We noted there that estimates of the 'sacrifice ratio' involved in disinflation have averaged about 3.5. This means that a country incurs a one-time loss of about 3.5 percentage points of *GDP* – in some year or other – for each percentage point of reduction in the full-equilibrium inflation rate. We argued that it is difficult to be dogmatic about what constitutes the optimal inflation rate, however, since estimates of the benefits of lower inflation are not at all precise, and they range both above and below this cost estimate. We add to that earlier analysis in this section in two ways, and both extensions are motivated by empirical considerations. For one thing, empirical studies suggest that the short-run Phillips curve is flatter at low inflation rates. For another, estimated sacrifice ratios vary a great deal, and one of the considerations that appears to be important is how abrupt or gradual the disinflation episode is (see Ball, 1994). In this section, we highlight analyses that address these issues.

One of the reasons for flatter Phillips curves at low inflation rates may be the fact that wages appear to be more 'sticky' in the downward direction than they are in the upward direction. The implications of this proposition can be appreciated by considering the short-run Phillips curves shown in Figure 7.1. They are 'curved' – that is, flatter in the lower quadrant than they are in the upper quadrant, to reflect relative downward rigidity.

Figure 7.1
Implications of a non-linear short-run Phillips curve

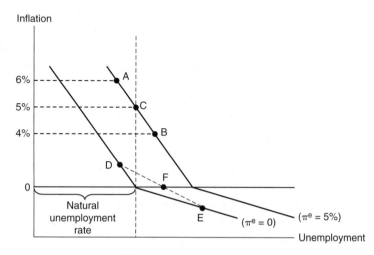

Consider a set of shocks that moves the economy's observation point back and forth along a given short-run trade-off line in this setting – alternating between positive and negative inflation shocks of equal magnitude. If an inflation rate of (say) 5 per cent is chosen, and the shocks never push the economy's observation point below the horizontal axis, the average inflation rate will be 5 per cent and the average unemployment rate will be the natural rate. If a zero-inflation target is chosen, however, shocks will push the economy's observation point into the lower quadrant for half of the time. Even if inflation averages zero, the fact that the Phillips curve is flatter in the lower part of the diagram means that the unemployment rate will average an amount given by distance *OF*, which is more than the natural rate. The moral of this story is that – with non-linear short-run Phillips curves and stochastic shocks – there *is* a *long-run* trade-off after all. When we are 'too ambitious' and aim too low on the inflation front, we risk having a higher average unemployment rate.

This risk can be limited by choosing something like 2 per cent as the target inflation rate. This consideration, along with the limited support for pushing inflation all the way to zero that was considered in Chapter 5 (section 5.4), suggests that the common practice of adopting an inflation target in the 2 per cent range has some merit. (Yet another consideration that supports such a target is the upward bias in the consumer price index. Since it is a fixed-weight index, this measure 'assumes' that individuals do not have the opportunity of shifting away from relatively expensive items. Since individuals do have this degree of freedom, the standard price index gives an exaggerated impression of the true rise in the cost of living. The size of this bias has been estimated to be about one-quarter to one-half of 1 percentage point on an annual basis.)

The remainder of this section reviews Barro and Gordon (1983), who apply the concept of dynamic consistency in policy making to monetary policy. Their model abstracts from the non-linearities and stochastic shocks that have been the focus of the analysis in the last three paragraphs. It emphasizes that monetary policy should deliver an entirely *predictable* inflation rate – *whatever* target value is selected. The reasoning is best clarified by considering the following two equations:

$$u = u^* - a(\pi - \pi^e)$$

$$L = (u - ju^*)^2 + b(\pi - 0)^2$$

The first relationship is an inverted expectations-augmented Phillips curve, which stipulates that the unemployment rate falls below its natural value, u^*, only if actual inflation exceeds expected inflation. This relationship is illustrated in Figure 7.2. The vertical line at $u = u^*$ indicates the set of

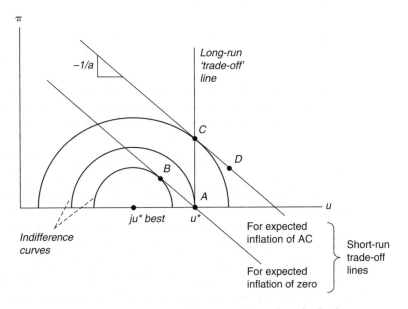

Figure 7.2 The superiority of stabilization rules without feedback

outcomes that are consistent with full equilibrium (that is, that expectations be realized). The fact that this line is vertical means that there is no trade-off between unemployment and inflation in the long run. The family of negatively sloped lines (each with a slope equal to $(-1/a)$) are the short-run trade-off curves. They indicate that – for as long as individuals' expectations of inflation are fixed – higher inflation will generate lower unemployment. As long as the central bank cares about unemployment, this short-run Phillips relationship will represent a temptation. By raising inflation, the bank can reduce unemployment. The problem is that – by raising inflation above what people were previously forecasting – the bank will cause problems in the longer run. Rising expectations of inflation shift the economy to a higher short-run trade-off line. In the end, citizens receive short-term gain (lower unemployment) in exchange for long-term pain (higher inflation).

A more formal analysis of this dynamic choice can be had by defining a specific objective function for the central bank. That is done in the second equation. It states that the bank suffers losses (L) whenever the unemployment rate differs from its 'best' value (ju^*) and whenever inflation differs from its 'best' value (assumed to be zero). To ensure that losses are incurred whether these targets are missed on both the high and low sides, the loss function stipulates that it is the square of each deviation that matters. Parameter b represents the relative importance citizens attach to low inflation – as opposed to suboptimal levels of unemployment. We assume that parameter j is a positive fraction. This ensures that the invisible hand has not worked. The unemployment rate that the market generates (on average, u^*) is higher than the value that is socially optimal (ju^*). Only if this is assumed can we interpret the unemployment as 'involuntary'. (The interpretation of unemployment as involuntary is discussed in much greater detail in Chapter 8. The analysis in that chapter provides a rigorous defence for the proposition that it is reasonable to specify parameter j as a fraction. This is important, since the analysis in the present section breaks down if j is not a fraction.)

The loss function is illustrated in Figure 7.2 by the indifference curves. Curves that are closest to the point marked 'best' represent higher utility. Suppose that the economy is at point A – with an undesirable level of unemployment (the natural unemployment rate) and the desirable amount of inflation (zero). The central bank will find it tempting to move to a point like B. This point is feasible – at least for a while – since it is on the currently relevant short-run trade-off line. This point is also desirable – since it is on a preferred indifference curve compared to point A. So the central bank will be tempted to print money to generate the inflation rate indicated by the height of point B.

The trouble with this strategy is that point B is not sustainable. It involves actual inflation (positive) exceeding expected inflation (zero). Individuals will be smart enough to revise upward their forecast of inflation. This will move the economy to a higher trade-off curve and so to less desirable indifference curves. Actually, if individuals are clever, they will be able to see immediately the point where the economy will come to rest. After all, a full equilibrium requires two things. First, it must be a point of tangency between a short-run Phillips curve and an indifference curve – since (by choosing point B) the central bank will have demonstrated that this is how it sets policy. Second, it must be a point where actual and expected inflation are equal; otherwise private agents will revise their forecast, and that means the economy has yet to reach a state of rest. The vertical line at $u = u^*$ represents all points that involve actual inflation equalling expected inflation. Thus, the long-run equilibrium is the point on this long-run Phillips curve that meets the central bank's tangency requirement – that is, point C in Figure 7.2.

This reasoning proves that it is not advisable for the central bank to try for point B – by falsifying the expectations that individuals had at point A. Once this attempt to move to B gets going, the system gravitates to point C – which is on the least desirable of the three indifference curves. The central bank will make the right decision if it focuses on the vertical long-run Phillips curve. If it does so, and tries to achieve the point of tangency between this constraint and the indifference map, the bank will realize that point A is that best tangency point. By focusing on the long run – and ignoring the fact that it can (but should not) exploit the fact that individuals have already signed their wage and price contracts and so are already committed to their inflationary expectations – the bank can deliver point A (and this is better than point C). The moral of the story is that the bank should focus on the long run, and not give in to the temptation to create inflation surprises in the short run.

A formal proof of this proposition can be developed as follows. The central bank has two options. First, it can be myopic and interventionist by revising its decision every period – capitalizing on the fact that the inflationary expectations of private agents are given at each point in time. Second, it can take a long-term view and be passive – just setting inflation at what is best in full equilibrium and not taking action on a period-by-period basis. In each case, the appropriate inflation rate can be calculated by substituting the constraint (the Phillips curve equation) into the objective function, differentiating that objective function with respect to the bank's choice variable, the inflation rate, and setting that derivative equal to zero. In the myopic version, inflationary expectations are taken as given (and that fact can be exploited), while in the passive version the bank subjects itself to the additional constraint that it not falsify anyone's expectations. In this case, the $\pi = \pi^e$ constraint is imposed before, not after, optimization by the bank.

In the myopic case the first-order condition is:

$$\partial L/\partial \pi = 2(u - ju^*)(-a) + 2b\pi = 0,$$

and, when the $\pi = \pi^e$ (which implies $u = u^*$) full-equilibrium condition is substituted in, this policy generates an equilibrium inflation rate equal to $\pi = au^*(1 - j)/b$. This expression gives the height of point C in Figure 7.2. When this value for inflation and $u = u^*$ are substituted into the loss function, we see that losses under the myopic interventionist approach are:

$$L(myopic) = (u^*(1 - j))^2(1 + a^2/b).$$

In the passive case the first-order condition is (by substituting $\pi = \pi^e$ and $u = u^*$ into the loss function before differentiation):

$$\partial L/\partial \pi = 2b\pi = 0,$$

so this policy generates $\pi = 0$ (the height of point A in Figure 7.2) and losses equal to:

$$L(passive) = (u^*(1 - j))^2.$$

By inspecting the two loss expressions, the reader can verify that losses are smaller with the 'hands-off' approach to policy.

Despite what has just been shown, individuals know that central banks will always be tempted by point B. When the central banker's boss (the government) is particularly worried about an electorate (which is frustrated by unemployment), there is pressure on the bank to pursue what has been called the 'myopic' policy. Following Fischer and Summers (1989), let parameter c be the central bank's credibility coefficient. If people believe that there is no chance that the bank will be myopic, its c coefficient is unity. If people expect the myopic policy with certainty, the bank's c coefficient is zero. All real-world central banks will have a credibility coefficient that is somewhere between zero and one. Thus, in general, social losses will be equal to:

$$L = cL(passive) + (1 - c)L(myopic), \text{ so}$$

$$L = (u^*(1 - j))^2(1 + (1 - c)a^2/b).$$

This expression teaches us three important lessons: that losses will be less with a higher c, a lower a and a higher b. Let us consider each of these lessons in turn.

Anything that increases central bank credibility is 'good'. This explains why all central bankers make 'tough' speeches – assuring listeners that, except when the overall stability of the entire financial system is in question and when unemployment threatens to rise to crisis levels, the bank cares much more about inflation than it does about unemployment. It also explains why some countries (such as New Zealand) link the central banker's pay to his or her performance (he or she loses the job if the inflation target is exceeded). In addition, it explains why particularly conservative individuals are appointed as central bankers – even by left-wing governments – and why central banks are set up to be fairly independent of the government of the day (such as in the United Kingdom). Finally, it explains why developing countries, and countries that have had a history of irresponsible monetary policy, often choose to give up trying to establish credibility – and just use another country's currency instead of their own.

Anything that makes the family of short-run Phillips curves steeper (that is, makes the slope expression $(-1/a)$ bigger) is 'good'. Thus, the analysis supports the wider use of profit sharing and/or shorter wage contracts. Finally, increased indexation is 'bad'. Thirty-five years ago, when various Western countries were debating the wisdom of fighting inflation, some argued that it would be best to avoid the temporary recession that accompanies disinflation. These individuals argued that it would be better to include a cost-of-living clause in all wage, pension and loan contracts. With indexed contracts, unexpected inflation would not transfer income and wealth in an unintended fashion away from pensioners and lenders to others. Thus, some people argued that embracing indexation and 'living with inflation' would have been better than fighting it. Our analysis can be used to evaluate this controversy, since widespread indexation would change parameter b. If we had indexed contracts, any given amount of inflation would result in smaller social losses. Thus, more indexation means a smaller parameter b. But the final loss expression indicates that a smaller b is 'bad'. This is because indexation makes it more sensible for the central bank to be myopic. There is always the temptation of point B, and indexation makes the cost of going for B seem smaller.

We can summarize as follows. More indexation is 'good news', since it makes any given amount of inflation less costly. But more indexation is 'bad news', since it tempts the central bank to choose more inflation. It is interesting (and perhaps unexpected) that – according to the formal analysis – the 'bad news' dimension *must* be the dominant consideration. (This is why economists often use formal analyses. Algebra is a more precise tool than geometry, and sometimes this means we can learn more from algebraic analysis. This analysis of indexation is an illustration of this fact.) Overall, the analysis supports disinflation over 'living with inflation'.

Before leaving this analysis of central bank credibility, it is worth noting several things. First, the analysis does *not* prove that zero inflation is best; it *assumes* it. Another point that is worth emphasizing is that what this central bank credibility analysis rules out is policy that creates surprises. It does not rule out discretionary policy that is well announced in advance. This distinction can be clarified as follows. Let the inflation term in the loss function be the average inflation rate, π^*, instead of just this period's inflation:

$$L = (u - ju^*)^2 + b(\pi^* - 0)^2.$$

Assume that the central banker follows an ongoing reaction function:

$$\pi = \pi^* + d(u - u^*),$$

which states that the bank raises aggregate demand (and therefore inflation) whenever unemployment rises above the natural rate. It is assumed that this reaction is announced in advance – as an ongoing decision rule. Thus, it is a policy that is not based on causing private sector forecasts to be incorrect. If we eliminate π by substituting this policy-reaction function into a standard Phillips curve:

$$u = u^* - h(\pi - \pi^e),$$

the result is:

$$u = u^* - a(\pi^* - \pi^e)$$

where $a = h/(1 + dh)$. The analysis proceeds just as before – using the revised loss function and this revised Phillips curve. The only thing that is new is the revised interpretation of parameter a – which is defined in this paragraph. As before, anything that makes a small is 'good', and we see that embracing discretionary policy that is announced in advance (moving to a higher value for coefficient d) is therefore 'good'. Overall, then, this credibility analysis supports discretionary policy – *as long as* that policy is a pre-announced ongoing process, not a one-time event. This is why the policy analysis in earlier chapters of this book have involved functions that were assumed to be fully understood by the agents in the model.

More on central bank independence is available in Fischer (1995) and McCallum (1995). As a result of this basic model of policy credibility, we now have an integrated analysis of disinflation which combines important insights from both Keynesian and Classical perspectives. Keynesians have emphasized rigidities in nominal wages and prices to explain the recession that seems to always accompany disinflation. New Classicals have stressed the inability of the central bank to make credible policy announcements. Ball (1995) has shown that *both* sticky prices and incomplete credibility are necessary to understand the short-run output effects of disinflation. Indeed, if incomplete credibility is not an issue, Ball shows that disinflation can cause a temporary boom, not a recession. Only a fraction of firms can adjust their prices quickly to the disinflationary monetary policy. But, if the policy is anticipated with full credibility, firms that do adjust know that money growth will fall considerably while their prices are in effect. Thus, it is rational for them to reduce dramatically their price increases, and this can even be enough to push the overall inflation rate below the money growth rate initially. This is what causes the predicted temporary boom. However, since we know that such booms do not occur during disinflations, we can conclude that policy credibility *must* be a central issue.

The general conclusion to follow from this monetary policy analysis is that the only dynamically consistent – that is, credible – policy approach is one that leaves the authorities no freedom to react in a previously unexpected fashion to developments in the future. Discretionary policy that is not part of an ongoing well-understood rule can be suboptimal, because 'there is no mechanism to induce *future* policy makers to take into consideration the effect of their policy, via the expectations mechanism, upon *current* decisions of agents' (Kydland and Prescott, 1977, p. 627).

This argument for 'rules' (with or without predictable feedback) over 'discretion' (unpredictable feedback) has many other applications in everyday life. For example, there is the issue of negotiating with kidnappers. In any one instance, negotiation is appealing – so that the life of the hostage can be saved. But concessions create an incentive for more kidnapping. Many individuals have decided that the long-term benefits of a rule (no negotiations) exceed those associated with discretion (engaging in negotiations). Another application of this issue, which is less important but closer to home for university students, concerns the institution of final exams. Both students and professors would be better off if there were no final examinations. Yet students seem to need the incentive of the exam to work diligently. Thus, one's first thought is that the optimal policy would be a discretionary one in which the professor promises an exam and then, near the end of term, breaks that promise. With this arrangement, the students would work and learn but would avoid the trauma of the exam, and the professor would avoid the marking. The problem is that students can anticipate such a broken promise (especially if there is a history of this behaviour), so we opt for a rules approach – exams no matter what. Most participants regard this policy as the best one. (For further discussion, see Fischer, 1980.)

We close this section on dynamic consistency by returning to disinflation policy. In this further treatment of the issue, we integrate political and macro-economic considerations. We include this material for two reasons. First, it shows how political uncertainty can be a source of incomplete credibility in economic policy making. Second, it provides a framework for examining whether gradualism in policy making is recommended or not.

Blanchard (1985a) has presented a simple model which highlights this interplay. His analysis focuses on the possibility of two equilibria – both of which are durable, since both are consistent with rational expectations. The essence of this model is that disinflation policy only works if agents expect low money growth in the future. If a 'hard-line' political party is in power and it promises disinflation, two outcomes are possible. On the one hand, agents can expect that the disinflation will succeed and that the anti-inflation party will remain in power. Since both these expectations will be realized, this outcome is a legitimate equilibrium. On the other hand, agents can expect that the disinflation will fail, and that (perhaps as a result) the anti-inflation party will lose power. Since the change in government means that the dis-inflation policy is not maintained, once again, the results validate the initial expectation, and this outcome is another legitimate equilibrium. Blanchard formalizes this argument, to see what strategy is advised for the hard-line party.

The basic version of the model is straightforward. Unemployment depends inversely on the excess of the money growth rate, g, over the inflation rate, π: $u = -\gamma(g - \pi)$. The inflation rate is a weighted average of the current actual money growth rate and what growth rate is expected in the future, g^e: $\pi = \phi g + (1 - \phi)g^e$. The hard-line party (which is in power initially) sets $g = \bar{g}$. The political opponent, the 'soft' party, sets $g = g^*$, where $g^* > \bar{g}$.

If agents expect the hard-liners to stay in power, $\pi = \bar{g}$, so unemployment is zero. If agents expect the soft party to gain power, $\pi = \phi\bar{g} + (1 - \phi)g^*$.

Combining this relationship with the unemployment equation, we have a summary of how unemployment and inflation interact:

$$u = - (1 - \phi) (\gamma/\phi) (\pi - g^*).$$

Any of this infinity of combinations of unemployment and inflation rates are equilibria, assuming the soft party wins power. In the simplest version of his model, Blanchard assumes that the soft party does win power if inflation is pushed so low that unemployment is deemed the more serious problem; specifically the soft party wins if $\beta u > \pi$. Using $u = (1/\beta)\pi$ to eliminate the unemployment rate from the previous equation, we determine the minimum inflation rate that the hard-liners can afford to promise and still be certain of remaining in power:

$$\pi^* = [(\beta\gamma(1 - \phi))/(\phi + \beta\gamma(1 - \phi))]g^*.$$

To recap – for inflation rates between $\bar{g}$ and π^*, the hard-liners stay in power and disinflation succeeds. For all inflation rates lower than π^*, there are two equilibria. If the hard-liners are expected to remain in power, any chosen inflation rate below π^* and $u = 0$ is the outcome and the hard-liners do remain in power. However, private agents may expect the hard-liners to lose, and in that case we observe the same chosen inflation rate along with positive unemployment (the value given by the second-last indented equation) and the hard-liners do lose power.

Three reactions to this two-equilibria feature are possible. One is to interpret it as a theoretical underpinning for gradualism: the hard-liners can avoid any chance of losing power (and therefore ensure that the two-equilibria range of outcomes never emerges) by only disinflating within the $\bar{g}$ to π^* range. (This is Blanchard's reaction.) A second reaction is to argue that the model should be re-specified to eliminate the two-equilibria possibility. (Blanchard notes that this is achieved if the probability of the hard-liners retaining power is less than unity even if unemployment never exceeds zero.) The third reaction is to argue that we must develop more explicit learning models of how agents' belief structures are modified through time. (This is the reaction of Farmer, 1993, as he exhorts macroeconomists to focus directly on self-fulfilling prophecies rather than to avoid analysing these phenomena.)

Blanchard's analysis is not the only one to provide a rationale for gradualism. Our study of stabilization policy when the authority is uncertain about the system's parameter values (Chapter 3, section 3.2) showed that uncertainty makes optimal policy less activist. Drazen and Masson (1994) derive a very similar result to Blanchard's, in an open-economy model that stresses the duration of the hard-line policy. It is commonplace to assume that a central bank's credibility rises with the duration of its hard-line position. This presumption does not always hold in Drazen and Masson's study, since the larger period of (temporary) suffering can so undermine support for the central bank's policy that it becomes rational for everyone to expect that a softening of its stand must take place. The bank can avoid this loss of credibility only by being less hard-line in the first place. Drazen and Masson compare their model to a person following an ambitious diet. When such a person assures us that he will skip lunch today, is the credibility of that promise enhanced or undermined by the observation that the individual has not eaten at all for three days? On the one hand, there is clear evidence of the person's determination; on the other hand, the probability is rising that the individual will simply have to renege on his promise. Again, credibility may be higher with gradualism.

For a more thorough sampling of the literature which integrates macro theory, credibility and considerations of political feasibility, see Persson and Tabellini (1994). Another study that is similar to Blanchard's is Loh (2002). Also, King (2006) provides a very general and concise explanation of why discretionary policy creates a multiple-equilibria problem that a rules approach avoids.

7.3   A constraint on monetary policy: currency union

This section of the chapter uses the New Neoclassical Synthesis approach to consider the implications for output volatility of alternative exchange-rate regimes. We want to evaluate how well each exchange-rate policy insulates our economy from *ongoing* foreign developments, without having to draw a multiple-dimension phase diagram or without having to confront a much more complex version of the stochastic-shock analysis that was presented in section 6.5. We avoid both of these complications by focusing on a continuous-time model that involves an ongoing variation in export demand. The model is defined by equations 7.1 to 7.5. These equations define (respectively) the new *IS* relationship, the new Phillips curve, interest parity, monetary policy (assuming flexible exchange rates), and an exogenous cycle in autonomous export demand. The definition of variables that readers have not encountered in earlier chapters is given following the equations:

$$\dot{y} = \alpha(r - \bar{r}) + \Omega(\dot{f} + \dot{e} - \dot{p}) + \beta \dot{a} \qquad (7.1)$$

$$\ddot{p} = -\lambda(y - \bar{y}) + \gamma((f - \bar{f}) + (e - \bar{e}) - (p - \bar{p})) + \psi(a - \bar{a}) \quad (7.2)$$

$$r = \bar{r} + \dot{f} + \dot{e} - \dot{p} \quad (7.3)$$

$$p + \mu y = 0 \quad (7.4)$$

$$a = \bar{a} + \delta \sin(t) \quad (7.5)$$

The variables that may be less familiar are: a – autonomous export demand, e – nominal exchange rate (the domestic currency price of foreign exchange), and f – the price of foreign goods. As usual, p is the price of domestically produced goods.

This open-economy version of the new *IS* relationship is based on a log-linear approximation of the economy's resource constraint, $y = \alpha c + \beta a + (1 - \alpha - \beta)x$, where c is the log of domestic consumption expenditure, a is the log of the autonomous part of exports and x is the log of the part of exports that is sensitive to the real exchange rate. As is now customary, the Ramsey model is used to define the behaviour of forward-looking domestic households. Following McCallum and Nelson (1999), the rest of the world is not modelled; it is simply assumed that $x = \xi(f + e - p)$. Equation 7.1 follows by taking the time derivative of the resource constraint, substituting in the domestic consumption and the export functions, and interpreting parameter Ω as $\xi(1 - \alpha - \beta)$.

As derived in Chapter 4, equation 7.2 is based on Calvo's (1983) model of sticky prices. In this open-economy setting, we assume a Leontief production relationship between intermediate imports and domestic value added; is the unit requirement coefficient for intermediate imports, and θ is labour's exponent in the Cobb–Douglas domestic value added process (so that $y = \theta n$, and the marginal product of labour, MPL, equals $\theta Y/N$). The associated definition of marginal cost, $MC = W/[MPL(1 - \phi(FE/P))]$, is used in a derivation just like that reported in sections 4.5 and 6.5 to arrive at equation 7.2. We report only one detail from that derivation; it yields the following restriction concerning the summary parameters: $\beta\lambda/\psi = 1 + (\alpha/2)(2 - \theta)$. This restriction implies that $\beta\lambda/\psi$ must exceed unity, and we rely on this fact below. For a closed economy with no autonomous spending term, only the output gap appears in the new Phillips curve. But, in this open-economy setting, there are direct supply-side effects of the exchange rate (stemming from the intermediate imports) and a direct supply-side effect of the exogenous variation in exports (stemming from using the resource constraint to establish the link between real marginal cost and the output gap).

There is much discussion of the importance of exchange-rate 'pass-through' in the literature that compares the efficacy of fixed and flexible exchange rates. One advantage of specifying imports as intermediate products is that no independent assumption concerning exchange-rate pass-through needs to be made. Indeed, the Calvo nominal flexibility parameter also stands for the proportion of firms that pass changes in the exchange rate through to customers at each point in time.

Equation 7.3 defines interest arbitrage. With perfect foresight, the domestic nominal interest rate, $r + \dot{p}$, must exceed the foreign nominal interest rate, $\bar{r} + \dot{f}$, by the expected depreciation of the domestic currency, $\dot{e}$. Price stability exists in the rest of the world ($f = \dot{f} = \ddot{f} = 0$), so the domestic central bank can achieve domestic price stability in two ways. One option is to fix the exchange rate. This option is best thought of as opting for currency union, so it does not generate speculation about changes in the value of the peg. This option is imposed in the model by assuming $e = \bar{e} = \dot{e} = 0$ and by ignoring equation 7.4. The second option is to peg a linear combination of the domestic price level and domestic real output (imposed in the model by assuming equation 7.4). Equation 7.4 encompasses two interesting cases: targeting the price level ($\mu = 0$) and targeting nominal GDP ($\mu = 1$).

We assume that business cycles in this small open economy are caused by exogenous variations in export demand, as defined by the sine curve in equation 7.5. We now proceed to derive the reduced form for real output, to see how the amplitude of the resulting cycle in y is affected by picking one exchange-rate regime or the other. We explain the derivation of the reduced form for real output in the flexible exchange-rate case (and we assume that readers can use similar steps to verify the result that we simply report for fixed exchange rates).

First, we simplify by setting $f = \dot{f} = \ddot{f} = 0$. Next, we take time derivatives of equation 7.4 and use the result to eliminate the first and second time derivatives of p. Then, we substitute equation 7.3 into equation 7.1 to eliminate the interest rate, and use the result to eliminate the term involving the time derivative of the exchange rate in the time derivative of equation 7.2. The result is:

$$-\mu\ddot{y} = A_1\dot{y} + A_2\dot{a} \tag{7.6}$$

$$A_1 = \gamma\mu - \lambda + (\gamma/(\alpha + \Omega))(1 - \mu(\alpha + \Omega))$$

$$A_2 = \psi - (\gamma\beta/(\alpha + \Omega))$$

We use the undetermined coefficient solution procedure. Following the same approach that we used in Chapter 4 (section 4.3) and Chiang (1984, p. 472), the trial solution for output can be written as:

$$y = \bar{y} + B[\cos(t)] + C[\sin(t)] \tag{7.7}$$

The time derivatives of equation 7.7, $\dot{y} = -B\sin(t) + C\cos(t)$, $\ddot{y} = B\sin(t) - C\cos(t)$, and the derivative of equation 7.5, $\dot{a} = \delta\cos(t)$, are substituted into equation 7.6. The resulting coefficient-identifying restrictions are $B = 0$, and:

$$C_{flex} = \delta A_3/(A_4 + \mu(\alpha + \Omega)), \tag{7.8}$$

$$A_3 = \psi(\alpha + \Omega) - \gamma\beta$$

$$A_4 = \lambda(\alpha + \Omega) - \gamma.$$

The similar expression for the fixed-exchange-rate version of the model is:

$$C_{fix} = \delta(A_3 + \beta)/(A_4 + 1). \tag{7.9}$$

Since reduced-form parameter C represents the amplitude of the cycle in real output, it is our summary measure of output volatility. To evaluate the relative appeal of flexible versus fixed exchange rates, we compare expressions 7.8 and 7.9. Subtracting the former from the latter, we have:

$$C_{fix} - C_{flex} = [\delta(\alpha + \Omega)(1 + \mu\psi(\alpha + \Omega) + \beta(1 - \gamma))(\beta\lambda - \psi)]/[(1 + A_4)(A_4 + \mu(\alpha + \Omega))] \tag{7.10}$$

The reader can verify that a sufficient, though not necessary, condition for A_4 to be positive is that intermediate imports be less than half of *GDP*. Taking this to be uncontroversial, we make this assumption. Then, a sufficient, though not necessary, condition for equation 7.10 to be positive is $(\beta\lambda - \psi) > 0$. As noted above, the micro-foundations imply that this restriction *must* hold. We conclude that the model supports a flexible exchange rate. It is noteworthy that this conclusion is warranted for quite a range of monetary policies followed under flexible exchange rates – all the way from a hard-line approach (absolute price-level targeting) to a policy that pays significant attention to real-output outcomes (nominal *GDP* targeting). Since each one of these options delivers lower output volatility – with no trade-off in terms of long-run price stability – the flexible exchange-rate policy is supported.

There is a vast pre-new-synthesis literature on this question. The original analysis – the Mundell–Fleming model – predicted that a flexible exchange rate would serve as a shock absorber in the face of demand shocks. As complications such as exchange-rate expectations and supply-side effects of the exchange rate were added as extensions to this descriptive analysis, the support for flexible exchange rates – as a mechanism for achieving lower output volatility – was decreased but (in most studies) not eliminated. The analysis in this section allows for all these extensions, and for the dynamic structure that is imposed by the micro-foundations and inter-temporal optimization that forms the core of the new synthesis approach. For those who have maintained a preference for flexible exchange rates throughout this period, the robustness indicated by our conclusion is reassuring. As we found in the previous chapter, both old and new analyses often complement each other – at the level of policy implications.

A number of recent studies have focused on monetary policy in small open economies. Kirsanova et al. (2006) focus on the question of which price level the central bank should attempt to keep on a target – the price of domestically produced goods or the overall consumer price index. The former is a sticky variable, while the latter has a jump dimension since it is affected directly by the exchange rate (through its effect on the price of imports). Similar closed-economy analyses have addressed the question: should the price level or the wage level be targeted by monetary policy? The general answer to these questions is that the central bank should target whichever nominal variable is the stickiest. After all, welfare costs arise when the sticky variable cannot adjust to its equilibrium value. If the central bank never lets that variable get very far from that desired value, its stickiness cannot matter much.

Devereux et al. (2006) apply the new synthesis approach to models of developing economies; they provide a detailed account of how optimal monetary policy depends on the extent of exchange-rate pass-through. Calvo and Mishkin (2003) offer a less model-specific discussion of the options for developing countries. They argue that the choice between fixed and flexible exchange rates is likely to be less important than whether or not the country possesses good institutions and a set of sound fiscal policies. Finally, Edwards and Levy (2005) provide a summary of the empirical evidence. By comparing the group of countries that have adopted flexible exchange rates with those that have not, they find that – despite the differences in monetary policy strategies within the first group – a flexible exchange rate acts as a shock absorber.

This issue has surfaced in the discussions surrounding the extreme austerity that has characterized some European economies, such as Greece. The concern is that, with being in a currency union and therefore being unable to have a depreciation in its own currency (which would make it clear to all citizens that everyone was truly sharing the pain), these countries suffer much more than they would if they had the option of a flexible exchange rate. But this view has been challenged by Farhi et al. (2012), who use an open-economy new synthesis model to show how a revenue-neutral fiscal policy package can duplicate the effects of a currency devaluation. So, while achieving political agreement for complicated fiscal actions is more difficult than simply pursuing a monetary policy that depreciates the home currency, at least there is scope – in principle – for replacing a monetary policy initiative with a fiscal one.

7.4 A constraint on monetary policy: the zero lower bound on nominal interest rates

Even in a closed economy there can be a constraint on monetary policy: the zero lower bound on nominal interest rates. A review of the material in Chapter 2 will readily confirm for readers that, if the central bank is unable to lower the interest rate when the price level is below target (a situation which can be imposed in the model by setting the bank's aggressiveness coefficient to zero), then the aggregate demand curve is vertical and the economy cannot converge back to full equilibrium following a negative shock to the level of economic activity. The general relevance of this problem in recent years has stimulated analytical work on two questions: Can monetary policy be conducted in a different way to avoid the zero lower bound problem? Can fiscal policy be used if monetary policy cannot operate in this environment? We consider both these issues in this section, but first we note that both Mankiw and Weinzierl (2011) and Eggertsson (2011) have used modern micro-based macro theory to verify that, without the zero lower bound problem, the standard view – that monetary policy should be the policy maker's first line of defence – is warranted.

Central banks have adopted two main ways of trying to cope with the zero lower bound on the short-term nominal interest rate: quantitative easing and forward guidance. In the former, the central bank shifts from its normal practice of buying short-term paper when it wants to lower the short rate to buying long-term bonds in an attempt to lower long-term rates (which are still above zero). The challenge comes from what is known as the expectations theory of the term structure, which we discussed in Chapter 6 (section 6.4). According to that theory, if bond holders are risk neutral, the long rate should be equal to an average of the current and the expected future short rates. This follows from the fact that bond holders have two options – to hold a long bond or a series of short bonds over the same longer holding period – and equilibrium requires that they be indifferent between these two options. For example, using R to denote a one-year rate and r to denote quarterly rates, the equilibrium condition is:

$$(1 + R) = (1 + r_1)(1 + r_2^e)(1 + r_3^e)(1 + r_4^e).$$

The zero lower bound means that the authority cannot lower r_1. Quantitative easing is based on the hope that asset holders do not expect future short rates to be zero. But, if they do expect the zero lower bound to last for all four quarters that are considered here, then the arbitrage condition implies that the long rate cannot be affected by the central bank's open-market operations. Clearly, there is some scope for an effect, since individuals may not expect future short rates to stay low indefinitely. But experience has shown that the policy maker is quite limited. Both the United States and Canada engaged in what were called large 'Operation Twist' policies in the early 1950s. The policies involved financing a very large open-market operation at the short end by performing an open-market operation at the long end of an equal magnitude in the opposite direction. The econometric studies indicated that this dramatic change in the quantities of long and short bonds outstanding had almost no effect at all on the yield curve. This historical experience should limit our expectations concerning how much quantitative easing can offer.

Of course, the policy may still generate important confidence effects, but this possibility is not included in the standard new synthesis model. As long as people are convinced by an energetic embracing of quantitative easing that the authorities will do whatever it takes to preclude a serious recession, then investors' 'animal spirits' may be pushed in the desirable direction. Hill (2009) has recently reminded us of Leijonhufvud's insight – that the problem Western economies faced following the recent recession 'is the lack of a truly comprehensive futures market in which firms with excess capacity and workers with excess leisure could make conditional commitments'. Since we have adopted the convention that money is one half of each of these transactions, making more money available is a blunt way of trying to address this problem. Hill is appealing to the literature on multiple-equilibria models such as Woodford (1991) and Howitt and McAfee (1992). These analyses involve thoroughgoing micro-foundations and rational expectations, and they show that it is possible for the policy maker to improve welfare solely by committing to intervene if ever necessary. Knowledge of that commitment can be sufficient to cause agents to expect that a deep recession will be avoided, and therefore (when they act on that belief) to achieve that outcome.

Forward guidance involves the central bank simply promising to keep the short rate at a low level for a noticeable period into the future. If individuals expect that the economy may have recovered before that period has ended, they will expect inflation in the future. After all, the central bank has just promised not to raise rates to stop that inflation. Expectations of inflation are precisely what we want to generate in a recession, so that individuals are tempted to buy now to beat the price increases. But this policy is dynamically inconsistent. If it is believed, and individuals do increase spending and the recession ends well before the period of promised low interest rates has elapsed, the central bank will be tempted to renege and raise rates after all. At that point in time, it would be desirable to limit the inflation. Knowing that the policy maker will face this temptation, private individuals may ignore the announcement in the first place. If so, forward guidance has limited power as well. Eggertsson (2010b) discusses this up-to-date application of the dynamic consistency challenge for monetary policy, while Andersson and Hofmann (2009) report econometric results that suggest very limited success emerging from actual forward-guidance policy episodes.

How might a policy maker react to this mixed, but perhaps disappointing, verdict concerning the scope for monetary policy when the zero lower bound matters? It would seem prudent to do as many actual policy makers have done in recent years – by turning to fiscal policy, even if (in normal times) that is not the preferred option. Macro theorists have done the same, for example Eggertsson (2010a) and Denes et al. (2013). For the remainder of this section we provide a very simplified version of this work.

Which fiscal policy instrument is most appealing for conducting short-run stabilization policy? The theory behind the new *IS* relationship suggests that the government should not engage in a series of short-run changes in the personal income tax rate. According to the permanent-income hypothesis, temporary changes in this levy are absorbed within savings. Indeed, the more temporary an income tax change is, the less it affects a household's long-run average income, so households use variations in their savings as a buffer to smooth consumption and avoid disruptions in their living standards. Much evidence has accumulated over the years to support this theory. But does this negative verdict apply to all tax policy initiatives? An alternative is that the government can arrange that the temporary tax changes be reflected in the level of sales taxes, instead of income taxes. Such a policy is not designed to affect households by changing their perception of their long-run average income. Instead, it is designed to affect the *timing* of their replacement expenditures on durables. In this case, the more temporary are the tax changes, the more they affect the timing of expenditures that were to be made relatively soon in any event.

As is often emphasized, stabilization policy initiatives need to be temporary, timely and targeted: temporary, since recessions and booms do not last; timely, since the initiative must have its effect when needed, not later on when the opposite phase of the business cycle is occurring; and targeted, so the government's limited funds can be directed to those most in need. Considering the recession phase of the cycle, it would appear that vouchers – which have value only as waivers for sales tax obligations, and which expire (say) within one year from the inception of the programme – would satisfy these requirements. Such vouchers are temporary (and can be believed to be temporary), and they can be targeted, since they can be distributed only to relatively poor families. Finally, they can be timely as well, since they can be distributed without much lag and new administrative arrangements. Overall, sales tax waiver vouchers represent a convenient way of implementing the standard proposition that what we need in a recession is *expectations of inflation*. Vouchers that expire in the near future generate precisely these expectations, and they are all the more necessary if households and firms come to doubt how monetary policy that is constrained by the zero lower bound problem can limit deflation.

But it is precisely on expectations grounds that some economists have expressed scepticism concerning fiscal initiatives. Applied to the suggestion that sales tax rates vary pro-cyclically, this criticism runs as follows. If households know that a cut in the sales tax is coming because there is concern that a recession may be approaching, they are likely to postpone spending on durables until this policy is delivered. This very delay in spending can precipitate the recession that was feared, or at least make worse a recession that would have occurred in any event. As a result, despite its good intentions, the suggested fiscal strategy could be destabilizing. The purpose of the remaining material in this section is to provide a compact new synthesis analysis of forward-looking agents to assess the sales tax initiative. We examine the following model:

$$\dot{y} = \alpha(r - \bar{r}) + (1 - \alpha)\dot{a} \qquad (7.11)$$

$$\dot{p} = -\lambda(y - \bar{y}) + \psi(a - \bar{a}) \qquad (7.12)$$

$$r + \dot{p} + \dot{s} = \bar{r} \tag{7.13}$$

$$\dot{a} = -\theta(a - \bar{a}) \tag{7.14}$$

The notation is standard: y, a and p denote the logarithms of real output, autonomous spending and the producer price of goods; r and s are the real interest rate and the sales tax rate, and bars above variables indicate full-equilibrium values. Equations 7.11 and 7.12 are the new IS and Phillips relationships. Equation 7.13 takes the place of a central bank reaction function. This equation simply stipulates that the nominal interest rate (the left-hand side) is fixed. The nominal interest rate is the real rate plus the inflation rate of consumer prices (which includes sales tax changes), as explained by Eggertsson (2010a). Equation 7.14 defines the exogenous event that causes a temporary deviation of output from its natural-rate value in this analysis. We assume that autonomous expenditure falls initially and then gradually returns to its initial value according to this equation.

For simplicity, we assume that the policy maker targets the sticky (producer) price and manages to keep this measure absolutely constant. We use the model to determine what sales tax policy is required to have achieved this outcome. Since this policy precludes inflation, the impact effect of the drop in autonomous spending on real output follows immediately from the simplified version of equation 7.12: $\lambda(y - \bar{y}) = \psi(a - \bar{a})$. The impact effect is $dy/da = \psi/\lambda$. What happens after this first instant is determined by taking the time derivative of this simplified version of equation 7.12 and then substituting out the time change in y by using equation 7.11. The result is:

$$\alpha(r - \bar{r}) = (\psi/\lambda)[(1 - \alpha)\lambda/\psi - 1]\dot{a}. \tag{7.15}$$

We have encountered the term in square brackets in section 7.3. We noted in the third paragraph of that section that the micro-foundations of the new Phillips curve stipulate that this term must be positive. As a result, since our thought experiment involves a being positive for the entire time path following the initial drop, equation 7.15 implies that the real interest rate must be below its full-equilibrium value throughout that adjustment period. This outcome is what we normally expect the monetary authority to deliver. In this case, it is what the fiscal authority needs to accomplish. The necessary time path for the sales tax rate follows from equation 7.13: $\dot{s} = -(r - \bar{r})$. Since the right-hand side is positive throughout the adjustment period, so must be the left-hand side. This is possible only if the sales tax is initially reduced below its full-equilibrium value and then allowed to rise gradually back up thereafter. This analysis confirms that the pre-new-synthesis policy advice is still appropriate in this new synthesis setting.

This analysis has been simplified by our not specifying how the government covers the forgone revenue while the sales tax is temporarily reduced. Several responses are possible on this score. First, the government could issue money to cover the deficit, and it is common practice for money issue to be ignored in the new synthesis literature. Second, the government could issue bonds to cover the deficit, and, given that Ricardian equivalence is implied by the standard version of the new *IS* relationship, this can be ignored as well. (For a new synthesis analysis that does not assume Ricardian equivalence, see Blake and Kirsanova, 2004.) Finally, the government could raise another tax to make up the lost revenue. Correia et al. (2013) analyse this option and show, for example, that a temporary rise in the payroll tax would maintain a balanced budget while the sales tax rate is low, and still provide the desired temporary stimulus. It may be difficult to explain to the electorate why payroll taxes are raised during the recession in this balanced-budget case. This is a common challenge that emerges in this literature – that unconventional fiscal policies are necessary components of policy packages that receive support from new synthesis analysis. Governments can avoid these communication challenges if they opt for bond-financed temporary deficits. But the ever-rising debt-to-*GDP* ratios that have plagued many countries suggest that an analysis of the sustainability of the attempt to cover what are intended to be temporary deficits is very much called for. It is to this issue that we turn in the next section.

7.5 The feasibility and desirability of bond-financed government budget deficits

Government debt has accumulated in many Western countries – both in absolute terms and as a proportion of *GDP*. Many governments are trying to contain this development in recent years, as they stabilize, and sometimes reduce, their debt ratios. We explore these attempts in this section.

Government debt would not have accumulated if governments had taken the advice that follows from the standard theory of fiscal policy. That advice is to run a deficit during the recessionary phase of each business cycle and to run a surplus during the boom half of each business cycle. According to conventional wisdom, this policy would help to balance the economy over the cycle, and it would balance the budget over the interval of each full cycle. As a result, this strategy would be sufficient to keep the debt from increasing over the long term.

Starting around 1970, many governments drifted into a pattern whereby they followed only half of this Keynesian plan. They took the advice that deficits are to be accepted, and even encouraged, during recessions. But these governments chose to disregard the other half of the plan, for they did not run surplus budgets for anything like half the time. By the 1990s, many governments had started to react to their exploding debt-to-*GDP* ratios. Many became so preoccupied with stopping the growth in debt that they no longer made any attempt to help balance the economy. Indeed, Europe's Stability Pact was much criticized for forcing this outcome on member governments. And, more recently, the insistence on the part of those making loans to the highly indebted European governments that those governments must pursue rigid austerity despite being in very deep recessions has also been much debated. We wish to outline how modern analysis can be used to evaluate this issue. As far as the long-run benefits of debt reduction are concerned, we provide a micro-based estimate in Chapter 10 (section 10.4). These benefits turn out to be substantial. In the present chapter, we restrict our attention to an investigation of how it has turned out that some governments have been able to re-establish control of their debt levels, while others have not, and whether the short-run built-in stability features of our economy are enhanced or not by governments following a rigid commitment to balanced budgets.

The basic issue is that short-term pain must be incurred to achieve the long-run benefits of debt reduction unless we can somehow 'grow our way out' of the rising debt-ratio problem. It would seem as if this might be possible, since the denominator of the debt-to-*GDP* ratio is growing through time, and, even with small annual deficits, the numerator may grow at a slower rate. The governments that have achieved a turnaround in their financial affairs are the ones that did not expect too much from this 'less painful' approach of hoping that growth could substitute for tough budget decisions. To defend this assertion, we now compare two fiscal policies – one that keeps a tight rein on the *primary* deficit, and the other that keeps the *overall* budget deficit as an exogenous target. How do such targets affect the stability of government finances?

To answer this long-run stability question, we simplify by ignoring money issue, the tax revenue collected on bond interest, and short-run deviations of real output from its natural rate. If we define G and T as real programme spending and real taxes, i as the nominal interest rate, and B as the number of non-indexed government bonds outstanding, the nominal deficit, D, is then defined by:

$$D = PG - PT + iB.$$

Using lower-case letters to define proportions of GDP: $d = D/PY, g = G/Y, t = T/Y, b = B/PY$, we have:

$$d = g - t + ib \qquad (7.16)$$

Under pure bond financing, the deficit is financed through bond issue: $\dot{B} = D$. Using the time derivative of the definition of the debt ratio, and introducing notation for the inflation rate and the real GDP growth rate: $\pi = \dot{P}/P, n = \dot{Y}/Y$, this accumulation identity can be re-expressed as:

$$\dot{b} = d - (\pi + n)b \qquad (7.17)$$

We consider two fiscal regimes – first, one that involves the government maintaining a fixed structural, or primary, deficit-to-GDP ratio. This policy means that $(g - t)$ remains an exogenous constant, and the overall deficit, d, is endogenous (determined in equation 7.16). Substituting equation 7.16 into equation 7.17 to eliminate d yields:

$$\dot{b} = (g - t) + (r - n)b$$

where $r = i - \pi$ is the real interest rate on government bonds. Assuming Ricardian equivalence, both the interest rate and the growth rate are independent of the quantity of bonds outstanding. With this simplification, we can use this last equation to determine $\partial\dot{b}/\partial b$. Convergence to a constant debt ratio occurs only if this expression is negative, so the stability condition is $n > r$. With a fixed primary deficit, then, a programme of bond-financed fiscal deficits is feasible only if the economy's long-run average real growth rate exceeds its long-run average real interest rate. We assess the likelihood of this condition being met for much of the remainder of this section. But first we consider an alternative fiscal regime.

Fiscal authorities can adopt a target for the *overall* deficit instead of the primary deficit. This regime makes d an exogenous variable. In this case the two-equation system defined by equations 7.16 and 7.17 becomes segmented. The dynamics of the debt ratio is determined by equation 7.17 alone. It implies that stability is assured if the *nominal* growth rate of GDP is positive. As long as the central bank does not try for deflation, the nominal growth rate is surely positive as a long-run-average proposition (for example, any positive n along with $\pi = 0$ will do). Thus, the debt ratio converges to $b = d/(n + \pi)$. We assume that this fiscal regime is in place when we use a calibrated model to estimate the size of the long-run benefits of deficit and debt reduction in Chapter 10.

The Canadian situation provides an interesting application of this analysis. For the 1968–83 period, the Liberal government of Pierre Trudeau ran large primary deficits every year, and, as this analysis suggests, the debt ratio exploded. Then, for the next ten years (1983–93), the Conservative government of Brian Mulroney maintained an average primary deficit of zero, hoping that this contraction in fiscal policy would be sufficient to permit the country to grow its way out of its debt-ratio problem. However, since interest rates exceeded the economy's growth rate, the analysis suggests that this hope would not be realized. Indeed, it was not; the debt ratio continued to increase in dramatic fashion. Finally, the Liberals (under Jean Chrétien and Paul Martin) returned to power for 13 years (1993–2006). During this period, the Liberals adopted a strict target for the overall deficit ratio. After that target was brought down over a five-year period, it remained constant (at a small surplus of about one-half of 1 percentage point of *GDP*) thereafter. Again, just as the analysis predicts, the debt ratio has fallen (by about 40 percentage points). So, with this policy, we *can* grow our way out of the debt problem. But this more appealing outcome required much pain initially, since getting the overall deficit to zero was much tougher than eliminating just the primary deficit. In any event, we conclude that – as simple as it is – a model that contains nothing but the basic accounting identities for government budgets and debt provides an excellent guide for interpreting actual policy.

Before focusing on the central question concerning the relative magnitude of the growth rate and the interest rate, two final points about the Canadian episode are worth making. First, by the turn of the century, the focus was on a much rosier scenario. People were speaking of the 'fiscal dividend', which referred to the extra room in the budget created by the shrinking interest payment obligations. With the prospect of the debt ratio falling from its peak to the government's announced long-run target by 50 percentage points, analysts expect significant interest payment savings. A drop in the debt ratio of 0.5 times an interest rate of 0.05 means a saving of 2.5 per cent of *GDP every* year. There has been no shortage of people ready to advise the government about how to spend this fiscal dividend – some arguing for better-funded programmes and others advocating tax cuts. To have some idea of the magnitudes involved in this debate, we should note that an annuity of 2.5 per cent of *GDP* would permit a *permanent* elimination of one-third of the federal government's total collection of personal income taxes. With so much at stake, we can expect ongoing debate about how best to use the fiscal dividend. With the recession in 2008, however, this debate was put on hold for a few years, since the government chose to let the debt ratio rise temporarily by about 5 percentage points.

The second interesting question concerning the Canadian case is how long it may take for the debt ratio to be brought back down by these 5 percentage points. Of course, the answer depends on whether the government completely eliminates the deficit for a few years or whether it chooses to be less draconian and reduce the deficit only back down to the value that is consistent with its debt-ratio target. In all the public rhetoric about eliminating deficits, it is often not appreciated that equation 7.17 implies that an ongoing deficit *must* exist if both the chosen debt-ratio target and the nominal *GDP* growth rate are positive. For example, for the Canadian debt-ratio target of 25 per cent and a nominal growth rate of 4 per cent, in full equilibrium, the government *must* run an ongoing deficit of 1 per cent of *GDP*. It is instructive to simulate with a discrete-time version of equation 7.17 and an assumed growth rate of 4 per cent: $b_{t+1} = d_t + 0.96b_t$. Consider starting in full equilibrium ($b = 0.25$, $d = 0.01$) and then disturb that equilibrium by what might happen during and following a recession (that d rises to 3 per cent for two years and then falls to 2 per cent for a year, to 1 per cent for a year, and then to zero for five years). This pattern of deficits is just enough to get the debt ratio rising by 5 percentage points and then falling back to its long-run target. It takes a full decade for the government finances to recover from the recession, and fully half of this decade requires 'austerity' ($d = 0$ instead of 1 per cent). But at least the austerity period does not involve having to run a surplus. We see that, with underlying growth, we need to modify the standard summary of the Keynesian strategy. With growth in the denominator, to avoid explosion in the debt *ratio*, we do not need to run surpluses as often as we run deficits. Indeed, as we see in this illustration, we may not need to run surpluses at all.

We return now to the fundamental question: was the fact that interest rates exceeded the economy's growth rate in the Canadian episode an unusual situation, or should we expect that as normal? An extensive literature addresses this question – known as the question of dynamic efficiency – and we discuss that analysis for the remainder of this section. McCallum (1984) analyses a model involving agents with infinite lives and money that enters the utility function; his conclusion is that the conditions of optimizing behaviour preclude the growth rate's exceeding the interest rate. Burbidge (1984) reaches the same conclusion with an overlapping generations model. The logic of this result follows from the fact that, in full equilibrium, the marginal product of capital equals the real after-tax interest rate (as long as we ignore depreciation). If the growth rate exceeds capital's marginal product, society has sacrificed too much and over-accumulated capital. In such a situation, the return on capital is an amount of future consumption that is less than the amount that can be had by just allowing for ongoing growth, and the current generation of consumers can gain (and no other generation of consumers will lose) by consuming some of the nation's capital stock. An equilibrium based on optimization involves exhausting such opportunities until the marginal product of capital is driven upward.

The economy is said to be dynamically efficient if it is impossible to make one generation better off without making at least one other generation worse off. As we note in Chapter 10, Abel et al. (1989) have tested for dynamic efficiency. The essence of their test can be explained as follows. Dynamic efficiency obtains if the return on capital, F_K, exceeds the real growth rate, n. Since all aggregates must grow at the same rate in a balanced growth equilibrium, we have $\dot{K}/K = n$. Thus, the dynamic efficiency inequality, $F_K > n$, can be re-expressed as $F_K > \dot{K}/K$ or $F_K K > \dot{K}$. In words, this last representation is: profits must exceed investment. Abel et al. compare profits and investment for many countries and for many years, and they find that the former exceeds the latter in *every* case. Thus, their analysis supports dynamic efficiency. While aspects of this empirical analysis have been questioned (Barbie et al., 2004), it is worth stressing two policy implications that follow from the observation that profits exceed investment. First, our economies have not accumulated enough capital to maximize steady-state consumption per head, and (given this objective function) any policy that stimulates saving can be defended on efficiency grounds. (Much more detailed discussion of these issues is given in Chapters 10–12.) The second implication of dynamic efficiency is that, as we have noted already, bond-financed budget deficits must render the macroeconomy unstable – at least if the rate of interest that is relevant for government policy decisions is of the same order of magnitude as the marginal product of capital.

It is clear that applied microeconomic policy decisions involve the government using interest rates of this order of magnitude. Indeed, in this context it is not at all appealing to assume that the growth rate exceeds the interest rate. If such a proposition were taken as true by people who carry out cost–benefit studies, they would calculate the present value of many of the component costs and benefits as infinity! To see this point, suppose that some cost or benefit item is estimated to be x per cent of *GDP*. The present value of this item is then $\int_t^\infty x e^{(n-R)} dt$, where R is the after-tax real interest rate. Clearly, if $n > R$, this present value is infinite. To avoid such a situation in cost–benefit studies, analysts *always* assume $R > n$.

Does internal consistency demand that we make the same assumption ($R > n$) when considering macroeconomic policy (for example, when assessing the stability or instability of bond-financed budget deficits) as we do when conducting microeconomic policy analysis (for example, when conducting cost–benefit studies)? If so, we must conclude that bond financing of budget deficits with an exogenous primary deficit involves instability, and so this fiscal regime should be avoided. But a number of analysts answer this question in the negative. They note that different rates of interest are involved both in firms' and the government's investment decisions on the one hand and in the financing of the government debt on the other. Investment decisions involve risk, and it is customary to account for risk in cost–benefit calculations by using a 'high' discount rate. Thus, it is not surprising that estimates of the marginal product of capital are noticeably higher than the rate of return paid on a safe government bond. It is possible for the average real growth rate to be consistently below the former and consistently above the latter. If so, it may be possible to argue that there is no inherent inconsistency involved in following standard cost–benefit practice, while at the same time maintaining that a bond-financed deficit – with exogenous programme spending and tax rates – is feasible.

It is difficult to react to this proposition formally, since our discussion has not involved uncertainty, and so it contains no well-defined mechanism for maintaining any gap between the marginal product of capital and a risk-free yield. We can say that, during the final quarter of the twentieth century, government bond yields exceeded real growth rates in many countries. In this environment, the entire distinction between safe and risky assets ceases to be important, since there is no doubt that bond financing (along with an exogenous primary deficit) involves instability. The take-off of government-debt-to-*GDP* ratios during much of that time is, of course, consistent with this interpretation.

In the end, over long time intervals at least, it seems fair to say that there is serious doubt concerning the relative magnitude of the growth rate and the level of government bond yields. Bohn (1995), Ball et al. (1995) and Blanchard and Weil (2003) have developed models of bond-financed deficits that involve explicit modelling of uncertainty. Ball et al. consider historical evidence for the United States since 1871. They estimate that this experience is consistent with being able, with a probability in the 80–90 per cent range, to run temporary deficits and then roll over the resulting government debt forever. The country can likely grow its way out of a large debt problem without the need for ever having to raise taxes. As a result, the welfare of all generations can be improved. This result is not certain. Nor does it violate the evidence in favour of dynamic efficiency, since there is still a positive probability that some generations will be worse off if growth is insufficient to lower the debt-to-*GDP* ratio.

Ball et al. use their result to argue that the usual metaphor concerning government deficits – that they are like termites eating one's house – is inappropriate. The termite analogy suggests very gradual but inevitable disaster. They advocate thinking of deficits as for a homeowner's decision not to buy fire insurance. Living standards can be higher as long as no fire occurs, but there is a large adverse effect if the fire does occur. They prefer the fire insurance metaphor, because the occurrence of a fire is not inevitable. Of course, reasonable people can disagree about the likelihood of the fire. Since we are not sure what caused the productivity slowdown in the mid-1970s, for example, it may be that extrapolating the more rapid average growth rates of the previous century into the future is ill advised. Similarly, with world capital markets now integrated, and with the high demand for savings stemming from the developing markets in Asia and elsewhere, world (real) interest rates may rise above historical norms for a prolonged period of time, once the aftermath of the 2008 recession is behind us. In short, it may be quite imprudent to put much weight on the 1945–75 historical experience (which was a historical anomaly, since it involved $n > r$). If so, the termite analogy is not so bad after all.

We close this section with a brief evaluation of balanced-budget rules such as the European Stability Pact. We have learned that, as long as the government either cuts programme spending or raises taxes as government debt rises, with a factor of proportionality that exceeds $(r - n)$, the instability problem can be solved. Thus, it is *feasible* to depart from a rigid balanced-budget rule. What we now consider is whether it is *desirable*: should the debt ratio be allowed to vary over the business cycle? As noted above, Keynesians have long assumed that one of the central lessons of the Great Depression was that adjusting *annual* spending and taxation with a view to maintaining a fixed budget-balance target 'come hell or high water' increases output volatility: spending has to be cut and taxes raised as the economy slows down, which is exactly the time we do not want that to happen. The Keynesian message was that it is better to help balance the economy by balancing the budget over the time horizon of one full business cycle, not over an arbitrary shorter period such as one year. Thus, for at least a half-century following the Depression, it was assumed that a rigid annually balanced-budget approach was 'obviously' to be avoided. But the Keynesian message has been increasingly ignored in recent years. As the 'hell or high water' quotation from the Canadian finance minister in 1994 indicates, governments have reverted (except when they feared a complete collapse of our financial system) to annual budget-balance targets that permit only very small departures from a more rigid regime. Adoption of the Stability and Growth Pact in Europe applied similar pressure. Long before the troubles in recent years, *The Economist* magazine editorialized on this topic: 'as the euro area faces the possibility of its first recession . . . the stability pact must not only preclude any fiscal easing but even trammel the operation of fiscal "automatic stabilizers". That could mean that these countries are required to increase taxes or cut public spending even as their economies slow. That smacks of 1930s-style self-flagellation' (25 August 2001, p. 13).

Are *The Economist*'s editorial writers correct or are they putting too much stock in an 'old' analysis that has not been modified to make it consistent with modern standards of rigour? Is it, or is it not, appropriate for the government to allow cyclical variation in its debt ratio by running deficits during recessions and surpluses during booms? There is a long literature assessing the usefulness of Keynesian-style 'built-in stabilizers'. For example, 40 years ago, Gorbet and Helliwell (1971) and Smyth (1974) showed that these mechanisms can serve as *de*stabilizers. Running a deficit budget during a downturn may well decrease the size of that initial recession. But over time the government debt must be worked back down, so the overall speed of adjustment of the economy is reduced. The initial recession is smaller, but the recovery takes longer. So this question is best thought of as another application of Figure 2.2 (in Chapter 2). In this application, the solid-line time path represents the outcome with the Keynesian policy, while the dashed-line time path is the outcome with a rigid balanced-budget rule in place. The (undiscounted) overall output loss may not be smaller when the Keynesian strategy is embraced.

While the early-1970s studies identified this trade-off between a favourable initial impact effect and an unfavourable persistence effect, they are dated; expectations are not modelled as we now deem appropriate, and the behavioural equations are descriptive, not formally micro-based. But more recent studies, for example Lam and Scarth (2006), OECD (2009) and Scarth (2010b), have investigated this trade-off in settings that respect the requirements of the modern approach to business cycle theory. The conclusion these authors reach is that only about one-third of the output volatility that emerges with a rigid balanced-budget rule is removed by following the more Keynesian approach. We conclude that the adoption of rigid budget-balance rules may not involve as dramatic a loss of built-in stability after all. This result is consistent with the empirical results of Levinson (1998), who compares US states that have the flexibility to run unbalanced budgets with those that do not. He found only a very slight reduction in output volatility in the states that did operate with a no-deficits constraint. Perhaps even more surprising, Fatas and Mihov (2003), who study data for 91 countries, conclude that institutional constraints on governments actually *decrease* output volatility. Broadly speaking, it appears that the New Neoclassical Synthesis approach can rationalize these mixed empirical findings.

The entire discussion in the last three paragraphs has focused on whether or not we should allow what used to be called 'built-in stabilizers' to operate. There is a related, but distinct, question: beyond the built-in stabilizers, should the fiscal authority take additional discretionary action in an attempt to stimulate aggregate demand during a recession? Since there will be the standard cost in the longer term – the need to work the accumulated government debt back down – sceptics argue that there had better be a short-term gain. And there will not be if the multiplier that attaches to these fiscal initiatives is very small. Barro (2009) is very critical of 'Team Obama' for their fiscal response to the recent recession, since in their plans they assumed that the short-term expenditure multiplier is 1.5. Barro argues that it is much lower – so much so that discretionary policy is simply not worth it. De Long and Summers (2012) address this criticism in some detail. Since this study is accompanied by extensive comments by others, and since it is so central to the stimulation-versus-austerity debate, readers are encouraged to consult this reference.

As noted in earlier chapters, there is a debate in the theory of monetary policy about whether a price-level targeting strategy represents a 'free lunch' – in that it may provide improved outcomes in terms of *both* lower inflation volatility *and* lower output volatility. We have seen in this section that a similar debate has emerged in the theory of fiscal policy. A 'free lunch' may be possible in this realm of policy as well if budget-balance rules can deliver both more stable debt-ratio time paths in the longer term and no appreciably higher output volatility in the short term. As we have seen, the aspect of the Keynesian approach that makes this counter-intuitive outcome emerge is that the Keynesian policy creates a need for the government to work the debt ratio back to its full-equilibrium value following temporary disturbances. This need slows the economy's speed of adjustment back to the natural rate. Historically, it has been difficult for macroeconomists to evaluate dynamic issues when their models have had only limited micro-foundations. With its increased grounding in inter-temporal optimization, however, the New Neoclassical Synthesis gives some analysts more confidence in their ability to assess dynamic considerations of this sort. The fact that the speed of adjustment outcome can be a quantitatively important consideration in this fiscal policy debate means that what is now mainstream macroeconomics offers some support for Europe's Stability Pact and the more recent drive for fiscal austerity.

7.6 Conclusions

Some of the most central questions that have been debated in the stabilization policy field over the years are: Is following a rule preferred to discretionary policy? Is a flexible exchange rate a shock absorber? What can be done to limit a recession if we are at the zero lower bound on interest rates? Are rigid budget-balance rules required to avoid an exploding debt-to-GDP ratio? Does the adoption of a budget-balance rule decrease the effectiveness of fiscal built-in stabilizers? Now that modern macroeconomics has a new paradigm – the New Neoclassical Synthesis – analysts are returning to these long-standing issues, and checking to see if the conventional wisdom – which is based on earlier, less micro-based models – is threatened by the sensitivity test that the new modelling approach makes possible. The purpose of this chapter has been to explain how these questions have been pursued within this new framework.

Some very central insights have emerged – such as the whole question of dynamic consistency in policy making. Part of the chapter focused on the financing of government budget deficits. We learned how one common specification of bond-financed fiscal deficits is infeasible. Not only does this help us interpret fiscal policy, but it can bring useful insights concerning monetary policy. For example, some economists have relied on this result to offer an explanation of why the disinflation policy of the early 1980s took so long to work. Sargent and Wallace (1981) note that, if the fiscal deficit is exogenously set and if bond financing can be used only temporarily, a reduction in money issue today must mean an increased reliance on money issue in the future. They show that, therefore, rational agents would not necessarily expect the inflation rate to fall along with the current money growth rate. Even in the short run, in the Sargent and Wallace model, inflation can rise as money growth falls.

The ultimate issue raised by Sargent and Wallace is which policy variables – the fiscal or the monetary instruments – should be set residually. In the 1980s, macroeconomic policy in many countries involved imposing monetary policy as a constraint on fiscal decisions – an approach that led to extreme reliance on bond-financed deficits and a dramatic increase in debt-to-GDP ratios. The analysis in part of this chapter indicates that it might have been more appropriate for monetary policy to be determined residually, as Friedman originally proposed in 1948. As long as fiscal parameters are set so that the budget deficit averages zero, this arrangement would control the longer-run growth in the money supply and, therefore, the underlying inflation rate. It would also have the advantage of avoiding the instabilities associated with inordinate reliance on bond financing. But these benefits can be had only if the fiscal policy record is consistent and credible. Friedman gave up expecting this in 1959, and he switched to supporting an exogenous monetary policy. Yet the analysis of this chapter suggests that this exogenous monetary policy *can* involve a decrease in the built-in stability properties of the macroeconomy. Increased reliance on bond financing can lead to instability (an unstable time path for the debt-to-*GDP* ratio). This problem can be avoided by embracing a rigid rule for the annual budget balance, but, as we have seen, the rigid fiscal regime probably worsens short-run macroeconomic performance to some degree.

8 Structural unemployment

8.1 Introduction

In earlier chapters, we examined cyclical (temporary) unemployment. For example, when actual output falls below the natural rate of output, unemployment is temporarily above its natural rate. In this chapter, we ignore cycles; instead, we focus on equilibrium, or permanent, unemployment. We assume that unemployment can persist in full equilibrium for three reasons:

- Asymmetric information problems cause the equilibrium wage to exceed the market-clearing level.
- The market power of unions, or a general belief in society that wages need to be 'fair', causes the equilibrium wage to exceed the market-clearing level.
- Transaction costs and friction in the labour market result in the simultaneous existence of both unemployed individuals and unfilled job vacancies.

We discuss each of these approaches to modelling the labour market in a separate section of the chapter. Much of this work has been pursued by a group of economists who are often called 'New Keynesians' – economists who believe that there is market failure in labour markets, but who also believe that explicit micro-foundations are essential to rigorous macroeconomics. Some New Keynesians have shown that real rigidities – such as the phenomena we study in this chapter – can make any given degree of nominal price rigidity more important from a quantitative point of view. We end this chapter with a discussion of this complementarity between the several strands of New Keynesian work. In the next chapter, we return to the three alternative (non-competitive) models of the labour market, and we focus on identifying fiscal policy initiatives that can be expected to lower the natural unemployment rate in all three settings.

8.2   Asymmetric information in the labour market: efficiency wages

To start, we consider structural unemployment that results from the first of the three considerations listed above: incomplete information. Workers know whether they are trying their best on the job, while employers can monitor this worker effort only incompletely. This differential access to information may lead firms to use wage policy as a mechanism for inducing higher productivity from their employees. Since a 'happy worker is a good worker', firms can have workers who put forth higher effort if they make it the case that workers really want to keep their current job. But one price – the wage rate – cannot clear two markets. Thus, if firms use the wage to 'clear' the 'effort market', society cannot use the wage to clear the workers market. Selfishness, in the form of profit-maximizing firms (the invisible hand), does not deliver what an all-knowing social planner would arrange (full employment), because – at the individual level – firms care about the productivity of their workers, not the nation's unemployment rate. In this setting, therefore, the invisible hand breaks down.

This section of the chapter is devoted to following up on this simple idea. Because this approach focuses on worker efficiency, it is known as efficiency-wage theory. Firms think of two considerations when deciding what wage to set. The direct effect on profits is that a higher wage raises labour costs, so high wages are undesirable. But there is an indirect effect on profits, since higher wages raise worker productivity and so raise profits. If this second effect dominates – at least over some range of wage rates – it is in the firm's interest to raise the wage above the competitive level. When all firms do this, the market involves unemployed individuals. This unemployment is involuntary, since individuals cannot convince firms to accept an offer to work for less. Firms reject such offers, since they represent a request that firms pay a wage that is inconsistent with profit maximization. Thus, one appealing feature of efficiency-wage theory for Keynesians is that we have some rigour behind the common notion that unemployment is a public-policy problem.

We pursue these ideas more carefully by explaining first Solow's (1979) and then Summers's (1988) theory of efficiency wages. Both Solow and Summers define profits as follows:

$$profits = F(qN) - wN.$$

Profits equal sales of goods (produced via the production function, F) minus the wage bill (all items measured here in real terms). For simplicity in this exposition, we follow these authors by ignoring capital, until the extended analysis in the next chapter. The overall quantity of labour is measured in efficiency units – as the product of the number of workers, N, times the effort expended by each worker, q. Solow followed the development literature and assumed that worker quality was a positive function of the level of the workers' happiness (and perhaps even basic nourishment), as measured by the workers' real wage: $q = H(w)$. It is assumed that diminishing returns are involved in this worker-productivity relationship: $H' > 0, H'' < 0$. Summers's specification stresses the relative, not absolute, income of the workers. His worker quality index is assumed to be higher, the bigger is the gap between what the worker gets at this firm, w, and what she receives if she separates from this firm. We denote this outside option as b, and we define it more fully below. Thus, for Summers, the index of worker effort is defined as:

$$q = ((w - b)/b)^a.$$

One handy feature of this specification is that, if we wish to ignore the variability in worker effort in what is derived below, we can set parameter a equal to zero. This makes $q = 1$, and the entire mechanism of variable worker productivity is suppressed. But, if a is a positive fraction, the work-effort index falls below unity, and effort varies directly with the gap between the current wage and the outside option.

In both specifications, firms have two choice variables – what quantity of workers to hire and what wage to set. We can determine the best values for both these things by: substituting the variable-worker-effort constraint into the definition of profits, differentiating the resulting objective function with respect to the firm's two choice variables, N and w, and setting these partial derivatives to zero. We now do just that. To decide on the best level of employment in both models, we work out:

$$\partial profits/\partial N = F'q - w = 0,$$

which states that firms should hire labour up to the point that its marginal product has been pushed down to the rental price of labour (the wage). This is the standard optimal hiring rule (encountered in basic price theory) except that, here, the marginal product expression involves the work-effort index.

To decide on the best wage, firms set the derivative of profits with respect to the wage equal to zero. In Solow's case, we get $F'H' = 1$. After using the other first-order condition to substitute out F', we are left with $wH'(w)/H(w) = 1$.

This condition implies that, to achieve profit maximization, firms must keep the real wage constant. It is straightforward to show that, in a sticky-nominal-price environment, where firms cost-minimize for an exogenous level of expected sales, this same sticky-real-wage feature emerges, and this is the micro-foundation that we appealed to back in Chapter 1 (section 1.5).

In Summers's version of efficiency wages, the derivative of the profit function with respect to the wage is:

$$\partial profits/\partial w = F'Na((w-b)/b)^{a-1}/b - N = [F'qa/(w-b)] - 1 = 0.$$

To appreciate the intuition behind this wage-setting rule, we again use the other first-order condition to substitute out $F'q = w$ and get:

$$w = b/(1-a).$$

According to this rule, firms must set the wage equal to their workers' outside option if there is no variability in worker effort (if a equals 0). This is what is assumed in the standard competitive model of the labour market. But, with variable worker productivity ($a > 0$), it becomes optimal to set the wage above the outside option – to induce workers to work hard (to lower the probability of getting fired by shirking less).

The implications for the unemployment rate can be determined once the workers' outside option is defined. Following Summers, we assume:

$$b = (1-u)w + ufw.$$

With u standing for the unemployment rate, there is a probability equal to the employment rate $(1-u)$ that fired workers will find a job with another firm (which in full equilibrium pays the same wage). There is a probability equal to the unemployment rate that the individual will be without a job. We assume a simple unemployment insurance programme in which individuals receive fraction f of their wage as an unemployment insurance benefit (without any waiting period or time limit) in this eventuality. The b equation above defines the outside option as this weighted average. When this relationship is substituted into the wage-setting rule, we have:

$$u = a/(1-f).$$

This solution for the unemployment rate teaches us three things. First, unemployment is zero if there is no variability in worker effort (that is, if parameter *a* is zero). Second, increased generosity in the unemployment insurance system (a higher value for parameter *f*) raises unemployment. This is because higher unemployment insurance shrinks the relative pay-off that individuals get by keeping their jobs. As a result, they choose to shirk more. Knowing this, firms raise the wage in an attempt to lessen this reaction of their employees. With higher wages, firms shift back along their (downward-sloping) labour demand curve and hire fewer workers. (By the way, this does not mean that unemployment insurance is 'bad'. After all, with unemployment insurance, any one unemployment spell hurts the individual less. It is just that there is a trade-off; this beneficial effect induces an increased frequency of unemployment spells.) The third implication of the solution equation for the unemployment rate follows from the fact that it does not include a productivity term, F'. Thus, the proposition that investment in education (which raises overall productivity) would lower unemployment is not supported by Summers's analysis. Higher productivity is desirable because it raises the wages of those who already have jobs, not because it brings more people jobs. This prediction is consistent with centuries of economic history. Vast productivity growth has led to similar increases in real wages, without any significant long-term trend in the unemployment rate.

We have focused on efficiency-wage theory so that we have at least one rigorous framework for arguing that some unemployment is involuntary. We have focused on Summers's specification in particular, since it leads to a straightforward closed-form solution equation for the structural unemployment rate. We will use this theory to evaluate how fiscal policy might be used to lower this 'natural' unemployment rate in the next chapter. Before closing the present discussion of efficiency-wage theory, however, it is useful to extend Summers's analysis by considering optimization on the part of households (not just firms). It is preferable that the household variable-work-effort function be derived, not assumed. This can be accomplished by assuming that households maximize $(\pi w + (1 - \pi)b - \beta b q^{\gamma})$. The proportion of time that the individual is employed in her current job is π, and this proportion rises with worker effort: $\pi = q^{\psi}$. The first two terms in the objective function define the individual's income; she receives w if she keeps her current job, and she receives b if she does not. The final term defines the disutility associated with putting effort into one's job. To be compatible with the income components of the objective function, this term is scaled by b. Since it is reasonable to specify that higher work effort increases the probability of keeping one's job, but at a decreasing rate, ψ must be less than one. Similarly, since it is appealing for higher effort to decrease utility at an increasing rate, γ must exceed unity. Household behaviour follows from substituting in the constraint and differentiating the objective function with respect to q. The result is the effort function given above, if a is interpreted as $1/(\gamma - \psi)$ and units are chosen so that $\psi/\gamma\beta = 1$.

We pursue several policy implications of this model of efficiency wages in the next chapter. But, for much of the remainder of this chapter, we consider alternative ways to model the labour market.

8.3 Imperfect competition in the labour market: unions

The literature on the macroeconomic effects of unions focuses on two different models, which are referred to as the non-cooperative and the cooperative theories of union–firm interaction. The non-cooperative model involves firms maximizing profits defined by $F(N) - wN$. This is achieved when the familiar condition $F' = w$ holds. This labour demand function is shown in Figure 8.1, as the locus of all points that are at the apex of an iso-profit curve. The slope of the iso-profit lines can be derived by setting the total differential of the definition of profits equal to zero. The slope of an iso-profit line is $dw/dN = [F'(N) - w]/N$, which is positive for low levels of N and negative for high levels of N (when the marginal product is low).

Figure 8.1 Models of union–firm interaction

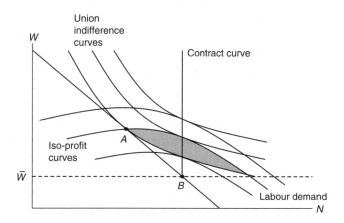

Unions are assumed to maximize the income of a representative member of the group. This can be defined as $w(N/L) + \bar{w}(L - N)/L$, where N and L denote employment and size of union membership respectively, w is the wage paid to union members if they are employed, $\bar{w}$ is the wage they receive if they are unemployed (which could be interpreted as unemployment insurance), and N/L is the probability of employment. The slope of the union's indifference curves is derived by setting the total differential of the expected income definition to zero. The result is $dw/dN = -(w - \bar{w})/N$, which is negative since the union wage cannot be less than the individual's reservation wage.

The union achieves the highest indifference curve by picking the wage that corresponds to the point at which the labour demand curve is tangent to an indifference curve (point A in Figure 8.1). Once the wage is set, firms are free to choose employment. But, since the union has taken the firm's reaction into account, its members know that point A will be chosen. We can derive what this model predicts concerning the real wage and employment by including a shift variable – such as A in a revised production function: $AF(N)$. Comparative static predictions are calculated by taking the total differential of the labour demand curve and the equal slopes condition. It is left for the reader to verify that the model does not predict real wage rigidity. One purpose of examining this model was to see whether the existence of unions in labour markets leads to wage rigidity and/or involuntary unemployment. Since the model contains no explicit explanation of why individuals deal with the firm exclusively through the union (Are they forced to? Did they choose to?), it is not possible to say whether lower employment means higher involuntary unemployment.

Let us now investigate whether wage rigidity occurs in the cooperative model of union–firm interaction. The outcome in the previous model is inefficient, since there are many wage/employment outcomes – all the points within the shaded, lens-shaped region in Figure 8.1 – that can make both the firm and the union better off than they are at point A. Non-cooperative bargaining leaves 'money on the table'. The cooperative model assumes that the two parties reach an agreement and settle at one of the Pareto-efficient points that lie along the contract curve. Completing the model now requires some additional assumption that defines how the two parties divide the gains from trade. The additional assumption that is most common (see McDonald and Solow, 1981) is that the two bargainers reach a Nash equilibrium. Without specifying some rule of this sort, we cannot derive any predictions about how the wage level responds to shifts in the position of the labour demand function.

Employment effects can, however, be derived without any such additional specification. The equation of the contract curve is had by equating the slope expressions for the iso-profit and the indifference curves. With the shift variable for labour's marginal product inserted, this equal slopes condition is $(AF' - w)/N = -(w - \overline{w})/N$, or $AF' = \overline{w}$. The contract curve is vertical, since w does not enter this equation. From this equation of the contract curve, we see that we can determine the effects on employment of changes in

A and $\bar{w}$ without having to specify the bargaining model that is required for the model to yield any real wage predictions. It appears that this cooperative union model does not support the hypothesis of real wage rigidity, but we can derive the employment effects that follow from this theory if we impose real wage rigidity in a macroeconomic context. For macroeconomic employment effects, it is *as if* real wages were fixed.

We complete our analysis of the cooperative model by using the standard Nash product to derive the condition which determines the division of the rents between the union and the firm. The function that is delegated to the arbitrator to maximize involves the product of two items: first, what the firm can earn in profits if cooperation is achieved (minus what it gets with no cooperation – zero), and, second, the similar differential for workers. This product can be written as $[(w - \bar{w})N^\psi]^\theta V^{1-\theta}$, where V is profits: $V = AF(N) - wN$, θ is the bargaining power parameter ($\theta = 1$: unions have all the power; $\theta = 0$: firms have all the power), and ψ is a union preference parameter ($\psi = 1$: the union is utilitarian in that it values all its members, not just the currently employed; $\psi = 0$: the union is seniority oriented, as only the wages of those currently employed are valued).

After differentiating the arbitrator's objective function with respect to w and N and simplifying, we have two labour market equations (which are the imperfect competition analogues for supply and demand curves) to determine wages and employment. McDonald and Solow call these two relationships the efficiency locus and the equity locus. The equation that defines the contract curve is the efficiency locus. It is $AF' = \bar{w}$ with a utilitarian union, while it is $AF' = w$ with a seniority-based union. With the seniority-based union, the negotiations pay no attention to employment, and the union indifference curves are horizontal lines. Thus, in this case, the labour demand curve and the contract curve coincide, and this version of the system essentially replicates the non-cooperative model. Finally, the equation which defines the division of the rents (the equity locus) is $\theta V = (1 - \theta)(w - \bar{w})N$, whether unions are utilitarian or not.

Pissarides (1998) uses a model of union–firm interaction that combines features of the two different approaches that have just been summarized. His model follows the 'right to manage' aspect of the non-cooperative approach, in that it is the firm that chooses the employment level *after* the wage has been determined. But the model involves a key feature of the cooperative approach as well, since the wage is not set unilaterally by the union. Instead, it is the result of a bargaining process involving both the union and the employer.

A simplified version of Pissarides' model (involving risk neutrality on the part of the union and a Cobb–Douglas production function) is explained here. In the first stage, an arbitrator is appointed to choose the wage which maximizes the following Nash product function: $(I - \bar{I})^\theta (V - 0)^{1-\theta}$. I is the index of the workers' net benefit from the contract. Pissarides' definition of this net benefit is $I = wN + (L - N)[(1 - u)w^* + u\bar{w}]$. As above, N is employment in this firm, and L is union membership. It is assumed that those who do not find employment in this firm seek employment elsewhere. These individuals face probabilities equal to the employment rate, and the unemployment rate, concerning whether they secure another job (and are paid w^*) or whether they are without work (and receive employment insurance equal to $\bar{w}$). $\bar{I}$ is what individuals receive if employment at this firm, N, is zero. Thus, $(I - \bar{I}) = N(w - (1 - u)w^* - u\bar{w})$. As far as the firm's profit is concerned, we have $V = Y - wN$, and the production function is $Y = AN^\gamma$.

Differentiating the arbitrator's objective function with respect to w, and then substituting in the equations that define full equilibrium ($w = w^*$) and the unemployment insurance system ($\bar{w} = fw$), we have: $u = a/(1-f)$, where $a = [\theta(1 - \gamma)/\gamma(1 - \theta)]$. We see that this version of imperfect competition in the labour market yields the *same* equation for the natural unemployment rate as did Summers's efficiency-wage model. Despite this similarity, there are some new results embedded within this alternative derivation of this reduced form. For example, in this union–firm interaction interpretation, we see that the natural unemployment rate is predicted to rise, the higher is the degree of union power. Thus, if lower structural unemployment is the goal, we might view the model as providing some support for legislation that is designed to limit workers' rights.

The more general point is that many policies that are designed to lower the natural unemployment rate (some of which we stress in the next chapter) receive equivalent analytical support – whether one appeals to efficiency-wage theory or union–firm interaction theory. We can have more confidence about making applied policy advice when the underlying rationale for that policy proposal is *not* dependent on just one interpretation of the labour market or the other.

Further, it is likely that we can apply the union–firm interaction model to settings that do not involve formal unions. In many Western countries, wages are settled in a manner that involves an implicit appeal to arbitration in which societal norms regarding 'fair' wages are given serious consideration.

Thus, we think it is instructive to apply this analysis and, in particular, the Pissarides specification of arbitration combined with firms' right to manage employment, beyond its original focus on unions.

8.4 Transaction frictions in the labour market: search theory

We continue our examination of 'natural' unemployment rate models by considering one more source of market failure. In this case, instead of incomplete information (and efficiency wages) or market power (and unions), we focus on *frictions* in the labour market. This analytical framework highlights the fact that job seekers and employers meet in a series of decentralized one-on-one settings. Since matches do not occur instantaneously, this setting generates an equilibrium amount of frictional unemployment. This section follows D. Romer (2001, pp. 444–53) and Hall (2003) very closely in outlining as simple a summary of search theory as is possible.

First, we define some notation; E, U and L stand for the number of individuals who are employed, unemployed and in the labour force. The labour force is taken as an exogenous constant. In this section of the chapter, we use f and s to denote the job-finding rate and the job separation rate. This notation can be used to define equilibrium. The labour market is in equilibrium when the unemployment rate is constant, and this, in turn, requires that the number of individuals leaving the unemployment pool each period be just balanced by the number who are entering that pool. In symbols, this is: $fU = sE$. Since $E = L - U$, and since the unemployment rate, u, is U/L, this equilibrium condition can be solved for the unemployment rate:

$$u = s/(s + f).$$

What search theorists have done is to build a model that makes the job-finding rate, f, endogenous (and based on optimizing behaviour). The resulting solution for f is then substituted into the unemployment rate equation just presented, so that the determinants of the natural unemployment rate are then exposed.

We need additional notation to define this theory (and we use Romer's): A, the marginal product of each employed worker; C, the fixed cost of maintaining a job; and w, the wage rate. It is assumed that there is no cost of posting a vacancy. The profit associated with each filled job is given by $(A - C - w)$, and the profit associated with each job vacancy is $(-C)$. We assume static expectations, so that we can represent the present value of receiving these flows indefinitely, by simply multiplying them by $(1/r)$.

The technology of the matching process is specified by:

$$M = \alpha U^\beta V^\gamma,$$

where M is the number of matches. If $\beta + \gamma < 1$, it is said that there is congestion or crowding in the labour market (the more individuals and firms there are in the market, the less chance there is that any one match can be made). If $\beta + \gamma > 1$, it is said that there is a 'thick market' externality involved (the more individuals and firms there are in the market, the more likely it is that a good match will be found). This is the assumption made by Howitt (1985) and Diamond (1984) in the multiple-equilibria models that are discussed in Chapter 9. Finally, if $\beta + \gamma = 1$, we rule out both negative and positive externality effects. Since the empirical evidence weakly favours this case, we proceed with this assumption below. Specifically, defining the vacancy rate, the unemployment rate, and the ratio of these two measures as $v = V/L$, $u = U/L$ and $x = u/v$, we can define the job-finding rate as:

$$f = M/U = \alpha U^{\beta-1} V^{1-\beta} = \alpha (u/v)^{\beta-1} = \phi(x).$$

Similarly, the job-filling rate can be represented as:

$$\theta = M/V = \alpha U^\beta V^{-\beta} = \alpha (u/v)^\beta = \alpha (u/v)(u/v)^{\beta-1} = x\phi(x).$$

We complete the model by defining the utility function of individuals. For simplicity, it is specified that individuals are risk neutral and that they do not save, so utility equals current income. Thus, the level of utility is w if an individual is employed, and utility is zero if she is unemployed.

Dynamic programming is used to define optimal behaviour. In this approach, we consider (for example) the 'annual return' that an individual receives from being employed. This value is denoted by rV_E, and it is equal to the sum of a 'dividend' and a 'capital loss':

$$rV_E = w - s(V_E - V_U). \tag{8.1}$$

This equation defines the annual dividend of having a job as the wage received, and the capital loss as the difference between the value of a job and the value of not having one (being unemployed). The probability of sustaining this capital loss is the job separation rate. The annual return that is associated with other states is defined in a similar manner.

The value to a firm of maintaining a filled job is:

$$rV_F = (A - C - w) - s(V_F - V_V) \tag{8.2}$$

The firm's annual profit is the 'dividend', and the difference between the value of a filled job and the value of an unfilled vacancy is the 'capital loss'. Again, the separation rate is the probability of sustaining this capital loss.

The annual return of being unemployed is given by:

$$rV_U = 0 + f(V_E - V_U) \tag{8.3}$$

since, without unemployment insurance, the dividend is zero, the capital gain is the increase in utility that comes with the possibility that the individual becomes employed, and the probability of receiving this gain is the job-finding rate.

Finally, the annual return to the firm of maintaining an unfilled vacancy is:

$$rV_V = -C + \theta(V_F - V_V) \tag{8.4}$$

The dividend is negative (the cost of maintaining any position), the capital gain is the extra profits that are received if the position is filled, and the probability of receiving this gain is the job-filling rate.

The remaining equations define different aspects of full equilibrium. As noted above, a constant unemployment rate requires that the flows out of, and into, the unemployed pool must be equal:

$$M = sE, \quad \text{or} \quad fU = sE. \tag{8.5}$$

Given that the cost of posting a vacancy is zero, firms must have posted a sufficient number to ensure that the marginal benefit is zero:

$$rV_V = 0 \tag{8.6}$$

Finally, the wage must be set so that the gains of the match are distributed between individuals and firms in a way that is consistent with the 'market power' of these groups. As in our models of union–firm interaction, we assume a Nash equilibrium, and for simplicity here we assume equal levels of bargaining power. This implies that the wage is set so that an individual's gain from a match is equal to the firm's gain from the relationship:

$$(V_E - V_U) = (V_F - V_V). \qquad (8.7)$$

The solution proceeds as follows. Subtracting equation 8.3 from equation 8.1, and equation 8.4 from equation 8.2, we have:

$$V_E - V_U = w/(f + s + r) \qquad (8.8)$$

$$V_F - V_V = (A - w)/(\theta + s + r) \qquad (8.9)$$

Substituting equations 8.8 and 8.9 into equation 8.7, and solving for w, we have:

$$w = A(f + s + r)/(f + \theta + 2(s + r)) \qquad (8.10)$$

and substituting equation 8.9 into equation 8.4:

$$rV_V = -C + [\theta(A - w)]/(\theta + s + r) \qquad (8.11)$$

Finally, substituting equation 8.10 into equation 8.11 to eliminate w, imposing $V_V = 0$, and substituting in $f = \phi(x), \theta = x\phi(x)$, and $z = A/C$, we end with:

$$((z - 1)x - 1)\phi(x) = 2(s + r) \qquad (8.12)$$

which is a non-linear equation in x, the ratio of the unemployment rate to the vacancy rate. Hall (2003) picks values for s, r, z, α and β, and solves for x. Once x is known, Hall solves for the unemployment rate:

$$u = s/(s + \phi(x)).$$

Part of Hall's calibration is that $\beta = 0.5$, so equation 8.12 becomes a quadratic equation. Hall chooses representative values for the other parameters as well, and as a result equation 8.12 becomes:

$$(0.62)y^2 - (0.913)y - 1 = 0,$$

where $y = \sqrt{x}$. Of the two solutions, only one is positive (that is, economically admissible). This one solution is used – in a version of the model that is extended to allow for several taxes – in Chapter 9. As with the other models of market failure in the labour market, we identify fiscal policies that can be expected to have favourable effects on the natural unemployment rate.

8.5 Related issues in New Keynesian economics: real versus nominal rigidities

Some of the labour market models that were surveyed in the three previous sections of this chapter provide support for the hypothesis of *real* wage rigidity, but a fundamental problem for business cycle theory is to explain why purely nominal shocks have real effects. The Keynesian and New Neoclassical Synthesis approaches to this question rely on *nominal* wage and/or price rigidity. Can the models of this chapter apply in any way to this question?

Some analysts have argued that the theories of real wage rigidity can apply to *nominal* wages in an indirect way. When wages are set, bargaining is *about* the real wage. But the item that is actually *set* as a result of these decisions is the money wage. It is set at the level intended to deliver the desired real wage, given inflationary expectations. With this interpretation, we can argue that the theories apply to money wage setting, although an additional assumption regarding indexation is required. We would expect agents to set the money wage with a full indexing clause so there would be no need to incur errors in forming inflationary expectations. But, given that catch-up provisions can roughly replace ex ante indexing formulae, and given that households and firms want to tie wages to different price indexes, the costs of full indexation are probably not worth the benefit (as McCallum, 1986, has stressed).

Quite apart from the preceding argument, some analysts are uneasy about applying an adjustment-cost model (such as the one we explored in Chapter 4) to explain sticky *goods* prices. Negotiation costs between buyers and firms are not a feature of reality for many commodities. Of course, the sale of many commodities involves posting prices, but it does not seem compelling to rest all of sticky-price macroeconomics on an item that seems rather trivial (such as the cost of printing new prices in catalogues – the so-called 'menu' cost – and the cost of informing sales staff about price changes). The response that one can make to the charge that adjustment costs for many nominal prices cannot be 'that important' is simply to demonstrate that even explicitly small price-change costs can lead to large welfare losses. Akerlof and Yellen (1985) and Mankiw (1985) provide analysis that is intended to support this view.

Let us examine a brief summary of the argument (along the lines suggested by D. Romer, 1993). Consider a monopolist who must set her nominal price before the relevant period but who can change that price later (during the period) at a 'small' cost. A situation in which the price has been set at too high a value is illustrated in Figure 8.2. When the firm set its price, it did not guess the then-future position of its demand curve perfectly. As it enters the period analysed in Figure 8.2, it has already posted a price equal to OA, but the appropriate price is OB. The firm must now decide whether making the change is worthwhile. As far as private profits are concerned, the firm loses an amount equal to area FGH by not lowering its price to OB. The cost to society of not adjusting the price is area $DGHE$ – potentially a much bigger amount. It is quite possible for even quite small adjustment costs to be larger than area FGH but much smaller than area $DGHE$. Thus, the social gains from price adjustment may far exceed the private gains.

Figure 8.2 Menu costs

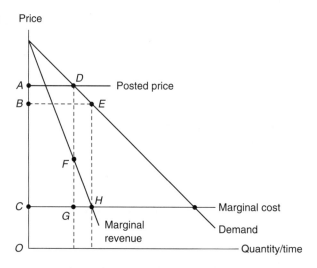

This analysis suggests that Keynesians may not have to assume 'large' nominal price-adjustment costs to sustain their simultaneous claims that:

1. prices may be sticky;
2. the welfare losses that follow from sticky prices may be large (at least if general equilibrium expectational effects – such as those stressed in Chapter 2 – are ignored);
3. government policy may be justified, since individual firms consider only the private benefits of price flexibility.

There are a couple of reasons why this analysis may not support such sweeping conclusions. For one thing, Figure 8.2 shows just the case involving prices remaining too high. It is left for the reader to draw a diagram in which the existing price is set at too low a value. It is still true that firms incur a small private cost (in terms of forgone profits) that may easily be dominated by the menu cost if they do not raise prices. And it is still true that the implications of not adjusting price are much larger for society. But, this time, that large area is a *gain* in welfare. Since prices may be too low just about as often as they are too high, it may be roughly the case that menu costs lead to *no* significant *net* effect on society welfare. While this normative issue has been overstated by some Keynesians, the positive point remains – even seemingly trivial menu costs may dominate the private benefits of incurring them.

A second issue that has been glossed over in our discussion of Figure 8.2 is a more detailed focus on how the demand and cost curves may have shifted to create an initial situation such as that illustrated. One possibility is that the vertical intercept of the demand curve and the height of the marginal cost curve shifted down by the same amount. But, if real wages are rigid, and the nominal price does not fall (given menu costs), the position of the marginal cost curve should *not* be shifted down at all. Such a redrawing of Figure 8.2 shrinks the size of area *FGH* and so makes it all the more likely that even small menu costs can be the dominant consideration. In short, *real wage rigidity* may increase the applicability of the menu-cost model to such an extent that the hypothesis can be said to play a central (if indirect) role in providing the micro-foundations for *nominal* rigidities.

The intuition behind this result is perhaps best appreciated by considering an oligopoly. Each firm finds it costly to change its relative price, since a higher *relative* price is immediately noticed by its current customers, while a lower relative price is not widely noticed by the other firms' customers. Thus, there is a *real* rigidity – in relative prices. Even if the nominal rigidity – the actual cost of changing its own nominal price – is very small, each firm will behave *as if* this is not the case, because of the real rigidity. Thus, real rigidities magnify the importance of a little nominal rigidity.

Alvi (1993) has presented a simple proof that this proposition is quite general, which we now summarize. Alvi assumes that each firm's profit function can be written as $V(P/\overline{P}, M/\overline{P})$, where P, $\overline{P}$ and M denote the firm's own price, the economy-wide average price and the nominal money supply. The first argument in this function captures imperfect competition, while the second captures aggregate effects. The fact that firms care only about relative prices and the real value of money means that no money illusion is involved. Each firm's optimum outcome can be written as:

$$P/\bar{P} = H(M/\bar{P}), \tag{8.13}$$

which indicates that the best value for the firm's price is simply a function of the two items which the firm takes as parameters: $\bar{P}$ and M. Note that real rigidity (that is, relative price rigidity) is prevalent if H' is small. We assume $P = \bar{P} = M = 1$ initially, and that $H' = h$. Then, the total differential of equation 8.13 implies:

$$dP/dM = h + (1-h)(d\bar{P}/dM). \tag{8.14}$$

Let $z = dP/dM$ be an index of nominal flexibility (so $z = 0$ implies complete nominal rigidity and $z = 1$ implies completely flexible nominal variables). Let proportion q of the firms be subject to nominal menu costs to the extent that their prices are not adjusted in response to a change in the money supply. Given this notation, we know that:

$$d\bar{P}/dM = (q)(0) + (1-q)(dP/dM) = (1-q)z.$$

Substituting this relationship into equation 8.14, we obtain:

$$z = h/(1-(1-q)(1-h)).$$

This final equation implies that $z = 1$ if there are no menu costs ($q = 0$). With menu costs, however, it implies $\partial z/\partial h > 0$, so a given amount of menu cost results in a high degree of overall nominal rigidity *if* real rigidities are prevalent. We conclude that it is not necessarily unreasonable to base a theory of business cycles on small nominal 'menu' costs.

Research continues on the microeconomics of menu costs. To some, the most appealing model of price changes at the individual level is known as the two-sided (S,s) adjustment rule. It involves the firm only incurring the fixed cost of adjustment when the gap between the desired price and the existing one exceeds a critical value (S on the high side, s on the low side). Heterogeneity among firms can take various forms, such as differing initial positions within common (S,s) bands, or firm-specific shocks. As is usual in the aggregation literature, not all specifications lead to well-defined macro implications.

Ball and Mankiw (1994) draw the distinction between time-contingent adjustment models and state-contingent adjustment models. The theory we covered in Chapter 4 is an example of the former, while the (S,s) models are examples of the latter. Ball and Mankiw note that no robust conclusions have emerged from the literature on state-contingent adjustment, but that this state of affairs is not necessarily upsetting. This is because time-contingent adjustment is optimal if the main cost is gathering information about the state rather than making the actual price adjustment. Also, in economies with two groups of firms – one making each kind of adjustment – it turns out that the sluggish adjustment on the part of the time-contingent firms makes it rational for those monitoring developments continuously according to the state-contingent model to behave much like the other group. Thus, it may well be that the quadratic adjustment-cost model of Chapter 4 is not such a bad approximation of a theory with much more detailed structure.

Another issue that is being researched is whether it matters to specify explicitly that it is the gathering of information, not the resetting of prices, that is costly. Mankiw and Reis (2002) have shown that a 'sticky-information' version of an expectations-augmented Phillips curve may fit the facts better than a 'sticky-price' version does. Further, they demonstrate that this version of a new synthesis model can lead to different conclusions regarding the relative appeal of alternative monetary policies.

8.6   Conclusions

In Chapters 1 to 4, we focused on the deviations of real output from its natural rate. We assumed that the natural output rate was unique and that we could think of it being determined by the Classical model. Further, we assumed – but had not formally shown – that, if we added some friction to the specification of the labour market, we could generate a unique, non-zero value for the associated natural unemployment rate. The primary task of this chapter has been to provide that more detailed set of analyses for the labour market. We have found that market failure can occur in the labour market for several different reasons – incomplete information, imperfect competition, and transactions costs. In some of these cases, these features allow us to interpret the resulting unemployment as involuntary, and so it is reasonable to investigate whether policy can improve the outcome. We proceed to address this very question in the next chapter.

There was one other purpose in surveying the several leading models that generate real rigidities in labour markets. We have seen that real rigidities – such as those highlighted in this chapter – magnify the importance of nominal rigidities. This is important since both New Keynesians and now all those who have adopted the New Neoclassical Synthesis have relied on this proposition to 'justify' their having their approach to business cycles depend on seemingly small 'menu' costs in an important way. Even New Classicals – such as Alexopoulos (2004), who has added a version of efficiency-wage theory to the real business cycle framework – have relied on this proposition to generate more persistence in real variables within their models.

There are three tasks that we address in the remaining chapters. First, as just noted, we use the models developed here to analyse a series of policy proposals designed to lower structural unemployment and to raise the economic position of those on low income. Second, we use some of these models to investigate the possibility of multiple equilibria. If theory leads to the possibility that there are two 'natural' unemployment rates – both a high-employment equilibrium and a low-employment equilibrium – there is an 'announcement effect' role for policy. It may be possible for the government to induce agents to focus on the high-activity outcome if agents know that the policy maker stands ready to push the system to that outcome if necessary. It is possible that no action – just the commitment to act – may be all that is necessary. Third, we would like to see whether policies that are geared to reducing structural unemployment have an undesirable long-run implication. Might these initiatives retard the productivity growth rate? We examine the first two issues in Chapter 9 and then devote the final three chapters to an analysis of long-term growth.

9

Unemployment and low incomes: applying the theory

9.1 Introduction

In the last chapter, we summarized three approaches to modelling the labour market – standard analyses of what determines the level of structural unemployment. While this is often called the 'natural' unemployment rate, this term is unfortunate, since all these theories suggest that the full-equilibrium unemployment rate can be affected by fiscal policy. The primary task for this chapter is to investigate precisely how. We consider several fiscal policies:

- replacing the income tax with an expenditure tax (section 9.2);
- taxing physical capital owners to finance a tax break for wage earners and/or employers (section 9.3);
- introducing low-income support policies, such as employment subsidies and a guaranteed annual income, in models of both developed and developing economies (section 9.4); and
- investigating how policy can both create and react to multiple equilibria (section 9.5).

9.2 Tax reform: direct versus indirect taxation

We begin by illustrating the possibilities for fiscal policy within the Summers (1988) version of efficiency-wage theory. First, we add an income tax to the model, which can be interpreted in two ways. First, it could be an employee payroll tax (which is levied on wage income but not on unemployment insurance benefits). Second, it could be part of a progressive personal income tax, which involves no tax on low levels of income (such as what individuals receive if all they have access to is the unemployment insurance benefit). With this tax, the specifications of the efficiency index and the outside option change compared to how they were specified in Chapter 8. These relationships are now given as $q = ((w(1-t) - b)/b)^a$ and $b = (1-u)w(1-t) + ufw$, where t is the wage-income tax rate. It is left for the reader to verify that these modifications change the unemployment rate solution to:

$$u = a/[1 - (f/(1-t))].$$

This equation implies that an increase in the tax rate raises the natural unemployment rate. This occurs because higher taxes reduce the relative pay-off individuals receive from work. To lessen the resulting increase in worker shirking, firms offer a higher wage, and they hire fewer workers at this higher price.

The importance of taxes can be illustrated by considering some illustrative parameter values. Realistic assumptions are: $u = 0.05, f = 0.50, t = 0.15$. These representative values are consistent with this model only if $a = 0.02$, which we therefore assume. Now consider fixing a and f at 0.02 and 0.5 respectively, while higher tax rates are considered. The reader can verify that the unemployment rate rises by 1 percentage point (to $u = 0.06$) when the tax rate rises by 10 percentage points to 0.25, and the unemployment rate rises by much more (2.67 percentage points, to 0.0867) when the tax rate rises by an additional 10 percentage points to 0.35. This thought experiment indicates that one does not need to have ultra-right-wing views to be concerned about efficiency in government. Only with such efficiency can we have the many valuable services of government with the lowest possible taxes, and (as this numerical example suggests) high taxes can very much raise unemployment.

It is instructive to examine the effects that several other taxes have (or, more precisely, do not have) within this basic version of the efficiency-wage model. With an employer payroll tax, , the firms' wage bill becomes $wN(1 +)$, and with a sales tax, λ, the wage that concerns households is $w^* = w/(1 + \lambda)$. It is left for the reader to verify that, when these changes are made in the specification of the efficiency-wage model, there is no change in the solution equation for the unemployment rate. It is useful to review the intuition behind why employee payroll taxes do, but these other taxes do not, affect unemployment. As already noted, both a more generous unemployment insurance system and a higher employee payroll tax increase unemployment. Both these measures lower the relative return from working. To compensate for the deterioration in work effort that results, firms must raise wages, and this makes a lower level of employment optimal.

The other taxes do not change the relative return of work compared to being unemployed. For example, sales taxes must be paid simply because goods are purchased; it makes no difference how the purchaser obtained her funds. This is why the natural unemployment rate is unaffected by the sales tax. Similar reasoning applies to the employer payroll tax. A cut in this levy increases both the ability of the worker's employer to pay higher wages and the ability of all other firms to pay that individual higher wages. Competition among firms for workers forces this entire increase in ability to pay to be transferred to those already working (in the form of higher wages). As a result there is no reduction in unemployment. The same outcome follows for anything that shifts the labour demand curve without having any direct effect within the workers' effort function. This is why we stressed in the previous chapter that increases in general productivity raise wages – and do not lower unemployment – in this efficiency-wage specification.

These results imply that we can have a lower natural unemployment rate if we rely more heavily on a sales tax, instead of an income tax. They also imply that investments in training and education lead to higher wages, but not to lower unemployment. But, before we can have confidence in such strong predictions and exhort real-world authorities to act on this advice, we need to know whether they are supported by the other theories of the natural unemployment rate.

To check the effects of various fiscal policies in our models of union–firm interaction, we add a wage-income tax (which, as above, can also be interpreted as the employee payroll tax), an employer payroll tax and a sales tax. As in Chapter 8, the function that is delegated to the arbitrator to maximize involves the product of two items: first, what the firm can earn in profits if cooperation is achieved (minus what it gets with no cooperation – zero); and, second, the similar differential in returns for workers. This product is $[(((1-t)w - \overline{w})/(1+\lambda))N^{\psi}]^{\theta} V^{1-\theta}$. $V = AF(N) - wN(1 + \tau)$ is profits. θ is the union bargaining power parameter, and ψ is the union seniority parameter.

After differentiating the arbitrator's objective function with respect to w and N and simplifying, we have the tax-included versions of the two labour market equations that determine wages and employment. The equation that defines the contract curve is $(1-t)AF' = \overline{w}(1+\tau)$ with a utilitarian union, while it is $AF' = w(1 + \tau)$ with a seniority-based union. The equity relationship is $\theta AF(N) = w(1 + \tau)N - (1-\theta)(1 + \tau)\overline{w}N/(1-t)$ whether unions are utilitarian or not. In both cases, the level of employment is unaffected by sales taxes, but it is affected by both the employer and the employee payroll tax (an increase in either tax raises unemployment).

We add the same set of taxes to the Pissarides (1998) model of union–firm interaction that combines features of the cooperative and non-cooperative approaches. The arbitrator's objective function is still $(I - \bar{I})^\theta (V - 0)^{1-\theta}$, and the production function is still $Y = AN^\gamma$. There are several changes: $(I - \bar{I}) = ((w - (1-u)w^*)(1-t) - u\bar{w})N/(1+\lambda)$, $V = Y - wN(1+\tau)$, and $\gamma AN^{\gamma-1} = w(1+\tau)$. Proceeding with the same steps as we followed in Chapter 8, we arrive at the revised solution equation for the unemployment rate:

$$u = a/[1 - f/(1 - t)],$$

where, as before, $a = [\theta(1 - \gamma)]/[\gamma(1 - \theta)]$. The policy implications are a little different from those that followed from the other models of union–firm interaction, but they are the same as those that followed from the efficiency-wage model. For all the models, we have found that the natural unemployment is increased by higher employee payroll taxes, but it is not increased by a higher sales tax. It appears that there is one general conclusion that has emerged from both efficiency-wage theory and union–firm interaction theory: if a lower unemployment rate is desired, we should reduce employee payroll and wage-income taxes, and finance these tax cuts by imposing a higher sales tax. It is reassuring that this move toward a heavier reliance on indirect taxes receives the same analytical support from both theories about labour markets. We can have more confidence about making applied policy advice when the underlying rationale for that policy proposal is not dependent on just one interpretation of the labour market or the other.

But our examination of this policy proposal is not complete; we must derive its implications in the search model as well. To pursue this sensitivity test, the same set of taxes is added to that model. It is left for the reader to verify that equations 8.10 and 8.12 are altered:

$$w = [A(f + s + r)]/[(f + s + r)(1 + \tau) + ((\theta + s + r)(1 - t)/(1 + \lambda))]$$

$$rV_V = -C + [\theta(A - w(1 + \tau))]/(\theta + s + r).$$

Proceeding with the solution, and Hall's (2003) calibration, we reach the several policy conclusions. Some are similar to the outcomes that we discovered in our analysis of efficiency wages and unions. For example, an increase in the employee payroll tax increases unemployment. Even the magnitude of this response is comparable to our earlier findings. (If t is raised from zero to 0.1, the unemployment rate rises by about one-half of 1 percentage point.) This finding means that our earlier conclusion is robust across alternative specifications of the labour market. For this policy, at least, it appears not to matter that there is controversy concerning how best to model structural unemployment. Policy makers can proceed without needing to wait for this controversy to be resolved.

But this assurance does not apply to all policy initiatives, since some of the implications of search theory are different from the policy theorems that followed from the other models. For example, in this specification, both the employer payroll tax and the interest rate affect the natural unemployment rate – predictions that are at odds with both the efficiency-wage model and Pissarides' model of union–firm interaction. But not all of these differences are important. For example, while the interest rate matters in the present specification (since a higher interest rate lowers the benefit of having a job and so raises equilibrium unemployment), the practical significance of this effect is non-existent. The reader can verify that, when Hall's calibration is used, and when the annual interest rate is raised by even 2 or 3 percentage points, the effect on the unemployment rate is truly trivial. Hence, some of the differences across models of the labour market are irrelevant for policy purposes, and we can proceed with the policy prescriptions that accompanied the earlier specifications.

However, not all the differences across natural unemployment rate models can be dispensed with in this way. For example, in this search model, the unemployment rate is increased by the existence of a sales tax. Again, for Hall's calibration, we find that increasing the λ variable from zero to 0.1 makes the unemployment rate rise by about one-half of 1 percentage point. This is a non-trivial effect, and it differs markedly from the zero response we discovered with efficiency wages and unions.

This different outcome is important for the general debate on whether we should follow the advice of many public-finance practitioners – that we should replace our progressive personal income tax with a progressive expenditure tax. According to growth theory (models which usually involve no unemployment, which we examine in Chapters 10–12), this tax substitution should increase long-run living standards. According to efficiency-wage and union theory, this tax substitution should bring the additional benefit of lowering the natural unemployment rate. But, as just noted, this fortuitous outcome is not supported by search theory. However, this search model indicates that the cut in the wage-income tax can be expected to lower unemployment by about the same amount as the increase in the expenditure tax can be expected to raise unemployment. Thus, even this model does not argue for rejecting the move to an expenditure tax. In this limited sense, then, the labour market models give a single message: with respect to lowering the natural unemployment rate, we either gain or at least do not lose by embracing a shift to expenditure-based taxation.

9.3 The globalization challenge: is mobile capital a bad thing to tax?

One of the primary concerns about the new global economy is income inequality. Compared with many low-wage countries, the developed economies (often referred to as the North) have an abundance of skilled workers and a small proportion of unskilled workers. The opposite is the case in the developing countries (the South). With increased integration of the world economies, the North specializes in the production of goods that emphasize their relatively abundant factor, skilled labour, so it is the wages of skilled workers that are bid up by increased foreign trade. The other side of this development is that Northern countries rely more on imports to supply goods that require only unskilled labour, so the demand for unskilled labour falls in the North. The result is either lower wages for the unskilled in the North (if there is no legislation that puts a floor on wages there) or rising unemployment among the unskilled in the North (if there is a floor on wage rates, such as that imposed by minimum wage laws and welfare). In either case, unskilled Northerners can lose income in the new global economy.

There is a second hypothesis concerning rising income inequality. It is that, during the final quarter of the twentieth century, skill-biased technical change has meant that the demand for skilled workers has risen while that for unskilled workers has fallen. Technical change has increased the demand for skilled individuals to design and program in such fields as robotics, while it has decreased the demand for unskilled workers, since the robots replace these individuals. Just as with the free-trade hypothesis, the effects of these shifts in demand depend on whether it is possible for wages in the unskilled sector to fall. The United States and Europe are often cited as illustrations of the different possible outcomes. The United States has only a limited welfare state, so there is little to stop increased wage inequality from emerging, as indeed it has in recent decades. Europe has much more developed welfare states that maintain floors below which the wages of unskilled workers cannot fall. When technological change decreases the demand for unskilled labour, firms have to reduce their employment of these individuals. Thus, Europe has avoided large increases in wage inequality, but the unemployment rate has been high there for many years.

Most economists favour the skill-biased technical change explanation for rising income inequality. This is because inequality has increased so much within each industry and occupation, in ways that are unrelated to imports. The consensus has been that only 11 per cent of the rising inequality in America can be attributed to the expansion of international trade. But, whatever the causes, the plight of the less skilled is dire.

Even if globalization is not the cause of the low-income problem for unskilled individuals in the North, it may be an important constraint on whether their governments can do anything to help them. This is the fundamental challenge posed by globalization. Citizens expect their governments to provide support for low-income individuals so that everyone shares the benefits of rising average living standards. The anti-globalization protesters fear that governments can no longer do this. The analysis in this section – which draws heavily on Moutos and Scarth (2004) – suggests that such pessimism is not warranted. To address this question specifically, let us assume that capitalists (the owners of capital) are 'rich' and that they have the ability to relocate their capital costlessly to lower-tax jurisdictions. Also, we assume that labour is 'poor' and that these individuals cannot migrate to other countries. Can the government help the 'poor' by raising the tax it imposes on the capitalists and using the revenue to provide a tax cut for the workers? Anti-globalization protesters argue that the answer to this question is 'obviously no'. They expect capital to relocate to escape the higher tax, and the result will be less capital for the captive domestic labour force to work with. Labour's living standards could well go down – even with the cut in the wage-income tax rate. It is worth reviewing the standard analysis, since it is the basis for recommending that we not tax a factor that is supplied perfectly elastically (such as capital is for a small open economy). Figure 9.1 facilitates this review. The solid lines represent the initial demand and supply curves for capital. The demand curve is the diminishing marginal productivity relationship that is drawn for an assumed constant level of labour employed. The supply curve is perfectly elastic at the yield that owners of capital can receive on an after-tax basis in the rest of the world. Before the tax on capital is levied to finance a tax cut for labour, the economy is observed at the intersection of these solid-line demand and supply curves, and *GDP* is represented by the sum of the five regions numbered 1 to 5.

When the government raises the tax on capital, capitalists demand a higher pre-tax return – an amount that is just enough to keep the after-tax yield equal to what is available elsewhere. Thus, the higher (dashed) supply curve in Figure 9.1 becomes relevant. Domestically produced output falls by regions 1 and 3. Capital owners do not lose region 1, since they now earn this income in the rest of the world. Labour loses regions 3 and 4, but, since the tax revenue is used to make an unconditional transfer to labour, their net loss is

Figure 9.1 A tax on capital

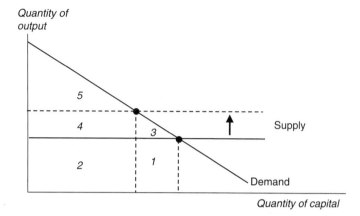

just region 3. But this is a loss, so the analysis supports the propositions that capital is a bad thing to tax and that it is impossible to raise labour's income.

But this standard analysis involves the assumption that the policy has no effect on the number of men and women employed. If the level of employment rises, capital *can* be a good thing to tax after all. If there is unemployment in the labour market, and no similar excess supply in the capital market, the economy involves a distortion before this policy is initiated. The existence of involuntary unemployment means that, before the policy, society's use of labour is 'too small' and that (from society's point of view) profit maximization has led firms to use 'too much' capital compared to labour. A tax on capital induces firms to shift more toward employing labour, and this helps lessen the initial distortion. But can this desirable effect of the policy package outweigh the traditional cost (the loss of income represented by region 3 in Figure 9.1)? Figure 9.2 suggests that this possible. As long as the wage-income tax cut results in lower unemployment, each unit of capital

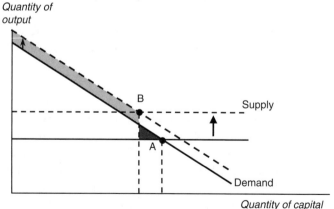

Figure 9.2 A tax on capital to finance a wage-income tax cut

has more labour to work with, and so it is more productive. This is shown in Figure 9.2 as a shift up in the position of the marginal product of capital curve (shown by the higher dashed demand curve). In this case, the total income available to labour is affected in two ways. It is reduced by the shaded triangle, and it is increased by the shaded parallelogram.

If the gain exceeds the loss, the low-income support policy is effective after all. It lowers unemployment, it raises the total income of the 'poor' (labour) and it does not reduce the income of the 'rich' (the owners of capital). This approach to low-income support is not a zero-sum game, in the sense that labour is not helped at the expense of capitalists. This is because the size of the overall economic 'pie' has been increased by policy. Labour receives a bigger slice, and capitalists get the same slice as before. And all of this appears possible – despite the fact that the government faces the constraint (perfect capital mobility) that is stressed by the anti-globalization protesters. The same result is stressed in Koskela and Schöb (2002). In their model, the unemployment results from unions, not asymmetric information, as is the case in our specification below. Related work, involving search theory instead of either efficiency wages or unions, is available in Domeij (2005).

There are two crucial questions. First, is it reasonable to expect that a cut in the wage-income tax rate will lower the long-run average unemployment rate? We addressed that question in the previous section of this chapter, and we discovered that the answer is 'yes'. The second question concerns whether it is reasonable to argue that the gain can be bigger than the loss. It is straightforward to answer this question by combining: one of our models of unemployment (we choose the efficiency-wage model), a production function that involves both capital and labour as inputs, a government budget identity, and the hypothesis of perfect capital mobility. We now define just such a model, and derive the condition that must be satisfied for this revenue-neutral tax substitution to provide the Pareto improvement that we have just discussed:

$$Y = (qN)^{1-\gamma} K^{\gamma}$$

$$q = [(w(1-t)-b)/b]^{a}$$

$$b = (1-u)w(1-t) + ufw$$

$$(1-\gamma) Y/N = w$$

$$\gamma Y/K = r$$

$$u = a(1 - t)/(1 - t - f)$$

$$N = 1 - u$$

$$r(1 - \tau) = r^*$$

$$G + fwu = \tau rK + twN$$

The equations are explained briefly as follows. The first is a Cobb–Douglas production function, which indicates that output is determined by the quantity of inputs – capital and effective labour. The labour effectiveness index is defined in the second equation – as in the Summers efficiency-wage model in Chapter 8. By combining the second, third and sixth equations, readers can verify that worker productivity turns out to be an exogenous constant – independent of tax and unemployment insurance generosity policy: $(q = (a/(1-a))^a)$. This fact simplifies the derivations that are referred to below. The third equation defines the average income of a labourer (which is equivalent to the outside option in the efficiency-wage model). The next three equations are the firms' first-order conditions for profit maximization. Firms hire each factor up to the point that the marginal product equals the rental cost. Also, when the firms' optimal wage-setting relationship is combined with the optimal hiring rule for labour, the solution for the unemployment rate (the sixth equation) emerges.

The next two equations define factor supplies. Labour supply is inelastic (at unity), so employment is one minus the unemployment rate. Capital is supplied completely elastically at the rate of return that this factor can earn in the rest of the world. This perfect capital mobility assumption is what imposes the globalization constraint – that capital can avoid paying any tax in this small open economy. Finally, the last equation defines a balanced government budget. The uses of funds (on programme spending and unemployment insurance) must equal the sources of funds (the taxes on capital and wage incomes). In this section of the chapter, τ refers to the tax on the earnings of domestically employed capital, not an employer payroll tax.

The equations determine Y, N, u, w, b, K, r, q and τ for given values of the other variables and $g = G/Y$. We use this system to derive the effects on the unemployment rate, u, and the average income of a labourer, b, of a cut in the wage tax rate, t, that is financed by a change in (presumed to be an increase in) the tax on capital, τ. To accomplish this, we take the total differential of the system and eliminate the other endogenous variable changes by substitution. The goal is to sign du/dt and db/dt.

It turns out that the second of these policy multipliers has an ambiguous sign. Nevertheless, we can show that the average income of a labourer *must* rise, as long as the government does not encounter an odd 'Laffer curve' phenomenon. What this means is that the government must raise one tax rate when the other is cut. Laffer believed that the opposite might be true – that a cut in one tax rate might so increase the level of economic activity (the overall tax *base*) that overall revenue collected would increase, despite the fact that the tax *rate* was reduced. Most economists read the evidence as being against this proposition, and so have concluded that tax cuts do not more than finance themselves. That is, most analysts are comfortable assuming that the other tax rate would have to be raised. We assume that here. To make use of this non-controversial assumption, we need to work out $d\tau/dt$ and to assume that this expression is negative. It is left for the reader to verify that this assumption is necessary and sufficient to sign the average-income response (to ensure that db/dt is negative). The unemployment rate response is unambiguous in any event.

The one troublesome feature of these results is that the revenue-neutral tax substitution causes a transfer from one group to another *within* the labour group (not between capitalists and the overall labour group). Both the decreased availability of the complementary factor of production (capital) and the reduction in the tax applied to wages lead to a reduction in the level of the pre-tax wage. Since the unemployment insurance benefit is indexed to this market wage, the unemployed suffer. Thus, while the total income of workers and the unemployed *taken as a group* increases, and while there are fewer individuals unemployed, there is still a problem. If there is a subset of individuals who are chronically unemployed, this group is worse off. The question arises, therefore: is there an alternative policy that can avoid this problem? The answer is 'yes', and it has been advocated by Phelps (1997). Phelps suggests that the government intervene on the demand side, not the supply side, of the labour market – subsidizing employers to hire unskilled individuals, rather than subsidizing unskilled individuals to accept low-wage jobs. The idea is to put upward, not downward, pressure on the level of market wages. Phelps has not examined his suggestion in a small open-economy environment, but we do so here.

Our model is amended in four ways. First, the employee payroll tax is eliminated. Second, the employer subsidy is introduced into the optimal hiring rule for labour (so that the right-hand side of the third equation becomes $w(1-s)$, where s is the subsidy rate). Third, the expression for the unemployment rate, the sixth equation, becomes $u = a(1-s)/(1-f)$. Finally, the government budget constraint (the last equation) becomes:

$$G + fwu + sw\,(1-u) = \tau r K$$

The derivations are a little messier in this case, since the level of worker effort, q, is no longer constant; it rises with the introduction of the subsidy to employers. It is left for energetic readers to verify that, when the employment subsidy is introduced and financed by an increase in the tax rate applied to the earnings of perfectly mobile capital, there are several results of interest. First, the tax rate on capital needs to rise to finance the Phelps initiative (so there is no odd Laffer curve outcome). Second, the unemployment rate falls. Third, wages rise, so both the expected income of an unskilled individual and the income of a permanently unemployed individual are higher. The effect on the wage rate is ambiguous *a priori*, since the government policy pushes wages up, while the flight of some capital to the rest of the world pushes wages down. But, for plausible calibrations of the model, wages rise. Indeed, a set of sufficient, though not necessary, conditions for the wage rate to rise is that the unemployment rate be less than one-half and the tax rate applied to capital be less than one-third. So Phelps's suggested policy can easily represent a Pareto improvement.

We conclude that low-income support policy by governments in small open economies is quite feasible – despite the constraint imposed by globalization – *as long as* the revenue that is raised from the attempt to tax capital is used to lessen the pre-existing distortion in the labour market. This result means that anti-globalization protesters have been premature in their verdict concerning the inability of governments in small open economies to raise the economic position of the low-income individuals within their countries.

Before closing this section, it is worth reviewing why a Pareto improvement is possible. For an initiative to be both efficiency-enhancing and equity-enhancing, the economy must be starting from a 'second-best' situation. Involuntary unemployment involves just this kind of situation. We can clarify by recalling an example introduced in the original paper on this topic (Lipsey and Lancaster, 1956). In a two-good economy, standard analysis leads to the proposition that a selective sales tax is 'bad'. With a tax on the purchase of just one good, the ratio of market prices does not reflect the ratio of marginal costs, so decentralized markets cannot replicate what a perfect planner could accomplish – achieve the most efficient use of society's scarce resources. Society is producing and consuming 'too little' of the taxed good and 'too much' of the untaxed good. But this conclusion assumes that there is no pre-existing market distortion – before the tax is levied. A different verdict emerges if it is assumed that there is an initial market failure. For example, if one good is produced by a monopolist who restricts output and raises price above marginal cost, a similar inefficiency is created (with society consuming 'too little' of this good and 'too much' of the competitively supplied good). There are two policies that can 'fix' this problem. One is to try to use the Competition Act to eliminate the monopoly; the other is to levy a selective excise tax on the sale of the *other* product. With this tax, *both* prices can be above their respective marginal costs by the same proportion, and society gets the efficient allocation of resources – even with the monopoly.

So the verdict concerning the desirability of a selective sales tax is completely reversed when we switch from a no-other-distortions situation to a with-other-distortions setting. The analysis in this section shows that this same logic applies in macroeconomics to factor markets. With the initial involuntary unemployment in the labour market, labour's price is 'too high' and firms employ 'too little' labour. By stimulating employment, we can increase overall efficiency – have higher *GDP* – as we improve equity (by lowering unemployment and raising unemployment insurance benefits). This sort of outcome is what led to the Bhagwati and Ramaswami (1963) theorem. This proposition concerns a second-best setting, and it states that we have the best chance of improving economic welfare if the attempt to alleviate the distortion is introduced at the very source of that distortion. Since the distortion in this case is that wages are 'too high' to employ everyone, one would expect that the government can improve things by pulling the wage that firms have to pay to hire labour back down. Another way of saying essentially the same thing is to note that the second-best problem is the existence of asymmetric information in the labour market, which leads to a level of employment that is 'too low'. By directly stimulating employment, the employment subsidy partially removes the original distortion at source, and this is why the analysis supports this initiative.

There are three broad ways that governments can offer support to those on low incomes. One method is to provide unemployment insurance. This method makes the government support conditional on the individual being unemployed, so it leads to higher unemployment. The second method is to provide basic income (see Van Parijs, 2000) – a guaranteed income for everyone that is *not* conditional on one's employment status. Proponents argue that the basic income policy is better than unemployment insurance, since it does not involve the incentive that leads to higher unemployment. As already noted, other macroeconomists, such as Phelps (1997), Solow (1998) and Freeman (1999), have taken this line of reasoning further and advocated that it is best if the government uses the funds it could have used for these other support programmes to provide subsidies to firms to employ low-skill individuals. By making the support policy conditional on employment, this policy is intended to be the one that provides the lowest unemployment rate. As we have just seen, this focus on a reduction in the unemployment rate is *required*, if an *equity*-oriented initiative is to meet its objective – without lowering *efficiency*.

Of course, there can be political-feasibility constraints that can also be the reason for our being in a second-best world. For example, policy makers may find it impossible to take funds away from existing programmes such as unemployment insurance, a guaranteed annual income or an earned-income tax credit (which is essentially equivalent to a low employee payroll tax rate) to finance transfer payments to large firms (even when these transfers are conditional on hiring more unskilled individuals). This is because 'trickle-down' has acquired a shaky reputation, and non-economists have become less willing to consider helping 'large corporations' instead of 'small individuals'. Scarth (2012) focuses on this political-feasibility issue by exploring calibrated versions of the models considered here. Unemployment insurance receives more support in this setting. While this initiative is inefficient, since it leads to higher unemployment, it is a more targeted policy when compared to (say) a guaranteed annual income. Less targeted initiatives are much more expensive, and so require a bigger increase in the tax rate nominally levied on capital. As a result, more capital is driven out of the country. So noticeably less low-income support emerges. The simulations show that it would not be unreasonable for policy makers to give up on the pursuit of a Pareto improvement and to opt, instead, for a policy that involves an equity–efficiency trade-off. In particular, they might opt for a small increase in the incidence of unemployment if the pay-off is much more generous low-income support for the most needy.

9.4 Low-income support policies in developing economies

In the previous section, we examined one way of providing support to those on low incomes – levying a tax that is nominally on the 'rich' to finance a subsidy to firms for hiring the 'poor'. But, since the problem of inadequate incomes is most acute in the developing countries, we need to explore some ways in which our analysis might be altered to increase its applicability in that setting.

Development economists have stressed two things about production possibilities in the lesser developed countries that we now insert into our analysis. First, they have stressed that developing countries often have a limited supply of some *crucial* input – a problem that cannot be highlighted if we restrict our attention to the Cobb–Douglas production function (which allows firms to produce each level of output with *any* ratio of factor inputs). Second, they have stressed that workers can be so undernourished that their effectiveness on the job can be compromised. The following adaptation of the earlier model allows for these considerations:

$$Y = \min(V, L/\theta)$$

$$V = (qN)^{1-\gamma}K^{\gamma}$$

$$q = [(w-b)/b]^a b^n$$

$$b = (1-u)w$$

$$(1 - v\theta)(1 - \gamma) Y/N = w(1 - s)$$

$$(1 - v\theta)\gamma Y/K = r$$

$$u = a(1 - s)$$

$$N = 1 - u$$

$$v = v^*$$

$$r(1 - \tau) = r^*$$

$$G + swN = \tau rK$$

The first two equations define the production process, and this two-part specification follows suggestions made by Moutos. The first equation is the overall production function. It is a Leontief fixed-coefficient relationship which states that output is equal to the minimum of two inputs – skilled labour, L, and remaining value added, V. The latter is a standard Cobb–Douglas function of unskilled labour, N, and capital, K. Skilled labour is the 'crucial' input; each unit of output *requires* θ units of this input. The remaining value added can be produced with an infinite variety of unskilled-labour-to-capital ratios. Development economists refer to this type of specification as an 'O-ring' theory of production. This label is based on the NASA disaster in which the travellers in the Columbia spacecraft perished all because of one tiny flaw – a damaged O-ring sealer. The basic idea is that – no matter how many and how good all other inputs are – if one is missing the entire enterprise amounts to nothing. Skilled labour is the analogue to the O-ring in our case, and this is a concise way of imposing the notion that the modern world involves knowledge-based economies. With profit maximization, firms do not hire unused factors, so we proceed on the assumption that $Y = V = (1/\theta)L$.

The third equation is the unskilled worker effort index. It is different from what was specified in section 9.3 in two ways. The non-essential way is that – for simplicity – we have removed the unemployment insurance system in this specification, and we have also set taxes on both forms of labour to zero. The novel feature in the effort relationship is the second argument on the right-hand side. We can think of this as a 'nourishment effect'; with parameter $n > 0$, it is the case that – other things equal – the higher is the unskilled labour wage, the more healthy, and therefore the more productive, are these individuals. As a result, the worker-quality index incorporates both the Summers and Solow specifications that were explained in Chapter 8. There is no variable-worker-effort function for skilled labour. For one thing, it is assumed that their wage is high enough for there to be no concern about their basic health and nourishment. Further, since these individuals have 'good' jobs, there is no reason for them to consider shirking; they enjoy their work too much. Thus, only the unskilled become unemployed.

The fifth, sixth and seventh equations are the first-order conditions that follow from profit maximization. Profits are defined as $Y - wN - vL - rK + SN$. After optimization, we substitute in the fact that the employment-subsidy payment is proportional to the going level of wages: $S = sw$. The next three equations define factor supplies; unskilled labour is stuck within the country (inelastic supply), and the other two factors are perfectly mobile internationally. Skilled labour can earn wage v^*, and capital can earn rent r^*, in the rest of the world. The last equation is the government budget constraint. Programme spending and the employment-subsidy expenses (paid to firms for hiring unskilled labour) are financed by a tax on capital.

We do not expect readers to work out the formal results of this model. Its structure is spelled out just so that readers are aware of how to adapt the analysis to a developing economy setting. We simply assert the result that emerges: the subsidy to firms for hiring unskilled labour brings both good and bad news. The good news is that the unemployment rate is reduced. The bad news is that sufficient capital is pushed out of the country (owing to the higher tax levied on capital to finance the employment initiative) for the average income of an unskilled individual, b, to fall. Thus, it is harder for governments to provide low-income support in the very set of countries where pursuing this objective is most compelling.

To keep exposition straightforward, we followed Moutos's specification of the O-ring feature in the production function (which is much simpler than the standard specification, as in Kremer, 1993a). Given this departure from the literature, it is useful to provide a sensitivity test. To this end, we report a different, less thoroughgoing, method of decreasing substitution possibilities within the production process. We revert to just the one (unskilled) labour and capital specification, but we switch from Cobb–Douglas to a CES production function with an elasticity of factor substitution equal to one-half (not unity as with the Cobb–Douglas). The production and factor demand functions become:

$$Y = \phi(qN)^{-1} + (1-\phi)K^{-1}$$

$$\partial Y / \partial(qN) = \phi(Y/qN)^2$$

$$\partial Y / \partial K = (1-\phi)(Y/K)^2$$

Again, we simply report the results, without expecting readers to verify them, since the derivations are quite messy. The outcomes for this specification of limited factor substitution are very similar to what has been reported for the O-ring model. This fact increases our confidence that the disappointing conclusion reached in that case is likely to be relevant for actual developing economies.

9.5 Multiple equilibria

The model of efficiency wages presented in Chapter 8 (section 8.2) is a convenient vehicle for illustrating the possibility of multiple equilibria. Sometimes, as formerly in Canada, the generosity of the unemployment insurance system is increased (up to a maximum) for regions of the country that have had high unemployment in previous periods. We can model this policy by specifying that the unemployment insurance generosity parameter, f, be higher if the previous period's unemployment rate is higher: $f_t = \alpha u_{t-1}$ if the previous period's unemployment rate is below some upper limit $(u_{t-1} < \bar{u})$, while $f_t = \bar{f}$ once that maximum upper limit is reached $(u_{t-1} \geq \bar{u})$. Since the solution equation for the unemployment rate is $u_t = a/(1 - f_t)$, in the simpler version of the model with no taxes, we can see (after eliminating the f variable by substitution) that the unemployment rate follows a first-order non-linear difference equation, as long as it is below the upper bound.

This relationship is shown as the heavy line in Figure 9.3. Since full equilibrium involves $u_t = u_{t-1}$, there are three values for the natural unemployment rate – given by the points A, B and C. But only points A and C represent stable outcomes. To see this, suppose the economy starts at point A. Consider a 'small' shock that makes the unemployment rate rise from 1 to 2. The time path beyond that first period is shown in Figure 9.3 by the steps back to point 1. Now consider a 'large' shock that makes the unemployment rate rise from 1 to 3. The time path in this case is the set of steps from 3 to 4. Thus, when near A or C, the economy converges to these points; convergence never occurs to point B. As stressed by Milbourne et al. (1991), models of this sort have awkward implications for disinflation policy. The 'temporary' recession involved in disinflation may be *permanent* if the recession is a 'large' shock.

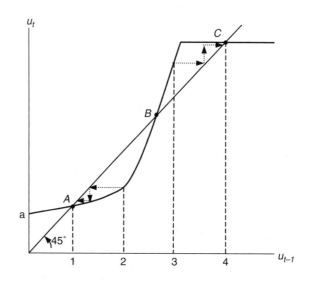

Figure 9.3 Two values for the natural unemployment rate

Through almost all of the first seven chapters of this book, we have assumed that the economy has just one long-run equilibrium (the natural rate of output). Often we have restricted our investigation of the role for government to questions of how alternative policy rules affect the speed with which the economy approaches that full equilibrium or how (if stochastic shocks are present) these rules affect the asymptotic variance of variables about their full-equilibrium values. Thus, our analysis has followed Tobin's (1975) suggestion that Classical models be accepted as descriptions of *the* long-run outcome and that Keynesian models be recognized as very helpful descriptions of the adjustment paths toward that full equilibrium. Now, however, we can see why Keynesians find multiple-equilibria models so exciting. They suggest that Keynesians should no longer concede the long run to the Classicals. With more than one natural rate, there is an additional role for policy – to try to steer the economy to the 'preferred' full equilibrium.

One advantage of the multiple-equilibria model that we have just discussed is its simplicity. This simplicity permits explicit derivations. But one disadvantage is that the existence of multiple equilibria depends on the presence of a particular government policy. The response of the New Classicals is simply to suggest that the policy maker avoid such policies. So this dependence of the multiple equilibria on policy itself has to temper the enthusiasm about reclaiming some relevance concerning the economy's full equilibrium on the part of Keynesians. But, as we shall see in the following brief (non-technical) review of other multiple-equilibria models, not all owe their existence to particular government policies.

Diamond (1984) and Howitt (1985) examine search theories, which analyse how households and firms interact to evaluate whether the individual is hired (or wants to be hired). A key feature of their versions of these models is the presence of a trading externality. The probability of obtaining a positive match between workers and jobs depends on the amount of resources firms devote to recruitment. But much of the benefit of increasing the information flow emerges as a general social benefit – a lower equilibrium level of frictional unemployment. There is no direct link between this general benefit and the individual decision process of any particular firm. It is rational for the individual firm to think that, if it increases expenditures on the hiring and searching process, the overall level of frictional unemployment will be unaffected. In any event, the firm is unable to appropriate any general benefits that occur. Since the private return to recruitment from the firm's point of view is less than the social return, the economy reaches an equilibrium that is inefficient.

One way to understand this class of search models is by focusing on the very simplified narrative suggested by Diamond. Consider a group of individuals who live on an isolated island by eating coconuts. Religious custom precludes eating the coconuts that each individual has collected herself. Before deciding how much to produce (that is, how many trees to climb and coconuts to collect), each individual must form an expectation about the probability that she will find another individual with whom to trade. To have *some* other traders is very valuable to the worker/trader, but, once there are a reasonable number, more traders bring only a very small additional benefit (since by then she is already almost certain to find a partner). Thus, with y denoting her own output and x her expectation of each other trader's output, she will set her own activity level according to the $y = f(x)$ relationship, like that shown in Figure 9.4 – which captures the increasing returns to the trading process in the AB range of the graph. Let expectations be adaptive: $\dot{x} = \lambda(a - x)$, where a is the actual behaviour of others. We can evaluate

$d\dot{x}/dx$ in the region of full equilibrium (when everyone is at the same activity level: $a = y$. Evaluating at $a = y = f(x)$, we have $d\dot{x}/dx = -\lambda(1 - f')$, so equilibrium is stable only if $f' < 1$. Equilibrium involves $a = y = x$, and these points occur along the 45-degree line in Figure 9.4. Points A and C are the two stable equilibria. Given that individual traders do not receive the full social benefit that follows from their entering the otherwise 'thin' market, there is an externality problem. This market failure allows us to rank the two stable equilibria; C is preferred. In principle, government involvement could switch the outcome to the Pareto-superior equilibrium.

Figure 9.4 Multiple equilibria with increasing returns to scale

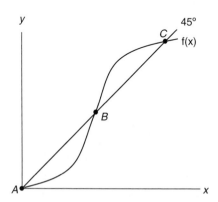

Howitt (1986, p. 636) summarizes the outcome as follows, stressing that both the more-preferred and the less-preferred equilibria involve rational expectations: 'if everyone believes that markets will be inactive they will anticipate a high cost of transacting; this will discourage them from undertaking transactions, and the initial beliefs will be self-fulfilling'. What Diamond and Howitt have done is to provide modern standards of analytical rigour to defend the very early summary of Keynesian economics – that, without policy intervention, the economy could remain stuck *indefinitely* with a suboptimal amount of unemployment.

Woglom (1982), Blanchard and Kiyotaki (1987), and Rowe (1987) have also constructed models involving multiple equilibria. One feature in some of these models is that firms face kinked demand curves. The reason for the kink is not the traditional oligopoly consideration based on rivals' reactions. Instead, the kink is based on Stiglitz's (1979) assumption of asymmetries in the dissemination of information to customers. Customers learn immediately about any price change at the firm with which they have been trading, but they learn only slowly of other price changes. Price increases are noticed by a firm's own customers (so an elastic response can occur), but price decreases are not noticed by customers who have been buying elsewhere (so an inelastic response occurs). The resulting kink in the demand curve causes a discontinuity in firms' marginal revenue curves. If marginal cost cuts through this discontinuity, almost any such point can be an equilibrium.

Individual firms face a free-rider problem when adjusting prices. They can understand that, when there is a general reduction in all firms' demand, it would be desirable to have all firms lower price. This would stimulate aggregate demand and avoid a recession. But, if only one firm lowers price, this general benefit is not forthcoming, since one firm is too small to matter. Every firm wants to keep its own price high while having all others pass on to it the 'macro' benefit of lowering their prices. This is the standard 'unstable cartel' or 'prisoners' dilemma' problem. Expansionary policy can internalize this externality problem.

It is not just that imperfect competition can lead to multiple equilibria; it is that the equilibria can be formally ranked. The high-activity equilibrium is preferred, since it lessens the standard efficiency cost associated with monopoly. Another implication of imperfect competition is noteworthy. Manning (1990) has focused on the increasing returns that characterize a natural monopolist. Increasing returns can make the labour demand curve positively sloped. As a result, it can intersect a positively sloped wage-setting locus more than once, and so there are multiple equilibria. Farmer (1993) has also considered increasing returns to scale – examining how the New Classical model is affected by this extension. Multiple stable equilibria emerge.

'Strategic complementarity' is a game-theoretic term which has been used to interpret many of the multiple-equilibria models. As Cooper and John (1988) have noted, there is a *general* reason that coordination fails in many of these New Keynesian models. The general feature is that the larger is aggregate production, the larger is the incentive for each individual to produce. They show that this feature provides a general underpinning for Keynesian multiplier effects, Oh and Waldman (1994) explain that it is a basis for slow adjustment, and Alvi (1993) proves that strategic complementarity can (along with real rigidities) accentuate the importance of any nominal rigidities that are present in the system.

The most general notion of multiple equilibria is found in models that involve *hysteresis*. The simplest model of this sort – provided by Blanchard and Summers (1986) – is based on the idea that the more senior members of a union (the 'insiders') are the ones who make the decisions on wages. These workers are assumed to give no weight to the preferences of members who are no longer seen – having become unemployed. The insiders' power stems from median-voter considerations. The wage is set equal to the value that makes the firm want to hire just the number of workers who were employed in the previous period. Thus, the expected employment in time t, denoted as $E(N_t)$, equals the last period's employment, N_{t-1}. An expression for expected employment can be had by specifying a labour demand function. Blanchard and Summers assume a simple aggregate demand function for goods, $Y_t = c(M_t - P_t)$, and constant returns to scale in production; thus, if units are chosen so that labour's marginal product is unity, $Y_t = N_t$ and $P_t = W_t$ (where Y stands for output, M for money supply, P for price and W for the wage rate). The implied labour demand function is $N_t = c(M_t - W_t)$. If the expectations operator is taken through this relationship and the resulting equation is subtracted from the original, we have $E(N_t) = N_t - c(M_t - E(M_t))$, since wages are set so that $W_t = E(W_t)$. Replacing expected employment by N_{t-1}, the time path for employment becomes:

$$N_t = N_{t-1} + c(M_t - E(M_t)).$$

This model is consistent with both the random-walk observation concerning output and employment rates (Campbell and Mankiw, 1987) and the 'money surprise' literature (Barro, 1977). Unexpected changes in aggregate demand affect employment, and there is nothing to pull the level of employment back to any particular equilibrium (because the preferences of laid-off workers no longer matter for wage setting). Blanchard and Summers consider several variations of this and other models to test the robustness of the hysteresis prediction. Some of these extensions allow the 'outsiders' to exert some pressure on wage setting, with the effect that the prediction of pure hysteresis is replaced by one of extreme persistence.

Another source of multiple equilibria is 'the average opinion problem' in rational expectations. The economy has many equilibria – each fully consistent with rational expectations – and each one corresponding to a possible view of what all agents expect all the others to take as the going market price (see Frydman and Phelps, 1983).

Ultimately, models such as these lead us to the proposition that the belief structure of private agents is part of the 'fundamentals' – much like tastes and technology – so that economists should study the several equilibria rather than search for some rationale to treat all but one as inadmissible. (Readers saw how common this practice is when learning phase diagram methods in Chapter 6.) This plea for further study inevitably forces analysts to explore how agents gradually achieve rational expectations. For example, consider even a very limited aspect of learning – *can* agents grope their way to knowing the actual values of a model's structural coefficients if all they start with is knowledge of the form of the model? Pesaran (1982) surveys some of the studies which pose this class of questions. Some plausible adaptive learning schemes converge to unique rational-expectations equilibria in some contexts, but not always. Despite the assumption that agents incur no decision-making costs, these plausible learning models sometimes lead to cycles and/or divergence from rational-expectations equilibria. With decision-making costs, Pesaran (1987) has stressed that agents can become trapped in a kind of vicious circle of ignorance. If agents expect further learning to be not economically worthwhile, insufficient information will be accumulated to properly test that initial belief and therefore to realize that the original decision may have been mistaken. This implies that systematic forecast errors may *not* be eliminated with *economically* rational expectations.

Most studies of multiple equilibria do not question the entire concept of rational expectations; instead, they stress how the economy might shift between them – resulting in fluctuations in aggregate demand that are ongoing owing to the self-fulfilling cycle of revised expectations (as in Woodford, 1991). This class of models is quite different from both traditional macroeconomics and New Classical work, where cycles are caused by exogenous shocks to fundamentals (such as autonomous spending in Keynesian models or technology in the real business cycle framework). In the standard approach, it is almost always the case that it is optimal for agents to absorb these shocks (at least partly) by permitting a business cycle to exist. After all, stochastic shocks are a fact of life. As we have seen in earlier chapters, attempts by the government to lessen these cycles can reduce welfare. But if cycles result solely from self-fulfilling expectations, then it is much easier to defend the proposition that the elimination of cycles is welfare improving. Indeed, government may not need to actually do anything to eliminate the cycles other than make a commitment to intervene to stabilize *if* that were ever necessary. Knowledge of that commitment may be sufficient to cause agents to expect (and therefore achieve) a non-cyclical equilibrium.

Howitt and McAfee (1992) build a similar model of endogenous self-fulfilling cycles. It is based on the theory of search behaviour in the labour market covered in Chapter 8 (section 8.4) – one that involves a supposedly 'non-fundamental' random variable called (in deference to Keynes) 'animal spirits'. A particularly interesting feature of the analysis is that the equilibrium involving ongoing cycles between the optimistic and pessimistic phases is stable in a learning sense. Bayesian updating induces convergence to this equilibrium with positive probability, even though agents start with no belief that animal spirits affect the probability of successful matches in the labour market search activity. Models such as this one provide a solid modern pedigree for even the most (apparently) non-scientific of Keynesian ideas – animal spirits.

There are many more models of multiple equilibria in the literature that focus on other topics. But enough has been covered for readers to appreciate how many public-economics terms – externality, incomplete information, missing markets, non-convexity, moral hazard, market power – appear in New Keynesian analyses. The intention is to meet the challenge posed by the New Classicals – have firmer micro-foundations for macro policies – which can then be motivated on the basis of some well-identified market failure (second-best initial condition). This means that the principles that underlie normative analysis in macroeconomics are becoming consistent with the principles that underlie microeconomic policy analysis – an outcome much applauded by New Classicals.

9.6   Conclusions

The purpose of this chapter has been to use some of the micro-based macro models of the natural unemployment rate that were developed in the previous chapter to assess several policies that have been used or advocated for reducing structural unemployment and/or raising the incomes of unskilled individuals. Here, we summarize a few of the key findings.

First, there is considerable analytical support for a policy of decreasing our reliance on income taxation and increasing that on expenditure taxes. This tax substitution can be expected to lower the natural unemployment rate. Second, involuntary unemployment creates a second-best environment in the labour market. In such a setting, it can be welfare-improving to impose a distorting tax – even one levied on capital that is supplied perfectly elastically – if the revenue can be used to reduce the pre-existing distortion in the other factor market (the labour market). This environment makes low-income support possible – even for the government of a small open economy that faces the 'globalization constraint'. This second-best analysis was extended so that the appeal of competing anti-poverty policies – providing employment subsidies to firms or providing basic income to individuals – could be compared to unemployment insurance.

Finally, we explored how natural unemployment rate analyses could be modified to consider some of the additional constraints that confront policy makers in developing economies and to consider the possibility of multiple equilibria. The possibility of multiple equilibria suggests an 'announcement effect' rationale for policy. With both a high-employment equilibrium and a low-employment equilibrium possible – and with both involving self-fulfilling rational expectations – policy can induce agents to focus on the high-activity outcome if agents know that the policy maker stands ready to push the system to that outcome if necessary. It is quite possible that no action – just the commitment to act – may be all that is necessary.

The natural unemployment rate is a long-run concept. There is another long-run aspect of real economies that we have ignored thus far in the book. This feature is the fact that there is ongoing growth – a long-run trend in the natural rate of output. We focus on this issue – productivity growth – in the remaining chapters of the book.

10

Traditional growth theory

10.1 Introduction

In our discussion of stabilization policy, we focused on short-run deviations of real *GDP* from its long-run sustainable value. We now shift our focus to the determinants of the trend in *GDP* and away from a focus on the deviations from trend. We care about the trend, since we wish to explore what policy can do to foster rising long-run average living standards. To highlight this issue, we now abstract from short-run deviations altogether. In this chapter, therefore, we consider a longer-term analysis in which it is reasonable to assume completely flexible wages and prices. In such a world, there is no difference between the actual and the natural rates. We focus on the long-run determinants of per-capita consumption.

All Western governments try to stimulate saving. Some of the initiatives are: taxing consumption instead of income (partially replacing the income tax revenue with the expenditure taxes); allowing lower taxes on capital gain and dividend income; allowing contributions to registered retirement saving plans to be made with before-tax dollars; keeping inflation low; and deficit reduction. One of the purposes of this chapter is to review the traditional economic analysis that is viewed as supporting initiatives such as these.

Growth theory is often described as 'old' or 'new'. The 'old' analysis refers to work that involves two features: (1) descriptive behavioural functions for agents (that are not explicitly based on inter-temporal optimization); and (2) productivity growth specified as an exogenous process. As a result, there are two sets of literature that qualify as 'new' growth theory. The first continues to specify productivity growth as exogenous, but, since micro-based decision rules are involved, the analysis respects the Lucas critique. The second branch of new growth theory – which is new in both senses – involves both micro-based behavioural functions and endogenous productivity growth. This 'new-new' analysis is also called endogenous growth theory. We examine old growth theory and the first class of new models in this chapter. We move on to endogenous productivity growth analysis in Chapter 11.

10.2 The Solow model

The standard model of exogenous growth is due to Solow (1956) and Swan (1956). It is defined by the following relationships:

$$Y = F(N, K)$$

$$S = I$$

$$S = sY$$

$$I = \dot{K} + \delta K$$

The first equation is the production function: output is produced by combining labour and capital. We assume that the production function is constant returns to scale. One implication of this assumption is that a doubling of both inputs results in an exact doubling of output. This assumption is necessary if we want the full equilibrium of the system to be what is referred to as a balanced growth path. This is a situation in which all aggregates (the effective labour supply, capital, output, consumption and investment) grow at the same rate – the sum of the population and productivity growth rates. This outcome implies that wages grow at the productivity growth rate and that the interest rate is constant. The constant-returns-to-scale assumption is an appealing one if the economy is already big enough for all the gains of specialization to be exhausted and if factors that are fixed in supply (such as land and non-renewable raw materials) are of limited importance. Standard growth theory abstracts from these issues; we consider them briefly in section 10.5 below.

The notation is standard; the second equation stipulates goods market clearing (saving equals investment), and the next two relationships define saving and investment. There are no adjustment costs for capital; firms invest whatever output is not consumed. N denotes labour measured in efficiency units, which is always fully employed (flexible wages are assumed implicitly). Labour grows at an exogenous rate, $\dot{N}/N = n = \gamma + z$, where γ is the productivity growth rate and z is the rate of population growth. As noted above, since γ is taken as exogenous, this is called an 'old' growth model involving exogenous technological change. The fourth equation states that the capital stock grows whenever gross investment, I, exceeds the depreciation of pre-existing capital, δK.

Since the production process involves constant returns to scale, we re-express it in what is called the 'intensive' format. We use lower-case letters to denote each variable on a per-effective-worker basis. For example, assuming a Cobb–Douglas function: $Y = K^\alpha N^{1-\alpha}$, we have $y = Y/N = (K/N)^\alpha = f(k)$. Using the time derivative of the $k = K/N$ definition, and substituting the other relationships into the result, the entire model can be summarized in a single differential equation:

$$\dot{k} = sf(k) - (n + \delta)k.$$

This dynamic process is stable if $\partial \dot{k}/\partial k < 0$; in other words, convergence to equilibrium requires $sf'(k) - (n + \delta) < 0$. We evaluate this requirement using full-equilibrium values. In full equilibrium, $y/k = (n + \delta)/s$, so convergence requires that the average product of capital exceed the marginal product of capital. This condition is satisfied for any well-behaved production function such as that shown in Figure 10.1; since the tangent at any point such as C is flatter than the ray joining point C to the origin, the marginal product is less than the average product.

Figure 10.1 The Solow growth model and the golden rule

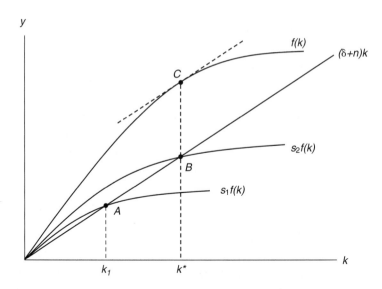

This definite stability property is easily seen in Figure 10.1. The production function is graphed (in intensive form) as the $f(k)$ curve. The lower curve, labelled $sf(k)$, is the nation's savings function – defined on a per-effective-worker basis. The final line in the figure is the ray coming out from the origin with a slope equal to $(n + \delta)$. This line can be interpreted as the 'required' investment line, if 'required' refers to what is necessary to keep the capital stock growing at the same rate as the effective labour supply. With no investment, the capital stock is shrinking through depreciation at rate δ. Thus, to make up for this, and to have capital grow at effective labour's growth rate, n, capital must grow at a rate equal to the sum of these two factors for the system to achieve balanced growth. Capital–labour ratio k_1 is the equilibrium, since it marks the intersection of the *actual* per-effective-worker saving/investment schedule with the *required* saving/investment schedule.

Suppose the economy starts with a capital–labour ratio that is smaller than value k_1 (that is, we start to the left of the equilibrium). In this region of the figure, the height of the actual saving/investment curve is greater than the height of the required saving/investment line. Thus, the economy is accumulating more capital than is necessary to keep the capital–labour ratio constant, and that ratio must, therefore, rise. The economy moves inexorably toward the k_1 level of capital intensity. Since convergence to $\dot{k} = 0$ is assured, we know that, in full equilibrium, output and capital must grow at the same percentage rate as does labour (measured in efficiency units). But, since that growth rate, n, is an exogenous variable, it cannot be affected by policy (which in this compact structure must be interpreted as variations in the savings rate, s). A tax policy which permanently raises the propensity to save pivots the $sf(k)$ curve up in Figure 10.1, making the equilibrium point move to the right. The economy settles on a higher capital–labour ratio. Assuming that this higher level of capital intensity raises per-capita consumption, the response is as shown in Figure 10.2. Consumption falls *initially*, since people save a bigger share of a *given* level of income. But, *through time*, the higher saving means that workers have more capital to work with, and there is higher output, and this is what permits *both* higher saving and higher consumption. Figure 10.2 shows both the short-term pain and the long-term gain. It also shows that the growth rate rises – but only in a transitional way. The lasting effect of the higher savings policy is an increase in the *level* of the capital–labour ratio (and therefore in the level of per-capita consumption),

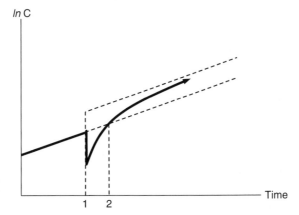

Figure 10.2 Per-capita consumption and lower interest taxation

not in the growth *rate*. Nevertheless, this can still represent a very significant increase in material welfare.

But can we be sure that there is long-term gain? By considering Figure 10.1, this appears to be possible when the *initial* equilibrium (before the pro-savings initiative is instituted) is on the left side of the diagram (as we have assumed). But it does not appear to be possible if the initial equilibrium is already well over to the right. This ambiguity raises the question: how can we determine the optimal value for the savings rate – at least as long as we restrict our attention to full-equilibrium considerations? At low capital–labour ratios, labour does not have enough capital to work with to achieve maximum efficiency. At high capital–labour ratios, diminishing returns with respect to capital sets in to such an extent that most of the extra output is not available for consumption – it is needed just to maintain the capital stock and to keep it growing at the same rate as labour. (With a fixed depreciation rate, a large capital stock requires a lot of replacement investment each period.)

The key to determining the 'best' savings rate is to realize that per-capita consumption is pictured in Figure 10.1 as the vertical distance between the output-per-capita curve, $f(k)$, and the required (for a constant k) investment-per-capita line, $(n + \delta)k$. That gap is maximized at the capital–labour ratio identified as k^*, where the tangent at point C is parallel to the $(n + \delta)k$ line. Thus, the rule which must be obeyed to maximize steady-state consumption per head – the so-called 'golden rule' – is that the marginal product of capital equal the sum of the depreciation rate and the rates at which the population and the state of technical knowledge are growing.

Is this condition likely to be met in modern developed economies? It is clear that all policy makers assume that it is not and that we are at a point to the left of the golden rule (as in Figure 10.1). If this were not the case, the analysis could not support the universal drive among policy makers to stimulate saving. Thus, the presumption appears to be that – in actual economies – the marginal product of capital exceeds $(n + \delta)$. As long as we believe that firms maximize profits, we have to believe that – in long-run equilibrium – they must be equating the marginal product of capital to its rental cost, $(r + \delta)$. Thus, the presumption must be that $(r + \delta)$ must exceed $(n + \delta)$, or that r must exceed $n = \dot{K}/K$. As noted in Chapter 7, Abel et al. (1989) have tested this presumption by comparing net profits, rK, and net investment, $\dot{K}$, by consulting the national accounts for many countries. For every country and every year, they found that profits exceeded investment. This finding has been taken as strong support for the proposition that all these economies are under-capitalized. Thus, Figure 10.2 correctly shows the time path for per-capita consumption following a pro-savings initiative.

So higher saving involves short-term pain during the time interval between points 1 and 2 in Figure 10.2, since – without the policy – per-capita consumption would have been higher (following along the lower dashed line). But, after point 2 in time, there is long-term gain. Old people are hurt by the pro-savings policy, since they could die within the 1-to-2 time period. But the young, especially those who are not born until after point 2 in time, are made better off. From the point of view of the elderly, higher saving is a policy of following the golden rule – doing unto others (the young) what the elderly would like others to have done for them.

While the Solow model is the analytical base for pro-savings policy initiatives, it is not without its critics. For one thing, it seems incapable of explaining the vast differences in living standards that we have observed, both across time and across countries at a point in time. Roughly speaking, the challenge is to explain the fact that citizens in the developed economies have a living standard that is ten times the level that was observed 100 years ago in these same countries. Similarly, the developed countries enjoy living standards that are roughly ten times what the poorer countries are making do with today. Differences of these magnitudes seem beyond the Solow model. To appreciate this fact, take the total differential of the steady-state version of the model's basic equation, replace k with y (by using the Cobb–Douglas production function given above), and evaluate the result at steady-state values. That result is:

$$(dy/y) = (\alpha/(1-\alpha))\,(ds/s).$$

If we consider a plausible value for capital's share of output, $\alpha = 0.33$, this result implies that per-capita output is increased by a mere 5 per cent when a substantial increase in the savings ratio (10 per cent) is undertaken and sustained indefinitely. This quantitative outcome is not in the league of what we need to explain.

A second empirical issue concerns the speed of convergence to full equilibrium. The model's speed of adjustment is the absolute value of the coefficient in the stability condition (the absolute value of the $\partial \dot{k}\,/\,\partial k$ expression). When this is evaluated at full equilibrium, we see that the speed of adjustment measure is $(n + \delta)(1 - \alpha)$. Taking one year as the period of analysis, plausible values are: $n = 0.02$, $\delta = 0.04$ and $\alpha = 0.33$, so the speed coefficient is 0.04. From the 'rule of 72', it takes $(72/4) = 18$ years for the model to get halfway from an initial steady state to a new steady state. Most empirical workers argue that adjustment speed in the real world is much faster than this, so there is concern about the applicability of the Solow model on this score as well.

Related to this, a great deal of empirical work has been done to test the 'convergence hypothesis' – an implication of the Solow growth model when it is combined with several assumptions concerning similar modes of behaviour across countries. Consider two countries for which the values of n, α, δ and s are the same. The Solow model implies that these two economies must eventually have the same levels of per-capita income, no matter what the size of their initial capital–labour ratios. Initially 'poor' countries will grow faster than the initially 'rich' countries, and they must converge (or 'catch up') to the same standard of living. Growth rates should correlate inversely with the initial level of per-capita income. Comparable data sets for some 138 countries (annual data since 1960) have been constructed, and this data appeared (initially at least) to reject this convergence hypothesis. This finding was one of the things which stimulated the new theories of endogenous growth – some of which do not imply convergence.

Mankiw et al. (1992) have shown that the Solow model is not necessarily threatened by this lack of convergence evidence. After all, countries do have different savings rates and population growth rates, so they are approaching different steady states. After accounting for this fact, and for the fact that countries have invested in *human* capital to different degrees, Mankiw et al. find stronger evidence of convergence. A number of studies have questioned the robustness of the Mankiw et al. conclusions. Thus, while a new approach to growth modelling *may* not be needed to rationalize the cross-sectional evidence, many economists remain dissatisfied with the fact that the Solow model does not attempt to endogenize, and therefore explain, the steady-state growth rate. We explore the simplest versions of some of these models in Chapter 11. Before doing so, however, we investigate how basic exogenous growth theory has been modified to respect the Lucas critique.

10.3 Exogenous growth with micro-foundations

The following equations define a model that has well-defined underpinnings based on constrained maximization:

$$\dot{c} = (r(1 - \tau) - \rho - n)c - p(p + \rho)k$$

$$f'(k) = r + \delta$$

$$\dot{k} + nk = f(k) - c - \delta k - g$$

$$g = \tau rk + tw$$

All variables are defined on a per-effective-unit-of-labour basis. This means, for example, that, in full equilibrium, c will be constant. Per-capita consumption will be growing at the productivity growth rate, but per-capita consumption measured in efficiency units, c, will not be growing.

The first equation was explained in Chapter 4; it involves inter-temporal utility maximization by finitely lived agents (individuals who face a constant annual probability of death, p, and a life expectancy of $(1/p)$ years).

The second equation follows from profit-maximizing firms that incur no adjustment costs while installing capital; capital is hired so that its marginal product equals the rental cost. For simplicity, there is no labour–leisure choice. The aggregate labour force is fixed at unity, so the population growth rate, z, is zero. Total labour income, w, is determined residually (and the associated equation is not listed above).

The third equation is the goods market clearing condition (often referred to as the economy's resource constraint); net investment is output minus household spending, replacement investment expenditure and government purchases.

Finally, the fourth equation is the government budget constraint; τ and t are the tax rates levied on interest and wage income (respectively). Government spending is taken as exogenous and constant. The wage income tax rate is determined residually by this equation, to balance the budget – given the permanent reduction in the interest-income tax rate, τ, that we examine.

It is noteworthy that all the model's parameters are 'primitive' in the Lucas sense. Assuming the same Cobb–Douglas production function as used above, the model involves seven parameters: ρ is a taste parameter, p, α and δ are technology parameters, and t, τ and g are policy parameters. There are no parameters in the equations defining private sector behaviour that could be mixtures of fundamental taste and technology coefficients and the parameters that define alternative policy regimes (such as 's' in the Solow model). Thus, more legitimate policy analysis is possible in the present setting.

Before proceeding with a formal analysis of the revenue-neutral tax substitution in this model, it is useful to consider some intuition concerning its full equilibrium. Ignoring ongoing productivity growth, the cost of forgoing consumption for a period is the rate of time preference, while the benefit of forgoing that consumption is the amount of output that an additional piece of capital can generate (the marginal product of capital). As a result, the stock of capital should be expanded to the point that its marginal product equals the agents' rate of time preference. Is this condition satisfied in a decentralized economy? Firms ensure that the (net of depreciation) marginal product of capital equals r, while households ensure that the rate of time preference equals $r(1-\tau)$. The social optimum is reached by decentralized agents only if τ is zero. Thus, the interest-income tax should be zero in the steady state. But should we not pay some attention to what occurs during the transition to that full equilibrium? To answer this question, we analyse a phase diagram.

We can ignore the fourth equation, since it simply solves for τw residually. Taking a total differential of the first three equations, eliminating the change in the interest rate by substitution, and evaluating coefficients at steady-state values, we have:

$$[d\dot{k} \quad d\dot{c}]' = \phi[dk \quad dc]' + [0 \quad -cr]' d\tau$$

where

$$\phi = \begin{bmatrix} (r-n) & -1 \\ c(1-\tau)f'' - p(p+\rho) & r(1-\tau) - \rho - n \end{bmatrix}$$

Here c can jump at a point in time, while k is predetermined at each instant, so unique convergence to full equilibrium requires a saddle path (which obtains as long as we assume that the determinant of ϕ is negative, and this is fully consistent with representative values of the model's parameters). The reader can use the entries in the ϕ matrix to pursue the methods explained in Chapter 6 (section 6.2), and verify the particulars of the phase diagram shown in Figure 10.3.

A cut in interest taxation shifts the $\dot{c} = 0$ locus to the right; the economy moves from point 1 to point 2 immediately, and then from point 2 to point 3 gradually, in Figure 10.4. The formal analysis confirms that there is short-term pain (lower c initially) followed by long-term gain (higher c in the new full equilibrium), so the result is similar to that pictured in Figure 10.2. The only difference stems from the fact that c in the present analysis is per-effective-worker consumption, not per-person consumption (which was the focus in Figure 10.2). As a result, there is no positive slope to the trend lines in the version of Figure 10.2 that would apply to variable c. Nevertheless, the

Figure 10.3 Phase
diagram

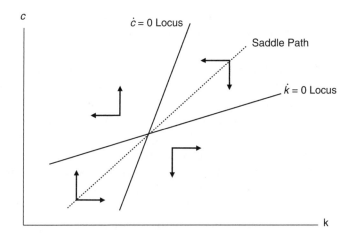

Figure 10.4 Dynamic
adjustment following
lower interest-income
taxes

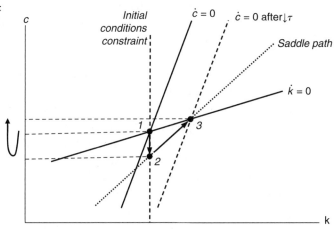

formal analysis accomplishes two things: it confirms that there is a short-
term pain followed by long-term gain outcome when the analysis is extended
to involve explicit dynamic optimization on the part of households and firms,
and it facilitates a calculation which determines whether the short-term pain
is or is not dominated by the long-term gain. To answer this question, we
calculate $dPV/d\tau$, where PV is the present value function:

$$PV = \int_{0}^{\infty} e^{-\lambda i} \ln c_i di$$

and λ is the social discount rate. This welfare function is based on the instantaneous household utility function that is already involved in the derivation
of the model's consumption function, so there should be no controversy

about this general form of social welfare function. But there is controversy concerning what discount rate to use.

One candidate is $\lambda = r(1 - \tau) - n$, the economy's net of tax and growth rate of interest. This is what is used in standard applied benefit–cost analysis – based as it is on the hypothetical compensation principle. Another candidate is $\lambda = \rho$, each individual's rate of time preference. For internal consistency, this option *must* be used if agents live forever (that is, if $p = 0$). But, in the overlapping generations setting that is our focus here, the $\lambda = \rho$ assumption is not so obviously appealing. It is not without any appeal in this context, however, since it has been shown that this discount rate is an integral part of the only time-consistent social welfare function to be identified in the literature as consistent with this overlapping generations structure (Calvo and Obstfeld, 1988). Given the uncertainty concerning what discount rate to use in public policy analysis, it is instructive to consider both these options. Two rather different conclusions emerge (and readers can verify this by following the procedure outlined in section 6.2).

If the time preference rate of any one generation is used as the social discount rate, we find that – even allowing for the short-term pain – agents are better off if the interest-income tax is eliminated. But, if the net market interest rate is used, there is less support for this initiative. This is because, with the net interest rate exceeding the time preference rate in the overlapping generations setting, this decision rule involves discounting the long-term gain more heavily. It turns out that $\partial PV / \partial \tau = 0$ in this case, so the pro-savings policy is neither supported nor rejected when the hypothetical compensation criterion is used. This result is consistent with Gravelle (1991), who argues that this tax substitution has more to do with distribution than efficiency. It follows from the fact that, when we use the rate at which the market permits agents to trade goods across time as the social discount rate, we are essentially just rediscovering the economy's inter-temporal resource constraint. But reliance on this hypothetical compensation principle is widespread in applied benefit–cost analysis, so it is unsettling that its application in this tax-substitution setting threatens conventional wisdom on this topic. And it is worth remembering our discussion in Chapter 4 (section 4.5), which indicated that surveys do not support the conventional presumption of exponential discounting – no matter what the rate.

We return to this broad issue – the support or lack thereof for pro-savings initiatives – in Chapter 12. In that chapter we will add interesting features to the tax-substitution analysis. First, the equilibrium growth *rate* will be endogenous, so fiscal policies will affect growth permanently. Second, we will consider two groups of households – one very patient and the other much less so. With each group having its own rate of time preference – one above the economy's net interest rate, and the other below it – we can be more explicit when we compare the short-term pain and the long-term gain of fiscal policies that raise national savings. In the meantime, we extend the present exogenous growth model with just one class of households to allow for government debt and open-economy features, so we can consider a policy of government budget deficit and debt reduction, for a small open economy.

10.4   A benefit–cost analysis of debt reduction

Thus far, we have used the optimization-based exogenous growth model to examine a balanced-budget tax substitution – a revenue-neutral switch in the tax system that involves the government relying more heavily on wage taxation and less heavily on interest taxation. In recent decades, however, many governments have not been balancing their budgets, and the pro-savings initiative that has become the centre of attention has been deficit and debt reduction. The purpose of this section is to bring our analysis to bear more squarely on this topic. To do so, we must add the deficit and debt variables (and another differential equation – the accumulation identity for the nation's foreign debt) to the model. This additional source of dynamics creates a problem. We do not wish to attempt the drawing of three-dimensional phase diagrams. Nor do we want to solve the set of differential equations in algebraic form. As a result, we make no attempt to analyse the entire time path of the economy's response to fiscal retrenchment. Instead, we confine our attention to a comparison of the initial and the final full equilibria. Since we wish to illustrate the importance of fiscal retrenchment in quantitative terms, we calibrate by selecting empirically relevant values for the model's slope coefficients.

The extended model is simplified slightly by our continuing to abstract from population growth, and by our now dispensing with interest taxation. The system is defined by the following five equations:

$$\dot{c} = (r - \rho - n)c - p(p + \rho)(k + b - a)$$

$$f'(k) = r + \delta$$

$$\dot{a} = (r - n)a - [f(k) - c - \dot{k} - (n + \delta)k - g]$$

$$\dot{b} = d - nb$$

$$d = rb + g - t$$

As above, all variables are defined as ratios – with the denominator being the quantity of labour measured in efficiency units. Units of output are chosen so that, initially, these ratios can be interpreted as ratios to GDP as well. The new variable is a, the nation's foreign debt ratio.

The first equation is the private sector consumption function – very similar to what has been discussed above. There is one difference here; there is an additional component to non-human wealth. In addition to the domestically owned part of the physical capital stock $(k - a)$, there is the stock of bonds issued by the government to domestic residents (b).

The second equation states that firms maximize profits and hire capital until the marginal product equals the rental cost. For this application, we focus on a small open-economy setting. As a result, the interest rate is determined from outside (it is pinned down by the foreign interest rate and the assumption of perfect capital mobility). Since k is the only endogenous variable in the second equation, this optimal-hiring-rule relationship pegs the capital stock. Thus, in analysing domestic policy initiatives, we take k as a constant (and set $\dot{k} = 0$).

The third equation combines the GDP identity with the accumulation identity for foreign debt (both written in ratio form). This version of the accumulation identity states that the foreign-debt-to-GDP ratio rises whenever net exports fall short of the pre-existing interest payment obligations to citizens in the rest of the world. The interest payment term reflects the fact that – even when net exports are zero – the foreign debt ratio rises if the growth in the numerator (the interest rate paid on that debt this period) exceeds the growth in the denominator (the GDP growth rate, n). Net exports are defined by the expression in square brackets in the third equation.

The final two equations define the government accounting identities (and they were discussed in Chapter 7, section 7.4).

As noted, to avoid advanced mathematics, we ignore the details involved in the dynamic approach to full equilibrium, and focus on the long run. Once full equilibrium is reached, all aggregates are growing at the same rate as overall GDP (at rate n), so ongoing changes in the ratios (all the dotted terms in these five equations) are zero. The five equations then determine the equilibrium values of c, k, a, b and one policy variable, which we take to be t. We take the total differential of the system, we set all exogenous variable changes except that in d to zero, and we eliminate the changes in a, b and t by substitution. The result is:

$$dc/c = [(r-n)\,p(p+\rho)\,dd]/[nc((r-n)\,(r-n-\rho)-p(p+\rho))].$$

We evaluate this expression by substituting in the following representative values for the parameters: $r = 0.05$, $\rho = 0.025$, $n = 0.02$ and $p = 0.02$. These values ensure a rising consumption-age profile for each individual generation. Also, they involve a life expectancy $(1/p)$ once an individual reaches her initial working age of 50 years.

The illustrative calculation requires that an assumption be made concerning the amount that the full-equilibrium deficit-to-*GDP* ratio is reduced. We take Canada as an example of a small open economy. Since Canada's debt-to-*GDP* ratio peaked in the mid-1990s, the government has announced a target (to be reached by 2020) that is 50 percentage points below the peak value. Thus, as an illustration, we consider a reduction in d that is just sufficient to generate this reduction in b. Since $d = nb$ in full equilibrium, this 50-percentage-point drop in b requires a drop in d equal to n times 0.5 (so the imposed change in d is −0.01).

Finally, the illustrative calculation requires an assumption concerning the initial ratio of private consumption to *GDP*. We assume 0.585, since this value emerges from two sets of consideration. First, it is consistent with Canadian data. Second, it is consistent with the full-equilibrium restrictions involved in this model and other parameter value assumptions that we need to make – those noted above and the following. We have assumed that: the aggregate production function is Cobb–Douglas with capital's share parameter equal to 0.3; the equilibrium capital-to-*GDP* ratio is 3.0; capital depreciates at rate 0.05 per year; the initial foreign-debt-to-*GDP* ratio is 0.5; and the size of government (as a proportion of *GDP*) is representative of the Canadian federal government in the early 1990s.

With all these assumptions, the percentage change in consumption turns out to be 3 per cent. This means that, according to the model, the fiscal retrenchment undertaken in Canada (which might have been completed had the recession in 2008 not occurred) can be expected to raise Canadians' standard of living by 3 per cent. In 2013 dollars, this amounts to an increase in material living standards of more than $6000 per year for each family of four. Since this sum is received every year into the indefinite future, it is an annuity, not a one-time benefit. As a result, this represents a significant change in living standards. Further, this analysis assumes that the country's risk premium is not reduced through deficit reduction – an assumption that is consistent with evidence in Canada's case (Fillion, 1996). If deficit reduction does lead to a lower domestic interest rate (and this assumption is appropriate for several highly indebted countries), the long-term benefit of debt reduction is even larger.

As far as it goes, this analysis supports the policy of many Western governments in recent years – that of government budget deficit and debt reduction. Of course, it must be remembered that all that has been established here is that the long-term benefits are significant. Two other considerations are integral parts of a complete benefit–cost analysis of debt reduction. First, there is the short-term pain that must be incurred to achieve this long-term gain. In the short run (while some prices are sticky), there will be a temporary recession. This may not be too large, however, since a flexible exchange rate can largely insulate real output from aggregate demand shocks (see Fleming, 1962; Mundell, 1963). But, even if there were no temporary recession involved, consumption would have to fall in the short run to 'finance' the higher national saving (as discussed in section 10.3). So there is short-term pain involved in debt reduction. The second broad issue concerns the distribution of the long-term gain. We shall now see that – unless the government uses the fiscal dividend to improve labour's position – all of the gain from debt reduction undertaken in a small open economy can be expected to go to the owners of capital!

The proposition that the benefits of higher national saving extend to individuals on lower incomes is often referred to as 'trickle-down' economics. We now evaluate this proposition.

Pro-savings initiatives often take the form of the government using the tax system to stimulate private saving, instead of boosting public sector saving via deficit reduction. Some people oppose these tax initiatives on equity grounds; they believe that only the rich have enough income to do much saving, and so they are the only ones who can benefit from these tax policies. Those who favour pro-savings tax concessions argue that this presumption is incorrect; indeed they argue that most of the benefits go to those with lower incomes. But, since the process by which these benefits 'trickle down' the income scale is indirect, they argue, many people do not understand it and thus reject these tax initiatives inappropriately. We now examine whether this trickle-down view is correct, first in a closed economy and then in a small open economy.

Figure 10.5 shows the market for capital; the demand curve's negative slope shows diminishing returns (the fixed quantity of labour being shared ever more widely), and the supply curve's positive slope captures the fact that savings are higher with higher returns. Equilibrium occurs at point E. With just two factors of production, capital and labour, the area under the marginal product of capital curve represents total output. Thus, GDP is the entire area under the demand curve up to point E in Figure 10.5. Further, since each unit of capital is receiving a rate of return equal to the height of point E, capital's share of national income is the rectangle below the horizontal line going through point E. Labour gets the residual amount – the triangle above this line. A tax policy designed to stimulate savings shifts the capital supply curve to the right, as shown in Figure 10.5. Equilibrium moves from point E to point A, and total output increases by the additional area under the marginal product curve (that is, by an amount equal to the shaded trapezoid in Figure 10.5). So the pro-saving tax initiative does raise per-capita output. But how is this additional output distributed? The owners of capital get the light-shaded rectangle, and labour gets the dark-shaded triangle. So, even if capitalists do all the saving and are the apparent beneficiaries of the tax policy, and even if workers do no saving, labour does get something.

Figure 10.5 Trickle-down economics in a closed economy

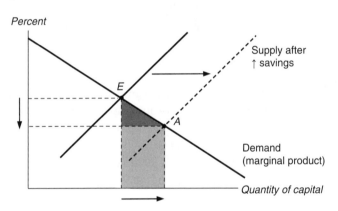

Furthermore, labour's benefit is not just the small shaded triangle in Figure 10.5. Being more plentiful, capital's rate of return has been bid down to a lower level. Since that lower rate is being paid on all units of capital, there has been a transfer from capital to labour of the rectangle formed by the horizontal lines running through points E and A. So, after considering general equilibrium effects, we see that capital owners may not gain at all; labour, on the other hand, must gain. We conclude that, in a closed economy (which can determine its own interest rate), the benefits of pro-savings tax initiatives *do* trickle down.

We now consider whether this same conclusion is warranted in a small open economy. In Figure 10.6, the marginal product of capital curve and the domestic supply curve appear as before; but the open-economy graph contains one additional relationship – a line that shows the supply of savings on the part of lenders in the rest of the world (to this economy). For a small economy, this world supply curve is perfectly elastic, at a yield equal to what capital can earn when it is employed in the rest of the world (assumed to be the height of the horizontal supply curve in Figure 10.6). Equilibrium occurs at point E, and GDP is the entire trapezoid under the marginal product curve up to point E.

Figure 10.6 The size and distribution of income: an open economy

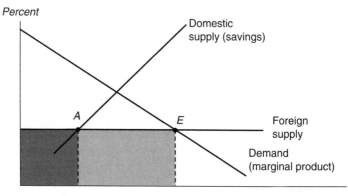

The rate of return for each unit of capital is given by the height of the foreign supply curve, so capital owners earn the shaded rectangles under that line, while labour receives the upper triangle. The domestic supply of savings curve indicates the proportion of capital's income that goes to domestically owned capital (the dark-shaded rectangle), as well as the proportion that is the income of foreign owners of capital (the light-shaded rectangle).

We now consider, as before, a tax break for domestic capitalists if they save more. This policy shifts the domestic supply curve to the right, as shown in Figure 10.7. In this case, equilibrium remains at E. There is no growth in the amount of goods produced. But there is growth in the amount of income that domestic residents receive from that activity, because the income of domestic individuals who own capital increases by the amount of the shaded rectangle between points A and B in Figure 10.7. Since labour is still working with the same overall quantity of capital, labour's income – the unshaded triangle – is unaffected. So the entire increase in national income goes to the owners of capital, and we must conclude that the critics of trickle-down economics are justified if they apply their critique to a small open economy.

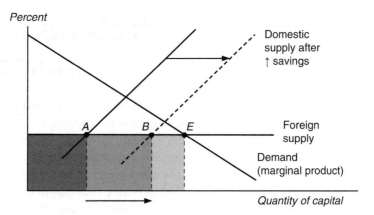

Figure 10.7 The failure of trickle-down in an open economy

10.5 Natural resources and the limits to growth

In all our models considered thus far in the book, we have assumed that there are only two inputs in the production process, and that both can expand without limit. Many concerned citizens see this as a fundamental limitation of mainstream economics. This section briefly considers this issue, by allowing for non-renewable resources, and asking whether ongoing growth in material living standards remains possible.

It seems that every generation involves a group that, like Malthus, is very concerned about our running out of something that is central and important. For Malthus, it was food. For the Club of Rome, a group of scientists who wrote the widely read short book entitled *Limits to Growth* (Meadows, 1972), it was minerals and fossil fuels. Today, this concern about many exhaustible resources remains, and added to it is an even more fundamental set of worries about species extinction, and the breakdown of the entire environmental and climatic patterns that have existed up to this point in time. How has mainstream economic analysis reacted to these concerns?

The reaction to the Club of Rome was immediate and highly critical. Economists asked why there is any interest in simulations of mineral and fuel usage in which it is assumed that there will never be any change in prices or in the pattern of demand. Surely, economists argued, as these items become more scarce, their prices will rise. And, as these prices rise, demand will fall and the supply of substitutes will rise, so voluntary conservation will naturally occur. After all, rising prices are the market's signal of increasing scarcity, and so the market system has a self-correction mechanism: rising prices automatically leading to a reduced rate of resource use. By assuming no such price increases would ever occur, the Club of Rome study was biased in the

246

Macroeconomics

direction of reaching its alarmist conclusion (just like Malthus, at least for developed economies).

Harold Hotelling wrote an important paper in 1931 that described this self-correction feature concerning exhaustible resource prices for the first time, and in a more precise fashion. To appreciate his argument, consider an owner of such a resource. She has two options: to sell a unit of the resource today and receive today's price, p_1, or to sell that unit next period and receive tomorrow's price. This second option has a present value equal to $p_2/(1 + r)$ (r denotes the interest rate and we simplify by ignoring taxes). In equilibrium, resource owners must be indifferent between these two options, so these returns must be equal. Simple manipulation of this equilibrium condition yields: $\Delta p/p = r$. Thus, if the supply of the resource truly is limited, and no substitutes are invented, we can expect that its price must rise at an exponential rate equal to the interest rate. This implies that the price will rise to infinity in finite time, and this development will provide a big incentive for individuals to look for substitutes on the demand side, and to invest in inventing substitutes on the supply side. Synthetic-rubber tyres, plastics and light-metal alloys are all examples of such substitutes. So mainstream economics displayed a complacent reaction to Club of Rome warnings.

Somewhat less complacency has emerged from macroeconomists who add non-renewable resources to their models. We consider briefly an example of this work here. Assume that each firm has the following production function, which involves both a man-made input (capital) and an impossible-to-reproduce input (energy):

$$y = f(k, e)M$$

Lower-case letters denote variables that have to do with the individual firm, and upper-case letters stand for aggregate (economy-wide) variables; y, k and e stand for output, the capital (both physical and human) input and the energy input, while M stands for 'manna' that arrives exogenously to the individual firm. We assume that both the individual production function and the manna relationship are Cobb–Douglas:

$$y = k^\alpha e^{1-\alpha}$$

$$M = AR^\beta$$

where all exponents are positive fractions. A stands for the level of technical knowledge, which is assumed to grow at a constant exogenously determined rate (as in Solow's model). R is the remaining stock of energy at each point in time. As this stock dwindles, individual producers are forced to use ever more expensive sources of energy, so, for any given level of resources employed at the individual level, the firm gets less output. This feature is imposed by parameter β being positive, and it is referred to as the 'depletion effect' in the literature. In aggregate, there is a definitional relationship between the remaining stock of the resource and the amount used each period. This relationship simply states that this period's use (E, which is the sum of all the individual es) equals this period's reduction in the remaining stock:

$$\dot{R} = -E.$$

But there is an externality effect present, since each individual firm regards itself as being too small for its energy use to have any appreciable effect on the nation's remaining stock of the resource. Thus, the identity just given is ignored at the individual level as firms and households optimize. This lack of taking account of the negative spillover effect on others is the initial 'second-best' problem that makes it possible for a government initiative that induces individuals to utilize the resource at a slower rate to have a positive effect on people's material living standards.

Profit maximization on the part of firms leads to standard optimal hiring rules – that factors be hired to the point that marginal products equal rental prices. Expressing these relationships in aggregate terms and using the Cobb–Douglas form, we have:

$$\alpha Y / K = r$$

$$(1 - \alpha)\, Y / E = p$$

where p is the price of a unit of energy. Households are assumed to maximize utility subject to two constraints: that their stock of capital grows each year by how much they save, and that their resource stock shrinks by how much is sold off and used that period by firms. Following Ramsey (1928), the utility function is:

$$\int e^{-pt}(\ln C)\,dt.$$

The optimization conditions are:

$$\dot{p} / p = r$$

$$\dot{C}/C = r - \rho$$

which are the (now) familiar Hotelling condition, and the proposition that consumption growth equals the excess of the interest rate over the rate of impatience. The latter makes intuitive sense, since consumption growth is possible only if households save, and saving occurs only if the benefit (the interest rate return the market offers) exceeds the psychic cost (the impatience preference factor).

We define u as the (assumed to stay constant) utilization rate of the non-renewable resource: $u = E/R$. Given the $\dot{R} = -E$ identity, we then know that $u = -\dot{E}/E = -\dot{R}/R$. We wish to focus on a balanced growth equilibrium where the growth in all major aggregates is the same. Let that growth rate be $n = \dot{C}/C = \dot{Y}/Y = \dot{K}/K$. We wish to investigate how variations in the resource utilization rate, u, affects this growth rate in material living standards, n. To pursue this objective, we first note that the time derivative of the $(1-\alpha)\,Y/E = p$ equation implies $\dot{Y}/Y - \dot{E}/E = \dot{p}/p$ or $n + u = \dot{p}/p$. Combining this relationship with the households' optimization conditions, we end with $u = \rho$. Thus, left to their own devices, decentralized households and firms choose a using-up rate for the non-renewable resource equal to their rate of impatience. We know that this rate of resource use is 'too fast', since none of these individuals is putting any weight on the 'depletion effect' that they all impose on each other. It can be shown that a central planner, who takes account of this externality, would choose a smaller resource utilization rate, equal to $\rho/(1 + (\beta/(1-\alpha)))$. Thus, focusing on the model's balanced growth full equilibrium, there is an increased-efficiency justification for the government to impose a utilization rate smaller than ρ.

The final step in the analysis is to show that, if the government did impose this pro-environment policy, the rate of growth of material living standards would increase – not decrease as it seems to be assumed in public debate of this issue. The expression for the equilibrium growth rate can be derived by taking the logarithm, and then the time derivative, of the aggregate production function: $Y = K^{\alpha}E^{1-\alpha}AR^{\beta}$. After following these steps, and then substituting in $\dot{A}/A = \gamma$, $\dot{E}/E = \dot{R}/R = -u$ and $\dot{K}/K = \dot{Y}/Y = n$, we have:

$$n = (\gamma - (1 - \alpha + \beta)u)/(1 - \alpha). \tag{10.1}$$

This result implies two important things. First, as long as the rate of technological advance, γ, is big enough, it is possible to have ever-rising living standards even though the exhaustible resource is inexorably vanishing. This possibility exists, since increased technical knowledge can be rapid enough to allow us to shift away from resource-intensive production toward capital-intensive production, and capital is man-made. Empirical studies (for example, Nordhaus, 1992) have suggested that reasonable values for these parameters imply that, historically, summary parameter γ has been big enough for n to be positive. However, as we shift ever more from a manufacturing-based economy to a service-based economy, we can expect that γ may well fall (since many services are one-on-one, making labour productivity increases difficult to achieve). Baumol (1967) has drawn attention to this phenomenon by calling it the 'cost disease of the service sector'. If society is committed to having the public sector distribute a number of these services, the cost disease phenomenon suggests that there may be no sickness indicated by our having a growing public sector. Indeed, in this setting, it would be inevitable if people's desires are to be met.

There is a related consideration that has been noted, in different contexts, by Moutos (2000) and Hall and Jones (2007). These authors stress that households' income elasticity for some items may exceed unity, and this implies that, as our incomes grow, the demand for traditional manufactured goods does not grow proportionately. Moutos argues that wealthier households will consume relatively more goods that require high-skilled labour to produce. If this is the case, there will be rising income inequality even if technical change is not skill-biased. Hall and Jones argue that health care is one of these 'superior goods', since diminishing returns set in more dramatically for consumer goods than they do for having a longer life. They use a calibrated model to pursue this idea, and conclude that, by 2050, the health sector in the United States should be about 30 per cent of the economy, not today's 15 per cent. Their analysis suggests that the popular concern about the 'unsustainable' health sector may be inappropriate. These authors have shown that the utility function of the representative agent must be quite different from that embraced by modern growth theorists and business cycle analysts. Something like the Stone (1954) and Geary (1950–51) function is required. Pursuing this fundamental departure from mainstream analysis is not appropriate within our brief exposition of the macroeconomics of natural resources. Given this, we consider a reinterpretation of the economy's resource constraint, instead of the agents' utility function. We assume that there are two reasons for the 'depletion effect': natural resources become more expensive as they become ever more scarce *both* because we must spend more for extraction *and* because people become ever more concerned about the environmental implications. Only the former consideration is involved in the existing calibrations (such as Nordhaus). Thus, allowing for the fact that environmental concern is a 'superior' good (by inserting a larger value for parameter β in equation 10.1) makes it ever more likely that n may not remain positive. Indeed, even the optimal value for the growth rate of material living standards, $n = (\gamma/(1 - \alpha)) - (1 + (\beta/(1 - \alpha)))\rho$, may be negative.

The second implication of equation 10.1 is that the long-run equilibrium growth rate in material living standards *increases* when a lower resource utilization rate is imposed. This government policy induces private agents to keep a bigger stock of the resource along the growth path. As a result, each unit of capital has a higher marginal product. This outcome increases the interest rate and so it widens the gap between the return on saving and the rate of impatience. Individuals react by saving more, so the economy has more capital along the balanced growth path. This is how living standards eventually become higher despite society using less of the resource.

This long-run balanced growth path analysis is an example of the 'win–win' possibility that can emerge from a second-best initial condition. When the government addresses a pre-existing market failure (the externality effect known as the 'depletion effect'), we can win both on the environmental front and on the material living standards front. There will, of course, be some short-term pain incurred as this long-term gain is achieved, since (as with all pro-savings initiatives) increased capital formation means less consumption for a while. And the initial pain that accompanies this move to a slower rate of resource utilization is bigger than what occurs with the standard pro-savings policies, since only in this case does current output fall. This can be verified by substituting $E = uR$ into the production function $Y = K^{\alpha} E^{1-\alpha} A R^{\beta}$. We can immediately see that the reduction in u means less initial output. So consumption falls both because savings are higher and because current income is lower. In addition, there is a second difference between standard pro-savings initiatives and the lower resource utilization rate policy, and this concerns the *duration* of the short-term pain involved in each case. The former policies cause some short-term pain but they do not slow the economy's speed of adjustment toward reaching the balanced growth path and the long-term gain. The latter policy does slow this adjustment speed, and this makes the short-term pain last longer in the lower-u case. With $\dot{R} = -uR$ being a key relationship in the non-renewable resource model, and with u being the adjustment speed parameter in this dynamic relationship, a smaller u means slower adjustment. The overall adjustment speed in the full model depends on the absolute value of all the stable (negative) eigenvalues, and $-u$ is one of these. So, despite the basic similarity between the standard tax reform and natural-resource policy initiatives – that they are both pro-savings policies – there are these two important differences: the short-term pain is bigger, and it lasts longer, with the resource preservation policy. As a result, there is not necessarily tension involved in the combination of views that many governments have with respect to tax policy and natural-resource policy. For example, in Canada, the federal government supports standard tax reforms but does not support resource conservation. Ultimately, we need to consider simulations involving numerically calibrated versions of these models. The simulations undertaken by the author indicate that the number of years it takes before we switch from pain to gain is dramatically bigger following the resource conservation policy initiative (compared to the number of years it takes to achieve this same crossover following a general increase in the savings rate). These results imply that there is a trade-off between our resource conservation and our rising-material-living-standards objectives after all.

Many individuals favour pursuing resource conservation, despite this trade-off, simply because they see the benefits as outweighing the costs. Two other considerations probably play a role as well. For one thing, some individuals see preservation of the environment as a moral imperative. And, secondly, a case can be made that the mainstream analysis of non-renewable resources has embraced assumptions that are far too optimistic. It assumes both that there is a convenient *ongoing* underlying growth in technology (the convenient 'manna') and that we can substitute one factor of production for another fairly easily. The Cobb–Douglas function involves an elasticity of factor substitution that may very much overstate how easy it is for firms to make do with less of the dwindling resources, and many analyses that rely on the CES production function with a low elasticity of factor substitution reach much less sanguine conclusions about the possibility of ongoing growth as resources are used up. Further, as noted above, the analysis has abstracted from pollution externalities. These forgiving assumptions (compared to what Malthus assumed) appear to be sufficient to take some of the 'dismal' features out of our science. But they are probably leading us to be too complacent on the limits-to-growth issue. As a result, it is worrying that concern about non-renewable resources is generally left out of the standard analyses of fiscal policy and growth. Despite this concern, space limitations and the fact that our primary goal is to provide a concise exposition of the existing fiscal policy growth literature make it necessary for us to follow this convention in the remaining two chapters of the book.

It is worth noting that this discussion of non-renewable resources has involved our switching from exogenous growth to endogenous growth analysis, since in this case the full-equilibrium growth rate is affected by a policy parameter, u. We pursue a more systematic exploration of endogenous growth in the next chapter.

10.6 Conclusions

The purpose of this chapter has been to position readers so that they can benefit from our exploration of 'new' growth theory in the remainder of the book. Traditional growth analysis is 'old' in that (originally) it lacked formal optimization as a basis for its key behavioural relationship – the savings function – and (even today) it involves a rate of technological progress that is exogenous. In the analysis that has been covered in this chapter, we have seen that the first dimension of oldness has been removed through the addition of micro-foundations. We consider ways of endogenizing the rate of technical progress in the next chapter.

The basic policy prescription that follows from both the original and the micro-based version of traditional analysis is that pro-savings policies can be supported. These initiatives result in a *temporary* increase in the growth *rate* of consumption, and a *permanent* increase in the *level* of per-capita consumption. Calibrated versions of these models support the conclusion that, even without a permanent growth-rate effect, higher saving leads to quite substantial increases in average living standards. If higher saving leads to capital accumulation (as it does in a closed economy), even poor labourers who do not save benefit from a pro-savings fiscal policy. Such individuals benefit indirectly, since they have more capital with which to work. But, if the higher saving leads only to increased domestic ownership of the same quantity of capital for residents in an open economy, the poor labourer is not made better off. So, in some circumstances, the increase in average living standards does not involve higher incomes for everyone. Our task in the next chapter is to establish whether this basic conclusion – that a pro-savings policy is supported in models that do not stress income distribution issues, but may not be otherwise – holds in an endogenous productivity growth setting.

11

New growth theory

11.1 Introduction

The Solow growth model (and all the extensions we considered in Chapter 10, except the last one involving non-renewable resources) has the property that savings/investment policies cannot *permanently* affect the economic growth *rate*. This property of the model stems from the fact that the man-made item that raises labour's productivity – physical capital accumulation – involves diminishing returns. Given our standard assumption of diminishing returns, as more capital is accumulated, its marginal product must fall. This makes it ever less tempting for households to acquire more capital. As this reaction sets in over time, the temporary rise in productivity growth that initially accompanies a rise in saving must eventually wither away. The only way we can have a model that avoids this prediction is by changing our assumption about the production process. We need to build a model in which there is a man-made factor of production that does not involve diminishing returns. The obvious candidate is 'knowledge'. There seems to be no compelling reason why we need assume that the more knowledge we have, the less valuable more knowledge becomes. Thus, to have a theory of endogenous productivity growth, economists have built models involving constant returns to scale in the production process. We consider three of these models in this chapter.

11.2 Endogenous growth: the basic model

The most straightforward way of eliminating decreasing returns is to assume a production function that is a straight line ray emerging from the input–output origin: $Y = AK$. For this reason, this approach is known as the 'AK model'. The problem with assuming such a production function at the level of the individual firm is that – with constant returns – the size of the individual firm is indeterminate, so formal micro-foundations cannot be provided. Given our desire to keep the analysis free from the Lucas critique, this is unacceptable. This problem is usually solved by assuming that there is an externality. Each individual firm is assumed to have a 'normal' production function:

$$Y_i = K_i^\alpha (B_i N_i)^{1-\alpha}$$

where the i subscripts denote individual-firm items and B is the worker effectiveness index. Worker effectiveness is assumed to be proportional to the 'state of knowledge' in the economy, and – to avoid the complications of specifying a separate 'knowledge-producing' sector – it is assumed that the amount of knowledge possessed by the workers in each individual firm is simply proportional to the *overall* level of economic development (as measured by the *aggregate* physical capital stock that has been accumulated):

$$B_i = aK$$

We can derive an aggregate version of the first equation by substituting in the second equation and defining $Y = qY_i$, and similar equations for the two inputs (where q is the number of firms). Ignoring population growth (assuming N is constant), the result is $Y = AK$, where $A = a^{1-\alpha} N^{1-\alpha}$. At the aggregate level, the full model consists of the following relationships:

$$Y = AK$$

$$wN = (1-\alpha)Y$$

$$(r + \delta)K = \alpha Y$$

$$\dot{C}/C = r(1 - \tau) - \rho$$

$$\dot{K} = Y - C - G - \delta K$$

$$G = \tau r K + t w N$$

The second and third equations follow from profit maximization; firms hire each factor up to the point that the marginal product equals the rental cost. Combining the first and third equations, we have: $\alpha A = (r + \delta)$. Since three variables in this relationship are technology coefficients, this equation fixes the pre-tax rate of interest. This simplifies the interpretation of the remaining three relationships.

The fourth equation is the standard micro-based consumption function (where there is an interest-income tax, τ). For simplicity we have assumed infinitely lived family dynasties (for whom the probability of death is zero). The fifth equation is the economy's resource constraint – indicating that the capital stock grows whenever more output is produced than is consumed. The final equation defines a balanced government budget. Spending is financed by the revenue that is collected from the interest-income tax (rate τ) and the wage-income tax (rate t).

When a balanced growth path is reached, capital, output and consumption all grow at the same rate, n. This growth rate in living standards is also the labour productivity growth rate; otherwise 'effective' labour would not be growing at the same rate as all other aggregates. We rewrite the final three equations to focus on this equilibrium growth rate. In doing so, we divide the fifth equation through by K, define x and g as C/K and G/Y respectively, and use the second and third equations to simplify. The results are:

$$n = r(1 - \tau) - \rho$$

$$n = A(1 - g) - x - \delta$$

$$g = \tau\alpha - (\tau\delta/A) + t(1 - \alpha)$$

We assume that the government sets g and τ exogenously, so the model determines the wage tax. The system is recursive. The first equation determines the growth rate. Then, given n, the second equation determines x. Finally, the third equation determines t.

Since one of the policy variables enters the growth-rate determining equation, policy can have a permanent effect on the growth *rate* in this model. To illustrate, we can take $dn/d\tau = -r$ from the first equation. A pro-savings initiative (a cut in τ) raises the growth rate. The size of this response is particularly noteworthy. With a 5 per cent interest rate and a 10 percentage point cut in the tax rate ($r = 0.05$, $d\tau = -0.1$), we conclude that the annual productivity growth rate can be increased by one-half a percentage point.

This is a very big effect. This interpretation can be defended if we calculate the present value of the benefit of living in a setting that involves a growth rate that is one-half of 1 percentage point higher. The first step is to evaluate how long it takes for the economy to reach its new higher-growth-rate steady state. It turns out that it takes absolutely no time at all to reach this outcome. For simplicity, we abstract from the government as we consider the transitional dynamics to defend this assertion. In this simplified case, we use the time derivative of the definition of $x = C/K, \dot{x}/x = \dot{C}/C - \dot{K}/K$. Without imposing a balanced growth outcome, the model can be summarized by just two equations:

$$\dot{C}/C = r - \rho$$

$$\dot{x}/x = r + x + \delta - \rho - A$$

The total differential of this system is:

$$d\dot{C} = \bar{n}dC$$

$$d\dot{x} = \bar{x}dx$$

where $\bar{n}$ and $\bar{x}$ are the steady-state values of the growth rate and the consumption–capital ratio. Since both these entities are positive, both the first-order differential equations represent unstable dynamic processes. If we drew a phase diagram in C-x space, all arrows showing the tendency for motion would point to outright instability. There is not even a saddle path to jump on to. But, since both variables are 'jump' variables, the economy is capable of jumping immediately to the one and only stable point – the full balanced growth equilibrium. In keeping with the convention that we limit our attention to feasible stable outcomes, we assume that the economy jumps instantly – the moment any exogenous shock occurs – to the new full-equilibrium growth path. In short, there are no transitional dynamics in this growth model. We exploit this fact in our growth policy analysis in the final chapter. We rely on this fact here as well, as we illustrate the significance of a slightly higher growth rate. Assume that today's GDP is unity. If n and r denote the GDP growth rate and the discount rate, the present value (PV) of all future GDP is:

$$PV = \int_0^\infty e^{-(r-n)t}dt = 1/(r - n).$$

For illustrative parameter values $(r = 0.05$ and $n = 0.02)$, $PV = 33.3$. How much is this PV increased if the growth rate is increased by one-half of 1 percentage point? When $r = 0.05$ and $n = 0.025$ are substituted in, the answer is $PV = 40.0$. Thus, the once-for-all equivalent of living in a world with a one-half-point higher growth rate is a one-time gift equal to 6.7 times the starting year's GDP.

To have some feel as to whether this is 'big' or 'small' we compare this estimate to what was a hotly debated issue in Canada 25 years ago – the free-trade arrangement with the United States. In that policy application, the benefits for Canada were estimated to be a per-period level effect of 3 per cent higher living standards every year into perpetuity. The one-time lump-sum equivalent of this annuity is $(0.03)/(r - n) = 0.03/0.03 = 1.0$. Thus, in the past, Canadians have treated a policy that delivers this much as a big issue. The pro-savings tax cut that we are examining here involves a benefit that is more than six times as big. When contemplating results such as this, Robert Lucas (1988) argued that it is hard to get excited about anything else in life!

11.3 Endogenous growth: human capital

Before immediately sharing Lucas's excitement, we should check how sensitive this 'big response' result is to the particular features of the basic AK model. To pursue such a sensitivity test, we explore the two-sector literature, in which a separate knowledge-producing sector of the economy is specified. This knowledge is called human capital, H, and it is distinct from physical capital, K.

It is assumed that both forms of capital are important in the manufacturing sector – that part of the economy that produces consumption goods and the physical capital. A standard production function is assumed in this sector:

$$Y = AK^\alpha (bH)^{1-\alpha}$$

The total stock of human capital in the economy is H. Proportion b is employed in the manufacturing sector. The output, Y, can take the form of either consumption goods or physical capital accumulation. In other words, the usual accumulation identity for physical capital applies:

$$\dot{K} = Y - C - G - \delta K. \tag{11.1}$$

Following Lucas (1988), it is assumed that physical capital is not important in the education sector. Only human capital is needed to produce knowledge, and the simplest form of a constant-returns (production function and accumulation identity) relationship is assumed:

$$\dot{H} = B[(1-b)H] - \delta H \tag{11.2}$$

B is the gross rate of return on each unit of human capital employed in the education sector. The total amount that is employed there is proportion $(1-b)$ of the total. The net rate of return is $(B-\delta)$, since, for simplicity, we assume that physical and human capital depreciate at the same rate.

It is not obvious how we should interpret the education sector. On the one hand, it can be thought of as 'home study' where individuals simply refrain from paid employment and use the time to learn more. On this interpretation, these individuals are receiving no income (when away from the manufacturing sector), so there is no taxable wage income generated in the knowledge sector. This interpretation is appealing when thinking of university students. The other way of thinking about the education sector is that it is a 'research institute' that employs researchers who generate new knowledge. This interpretation of the education sector is appealing when thinking about professors, since professors receive wages which the government can tax. We proceed in two stages. First, we follow the 'home study' interpretation; then, later in this section, we shift to the 'research institute' interpretation.

Households are assumed to optimize. One outcome is a standard consumption function (listed below). Another implication is that individuals arrange their portfolio of assets so that – in equilibrium and at the margin – they are indifferent between their three options: holding physical capital employed in the goods sector, holding human capital employed in the goods sector, and holding human capital employed in the education sector. Since there is no tax on home study activity, the after-tax yield and the before-tax yield on human capital in that sector are the same. We denote that return by:

$$r^* = (B - \delta).$$

It is clear from this relationship that, since there is no taxation in the home study sector, r^* is totally pinned down by two technology parameters.

The net-of-depreciation (but before-tax) rate of return on physical capital in the goods sector is:

$$r = (\alpha Y/K) - \delta. \tag{11.3}$$

For portfolio equilibrium, the after-tax yield, $r(1 - \tau)$, must equal what is available on human capital placed in the other sector:

$$r(1 - \tau) = r^*. \tag{11.4}$$

The model consists of the four numbered equations plus the consumption function (equation 11.5 below). Focusing on full equilibrium ($\dot{C}/C = n$) and recalling the derivation section 4.3 (in Chapter 4), we know that the consumption function is:

$$n = r^* - \rho. \tag{11.5}$$

Before deriving the full-model properties, we simplify equations 11.1 and 11.2. We start by dividing equation 11.1 by K and equation 11.2 by H. Next we substitute in the full-equilibrium condition that the growth rate for both K and H is n. Finally, we define $x = C/K$, and we assume a common tax rate on all factor earnings in the goods sector $(t = \tau)$. With government spending being determined residually $(G = t(Y - \delta K)$, the *GDP* identity can be simplified further. The compact versions of equations 11.1 and 11.2 become:

$$n + x = [r^* + (1 - t)(1 - \alpha)\delta]/\alpha \qquad (11.1a)$$

$$n = B(1 - b) - \delta \qquad (11.2a)$$

The five equations determine r, r^*, b, x and the productivity growth rate n. As already noted, in simplifying these five relationships, we have substituted in the assumption of balanced steady-state growth – that the growth rates of C, K and H are all equal. Thus, we are limiting our attention to full equilibrium, and, for a simplified exposition, we are ignoring the transitional dynamics (which are not degenerate in this case, as they were for the AK model). Readers interested in an analysis of the between-steady-states dynamics should read Barro and Sala-i-Martin (1995, p. 182).

It is worth taking stock of the model's structure. The taste parameter (ρ), the technology parameters $(\alpha, B$ and $\delta)$, and the exogenous policy variable (t) are all given from outside. We can use the model to determine the effect on the steady-state growth rate of a shift to a smaller government. If there is an exogenous cut in the tax rate (and a corresponding drop in the level of government programme spending), we would expect – on intuitive grounds – that there would be a higher growth rate. First, the lower tax rate can be expected to encourage growth, since interest taxation is a disincentive to accumulating capital. Further, with lower government spending, there is less wastage. After all, in this model, since G enters neither the utility function nor the production function, society loses whenever it has any government. We do not intend to argue that this is the most satisfactory way of modelling government activity. Instead, we are just pointing out that it is in this (standard) setting that the move-to-smaller-government initiative should be expected to be at its most powerful. It is alarming, therefore, that we find *no* growth-*rate* effects. All the smaller government facilitates is a one-time permanent increased-*level* effect on living standards – just as in the exogenous growth-rate literature. This result emerges since human capital is the engine of growth in this model, and the tax rate that has been cut is the one levied on the income derived from physical capital.

We now interpret the education sector as involving market activity, with the income being taxable. The two production functions are exactly as before, but the net-of-tax return on human capital in the education sector is now:

$$r^* = (B - \delta)(1 - t)$$

where t is the tax on wage income. (Since we are now highlighting the tax-ability of income in this sector, we revert to our earlier practice, followed in section 11.2 involving the AK model, of allowing for different rates of tax on the income derived from physical and human capital.)

Profit maximization in the goods sector requires:

$$\alpha Y/K = r_K + \delta \quad \text{and} \quad (1 - \alpha)Y/bH = r_H + \delta.$$

Portfolio equilibrium requires equal yields:

$$r_K(1 - \tau) = r^* \quad \text{and} \quad r_H(1 - t) = r^*.$$

Eliminating the pre-tax rates of return (the rs with the subscripts) from these relationships by substitution, we have:

$$(Y/K) = [r^* + \delta(1 - \tau)]/[\alpha(1 - \tau)]$$

$$(Y/H) = b[r^* + \delta(1 - t)]/[(1 - \alpha)(1 - t)]$$

These relationships (along with $G = \tau r_K + tr_H H$, the government budget constraint) are needed to proceed through the substitutions that lead to the same compact expression of the model that was our focus in the 'home study' version of the two-sector model. That compact set of equations for this 'research institute' version is:

$$r^* = (B - \delta)(1 - t)$$

$$n = r^* - \rho$$

$$n = B(1 - b) - \delta$$

$$n + x + \delta = [(1 - g)(r^* + \delta(1 - \tau))]/[\alpha(1 - \tau)]$$

$$g = [\tau r^* \alpha/(r^* + \delta(1 - \tau))] + [(tr^*(1 - \alpha)/b)/(r^* + \delta(1 - t))]$$

The five equations determine r^*, b, x, n and one of the two tax rates. The taste parameter (ρ), the technology parameters (α, B and δ) and the exogenous policy variables (g and one of the two tax rates) are all given exogenously. To illustrate, we consider using the model to determine the effect on the steady-state growth rate of a cut in the tax on wage income (financed by an increase in the tax on the earnings of physical capital). From the first equation, we see that the cut in t can result in the same large increase in r^* that we obtained in the AK model. Then, focusing on the second equation, we see that the productivity growth rate moves one for one with r^* (again, as in the AK setting). Hence, we are back to the Lucas level of excitement. With this version of the two-sector model, we can expect big and permanent growth-rate effects from fiscal policy.

But there is a critical difference. In this model it is the *wage-income* tax that needs to be cut to stimulate growth, *not* the interest-income tax. This is because – of the two man-made inputs that are part of the production processes – it is human capital that is the central one. Its production is the process that involves constant returns to scale (and it is the presence of constant returns to scale that makes endogenous growth possible). This means that the growth-retarding tax is the one that lowers the incentive for people to acquire human capital. Even when the cut in this tax is financed by a higher tax on interest income, growth is significantly stimulated. Thus, *neither* version of the two-sector human capital model supports the common presumption in applied tax policy circles – that it is physical capital that is the bad thing to tax.

For the growth policy analysis in the next chapter, we rely on a human capital model that involves several features. First, we follow Barro and Sala-i-Martin (1995, pp. 144–6) and collapse the two sectors (the physical and human capital producing sectors) into one. This yields a system which has the simplicity of the AK model, but which has a richer interpretation. Second, we follow (and extend slightly) Mankiw and Weinzierl (2006) by introducing imperfect competition. This extension makes it possible for us to combine human capital and creative destruction effects in a rudimentary fashion, while avoiding the complexity of the R&D class of endogenous growth models (which we consider in section 11.4). In the final chapter of the book, we extend the framework that is outlined here, to allow for a subset of households to be relatively impatient. Since these individuals never save, they remain at a lower level of living standards. With both 'rich' and 'poor' in the model, we can investigate the effect of redistributive policies on the overall growth rate. In addition, if society maintains a 'fair' wage for this poor group, unemployment results. Within this setting, then, we can investigate the effect of job-creation policies on growth.

As just indicated, compared to the literature surveyed thus far in this section of the chapter, the model we now outline involves a middle-of-the-road assumption concerning factor intensities. The standard *AK* model specifies that knowledge is proportional to the aggregate stock of *physical* capital, while the Lucas two-sector framework makes *human capital* the engine of growth. The former specification leads to the policy that interest-income taxes should not exist, while the second leads to the proposition that wage-income taxes should not exist. The set-up suggested by Barro and Sala-i-Martin is an appealing intermediate specification. It involves the assumption that physical capital and human capital are used in the same proportions when producing all three items: consumer goods, new physical capital goods, and new knowledge (human capital).

To outline this framework concisely, we suppress the possibility of monopolistic competition initially. National output, Y, is consumed privately, C, consumed in the form of a government-provided good, G, or used to accumulate physical or human capital, $\dot{K} + \dot{H}$:

$$Y = C + G + \dot{K} + \dot{H}.$$

For simplicity, we ignore depreciation of capital. Both forms of capital, and consumer goods, are produced via the following production function:

$$Y = F(K, H) = \beta K^{\alpha} H^{1-\alpha}$$

with α a positive fraction. By defining $B = H/K$ and $A = \beta B^{1-\alpha}$, the production function can be re-expressed as $Y = AK$.

Profit maximization on the part of firms results in factors being hired to the point that marginal products just equal rental prices (r is the rental price of physical capital, w that for human capital):

$$\alpha A = r$$

$$(1-\alpha)Y/H = w.$$

Households maximize utility:

$$\int [\ln C_t + \psi \ln G_t] e^{-\rho t} dt$$

subject to $C + \dot{K} + \dot{H} = rK + wH$. As usual, ρ is the rate of impatience, and we now specify that government programmes are valued by households.

For simplicity at this stage (until the next chapter), we ignore the taxes that are necessary to finance government spending. Households choose the time paths for C, K and H. The first-order conditions are:

$$n = r - \rho$$

$$r = w.$$

Here n is the percentage growth rate of consumption (which equals the percentage growth in all other aggregates – Y, K, H and G – in the balanced growth equilibrium, and, as in the original AK model, there are no transitional dynamics in this specification). The intuition behind these behavioural rules is standard. Households save as long as the return on capital exceeds their rate of impatience, and this saving generates the income necessary to have positive growth in consumption. In equilibrium, households must be indifferent between holding their wealth in each of the two forms of capital, and the equal-yields relationship imposes this equilibrium condition.

A compact version of the model can be specified by defining $g = G/Y$ and $x = C/K$, by equating the two marginal product expressions and by dividing the resource constraint through by K:

$$n(1 + B) = A(1 - g) - x$$

$$B = (1 - \alpha)/\alpha$$

$$A = \beta B^{1-\alpha}$$

$$r = \alpha A$$

$$n = r - \rho$$

Among other things, we add taxes to this system in the next chapter, to determine the method of government finance that is most conducive to raising growth and household welfare. In the present chapter, we simply pave the way for this analysis by outlining this middle-of-the-road specification and by considering imperfect competition.

The easiest way of allowing for some market power is to specify a two-stage production process. Intermediate goods are created by primary producers (competitive firms) employing both forms of capital. Then, final goods are produced by the second-stage producers. This second stage involves fixed-coefficient technology (each single final good requires one intermediate product and no additional primary factors). The final good is sold at a mark-up over marginal cost:

$$\text{price of final good} = (\text{mark-up})(\text{marginal cost})$$

Letting the price of final goods be the numeraire (set at unity), the mark-up be $m > 1$, and marginal cost be denoted by MC, this standard pricing relationship becomes:

$$1 = m(MC).$$

Given competitive conditions among primary producers, the marginal cost of the second-stage firms is:

$$MC = r/F_K = w/F_N.$$

Combining these last relationships, we have:

$$r = F_K/m$$

$$w = F_N/m.$$

The final sales of the second-stage producers constitute the GDP. Measuring this aggregate from the expenditure side of the national accounts, we know that it equals $C + \dot{K} + \dot{H} + G$. Measuring GDP from the income side, it is the sum of primary-factor incomes, $wH + rK$, plus the profits of the second-stage producers, π. Given the factor pricing equations, and the assumption that the production function involves constant returns to scale, the national income measure is $(F(K, H)/m) + \pi$. Profits are defined as the excess of final sales $F(K, H)$ over what must be paid to the primary producers, $F(K, H)/m$:

$$\pi = F(K, H)\left[(m - 1)/m\right]$$

Substituting this definition of profits into the national income definition, we end with $C + \dot{K} + \dot{H} + G = F(K, H)$. We conclude that no respecification of the economy's resource constraint is appropriate in this simple imperfect competition environment.

To complete the model, we allow for the possibility that the economy-wide productivity parameter, β, is a function of the share of GDP that goes to profits. The idea is that higher profits make more innovation possible, so we specify:

$$\beta = \phi[\pi/(K^\alpha H^{1-\alpha})]^\theta = \phi[(m-1)/m]^\theta$$

where $\theta > 0$. We do not formally model the imperfect competition. Instead, we simply interpret m as a parameter that can be affected by competition policy. Further, each individual firm takes β as given. Thus, we consider a slightly revised production function:

$$Y = \phi[(m-1)/m]^\theta[K^\alpha H^{1-\alpha}].$$

This is a short-cut or 'black-box' specification of the essence of the R&D models of endogenous growth that are considered more fully in the next section of this chapter. No optimizing basis for investment in research is offered in this section; instead we make the straightforward assumption that an exogenous increase in the availability of profits (relative to primary-factor earnings) results in a higher level of technological ability.

Removing the government for a more simplified exposition, we have the revised compact listing of the model:

$$n(1 + B) = A - x$$

$$B = (1 - \alpha)/\alpha$$

$$A = \phi B^{1-\alpha}[(m-1)/m]^\theta$$

$$r = \alpha A/m$$

$$n = r - \rho$$

This model determines A, B, r, n and x, and we are interested in the effect of the degree of monopoly on the growth rate:

$$dn/dm = [\alpha A/m^2(m-1)][\theta - (m-1)].$$

If profits do *not* act as an incentive for innovation, as assumed by Mankiw and Weinzierl (2006) and K.L. Judd (2002), and which we can impose by setting $\theta = 0$, then a more competitive economy involves less pulling scarce resources away from accumulating capital, and therefore higher growth ($dn/dm < 0$). But if profits *do* increase innovation (if $\theta > 0$), then a more competitive economy *can* involve lower ongoing growth. In this case, the pro-growth effect of pulling resources back into the production of more capital is dominated by the anti-growth effect of there being less technical change. Most applied competition policy discussions highlight this tension, and it is similar to the creative destruction tension in the imperfect competition models that offer an explicit structure for modelling the decision to invest in research. In any event, in the next chapter, we use the framework just outlined to explore how the existence of imperfect competition affects the implications of endogenous growth theory for tax policy.

11.4 Endogenous growth: R&D

There is an extensive literature that investigates how profit-oriented researchers can generate endogenous growth, and, to pursue this literature, readers are encouraged to consult Aghion and Howitt (1998), Jones (2002) and Helpman (2004). The analyses in these books share the goal of the two-sector literature, in the sense that more structure concerning the creation of productivity enhancements is offered (compared to the reduced-form or 'black-box' approach of the *AK* model). Inventors in these models take a profit-maximizing approach to investment in research. Successful research is a stochastic process, and more research raises the probability that a worthwhile innovation emerges. These models highlight externality problems. On the one hand, firms invest 'too little' in research because they cannot hang on to all the benefits (higher profits) that follow from a successful innovation. This is because, after a lag, the new knowledge becomes a public good, and all the firm's competitors can benefit. But, in another sense, each firm invests 'too much' in research, since no individual inventor puts any weight on a negative externality – that her invention destroys the remaining rents that would have continued to accrue to the previous successful inventor (had this new project not been successful). This literature has brought a new level of rigour to Schumpeter's (1942) famous concept – 'creative destruction'. When these micro-based models are calibrated with realistic parameter values, they suggest that the under-investment problem outweighs the over-investment problem (so that a policy of supporting research and development is called for). Later in this section, we outline a specific version of this R&D approach.

The creative destruction model is not the only part of the endogenous growth literature that has attracted much attention in recent years. There has been a big revival of interest in what Arthur Okun (1975) called 'the big trade-off' many years ago. The conventional wisdom has been that we face a trade-off between our equity and efficiency objectives. In common parlance, if (through government policy) we try to redistribute the 'economic pie' by giving a bigger slice to the poor, the rich react to the higher taxes by producing less, so the total size of the pie shrinks. Policy analysts get particularly excited if they can identify an exception to this standard trade-off. As we have seen in earlier chapters, for an initiative to be both efficiency-enhancing and equity-enhancing, we must be starting from a 'second-best' situation. Endogenous growth models open up similar possibilities.

It all boils down to whether higher inequality is good for growth or not. In the early stages of economic development, the particularly scarce input seems to be physical capital. Acquiring more of this input requires saving. Since only the rich do much saving, inequality is good for growth, and (in this setting) Okun is correct to presume that we face a trade-off. But, as development proceeds, diminishing returns for physical capital set in, with the result that limited physical capital ceases to be the binding constraint. The increased availability of physical capital also raises the return on human capital, and its scarcity starts to become the factor that is more important for limiting further development. The important fact of life at this stage seems to be that there are imperfections in capital markets. In particular, human capital is rather imperfect collateral, and loans are particularly necessary for most people, since investments in human capital are rather lumpy. (You do not gain much by going to university for just a couple of months.) The more unequal is the distribution of income, the higher is the proportion of the population that is blocked by these imperfections in the loan market. In this case, income redistribution can lower the number of loan-rationed individuals, and so relieve these constraints. The result is both lower inequality and higher economic growth.

Saint-Paul's (2006) recent study is less optimistic on this score. He focuses on the relationship between wages and productivity. For a long time, wages for less-skilled individuals have increased with advances in productivity, while more recently this correlation appears to have turned negative. Saint-Paul's model is designed to offer an explanation for this pattern, and it highlights the fact that people shift their demand away from the products that use low-skilled labour intensively as they become more wealthy. As a result, as growth continues, there is an ever-decreasing demand for unskilled labour – in relative terms – and this outcome stems from a change in the pattern of demand as the growth process continues, not from skill-biased technical change. But the implication is the same – disappointment for those wanting to pursue both equity and growth.

There is an extensive multiple-equilibria literature that highlights the possibility of escaping an equity–efficiency trade-off (see Aghion et al., 1999; and

Das and Ghate, 2005). Some studies, such as Galor and Zeira (1993), stress the possibility of 'poverty traps'. With non-linearities stemming from such phenomena as increasing returns, there can be two equilibria: both a low-growth and a high-growth outcome. Quite a few development economists have become convinced of the applicability of these models, and so they argue that limited programmes of foreign aid may be wasted. According to this view, the North must offer the South enough aid to move the trapped economies all the way to the neighbourhood of the higher-growth equilibrium. Some recent empirical work (Graham and Temple, 2006) suggests that about one-quarter of the world's economies are stuck in a low-growth equilibrium.

We turn now from policy implications to specification issues. There is controversy concerning the most appealing way of modelling the growth process. Some models (such as P. Romer, 1990) focus on R&D spending by firms. Romer stresses that research output is different from human capital, since it becomes common knowledge that is not lost to the production process if an individual retires or becomes unemployed. Despite this difference, Romer's model has an important similarity with the human capital model, since Romer assumes that each year's increase in knowledge is proportional to the pre-existing level of knowledge. It turns out that the number of useful discoveries depends on the size of the population. The factor of proportionality linking the new output of knowledge to the pre-existing level of knowledge is a function of the number of people. More people mean more research centres, so there is a bigger chance of successful research emerging. This result is known as the 'scale effect' – the bigger is the *level* of the population, the higher is the productivity growth *rate*.

Jones (2003) is critical of Romer's R&D model for two reasons. Despite Kremer's (1993b) influential study of growth over the last one million years, Jones argues that the empirical evidence does not support the scale-effect prediction. Second, he argues that it is quite arbitrary to locate the linearity assumption that is necessary for non-explosive endogenous growth within a production function. Why should the input–output relationship in either the human capital model or the R&D model be *precisely* linear? After all, data on individual establishments does not seem to support the assumption of absolutely constant marginal product relationships. Jones argues that it is more plausible to assume a linear relationship in the population growth part of the model. Defining b and d as the birth and death rates, and L as the size of the population, we can specify $\dot{L} = (b-d)L$, which implies $\dot{L}/L = z$, and this is *not* arbitrary. Indeed, this relationship is true by definition. As a result, Jones argues that this equation forms a more plausible, less arbitrary, basis for endogenous growth theory. Nevertheless, there has not been a convergence of views on this controversy. For one thing, Solow (2003) has noted that there is considerable evidence in favour of conditional convergence among OECD countries. These countries would have to be converging in demographic patterns for Jones's model is to explain this outcome.

Despite these controversies, Schumpeter's (1942) creative destruction idea has been the focus of many endogenous growth analyses. Accordingly, we devote the remainder of this section to summarizing a particular version of this popular approach, and follow Aghion and Howitt (2007) very closely. In this particular study, these authors simplify their earlier work by reverting to Solow's descriptive savings function (to avoid the more complicated Ramsey alternative). As a result, we take the full-equilibrium version of the basic equation of the Solow model as a starting point. Here it has been solved for k:

$$k = (s/(n + \delta))^{1/(1-\alpha)}.$$

This relationship can be drawn in a graph with the growth rate on the vertical axis and the capital–labour ratio on the horizontal axis. It is a negatively sloped line that shifts-to the right when the savings propensity is assumed to increase. In Solow's model, the growth rate is exogenous and so independent of the savings propensity. Thus, as this Solow equilibrium condition curve shifts to the right, its intersection with the horizontal given-growth-rate line moves to the right as well, and not to any higher point in the diagram. In the R&D model of endogenous growth, however, this second relationship drawn in $(n\text{-}k)$ space is positively sloped, not horizontal. Thus, in this extension to Solow's model, the equilibrium growth rate is raised when the Solow curve is shifted to the right via an increase in the savings propensity. For the remainder of this section, we explain how this second, upward-sloping, $n\text{-}k$ relationship can be derived.

Let A be the level of productivity. Each innovation raises the level of A to γA, where $\gamma > 1$. In particular, for any innovation that actually takes place, we have $(A_{t+1} - A_t)/A_t = (\gamma - 1)$. We assume that an innovation takes place with a probability equal to λg and so, shifting to continuous time, we can write the productivity growth rate, n, as the size of each innovation times the probability of it occurring: $n = (\gamma - 1)(\lambda g)$. The probability of a successful innovation emerging from the research process depends on the intensity of research activity. It is raised by increased expenditures on research, G, which (in aggregate) equals $Y - C - \dot{K} - \delta K$. In particular, research success is proportional to the ratio of G to the level of pre-existing productivity: $g =$

G/A. This specification imposes what is known as the 'fishing-out' effect. This is the idea that it takes more resources to make another breakthrough when all the easier-to-invent ideas have already been exploited.

The profit of an innovator equals the probability of a successful innovation times the value of that innovation, V, minus the cost of the resources used:

$$profits = (\lambda g)V - G = (\lambda v - 1)G$$

where $v = V/A$. Free entry drives profits to zero, so $\lambda v = 1$. The value of each innovation is the present value of the profit stream that accrues to the individual who pays the innovator for her invention, π. Thus:

$$v = \pi/(r + \lambda g)$$

where the denominator is the obsolescence-augmented discount factor. The final part of the set-up involves the definition of the profits that are received by the individuals who rent the machines to the final-goods-producing firms. These machines embody the new technology that these individuals have bought from the innovators, so these profits are defined by:

$$\pi = pk - (r + \delta)k$$

where p is the rental price of machines, which equals the marginal product of machines in the final-goods-producing sector, $\alpha k^{\alpha-1}$, since the production function for final goods is k^α. Profit maximization involves substituting in $p = \alpha k^{\alpha-1}$ and differentiating with respect to k. The first-order condition is:

$$\alpha^2 k^2 = (r + \delta)k.$$

We use this relationship in two ways. First, we combine it with the definition of π, and then substitute that revised expression for π into the v equation. The result, when combined with the full-equilibrium (zero-profit) condition for the innovators, is:

$$r + \lambda g = \gamma \lambda \alpha (1 - \alpha) k^\alpha \tag{11.6}$$

The other use of the first-order condition is to focus on how the interest rate varies with capital intensity:

$$r = \alpha^2 k^{\alpha-1} - \delta \tag{11.7}$$

Finally, we repeat (for convenience) the growth-rate equation from above:

$$n = (\gamma - 1)\lambda g \tag{11.8}$$

We now use equations 11.6 to 11.8 to determine how the R&D process generates a second relationship between n and k. The direct effect of a higher k on g is to raise g (see equation 11.6). The indirect effect of the higher k is that it lowers the interest rate (equation 11.7), and the lower interest rate puts additional upward pressure on g (equation 11.6). Finally, the higher g raises the growth rate (equation 11.8). Thus, there is an R&D-based relationship between n and k, which is a positively sloped line in $(n\text{-}k)$ space. An increase in the savings propensity shifts the negatively sloped Solow relationship to the right. The intersection of that Solow relationship with the positively sloped line that we have just derived is then located to the north-east of the original intersection. As a result, there is a permanent increase in *both* capital intensity (the standard Solow result) *and* the growth rate (the new outcome).

A brief review of this model at the intuitive level is worthwhile. As in the Solow model, a pro-savings initiative leads to capital accumulation. In this R&D model, the fact that firms are employing more capital means that there is an increased market for innovations. This development induces researchers to put more resources into R&D, for two reasons. First, there is a bigger direct pay-off, and, second, there is an indirect effect. Higher capital intensity leads to a lower interest rate, and the lower discount rate makes the present value of (and therefore the price people are prepared to pay for) an innovation higher. Finally, the probability of achieving an innovation, and therefore the overall rate of productivity growth, rises with more resources devoted to R&D.

We conclude that the analytical underpinning for pro-savings initiatives has received further support, since this policy can be defended by appealing to both the human capital and the R&D models of endogenous growth, and whether or not an optimization-based theory of the household consumption–savings decision is part of the analysis. This conclusion is reassuring, since some policy analysts are uncomfortable with the proposition that new knowledge has to be embedded within labour, as it is in the human capital approach.

But there remains a question concerning the likely size of this permanent effect of savings policy on the growth rate. To have some idea about this, we insert illustrative values for the model's parameters into the expression that we have derived for $(dn)/(ds/s)$. We leave it for the reader to work out this response expression and to insert the following parameter values (and others if there is a desire for sensitivity testing). Here we simply report what emerges for the following calibration. We assume $\gamma = 1.2$ and $\lambda g = 0.1$, so the initial growth rate $n = 0.02$. Further, we assume $\alpha = 0.4$ and $r = \delta = 0.04$, so the initial capital–output ratio is 2. Finally, we assume $\lambda = 0.31$, and that the initial values for output and the savings rate are 1.59 and 0.08. These parameter values are appealing for two reasons: taken individually, they are broadly consistent with actual observations, and taken together they satisfy all the model's equations. We consider a doubling of the savings rate. This calibration implies that we can expect the productivity growth rate to rise by just one-fifth of 1 percentage point. Given that this thought experiment involves a dramatically large pro-savings initiative, this outcome has to be interpreted as rather modest.

11.5 An evaluation of endogenous growth analysis

We have considered several endogenous growth models in this chapter. Since there are several differences across the modelling approaches and the policy implications, it would be helpful to have some sort of common-sense base for relating this overall literature to the world of actual policy making. Thus, in this section of the chapter, we provide a 'back-of-the-envelope' estimate of the pay-off from increased investment in education – an estimate that is not based on any specific or formal macro model.

By comparing people's incomes – people with and without further education – many labour economists have estimated the returns to more education. A typical result from these cross-section regression equations (involving earnings as a function of years of schooling) is that the annual return to education is in the 7.5 per cent range. We use this return to estimate the higher standards of living that we might enjoy if *everyone* were more educated. This is a controversial thing to do, since it may be that much of the estimated return in the cross-section regressions just reflects a signal – that smarter people can make it through school and less clever people cannot. So, even if school does nothing but visibly separate people into these two groups, employers will find it useful to use this signal of native intelligence to save decision-making costs. The education process itself may not raise productivity. If this is the case, and the high private return reflects just signalling, then we should not apply it in an economy-wide thought experiment. After all, a signal has no discriminating power if everyone has the credential. Despite this controversy, we assume that education is not just a signal. This means that the following calculation is biased toward finding too big a pay-off from more investment in education. This bias only supports the conclusion that we reach, however, since the estimated pay-off is very small – despite the upward bias.

Consider transferring 1 per cent of *GDP* out of current consumption and into education. This reallocation is like buying an equity that pays a dividend of 7.5 per cent of 1 per cent of *GDP* forever. The present value of the stream of dividends that accompanies this year's equity purchase is therefore:

$$(.075)(0.01)(a + a^2 + a^3 + \ldots)$$

where $a = (1 + n)/(1 + r)$, and today's *GDP* is unity. This present value expression can be simplified to:

$$(0.075)(0.01)V$$

$$\text{where } V = (1 + n)/(r - n).$$

The cost of this year's equity purchase is the lost consumption, which is 0.01. The net benefit, *NB*, is therefore:

$$NB = (0.01)[(0.075)V - 1].$$

If society embarks on a permanent shift of resources into the education sector, we are making one of these equity purchases every year. The present value, *PV*, of this entire sequence of purchases is $(NB)(V)$. We are interested in the percentage change in living standards that is achieved by moving from a *PV* value of *V* to the new *PV* value of $(NB)(V)$. The ratio of these two outcomes is simply *NB*:

$$NB = (0.01)[((0.075)(1 + n)/(r - n)) - 1].$$

Illustrative parameter values are $r = 0.05$ and $n = 0.02$. These values make *NB* = 1.55 per cent.

Given the amount that most Western countries are spending on education at this time – something in the order of 5 or 6 per cent of *GDP* – a permanent 1 percentage point increase in the share of *GDP* going to education has to be regarded as a very big investment. Yet this investment is estimated to bring a series of annual benefits that is equivalent to a one-time pay-off equal to 1.55 per cent. The interesting question is: what increase in *n* (from a starting value of 0.02, with an r value of 0.05) is required to raise $V = (1 + n)/(r - n)$ by 1.55 per cent? The answer is that n must rise to 0.0205. In other words, when measured in terms of the equivalent permanent annual growth-rate increase, a truly large investment in education can be expected to raise living standards by just one-twentieth of 1 percentage point. This back-of-the-envelope exercise suggests that we temper our enthusiasm – compared to Lucas's. For an alternative defence of this same recommendation, see Easterly (2005).

We close this section with a brief reference to some empirical studies. Have economists found any evidence that policy can permanently affect growth rates? At a very basic level, the answer surely has to be 'yes'. The experience of the formally planned economies has shown dramatically that a market system cannot work without a set of supporting institutions (such as a legal system that creates and protects property rights). These institutions – which induce people to be producers and not just rent seekers – are the outcome of policy.

But, at a more specific level, there is evidence against policy mattering. An example pointed out by D. Romer (2001) involves three countries. During the 1960–97 period, the United States, Bolivia and Malawi had essentially the same growth *rates* and very different fiscal policies. These differences have resulted in very different *levels* of living standards (as predicted by exogenous growth theory) but not different growth rates. Another problem concerns estimated production functions. As these estimates vary the definition of capital from a narrow physical capital measure to an ever more broad measure of capital (including human capital), capital's estimated share ranges between one-third and eight-tenths. No study has found a value of unity (which is required to support the linear differential equation that lies at the core of the endogenous growth framework).

Finally, Jones (1995) has presented some interesting projections. He used the pre-1940 growth experience of the United States as a basis for making a simple projection of how much per-capita incomes would grow over the next 45 years. He replicated what someone might have predicted back then – without taking any account of later developments. He expected these projections to underestimate actual growth, since they ignore the vast increase in human capital that has been accumulated during the later period. For example, the share of scientists and engineers in the labour force has increased by 300 per cent. In addition, now 85 per cent of individuals, not 25 per cent, finish high school. But, despite all this, the simple projections *over* estimated the actual growth in living standards. This exercise has created a challenge for new growth theory to explain.

What advice can be given to policy makers, given all this controversy? It would seem that – if a policy involves definite short-term pain and *uncertain* long-term growth-*rate* gains – it may be prudent to postpone implementing that policy until the insight from further research can be had. This cautious strategy does not mean that nothing can be recommended in the meantime. After all, a number of policies can be present-value justified if they deliver a (much less uncertain) one-time *level* effect on living standards. This may not be as 'exciting' as a permanent growth-rate effect, but it is still very worthwhile. For example, the increase in living standards that we estimated to follow from government debt-reduction policy (see Chapter 10, section 10.4) is a very worthwhile outcome. This analysis assures us that there is a large scope for relevant policy analysis – even if it is too soon to base advice on an area of inquiry – endogenous growth theory – that is still 'in progress'.

11.6 Conclusions

We are leaving our introduction to growth theory in a somewhat untidy state. For one thing, we have had to acknowledge that there are empirical issues that both exogenous growth and endogenous growth models have trouble explaining. For another, our coverage of both the two-sector human capital and the R&D endogenous growth models has been simplified by our focusing entirely on balanced growth outcomes, that is, by our ignoring what happens along the transition path between full equilibria. We make no attempt to rectify this shortcoming in the book's final chapter. Instead, we focus on the reinterpretation of the *AK* model that was explained in section 11.3. There are two reasons for this focus. First, there are no transitional dynamics to be abstracted from in that model. Second, that specification is rich enough to allow for both 'rich' and 'poor' groups to be identified, with the poor owning just some human capital and no physical capital. This set-up is a convenient way to facilitate the consideration of *equity* issues, within the same analytical framework that addresses the overall question of how the growth rate in *average* living standards is affected by policy. The overriding intent is to be able to focus in a simplified but rigorous way on some of the most central questions: Does a pro-growth tax structure hurt those on low incomes? Do policies that reduce unemployment retard growth? Does an ageing population lead to lower growth? It is to these questions that we turn in our final chapter.

12
Growth policy

12.1 Introduction

The purpose of this chapter is to assess the analytical support for several propositions advocated by policy advisers, using a simple version of endogenous growth theory. We proceed through the following steps. First, we consider the optimal tax question by comparing income taxes to expenditure taxes. Without any market distortions allowed for in the analysis, we show that expenditure taxes are recommended. This basic analysis has been very influential. For example, the President's Advisory Panel on Federal Tax Reform in the United States (issued in 2005) argues for a wholesale replacement of the income tax with an expenditure tax. Our analysis indicates how the analytical underpinnings for this proposal are sensitive to the existence of other sources of market failure. For example, in section 12.2, we consider a second-best setting in which the government is 'too big'. In this situation, it is appropriate for the government to levy distorting taxes, so the income tax should not be eliminated. Many policy analysts argue *both* that government is 'too big' and that income taxes are 'bad'. This section of the chapter challenges these analysts to identify the analytical underpinnings of their views. A related finding follows from an extension that allows for two groups of households, one so impatient that these individuals do not accumulate physical capital. Progressive taxation is analysed by taxing only 'rich' households to finance transfers to the 'hand-to-mouth' group. The analysis does not support replacing a progressive income tax with a progressive expenditure tax – again, a challenge to conventional wisdom.

Other second-best considerations are considered in later sections of the chapter. In section 12.3, we focus on consumption externalities. This consideration pushes the conclusion for tax policy in the opposite direction; it strengthens the case for the expenditure tax. Some analysts (such as Frank, 2005, 2012) argue that consumption externalities are very important from an empirical point of view. How else, asks Frank, can we explain the fact that survey measures of subjective happiness show no increases over a half-century, when this period has involved significant increases in the standard measures of economic growth (such as per-capita GDP)?

Unemployment is added in section 12.4. In this second-best situation, an employment subsidy is supported as a mechanism for simultaneously lowering unemployment and raising the growth rate. This result represents a counter-example to those policy analysts who argue that we face a trade-off in the pursuit of low-income support policy (our equity objectives) and higher-growth policy (our efficiency objective). It is interesting that basic endogenous growth theory can provide examples such as this one, which illustrate the relevance of what Alan Blinder (1992) has called 'percolate-up' economics. In this class of models it seems relatively easy to find settings in which a fiscal policy that is designed to help those lower down on the 'economic ladder' has indirect benefits for those up the ladder. This is similar in spirit, but opposite in direction, to the more widely known approach known as 'trickle-down' economics, in which a fiscal policy designed to help the rich generates indirect benefits for those further down the economic ladder.

Finally, in section 12.5, we outline what basic growth models imply about how future living standards may be affected by a major demographic event that is much discussed. We consider the increase in the old-age dependency ratio that will accompany the ageing of the population that will occur as the post-war baby-boom generation moves on to retirement.

12.2 Tax reform: income taxes versus the progressive expenditure tax

Many economists and tax-reform panels have called for a shift in tax policy: a decreased reliance on income taxation and an increased reliance on expenditure taxes. The standard analytical underpinning for this tax-reform proposal is endogenous growth theory. While less emphasis is given to equity considerations in the theory (since standard growth theory involves a single representative agent), policy analysts sometimes call for a *progressive* expenditure tax, to avoid the regressivity that would otherwise accompany the use of sales taxes. The purpose of this section of the chapter is to use a simple version of endogenous growth theory to review this debate.

We begin with the proposition that total output produced each period, Y, is used in two ways. First, it is purchased by households to be consumed that period, C. Second, it is purchased by households to add to their stock of capital, K. $\dot{K}$ refers to that period's increase in capital. The supply-equals-demand statement (the economy's resource constraint) is:

$$Y = C + \dot{K}. \tag{12.1}$$

Next we specify the production process; in this initial case, it is very simple – output is proportional to the one input that is used in the production process, K:

$$Y = AK. \tag{12.2}$$

$A = r$, the rate of return on capital, is the amount that output increases as additional units of the input are hired (the average and marginal product of capital). A is the pre-tax return that households earn on their saving. There are two potentially controversial aspects of this specification of the nation's input–output relationship. First, there are no diminishing returns (as more capital is employed, its marginal product does not fall). As explained in Chapter 11, the economy's equilibrium growth rate is independent of fiscal policy if this assumption is not made, so we follow that standard practice in presenting the standard policy-oriented analysis here. Second, once the output emerges from this production process in the form of consumer goods, it is costless for society to convert that new output into additional capital. Again, this assumption is made to keep the analysis consistent with standard practice. Also, for simplicity, we ignore depreciation of capital.

In this initial specification, the government has just one function; it levies a proportional income tax rate, τ, on the income that households earn by employing their capital, and a proportional sales tax rate, s, on household consumption spending. The government uses this revenue to finance transfer payments, R, to households. The government's balanced-budget constraint is:

$$R = \tau rK + sC. \tag{12.3}$$

This specification of government is rather contrived, since all households are identical. There seems little point in having the government impose taxes that can distort each household's decisions when the only use for that revenue is to transfer the funds back to that same household. We make this assumption simply because it is standard in the tax policy literature. Also, it serves as a base upon which we can build a more interesting analysis of government policy in later sections of the chapter.

The only other relationship that is needed to complete this initial analysis is the one that describes how households make their savings-versus-consumption decision. We assume that their objective is to maximize their utility, which is defined by the following standard function:

$$utility = \int_{i=0}^{\infty} e^{-\rho i} \ln C_i \, di$$

subject to their budget constraint:

$$C + \dot{K} = rK + R - \tau rK - sC.$$

This constraint states that households pay for their consumption and capital accumulation (saving) by spending all their after-tax income and their transfer payment. As we discovered in Chapter 4, the decision rule that follows from this optimization is:

$$\dot{C}/C = r(1 - \tau) - \rho \tag{12.4}$$

The intuition behind this behavioural rule is straightforward. Households save as long as the after-tax return on capital exceeds their rate of impatience, and this saving generates the income that permits positive growth in consumption.

We now write the four numbered equations in a more compact form. We focus on a balanced growth equilibrium in which all aggregates – consumption, output and the capital stock – grow at the same rate $n = \dot{C}/C = \dot{Y}/Y = \dot{K}/K$, with the tax rates, τ and s, the ratio of consumption to capital, $c = C/K$, and the ratio of transfer payments to GDP, $z = R/Y$, all constant. To accomplish this, we divide equations 12.1 and 12.3 through by K and Y respectively, and use equation 12.2 and the balanced growth assumption to simplify the results:

$$r = c + n \tag{12.5}$$

$$z = \tau + sc/r \tag{12.6}$$

$$n = r(1 - \tau) - \rho \tag{12.7}$$

Equations 12.5 to 12.7 solve for the economy's growth rate, n, the consumption-to-capital ratio, c, and one of the tax rates (we assume that the sales tax rate, s, is residually determined by the model). The equations indicate how these three variables are affected by any change we wish to assume in the technology parameter, r, the taste parameter, ρ, and the government's exogenous instruments: the transfers-to-GDP ratio, z, and the income tax rate, τ.

Given the existing debate on tax reform, we focus on cutting the income tax rate, and financing this initiative with a corresponding increase in the sales tax rate. The effect on the growth rate follows immediately from equation 12.7: $dn/d\tau = -r < 0$. Thus, shifting to the sales tax raises the *ongoing growth rate* of living standards. But there is a *one-time level* effect on living standards (consumption) as well, and from equation 12.5 we see that this outcome is adverse: $dc/d\tau = -dn/d\tau = r > 0$. So a shift away from income taxation toward an increased reliance on expenditure taxes shifts the time path of household consumption in the manner shown in Figure 12.1. (We noted in Chapter 11, section 11.2, that this model involves no transitional dynamics; that is, the time path for living standards moves *immediately* from its original equilibrium path to its new one.)

Figure 12.1 Shifting to expenditure taxation – short-term pain for long-term gain

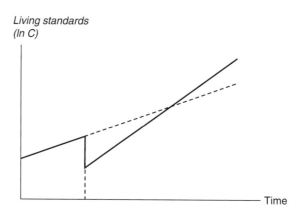

Given that there is short-term pain to achieve long-term gain, it is not immediately clear that this tax substitution is supported. But we can address this issue by using the household utility function. It is shown later in this section that, when the household utility integral is worked out, overall social welfare (SW) is:

$$SW = [\ln C_0 + (n/\rho)]/\rho \qquad (12.8)$$

where $C_0 = cK_0$ and K_0 is the initial capital stock, at the time when the tax substitution takes effect. From equation 12.8, we can determine the effect on overall welfare of the tax substitution:

$$dSW/d\tau = [(1/c)(dc/d\tau) + (1/\rho)(dn/d\tau)]/\rho$$

Using the one-time-level and ongoing-growth-rate effects reported above, we have:

$$dSW/d\tau = r(\rho - c)/(c\rho^2)$$

which can be simplified by using equations 12.5 and 12.7:

$$dSW/d\tau = -(\tau r^2)/(c\rho^2) < 0.$$

The fact that this expression is negative indicates that the government can raise people's material welfare by cutting the income tax rate – all the way to zero. This is the standard proof that we should rely on expenditure, not income, taxes to finance the transfer payments. Because the generosity of the transfer does not affect the household's consumption–saving choice, there is no such thing as an 'optimal' value for transfers. Whatever level is arbitrarily chosen has to be financed by expenditure taxes if the government wishes to maximize the material welfare of its citizens.

We now consider a sensitivity test, by asking how the optimal tax conclusion is affected by our replacing the government transfer payment with a programme whereby the government buys a fraction of the GDP and distributes it free to users (as in the case of government-provided health care). We continue to assume that no resources are needed to convert newly produced consumer goods into new capital or (now) into the government service. Thus, the economy's production function remains equation 12.2, and the resource constraint becomes:

$$Y = C + \dot{K} + G \tag{12.1a}$$

where G is the level of the government-provided good each period. The government budget constraint becomes:

$$G = \tau r K + sC. \tag{12.3a}$$

Finally, we assume that households value the government-provided good, so there are two terms in each period's utility function:

$$utility = \int_{i=0}^{\infty} e^{-\rho i}[\ln C_i + \gamma \ln G_i]di$$

Parameter γ indicates the relative value that households attach to the government service. Since the government imposes the level of government spending, individual households still have only one choice to make; they must choose their accumulation of capital with a view to maximizing the present discounted value of private consumption. The solution to that problem is still equation 12.4.

The model is now defined by equations 12.1a, 12.2, 12.3a and 12.4. Defining $g = G/Y$ as the ratio of the government's spending to GDP, these relationships can be re-expressed in compact form:

$$r(1 - g) = c + n \qquad (12.5a)$$

$$g = \tau + sc/r \qquad (12.6a)$$

$$n = r(1 - \tau) - \rho \qquad (12.7)$$

and the modified overall material welfare function is:

$$SW = [\ln C_0 + \ln G_0 + (1 + \gamma)(n/\rho)]/\rho \qquad (12.8a)$$

It remains true that $dc/d\tau = -dn/d\tau = r$, but, before we make use of these outcomes, we focus on the question of the optimal level of government programme spending. The criterion used to set government spending optimally is to arrange the outcome so that the following condition holds for households:

$$(MU/price)_{private\ consumption\ good} = (MU/price)_{government\ provided\ good}$$

With the price of both goods being unity, and the utility function that has been assumed, this condition requires $1/C = \gamma/G$; that is, the optimal programme-spending-to-GDP ratio is $g^* = \gamma c/r$. This definition is used to simplify the overall welfare effect of varying the income tax rate. The result is:

$$dSW/d\tau = [r^2/(c\rho^2)][(g - g^*) - \tau].$$

As before, material welfare is maximized when this expression is zero, and this requires no income tax ($\tau = 0$) only if government is set optimally ($g = g^*$). If, however, government spending is 'too big' ($g > g^*$), there should be an income tax.

What is the intuition behind the result that income taxes should be used to finance some of the government when government is too big? The answer hinges on the fact that this resource misallocation is in terms of a fixed *proportion* of a *growing* GDP. With growth, the magnitude of the distortion is being magnified. In this case, then, growth has a 'bad' dimension. This is why it becomes 'good' to rely, to some extent, on the anti-growth instrument for raising tax revenue (the income tax rate). Barro and Sala-i-Martin (1995, pp. 144–61) and Marrero and Novales (2005) consider similar models. Their government good is infrastructure, and it enters the production function instead of the utility function. Nevertheless, the same dependence of the optimal tax question on second-best considerations – whether the government has set its expenditure 'properly' – is stressed. A related result is also available in Garcia-Penalosa and Turnovsky (2005) in a developing economy setting. The fact that the government cannot levy taxes on workers in the traditional sector creates a second-best situation, with the result that capital taxation is appropriate.

Returning to our specific analysis, we conclude that we cannot know whether the actual economy involves the 'preferred' ratio of income to sales tax rates or not unless we know whether the government is 'too big' or not, and by how much. Many pro-growth policy analysts defend two propositions: (1) that income taxes are too high relative to sales taxes; and (2) that the government sector is too big. Our analysis has shown that the more correct these analysts are concerning the second proposition, the less standard growth theory supports their first proposition. One purpose of this section of the chapter is to identify this tension that policy analysts do not appear to be aware of.

Thus far, there has been just one input in the production process, and we have interpreted that input quite broadly – as including both physical and human capital. For most of the rest of this chapter, we wish to contrast patient households who plan inter-temporally and acquire physical capital (as discussed above) with households who always spend their entire labour income and transfer payments. To make this comparison explicit, we must distinguish physical capital (K) from human capital (H). As outlined in Chapter 11 (section 11.4), the nation's resource constraint becomes:

$$Y = C + \dot{K} + \dot{H} + G$$

since output is consumed privately, consumed in the form of a government-provided good, or used to accumulate physical and human capital.

Both forms of capital, the government service and consumer goods are produced via the standard Cobb–Douglas production function:

$$Y = \beta K^{\alpha} H^{1-\alpha}$$

By defining $B = H/K$ and $A = \beta B^{1-\alpha}$, the production function can be re-expressed as $Y = AK$ – the same form as that used above.

As explained in Chapter 11 (section 11.4), it is assumed that households rent out their physical and human capital to firms (which are owned by other households). Profit maximization on the part of firms results in factors being hired to the point that marginal products just equal rental prices (r is the rental price of physical capital, w that for human capital):

$$\alpha A = r$$

$$(1 - \alpha)Y/H = w.$$

Households maximize the same utility function. In this case, the constraint involved is: $(1 + s)C + \dot{K} + \dot{H} = r(1 - \tau)K + w(1 - \tau)H$. In addition to the familiar consumption-growth rule, $n = r(1-\tau) - \rho$, the optimization leads to $r = w$. In equilibrium, households must be indifferent between holding their wealth in each of the two forms of capital, and the equal-yields relationship imposes this equilibrium condition. Finally, the government budget constraint is $G = \tau r K + \tau w H + sC$, and the compact version of the full model is:

$$A = \beta B^{1-\alpha}$$

$$r = \alpha A$$

$$n = r(1 - \tau) - \rho$$

$$B = (1 - \alpha)/\alpha$$

$$n(1 + B) = A(1 - g) - c$$

$$g = \tau + sc/A.$$

The endogenous variables are: A, B, r, n, c and one of the tax rates. It is left for the reader to verify that all the conclusions that we noted earlier in this section continue to hold in this slightly extended setting. The reason that the distinction between physical and human capital does not yield different conclusions is because the economy uses the two forms of capital in exactly the same proportions when producing all four items: consumer goods, the government good, new physical capital goods, and new knowledge (human capital).

Perhaps the only result that readers might need help with concerns the effect of the tax substitution on social welfare. The social welfare function is the utility function of the representative household:

$$SW = \int [\ln C + \gamma \ln G] e^{-\rho i} di.$$

We know that $C_i = C_0 e^{ni}$ and that $G_i = G_0 e^{ni}$, so the social welfare expression can be simplified to:

$$SW = [(\ln C_0 + \gamma \ln G_0)/\rho] + (1+\gamma) \int_0^\infty \ln(e^{ni}) e^{-\rho i} di.$$

The integral in this last equation can be re-expressed as n times $\int i e^{-\rho i} di$, and this expression, in turn, can be simplified by using the standard formula $\int u dv = uv - \int v du$, to yield:

$$(-1/\rho)[i + \int -e^{-\rho i} di] = -e^{-\rho i}[(1+\rho i)/\rho^2]_0^\infty.$$

When this solution is evaluated at the extreme points in time, and the result is substituted into the expression for SW, equation 12.8a above is the result. When differentiating that equation with respect to the tax rate, we use $c = C/K$, which implies that $(dC_0/C_0)/d\tau = (dc/c)/d\tau$, since K cannot jump (K_0 is independent of policy). Also, since $G_0 = grK_0$, we know that $dG_0/d\tau = 0$ as well. The $g^* = \gamma c/r$ result emerges from maximizing SW subject to the resource constraint, that is, by evaluating $dSW/dG = 0$.

We now move on to consider income-distribution issues. Mankiw (2000) has suggested that, for the sake of realism, all fiscal policy analyses should allow for roughly half of the population operating as infinitely lived family dynasties and the other half operating hand to mouth. Thus far in this tax policy analysis, we have not followed this advice. Further, since all households have been identical, progressive taxes could not be considered. We now extend our analysis so that we can follow Mankiw's suggestion – both to increase the empirical applicability of the analysis and to make it possible to investigate progressive taxes.

Since the poor consume a higher proportion of their income than do the rich, a shift from a proportional income tax to a proportional expenditure tax makes the tax system regressive. For this reason, policy analysts are drawn to the progressive expenditure tax. It is hoped that this tax can avoid creating an equity problem, as we take steps to eliminate what is perceived to be an efficiency problem. For the remainder of this section of the chapter, we use our otherwise standard growth model to examine shifting between income and expenditure taxes when both taxes are strongly progressive. To impose progressivity in a stark fashion we assume that only 'Group 1' households – the inter-temporal consumption smoothers who are 'rich' – pay any taxes. 'Group 2' households – the 'poor' individuals who live hand to mouth – pay no taxes. In this section, we revert to our original specification concerning the expenditure side of the government budget. Once again we assume that there is no government-provided good; the taxes collected from the rich are used to make a transfer payment to the poor.

Group 2 households have a utility function just like the Group 1 utility function, except that Group 2 people are more impatient. Their rate of time preference is ϕ, which is sufficiently larger than the other group's rate of impatience, ρ, that Group 2 people never save voluntarily, so they never acquire any physical capital. It is assumed that they simply have to do some saving, in the form of acquiring the human capital that is absolutely required for employment. But beyond that 'compulsory' saving (which can be considered as compulsory schooling), they do none. Thus, this group's consumption function is simply their budget constraint. Using E to denote total expenditure by this portion of the population (assumed to be one-half of the total), we have $E = R + (wH-H)/2$, since this group receives no interest income and it pays no taxes, but it does receive the transfer payment. Since only Group 1 pays either tax, both the income and the expenditure tax are progressive. The government budget constraint is $R = \tau[rK + (wH/2)] + sC$. We re-express the Group 2 expenditure relationship and the government budget constraint by using the optimization conditions for firms and the rich households, and by defining $e = E/K$ and $z = R/Y$. The compact form of the model is:

$$A = \beta B^{1-\alpha}$$

$$r = \alpha A$$

$$n = r(1 - \tau) - \rho$$

$$B = (1 - \alpha)/\alpha$$

$$n = r - \alpha(c + e)$$

$$e = zA + [(1 - \alpha)A - Bn]/2$$

$$z = ((1 + \alpha)\tau/2) + (sc/A)$$

We assume that the initial situation involves only an expenditure tax ($\tau = 0$ initially), and we use the model to determine the effects of moving away from this initial situation by introducing the income tax (and cutting the expenditure tax by whatever is needed to maintain budget balance). If the conventional wisdom (that a progressive expenditure tax is preferred to a progressive income tax) is to be supported, the analysis must render the verdict that undesirable effects follow from the introduction of the income tax. We focus on the effects of the tax substitution on the two social welfare expressions:

$$(dSW_1/d\tau) = [(1/c)(dc/d\tau) + (1/\rho)(dn/d\tau)]/\rho$$

$$(dSW_2/d\tau) = [(1/e)(de/d\tau) + (1/\phi)(dn/d\tau)]/\phi$$

It is convenient to assume that the government adjusts the transfer payment, z, as it introduces the income tax and partially removes the expenditure tax, by just the amount necessary to keep the Group 2 households completely unaffected (by ensuring that $(dSW_2/d\tau) = 0$. Since $(dn/d\tau) = -r$, this makes it the case that $(de/d\tau) = er/\phi$. Finally, using $n = r - \alpha(c + e)$, we have $(dc/d\tau) = r(1 - \alpha e/\phi)/\alpha$. When this and the growth-rate effect are substituted into the overall welfare effect for the Group 1 households, and the result is simplified by using the $n = r - \alpha(c + e)$ and $n = r(1 - \tau) - \rho$ equations, with the initial condition that $\tau = 0$, we have:

$$(dSW_1/d\tau) = (er/\alpha c\rho^2)(1 - \rho/\phi).$$

Since the Group 2 households are more impatient than the Group 1 households ($\phi > \rho$), we know that Group 1 households *must* be made better off by introducing a progressive income tax (to partially replace the pre-existing progressive expenditure tax).

The intuition behind this finding runs as follows. From the selfish perspective of the rich, the optimal transfer to the poor is zero. Thus, with a positive transfer, the government is 'too big', and, since this problem is a constant proportion of a growing *GDP*, less growth is preferred. Thus, we have an additional application of the general principle that emerged earlier in this section. The reason that this result is not well known is that standard theory rarely moves beyond an analysis based on a single representative agent. This convention precludes considering equity issues and progressive taxes. When the regressivity of retail sales taxes is raised as an argument against a move to expenditure taxation, the reaction of proponents is to stress that an income tax with unlimited deductions allowed for documented saving is a form of expenditure taxation which can be progressive after all. So the equity concern is dispensed with as an issue that can be overcome with proper administrative design. But, to address the equity issue properly, it has to be introduced back at the level of analytical underpinnings of the contemplated tax reform. That has been the approach taken here, and, as we have discovered, the analysis does not provide the support for conventional policy advice that has been presumed would be forthcoming.

But we must remember that the analysis in this section has involved numerous simplifying assumptions. With a view to providing a little balance, we consider one such assumption in the remainder of this section. By doing so, we reiterate Judd's (2002) point that the presence of imperfect competition strengthens the case for an increased reliance on expenditure taxation. Here we add taxes to the monopolistic competition model that was explained in Chapter 11 (section 11.4). We assume that there is no government-provided good, that the government returns all revenue to private agents as a lump-sum transfer and that all forms of income (including monopoly profits) are taxed at the same rate. As a result, the government budget constraint is $R = \tau Y + sC$. To focus exclusively on the role of imperfect competition we revert to there being just proportional taxes and no hand-to-mouth group of households. The compact listing of the model is quite similar to that discussed in earlier parts of this section, except that the monopoly mark-up parameter, m, appears here in the fourth equation:

$$n(1 + B) = A - c$$

$$B = (1 - \alpha)/\alpha$$

$$A = \beta B^{1-\alpha}$$

$$r = \alpha A/m$$

$$n = r(1 - \tau) - \rho$$

$$z = \tau + sc/A$$

This model determines A, B, r, n, s and c, and we are interested in the effect of a change in the income tax rate, τ, on n, c and social welfare. Thus we derive $dn/d\tau = -r < 0$ and $dc/d\tau = r/\alpha > 0$, and substitute these results into:

$$dSW/d\tau = (1/\rho)\left[\,(1/c)\,(dc/d\tau) + (1/\rho)\,(dn/d\tau)\,\right].$$

After simplifying, the result is:

$$dSW/d\tau = (r^2/c\alpha\rho^2)\,(1 - \tau - m).$$

The best value for the income tax rate is that which makes this expression zero. Since m exceeds unity, that best value for τ is a negative number. Not only should positive income taxation be eliminated; the ownership of capital should be subsidized. This outcome follows from another second-best situation. With imperfect competition, there is the opportunity for profit income. This possibility means a reduced incentive to earn income by acquiring and employing capital (compared to what exists in a competitive economy). If there is no other source of market failure, it is optimal for the government to remove this incentive – by subsidizing the non-profit source of income (that is, by subsidizing capital accumulation).

In the real economy, there are probably several market failures, for example both imperfect competition and an over-expanded government (at least as viewed from the perspective of the rich). As we have seen in this section of the chapter, the former distortion calls for a negative τ value, while the latter distortion calls for a positive τ value. Without further empirical analysis, it seems difficult to defend the proposition that the best value for the income tax rate is zero.

12.3 Economic growth and subjective happiness

In this section, we address Frank's (2005) concern that standard growth theory ignores the findings of the subjective happiness literature. Despite the dramatic increase in statistics such as per-capita GDP and per-capita consumption over the last 60 years, citizens in all developed economies are telling us in surveys that they do not feel any happier. Frank's explanation for these results is that much of our higher consumption expenditure has been on 'positional goods'. If everyone acquires more of these goods, any one person's relative position is not improved by economic growth. We offer a simple formalization of this argument in this section. As with imperfect competition, increased support for a shift toward expenditure taxation emerges.

Thus far (except when we considered a government-provided good), we have assumed that only one thing affects utility – the household's own level of consumption. We now extend this specification by allowing utility to depend on the amount of leisure that the household chooses. Further, we allow one household's utility to depend inversely on the level of consumption of other households. This last feature is necessary if we are to explore Frank's suggestion that positional goods be taken more seriously in otherwise standard analysis. To simplify the exposition, and to highlight these extensions, we introduce them into the most basic model that was considered in the first few paragraphs of section 12.2. In particular, there is perfect competition, only one composite form of capital, and no hand-to-mouth individuals or government-provided good.

For the present discussion, it is best to think of capital as human capital. Letting x denote the fraction of each household's time that is spent at work, xH is employed capital, and the remainder, $(1 - x)H$, is what is devoted to leisure. The resource constraint, the production function and the government budget constraint are:

$$Y = C + \dot{H}$$

$$Y = rxH$$

$$R = \tau rxH + sC$$

The remaining equations that define the model are the first-order conditions that emerge from the following optimization. Households are assumed to maximize:

$$\int_0^\infty [\ln(C/\overline{C}^\lambda) + \psi \ln((1 - x)H)]e^{-\rho i}di$$

subject to $(1 + s)C + \dot{H} = r(1-\tau)xH + R$, by choosing C, H and x. Parameter λ allows for positional goods. $\overline{C}$ is the average level of consumption of other households. If $\lambda = 0$, no goods are positional, and each individual simply enjoys the direct benefit of what she consumes. But, if $\lambda > 0$, there is some positional element to her consumption, since any given level of consumption is less valuable to her, the higher is everyone else's level of consumption (meaning that she is relatively less well off). If $\lambda = 1$, higher consumption brings this individual no utility if others' consumption rises by the same amount as hers. The standard analysis in the previous section of this chapter implicitly assumes that $\lambda = 0$. In terms of this formalization, Frank recommends an analysis of the $\lambda > 0$ case (which we now provide).

The second argument in the utility function can be interpreted as leisure. Utility is higher, the larger is the fraction of time that the household spends away from work. Since human capital is embedded within each individual, taking leisure means withholding capital from the production process. It is assumed that the ability to enjoy leisure rises with the opportunities that are available and that this range of abilities and options is proportional to the individual's stock of human capital. This specification makes it possible for both arguments in the utility function to grow over time in a balanced fashion.

Optimization yields $\dot{C}/C = r(1-\tau)-\rho$ and $\psi c(1 + s) = r(1-\tau)(1-x)$, so the entire model can be written in compact form as follows:

$$n = r(1 - \tau) - \rho$$

$$\psi c(1 + s) = r(1-\tau)(1-x)$$

$$rx = c + n$$

$$z = \tau + sc/rx$$

where c is now C/H. These four equations define the behaviour that takes place in the decentralized market economy. They can be compared to the four equations that define the outcome that would obtain if a benevolent planner were in charge. The planner would maximize the same utility function, but she would recognize that C could not differ from $\bar{C}$. Formally, this optimization involves maximizing:

$$\int_0^\infty [\ln(C^{1-\lambda}) + \psi \ln((1-x)H]e^{-\rho i}di$$

subject to the economy's resource constraint, $C + \dot{H} = rxH$, by choosing C, H and x. This optimization, along with the associated definitions as before, leads to the following set of relationships:

$$n = r-\rho$$

$$\psi c = r(1-\lambda)(1-x)$$

$$rx = c + n$$

$$z = \tau + sc/rx$$

How can we ensure that the planner's outcome and the decentralized market outcome coincide? We answer this question in two stages. First, if goods are not positional at all ($\lambda = 0$), the outcomes are the same only if $\tau = s = z = 0$. Intuitively, if there is no market failure, there is no role for government. Second, if goods have a positional feature ($\lambda > 0$), the outcomes are the same only if $\tau = 0$, $s = \lambda/(1 - \lambda)$, and $z > 0$. Intuitively, if there is a market failure (a negative externality arising from consumption), consumption should be discouraged. There is no role for an income tax.

Ignoring all the other issues that have been considered in earlier sections of this chapter, then, we can conclude as follows: if goods have a positional feature, then the government should rely on expenditure taxes, not income taxes. But (just as we noted at the end of section 12.2) it is difficult to reach a firm conclusion regarding tax policy if there are *two* sources of market failure in the economy.

12.4 Unemployment and growth

As noted in previous chapters, there has been a revival of interest in what Arthur Okun (1975) called 'the big trade-off' between our equity and efficiency objectives. As a review, consider an employment subsidy – an initiative we considered in Chapter 9 – that is intended to lower unemployment and thereby help the poor. The government has to finance this set of payments, and, if this is accomplished by an increase in general income taxes, there is an increase in the tax burden on the rich. The rich react to the higher taxes by investing and producing less, so that there is a reduction in the average person's material living standards. Okun introduced the metaphor of the leaky bucket to describe the loss of efficiency that is part of the redistribution process – *if there are no pre-existing market failures that redistribution can alleviate*. Okun (1975) argued that 'money must be carried from the rich to the poor in a leaky bucket. Some of it will disappear in transit, so the poor will not receive all the money that is taken from the rich.' This loss involved in the redistribution process is thought to be particularly high if the economy's *ongoing* productivity growth *rate* is reduced by higher taxation.

Endogenous growth theory has shown that we may not have to face the big trade-off. The purpose of this section of the chapter is to argue that employment subsidies that help the poor turn out to raise – not lower – the productivity growth rate in an entirely standard model. Thus, modern analysis suggests that policy makers can pursue egalitarian measures of this sort with much more confidence than is usually thought appropriate. Trade-offs can be avoided if the economy starts from a second-best situation. In the analysis that follows (as in the analysis in Chapter 9, section 9.3), the second-best problem is involuntary unemployment. When labour's price is 'too high' and firms employ 'too little' labour, an employment subsidy can increase overall efficiency – even when that initiative must be financed in a way that increases another distortion. This is because the prospect of being unemployed reduces an individual's incentive to acquire human capital. An employment subsidy reduces this problem, and this is why policies that help the poor – by lowering unemployment – can be pro-growth after all. We pursue this simple idea for the remainder of this section of the chapter.

As in earlier sections, our analysis relies on a very simple version of endogenous growth theory. We follow Scarth (2005), and examine an employment subsidy paid to each firm (which lowers unemployment and so increases the incentive to accumulate human capital). The subsidy is paid for by levying an employee payroll tax. Since this levy reduces the incentive to earn wage income, the financing of the employment subsidy increases unemployment. A formal model is needed to determine whether the unemployment-reducing feature of the policy package (the employment subsidy to firms) dominates, or is dominated by, the unemployment-raising influence that is part of the financing of the employment subsidy. If unemployment is reduced, physical capital has more human capital to work with, so the marginal product of physical capital is higher. This outcome raises the incentive to save, and so increases the economy's growth rate. We now spell out the details of the model that allows us to compare the relative strength of these competing effects.

As usual, we start with the straightforward proposition that supply equals demand: $Y = C + E + \dot{K} + \dot{H}$. The supply of goods produced is either consumed by each of two groups of households – the 'rich' and the 'poor' – or used to accumulate physical and human capital. C is consumption spending by the rich (the Group 1 households), and E is the consumer expenditures of the poor (the Group 2 households).

Both forms of capital, and consumer goods, are produced via a standard production function. The inputs are the *utilized* stocks of physical and human capital. We follow the convention of standard growth theory by abstracting from short-run business cycles. Thus, physical capital is fully utilized. But, because there is structural unemployment, human capital is not. The utilized portion of the stock of human capital is $(1 - u)$, where u is the unemployment rate. The Cobb–Douglas production function is

$Y = \beta K^{\alpha}((1-u)H)^{1-\alpha}$, which is re-expressed as $Y = AK$, since we define $B = (1-u)H/K$, and $A = \beta B^{1-\alpha}$. Compared to standard endogenous growth theory, there is an important difference here. In this model, A is *not* a technologically determined constant. Instead, it rises if structural unemployment is lower, since physical capital has more labour to work with. Thus, parameter A is affected by the government's unemployment policy.

As usual, it is assumed that households rent out their physical and human capital to firms (which are owned by other households). Profit maximization on the part of firms results in factors being hired to the point that marginal products just equal rental prices. The expression for the marginal product of each factor input follows from the Cobb–Douglas production function: $\alpha A = r$ and $(1 - \alpha)Y/(1-u)H = w(1-\theta)$, where r, w and θ are the rental prices of physical and human capital, and the employment subsidy rate.

The remaining relationships that are needed to define the model are the ones that describe how households make their consumption-versus-saving (investment in capital) decision, how the unemployment rate is determined, and how the government finances its employment-creating initiative. We discuss each of these issues in turn.

As in section 12.2, we follow Mankiw (2000) and assume that there are two groups of households, with each representing one-half of the population. One group is patient and the other is not. The patient households save as long as the return on capital exceeds their rate of impatience, and this saving generates the income that is necessary to yield a positive percentage growth rate in consumption. This growth in living standards equals the economy's productivity growth rate. The simplest version of this outcome is the straightforward proposition that the productivity growth rate equals the excess of the interest rate over the household's rate of impatience: $\dot{C}/C = r-\rho$. The other condition that follows from household optimization concerning capital accumulation is that both physical and human capital must generate the same rate of return per unit, so households are indifferent between holding their wealth in each of the two forms of capital. This condition is $r = (1 - u)w(1 - t) + ufw$. In this setting, there is no tax on interest income, so the rate of return on physical capital is simply r. But there is a tax, levied at proportional rate t, on wage income. Individuals are employed $(1 - u)$ proportion of the time, so they pay that payroll tax for that portion of each period. They receive unemployment insurance, with the benefit equalling fraction f of the market wage, and they receive that income for proportion u of the time. So the rate of return on human capital is the weighted average expression just presented.

These forward-looking households make two separate decisions. As a group, each family makes the capital-accumulation decision by following the consumption-growth relationship that was just discussed. Following Alexopoulos (2003), we can think of this decision being executed by the family matriarch, who takes the labour market outcomes of the various family members as exogenous to her planning problem. She chooses the optimal capital-accumulation plan, and allocates the corresponding amount of consumption each period to each family member. Each family member is free to augment that level of consumption by adjusting her labour market involvement. The workers at each firm are assumed to rely on a group representative to negotiate wages with their employer. The negotiator pursues a wage that exceeds the workers' outside option, but only to a limited degree, since the negotiator values a high level of employment as well. As explained in Chapter 8 (section 8.3), unemployment emerges in this setting. Specifically, we have $u = \phi(1-t)(1-\theta)/(1-t-f)$, where $\phi = \alpha(1-v)/v(1-\alpha)$ and θ and $(1-v)$ are the employment subsidy and the weight on the workers' outcome in the arbitrator's Nash–product objective function. Of particular interest here is that the unemployment rate varies inversely with the level of the employment subsidy, and directly with the level of the payroll tax. Clearly, the growth model is not needed to arrive at these conclusions. What the growth-oriented part of the model does is facilitate an examination of how an employment subsidy affects the growth rate of living standards (the productivity growth rate).

Some macroeconomists might find the separate-decisions format for specifying the family unappealing. After all, for some time now, the goal when providing micro-foundations for macroeconomics has been to specify one overall optimization that simultaneously yields all behavioural equations for the agents. But, in the interest of tractability, it is now common to separate certain decisions. As already noted, in her model of efficiency wages and endogenous growth, Alexopoulos (2003) adopts precisely this same separation of the asset-accumulation and labour-market-involvement household decisions. Similarly, in the New Neoclassical Synthesis approach to stabilization policy analysis, modellers specify two separate firms: one to hire the factors and to sell 'intermediate' products, and the other to buy the intermediate products and to sell final products to households. These 'final goods' sellers have no costs at all, other than the menu costs that are incurred when changing prices. The two-stage process involving two separate firms is adopted solely to separate the optimization for gradual price adjustment from the optimization for determining factor demands. Thus, while it can be regarded as contrived, this practice of separating certain decisions appears to be accepted as a necessary way of proceeding in even the most central areas of study in modern macroeconomics. As noted, we follow this practice here.

The second group of households are impatient. They have such a high rate of time preference that they never save – beyond the investment in human capital that is necessary to have a job. As a result, this group simply consume all their income – which is half the after-tax labour income generated each period, minus their spending on acquiring human capital. This group interacts with employers in the same way as was described two paragraphs earlier. Thus, since this group constitute half the population, they represent half the unemployed. They are relatively poor, since by never acquiring any physical capital they receive no 'interest' income. The spending function for Group 2 households is given by $E = [w(1-t)(1-u)H + fuwH - \dot{H}]/2$.

Finally, we note the government's balanced-budget constraint. It is $tw(1-u)H = \theta w(1-u)H + fwuH$, a relationship which states that the payroll tax revenue pays for the employment subsidy and unemployment insurance. After dividing this relationship through by wH, and adding $(1-u)$ to both sides, it can be re-expressed as $(1-t)(1-u) + fu = (1-u)(1-\theta)$, and we use this version when simplifying the model. When the optimal hiring rules are substituted into the equal-yields condition, and this version of the government budget constraint is inserted into the result, we have $H/K = (1-\alpha)/\alpha$, so the introduction of the employment subsidy only affects B, and therefore A, through the $(1-u)$ term.

As usual, balanced growth is assumed, so $\dot{C}/C = \dot{K}/K = \dot{H}/H = n$. Also, we divide the resource constraint and the hand-to-mouth expenditure relationships through by K, and simplify the results by using $\alpha A = r$. The outcomes are $r = n + \alpha(c + e)$ and $e = (r-n)(1-\alpha)/\alpha$, where c and e are defined as C/K and E/K. Finally, we can simplify these relationships further by noting that $n = r - \rho$. We list the compact version of the model as follows:

$$r = \alpha A$$

$$A = \beta B^{1-\alpha}$$

$$B = (1-u)(1-\alpha)/\alpha$$

$$n = r - \rho$$

$$e = (1-\alpha)(\rho/2\alpha)$$

$$c = ((1-\alpha)/\alpha)\rho$$

$$u = \phi(1-t)(1-\theta)/(1-t-f)$$

$$t = \theta + (fu/(1-u))$$

The equations determine the responses of r, A, B, n, e, c, u and t, when the employment subsidy is introduced (θ is increased from an initial value of zero). The first four equations indicate that both the interest rate and the growth rate rise if the unemployment rate is reduced. The next two equations indicate that there is no change in the initial level of consumption for either group of households, so there is long-term gain without short-term pain. To determine whether the unemployment rate is reduced, we take the differential of the final two equations and substitute out the change in the tax rate. We evaluate the resulting expression at the initial value of $\theta = 0$, since we are considering the introduction of the employment subsidy. We have:

$$(du/d\theta) = [(u-\phi) - (\phi(1-t)][(1-f-t) - (f(u-\phi))/(1-u)^2]$$

We need to consider illustrative parameter values to evaluate the sign of this response. To that end, we consider an unemployment rate of 6 per cent and an unemployment insurance replacement rate of one-third, and we use the final two equations to determine the corresponding values for t and ϕ. The reader can readily verify that these values make the direct effect of the employment subsidy very much dominate the indirect effect of raising the payroll tax rate to finance this initiative, so unemployment *is* reduced. So this policy simultaneously helps the poor and raises productivity growth for all households.

As noted above, the intuition for this 'win–win' outcome is straightforward. Introducing the employment subsidy has a direct effect in the labour market – lower unemployment. As a result, physical capital has more labour to work with, and this raises physical capital's marginal product and so raises the interest rate. This represents an increased incentive to save, and the associated accumulation of capital raises the growth rate. The value of the formal model is that it allows us to see that, even when account is taken of how the initiative is financed, there is no short-term pain suffered by either the richer or the poorer households in order to secure the long-term gain (higher productivity growth). We conclude that basic endogenous growth analysis can support initiatives designed to reduce structural unemployment. As we noted when reporting a similar finding in Chapter 9 (section 9.3), this conclusion will not be regarded as too surprising if one recalls the Bhagwati and Ramaswami (1963) theorem – a proposition which states that we have the best chance of improving economic welfare if the attempt to alleviate a distortion is introduced at the very source of that distortion.

Many prominent economists, such as Phelps (1997), Solow (1998) and Freeman (1999), have advocated employment subsidies. As surprising as it may seem, given the high profile that is enjoyed by these advocates of employment subsidies, the investigation of this broad strategy within an endogenous productivity growth setting has not been researched at all extensively. This section of the chapter has been intended as a partial filling of this gap. Of course, much sensitivity testing is needed to see if similar results emerge in other formulations of endogenous growth. Also, it will be instructive to extend this analysis to an open-economy setting. Van der Ploeg (1996) and Turnovsky (2002) provide useful starting points for pursuing this agenda.

12.5 The ageing population and future living standards

There is widespread concern about the living standards that will be available for the generation that follows the baby-boom cohort. According to conventional wisdom, when the baby-boomers are old, the much smaller number of workers in the next generation will face high tax rates (and consequently lower living standards) if the pay-as-we-go public pension and public health care programmes are to be maintained. In this section of the chapter, we introduce readers to how our overlapping generations model can be adapted to make it useful for addressing these questions.

As noted, the challenge posed by the ageing baby-boomers is that the old-age dependency ratio is due to rise noticeably. To analyse this development within the context of the overlapping generations model that was introduced in Chapter 4 (section 4.2), we must introduce a retirement age. Nielsen (1994) has extended Blanchard's (1985b) model in this way. He shows that – with a constant probability of death (equal to p) and a constant overall population (equal to unity) – a retirement age of λ means that the proportion of the population that is in retirement must be $e^{-\lambda p}$ and the proportion of the population that is of working age is $(1-e^{-\lambda p})$. As long as the model is calibrated so that the retirement age (λ) is less than each individual's life expectancy $(1/p)$, each individual will make her life's plans on the assumption that she will need to finance her consumption needs during a retirement period. The old-age dependency ratio is $[e^{-\lambda p}/(1-e^{-\lambda p})]$. Within this framework, we can consider a higher old-age dependency ratio in the model economy by imposing a reduction in the retirement age.

It is a bit difficult to calibrate this model. For example, $p = 0.02$ and $\lambda = 40$ are reasonable specifications in and of themselves. (Recall that, in this framework, there is no separate 'youth' period, so individuals are born at working age, say 20 years; $p = 0.02$ then implies a life expectancy of $20 + 50$ years.) The unappealing thing is that these parameter values imply an old-age dependency ratio that is unrealistically large (roughly equal to the overall dependency ratio). Of course, it should not be surprising that a model which specifies that life expectancy is independent of age, and that people begin working at birth, has some difficulty fitting the facts perfectly. Why, then, do we use such a model? It is because the alternatives have some unappealing features as well.

One alternative is Diamond's (1965) two-period overlapping generations model. The problem with this specification is that each period is the length of one generation, say 35 years. This forces the modeller to specify that it takes 35 years for some output that has been produced but not consumed to actually be used in the production process as new capital. For this reason, Barro and Sala-i-Martin (1995) advise against using this specification. Despite this advice, many analyses are based on this framework. One accessible example is Scarth and Souare (2002). A number of studies (for example, Auerbach and Kotlikoff, 1987) have overcome the limitation of Diamond's two-period specification by analysing a multi-period, discrete-time, overlapping generations model. The disadvantage in this case is that analytical solutions are impossible, so complete reliance on numerical simulation is required. Since it is very difficult for other analysts to undertake sensitivity tests of this work, these other analysts tend to regard the conclusions as having been generated from a 'black box'. As a result, meaningful debate can be limited. It is for these reasons that there is widespread interest in extending Blanchard's continuous-time version of an economy with overlapping generations.

One such extension is by S. Jensen and Nielsen (1993). They allow some dependency of life expectancy on age, since they specify that the probability of death is zero for all individuals who are younger than the exogenous retirement age. Then, there is a constant probability of death once the retirement age is reached. This specification preserves our ability to generate analytical solutions, but not quite as easily as in Nielsen (1994). Other extensions of Blanchard's framework – designed to examine ageing populations and remain analytically tractable – are Faruqee (2003) and Bettendorf and Heijdra (2006). Another variation is offered by Gertler (1999). His model is similar to that of Jensen and Nielsen in that, while individuals are working, they face no probability of death, but they are subject to a constant probability of being retired. And, once retired, there is a constant probability of death.

Gertler focuses on avoiding an implication of logarithmic utility – that the degree of income risk aversion and the preference for inter-temporal substitution is pinned down by the same parameter. As a result, he assumes a more complicated preference function, but one that allows him to aggregate across the different age cohorts without having to assume that wages are constant – and with only one additional state variable entering the dynamic analysis. Nevertheless, since this framework is much messier than Nielsen's, we rely on the latter for the remainder of this section of the chapter.

Recall from Chapter 4 (section 4.2) that (ignoring taxes) the aggregate consumption function in the perpetual-youth version of the overlapping generations model is specified by the following aggregate relationships:

$$C = (p + \rho)(K + H)$$

$$\dot{K} = rK + w - C$$

$$\dot{H} = (r + p)H - w$$

These relationships can be combined to yield the standard aggregate consumption function:

$$\dot{C} = (r - \rho)C - p(p + \rho)K.$$

The Ramsey (1928) specification is nested within this model; it is the special case that exists when $p = 0$. Nielsen's contribution is to add life-cycle features to this model, so that Blanchard's model becomes a special case as well. In Nielsen's set-up, the first two equations are the same as in Blanchard's:

$$C = (p + \rho)(K + H)$$

$$\dot{K} = rK + w - C$$

It is the accumulation identity for human capital that is altered by the existence of retirement. By adding up over cohorts of all ages, and over the remaining years in each individual's life, this accumulation identity becomes:

$$\dot{H} = (r + p)H - w(1 - e^{-\lambda p}) + (w/r)[pe^{-\lambda p}(1 - e^{-\lambda r})].$$

The second term on the right-hand side is smaller than previously, since only a portion of the population is working (and therefore receiving wage income). The (new) third term on the right-hand side accounts for the fact that each individual receives the wage for only a portion of her remaining life. For a detailed derivation of this aggregate human capital accumulation identity, the reader must consult Nielsen (1994). Evaluation of the double integral (across cohorts of different ages and across the remaining years in any one person's life) is only possible if wages are constant. Perfect international capital mobility and constant-returns-to-scale technology are sufficient assumptions to deliver this independence of wages from changes in demography. As a result, it is prudent to limit our application of this particular model to small open economies. In any event, when the three relationships are combined, we have the revised aggregate consumption function:

$$\dot{C} = (r-\rho)C - p(p+\rho)(K-\Omega)$$

$$\Omega = (w/r)(1-e^{-\lambda r})(e^{-\lambda p})/(1-e^{-\lambda p}).$$

As can be seen, the aggregate consumption function is altered when a portion of the population is retired. This is because retirement lowers the aggregate stock of human capital (since human capital is embodied within workers), and it is also because people have an incentive to save more when they have to plan for a period of lower income later in life. As asserted above, this more general consumption function nests the earlier models. For example, when retirement is eliminated (when parameter λ goes to infinity), Nielsen's consumption function reduces to Blanchard's overlapping generations relationship. Then, when the probability of death falls to zero ($p = 0$), Blanchard's model reduces to Ramsey's (1928) analysis of the infinitely lived representative agent. The most general of these three frameworks is needed to consider rising old-age dependency.

As explained in Scarth (2004), a calibrated version of this model can be applied to Canada. The results indicate that Canadians need the government debt-to-GDP ratio to fall to about 25 per cent by 2020 if material living standards are to be increased by about the same amount that the ageing population can be expected to (other things equal) lower living standards. Of course, not all dimensions of the ageing population are captured in this model. For example, as van Groezen et al. (2005) have argued, since the elderly consume a higher proportion of services, and since it is more difficult to have productivity increases in the service sector, ageing can be expected to bring lower growth, and this mechanism is not included in this model. Despite this fact, the Canadian federal government has accepted the 25 per cent value as its target for the debt ratio, and officials have stated that this target is based on the desire to insulate living standards from the coming demographic shock. So it certainly is the case that policy makers do pay attention to the models that we have examined in this book.

12.6 Conclusions

How can our tax system be designed to promote both an increase in fairness (as we compare rich and poor today) and an increase in average living standards over the years to come? How can our structural unemployment problems be addressed without jeopardizing our desire to have more rapidly rising material living standards? What is needed to limit the threat to living standards that is posed by the ageing population? These questions are among the most disputed topics in public policy analysis today. It is the job of the policy-oriented economist to use the analytical structure of our discipline to help inform policy makers on these matters. It is important to identify both the trade-offs and the 'free lunches' that are possible, when confronting these issues. This chapter has been designed to help readers meet this challenge, by explaining how basic growth theory can be directly applied to help us understand these topical questions.

References

Abel, A., N.G. Mankiw, L.H. Summers and R.J. Zeckhauser (1989), 'Assessing dynamic efficiency: theory and evidence', *Review of Economic Studies*, **56**, 1–20.

Adelman, I. and F.L. Adelman (1959), 'The dynamic properties of the Klein–Goldberger model', *Econometrica*, **27**, 596–625.

Aghion, P. and P. Howitt (1998), *Endogenous Growth Theory*, Cambridge, Mass.: MIT Press.

Aghion, P. and P. Howitt (2007), 'Capital, innovation and growth accounting', *Oxford Review of Economic Policy*, **23**, 79–93.

Aghion, P., E. Caroli and C. Garcia-Penalosa (1999), 'Inequality and economic growth: the perspective of the new growth theories', *Journal of Economic Literature*, **37**, 1615–60.

Akerlof, G.A. and J. Yellen (1985), 'A near rational model of the business cycle, with wage and price inertia', *Quarterly Journal of Economics*, **100**, 823–38.

Alexopoulos, M. (2003), 'Growth and unemployment in a shirking efficiency wage model', *Canadian Journal of Economics*, **36**, 728–46.

Alexopoulos, M. (2004), 'Unemployment and the business cycle', *Journal of Monetary Economics*, **51**, 277–98.

Alvi, E. (1993), 'Near-rationality, menu costs, strategic complementarity, and real rigidity: an integration', *Journal of Macroeconomics*, **15**, 619–25.

Amato, J.D. and T. Laubach (2003), 'Rule-of-thumb behaviour and monetary policy', *European Economic Review*, **47**, 791–831.

Ambler, S. and L. Phaneuf (1992), 'Wage contracts and business cycle models', *European Economic Review*, **36**, 783–800.

Andersson, M. and B. Hofmann (2009), 'Gauging the effectiveness of central bank forward guidance', paper presented at the Viessmann European Research Centre Conference on Central Bank Communication, Decision Making and Governance, Wilfred Laurier University, available at: http://www.wlu.ca/viessmann/Conference_9.htm (accessed April 2009).

Andrés, J., J.D. López-Salido and E. Nelson (2005), 'Sticky-price models and the natural rate hypothesis', *Journal of Monetary Economics*, **52**, 1025–53.

Auerbach, A. and L. Kotlikoff (1987), *Dynamic Fiscal Policy*, Cambridge: Cambridge University Press.

Backhouse, R.E. and M. Boianovsky (2013), *Transforming Modern Macroeconomics: Exploring Disequilibrium Microfoundations, 1956–2003*, Cambridge: Cambridge University Press.

Ball, L. (1994), 'What determines the sacrifice ratio?', in N.G. Mankiw (ed.), *Monetary Policy*, Chicago: University of Chicago Press.

Ball, L. (1995), 'Disinflation with imperfect credibility', *Journal of Monetary Economics*, **35**, 5–23.

Ball, L. and N.G. Mankiw (1994), 'A sticky-price manifesto', *Carnegie-Rochester Conference Series on Public Policy*, **41**, 127–51.

Ball, L., D.W. Elmendorf and N.G. Mankiw (1995), 'The deficit gamble', *Journal of Money, Credit and Banking*, **30**, 699–720.

Ball, L., N.G. Mankiw and R. Reis (2005), 'Monetary policy for inattentive economies', *Journal of Monetary Economics*, **52**, 703–25.

Barbie, M., M. Hagedorn and A. Kaul (2004), 'Assessing aggregate tests of efficiency for dynamic economies', *Topics in Macroeconomics*, **4**.

Barlevy, G. (2004), 'The cost of business cycles under endogenous growth', *American Economic Review*, **94**, 964–91.

Barro, R.J. (1977), 'Unanticipated money growth and unemployment in the United States', *American Economic Review*, **67**, 101–15.

Barro, R. (2009), 'Voodoo multipliers', *Economists' Voice*, February, available at: http://www.bepress.com/ev.

Barro, R.J. and D.B. Gordon (1983), 'Rules, discretion and reputation in a model of monetary policy', *Journal of Monetary Economics*, **12**, 101–22.

Barro, R.J. and H.I. Grossman (1971), 'A general disequilibrium model of income and employment', *American Economic Review*, **61**, 82–93.

Barro, R.J. and X. Sala-i-Martin (1995), *Economic Growth*, New York: McGraw-Hill.

Basu, S., M.S. Kimball, N.G. Mankiw and D.N. Weil (1990), 'Optimal advice for monetary policy', *Journal of Money, Credit and Banking*, **22**, 19–36.

Baumol, W.J. (1967), 'Macroeconomics of unbalanced growth: the anatomy of urban crisis', *American Economic Review*, **57**, 419–20.

Benhabib, J., R. Rogerson and R. Wright (1991), 'Homework in macro-economics: household production and aggregate fluctuations', *Journal of Political Economy*, **99**, 1166–87.

Bernanke, B.S. and M. Gertler (1989), 'Agency costs, net worth, and business fluctuations', *American Economic Review*, **79**, 14–31.

Bernanke, B.S. and V.R. Reinhart (2004), 'Conducting monetary policy at very low short-term interest rates', *American Economic Review Papers and Proceedings*, **94**, 85–90.

Bernanke, B.S., M. Gertler and S. Gilchrist (1999), 'The financial accelerator in a quantitative business cycle framework', in M. Woodford and J. Taylor (eds), *Handbook of Macroeconomics*, Amsterdam: Elsevier, pp. 1341–93.

Bettendorf, L.J.H. and B.J. Heijdra (2006), 'Population ageing and pension reform in a small open economy with non-traded goods', *Journal of Economic Dynamics and Control*, **30**, 2389–424.

Bhagwati, J. and V. Ramaswami (1963), 'Domestic distortions, tariffs, and the theory of optimum subsidy', *Journal of Political Economy*, **71**, 44–50.

Bhattarai, S., G. Eggertsson and R. Schoenle (2012), 'Is increased price flexibility stabilizing? Redux', Federal Reserve Bank of New York Staff Report No. 540.

Blackburn, K. and A. Pelloni (2005), 'Growth, cycles, and stabilization policy', *Oxford Economic Papers*, **57**, 262–82.

Blake, A.P. and T. Kirsanova (2004), 'A note on timeless perspective policy design', *Economics Letters*, **85**, 9–16.

Blanchard, O.J. (1981), 'Output, the stock market, and interest rates', *American Economic Review*, **71**, 132–43.

Blanchard, O.J. (1985a), 'Credibility, disinflation and gradualism', *Economics Letters*, **17**, 211–17.

Blanchard, O.J. (1985b), 'Debt, deficits and finite horizons', *Journal of Political Economy*, **93**, 223–47.

Blanchard, O. (2009), 'The state of macro', *Annual Review of Economics*, **1**, 1–20.

Blanchard, O.J. and S. Fischer (1989), *Lectures on Macroeconomics*, Cambridge, Mass.: MIT Press.

Blanchard, O.J. and J. Galí (2010), 'Labor markets and monetary policy: a New Keynesian model with unemployment', *American Economic Journal: Macroeconomics*, **2**, 1–30.

Blanchard, O.J. and N. Kiyotaki (1987), 'Monopolistic competition and the effects of aggregate demand', *American Economic Review*, **77**, 647–66.

Blanchard, O.J. and L.H. Summers (1986), 'Hysteresis and the European unemployment problem', *NBER Macroeconomics Annual*, **1**, 15–78.

Blanchard, O. and P. Weil (2003), 'Dynamic efficiency, the riskless rate, and debt Ponzi games under uncertainty', *Advances in Macroeconomics*, **3**.

Blinder, A.S. (1973), 'Can income taxes be inflationary? An expository note', *National Tax Journal*, **26**, 295–301.

Blinder, A.S. (1981), 'Inventories and the structure of macro models', *American Economic Review Papers and Proceedings*, **71**, 11–16.

Blinder, A.S. (1987), 'Keynes, Lucas, and scientific progress', *American Economic Review Papers and Proceedings*, **77**, 130–35.

Blinder, A. (1992), 'Trickle down or percolate up?', Testimony before the United States Senate Appropriations Subcommittee for Labor, Health and Human Services, May 6.

Bohn, H. (1995), 'The sustainability of budget deficits in a stochastic economy', *Journal of Money, Credit and Banking*, **27**, 257–71.

Bouakez, H. and T. Kano (2006), 'Learning-by-doing or habit formation?', *Review of Economic Dynamics*, **9**, 508–24.

Bouakez, H., E. Cardia and F.J. Ruge-Murcia (2005), 'Habit formation and the persistence of monetary shocks', *Journal of Monetary Economics*, **52**, 1073–88.

Brainard, W. (1967), 'Uncertainty and the effectiveness of policy', *American Economic Review*, **57**, 411–25.

Brock, W.A., S.N. Durlauf and K.D. West (2003), 'Policy evaluation in uncertain economic environments', *Brookings Papers on Economic Activity*, **2003**, 235–322.

Buiter, W. and M. Miller (1982), 'Real exchange rate overshooting and the output cost of bringing down inflation', *European Economic Review*, **18**, 85–123.

Burbidge, J.B. (1984), 'Government debt: reply', *American Economic Review*, **74**, 766–7.

Cagan, P. (1956), 'The monetary dynamics of hyperinflation', in M. Friedman (ed.), *Studies in the Quantity Theory of Money*, Chicago: University of Chicago Press.

Calvo, G.A. (1983), 'Staggered prices in a utility-maximizing framework', *Journal of Monetary Economics*, **12**, 383–98.

Calvo, G.A. and F.S. Mishkin (2003), 'The mirage of exchange rate regimes for emerging market countries', *Journal of Economic Perspectives*, **17**, 99–118.

Calvo, G.A. and M. Obstfeld (1988), 'Optimal time-consistent fiscal policy with finite lifetimes', *Econometrica*, **56**, 411–32.

Campbell, J. and N.G. Mankiw (1987), 'Are output fluctuations transitory?', *Quarterly Journal of Economics*, **52**, 857–80.

Carlstrom, C. and T. Fuerst (1997), 'Agency costs, net worth, and business fluctuations: a computable general equilibrium analysis', *American Economic Review*, **87**, 893–910.

Carroll, C.D. (2001), 'Death to the log-linearized consumption Euler equation! (And very poor health to the second-order approximation)', *Advances in Macroeconomics*, **1**.

Chari, V., P. Kehoe and E. McGrattan (2009), 'New Keynesian models: not yet useful for policy analysis', *American Economic Journal: Macroeconomics*, **1**, 242–66.

Chiang, A.C. (1984), *Fundamental Methods of Mathematical Economics*, 3rd edn, New York: McGraw-Hill.

Christiano, L. and M. Eichenbaum (1992), 'Current real-business-cycle theories and aggregate labor-market fluctuations', *American Economic Review*, **82**, 430–50.

Christiano, L., M. Eichenbaum and C. Evans (2005), 'Nominal rigidities and the dynamic effects of a shock to monetary policy', *Journal of Political Economy*, **113**, 1–45.

Coenen, G., A. Orphanides and V. Wieland (2006), 'Price stability and monetary policy effectiveness when nominal interest rates are bounded at zero', *Advances in Macroeconomics*, **6**.

Cogley, T. and T. Yagihashi (2010), 'Are DSGE approximating models invariant to shifts in policy?', *B.E. Journal of Macroeconomics*, **10** (1), article 27.

Cooley, T.F. and G.D. Hansen (1991), 'The welfare costs of moderate inflation', *Journal of Money, Credit and Banking*, **23**, 483–503.

Cooper, R. and A. John (1988), 'Coordinating coordination failures in Keynesian models', *Quarterly Journal of Economics*, **103**, 441–64.

Cooper, R. and A. Johri (2002), 'Learning by doing and aggregate fluctuations', *Journal of Monetary Economics*, **49**, 1539–66.

Correia, I., E. Farhi, J.P. Nicolini and Pedro Teles (2013), 'Unconventional fiscal policy at the zero bound', *American Economic Review*, **103**, 1172–1211.

Cover, J.P. and P. Pecorino (2004), 'Optimal monetary policy and the correlation between prices and output', *Contributions to Macroeconomics*, **4**.

Das, S.P. and C. Ghate (2005), 'Endogenous distribution, politics, and the growth–equity trade-off', *Contributions to Macroeconomics*, **5**.

De Long, J.B. and L.H. Summers (1986), 'Is increased price flexibility stabilizing?', *American Economic Review*, **76**, 1031–44.

De Long, J.B. and L.H. Summers (2012), 'Fiscal policy in a depressed economy', *Brookings Papers on Economic Activity*, **2012** (Spring), 233–97.

Denes, M., G. Eggertsson and S. Gilbukh (2013), 'Deficits, public debt dynamics and tax and spending multipliers', *Economic Journal*, **123**, F133–63.

Devereux, M., A.C. Head and B.J. Lapham (1993), 'Monopolistic competition, technology shocks, and aggregate fluctuations', *Economics Letters*, **41**, 57–61.

Devereux, M.B., P.R. Lane and J. Xu (2006), 'Exchange rates and monetary policy in emerging market economics', *Economic Journal*, **116**, 478–506.

De Vroey, M. and P. Duarte (2013), 'In search of lost time: the neoclassical synthesis', *B.E. Journal of Macroeconomics*, **13** (1).

Diamond, P.A. (1965), 'National debt in a neoclassical growth model', *American Economic Review*, **55**, 1126–50.

Diamond, P.A. (1984), *A Search-Equilibrium Approach to the Micro Foundations of Macroeconomics*, Cambridge, Mass.: MIT Press.

Dixon, H.D. and E. Kara (2006), 'How to compare Taylor and Calvo contracts: a comment on Michael Kiley', *Journal of Money, Credit and Banking*, **38**, 1119–26.

Domeij, D. (2005), 'Optimal capital taxation and labour market search', *Review of Economic Dynamics*, **8**, 623–50.

Dornbusch, R. (1976), 'Expectations and exchange rate dynamics', *Journal of Political Economy*, **84**, 1161–76.

Drazen, A. and P.R. Masson (1994), 'Credibility of policies versus credibility of policymakers', *Quarterly Journal of Economics*, **90**, 735–54.

Driskill, R. (2006), 'Multiple equilibria in dynamic rational expectations models: a critical review', *European Economic Review*, **50**, 171–210.

Easterly, W. (2005), 'National policies and economic growth', in P. Aghion and S. Durlauf (eds), *Handbook of Economic Growth*, Amsterdam: Elsevier.

Edwards, S. and Y.E. Levy (2005), 'Flexible exchange rates as shock absorbers', *European Economic Review*, **49**, 2079–2105.

Eggertsson, G. (2010a), 'What fiscal policy is effective at zero interest rates?', *NBER Macroeconomics Annual*, **25**, 59–112.

Eggertsson, G. (2010b), 'The liquidity trap', *New Palgrave Dictionary in Economics*, 2nd edn, Houndmills, Basingstoke: Palgrave Macmillan.

Eggertsson, G. (2011), 'Commentary on optimal stabilization policy by G. Mankiw and M. Weinzierl', *Brookings Papers on Economic Activity*, **2011** (Spring).

Eggertsson, G. and P. Krugman (2012), 'Debt, deleveraging, and the liquidity trap: a Fisher–Minsky–Koo approach', *Quarterly Journal of Economics*, **127**, 1469–1513.

Eggertsson, G. and M. Woodford (2004), 'Policy options in a liquidity trap', *American Economic Review Papers and Proceedings*, **94**, 76–9.

Estralla, A. and J. Fuhrer (2002), 'Dynamic inconsistencies: counter-factual implications of a class of rational expectations models', *American Economic Review*, **92**, 1013–28.

Farhi, E., G. Gopinath and O. Itskhoki (2012), 'Fiscal devaluations', mimeo.

Farmer, R.E.A. (1993), *The Macroeconomics of Self-Fulfilling Prophecies*, Cambridge, Mass.: MIT Press.

Farmer, R.E.A. (2010), *How the Economy Works: Confidence, Crashes and Self-Fulfilling Prophecies*, Oxford: Oxford University Press.

Farmer, R.E.A. (2013a), 'Animal spirits, persistent unemployment and the belief function', in Roman Frydman and Edmund Phelps (eds), *Rethinking Expectations: The Way Forward for Macroeconomics*, Princeton, N.J.: Princeton University Press, pp. 251–76.

Farmer, R.E.A. (2013b), 'The natural rate hypothesis: an idea past its sell-by date', NBER Working Paper No. 19267.

Faruqee, H. (2003), 'Debt, deficits, and age-specific mortality', *Review of Economic Dynamics*, **6**, 300–312.

Fatas, A. (2000), 'Do business cycles cast long shadows? Short-run persistence and economic growth', *Journal of Economic Growth*, **5**, 147–62.

Fatas, A. and I. Mihov (2003), 'The case for restricting fiscal policy discretion', *Quarterly Journal of Economics*, **118**, 1419–47.

Favero, C.A. and F. Milani (2005), 'Parameter instability, model uncertainty and the choice of monetary policy', *Topics in Macroeconomics*, **5**.

Fillion, J.-F. (1996), 'L'endettement du Canada et ses effets sur les taux d'intérêt réels de long terme', Bank of Canada Working Paper 96-14.

Fischer, S. (1980), 'Dynamic inconsistency, cooperation, and the benevolent dissembling government', *Journal of Economic Dynamics and Control*, **2**, 93–107.

Fischer, S. (1995), 'Central-bank independence revisited', *American Economic Review Proceedings*, **85**, 201–06.

Fischer, S. and L. Summers (1989), 'Should nations learn to live with inflation?', *American Economic Review Papers and Proceedings*, **79**, 382–7.

Fisher, F.M. (2005), 'Aggregate production functions – a pervasive, but unpersuasive, fairytale', *Eastern Economic Journal*, **31**, 489–91.

Fisher, I. (1933), 'The debt-deflation theory of great depressions', *Econometrica*, **1**, 337–57.

Fleming, J.M. (1962), 'Domestic financial policies under fixed and floating exchange rates', *International Monetary Fund Staff Papers*, **9**, 369–79.

Frank, R.H. (2005), 'Positional externalities cause large and preventable welfare losses', *American Economic Review Papers and Proceedings*, **95**, 137–41.

Frank, R.H. (2012), *The Darwin Economy*, Princeton, N.J.: Princeton University Press.

Freeman, R. (1999), *The New Inequality: Creating Solutions for Poor America*, Boston: Beacon Press.

Friedman, M. (1948), 'A monetary and fiscal framework for economic stability', *American Economic Review*, **38**, 245–64.

Friedman, M. (1953), 'The case for flexible exchange rates', in *Essays in Positive Economics*, Chicago: University of Chicago Press.

Friedman, M. (1957), *A Theory of the Consumption Function*, Princeton, N.J.: National Bureau of Economic Research and Princeton University Press.

Friedman, M. (1959), *A Program for Monetary Stability*, New York: Fordham University Press.

Friedman, M. (1963), *Inflation: Causes and Consequences*, New York: Asia Publishing House.

Frydman, R. and E. Phelps (1983), *Individual Forecasting and Aggregate Outcomes: Rational Expectations Examined*, Cambridge: Cambridge University Press.

Galí, J. (2011), *Unemployment Fluctuations and Stabilization Policies: A New Keynesian Perspective*, Cambridge, Mass.: MIT Press.

Galí, J. and M. Gertler (1999), 'Inflation dynamics: a structural econometric analysis', *Journal of Monetary Economics*, **44**, 195–222.

Galí, J., M. Gertler and J.D. López-Salido (2005), 'Robustness of the estimates of the hybrid New Keynesian Phillips curve', *Journal of Monetary Economics*, **52**, 1107–18.

Galor, O. and J. Zeira (1993), 'Income distribution and macro-economics', *Review of Economic Studies*, **60**, 35–52.

Garcia-Penalosa, C. and S.J. Turnovsky (2005), 'Second-best optimal taxation of capital and labour in a developing economy', *Journal of Public Economics*, **89**, 1045–74.

Geary, R.C. (1950–51), 'A note on a constant-utility index of the cost of living', *Review of Economic Studies*, **18**, 65–6.

Gertler, M. (1999), 'Government debt and social security in a life-cycle economy', *Carnegie-Rochester Series on Public Policy*, **50**, 61–110.

Geweke, J. (1985), 'Macroeconometric modeling and the theory of the representative agent', *American Economic Review Proceedings*, **75**, 206–10.

Giannitsarou, C. (2005), 'E-stability does not imply learnability', *Macroeconomic Dynamics*, **9**, 276–87.

Goodfriend, M. (2004), 'Monetary policy in the New Neoclassical Synthesis: a primer', *Federal Reserve Bank of Richmond Economic Quarterly*, **90**, 21–45.

Goodfriend, M. and R.G. King (1997), 'The New Neoclassical Synthesis and the role of monetary policy', *Macroeconomics Annual*, **12**, 231–83.

Gorbet, F. and J. Helliwell (1971), 'Assessing the dynamic efficiency of automatic stabilizers', *Journal of Political Economy*, **79**, 826–45.

Graham, B.S. and J.R.W. Temple (2006), 'Rich nations, poor nations: how much can multiple equilibria explain?', *Journal of Economic Growth*, **11**, 5–41.

Gravelle, J.G. (1991), 'Income, consumption, and wage taxation in a life-cycle model: separating efficiency from distribution', *American Economic Review*, **67**, 985–95.

Grieve, R. (2010), 'Time to ditch AD-AS?', *Review of Radical Political Economics*, **42**, 315–20.

Groezen, B. van, L. Meijdam and H.A.A. Verbon (2005), 'Serving the old: ageing and economic growth', *Oxford Economic Papers*, **57**, 647–63.

Hahn, F.H. and R.M. Solow (1986), 'Is wage flexibility a good thing?', in W. Beckerman (ed.), *Wage Rigidity and Unemployment*, Baltimore: Johns Hopkins University Press.

Hall, R.E. (2003), 'Modern theory of unemployment fluctuations: empirics and policy applications', *American Economic Review Papers and Proceedings*, **93**, 145–50.

Hall, R.E. and C. Jones (2007), 'The value of life and the rise in health spending', *Quarterly Journal of Economics*, **122**, 39–72.

Hansen, G.D. (1985), 'Indivisible labor and the business cycle', *Journal of Monetary Economics*, **16**, 309–27.

Hansen, G.D. and R. Wright (1992), 'The labor market in real business cycle theory', *Federal Reserve Bank of Minneapolis Quarterly Review*, **16**, 2–12.

Hartley, J.E. (1997), *The Representative Agent in Macroeconomics*, New York: Routledge.

Helpman, E. (2004), *The Mystery of Economic Growth*, Cambridge, Mass.: Harvard University Press.

Hill, G. (2009), 'Letter: Misunderstanding Keynes: Robert J. Barro's "voodoo" multipliers', *Economists' Voice*, February, available at: http://www.bepress.com/ev.

Honkapohja, S. and K. Mitra (2004), 'Are non-fundamental equilibria learnable in models of monetary policy?', *Journal of Monetary Economics*, **51**, 1743–70.

Hotelling, H. (1931), 'The economics of exhaustible resources', *Journal of Political Economy*, **39**, 137–75.

Howitt, P. (1978), 'The limits to stability of full employment equilibrium', *Scandinavian Journal of Economics*, **80**, 265–82.

Howitt, P. (1985), 'Transaction costs in the theory of unemployment', *American Economic Review*, **75**, 88–100.

Howitt, P. (1986), 'The Keynesian recovery', *Canadian Journal of Economics*, **19**, 626–41.

Howitt, P. (2012), 'What have central bankers learned from modern macroeconomic theory?', *Journal of Macroeconomics*, **34**, 11–22.

Howitt, P. and R.P. McAfee (1992), 'Animal spirits', *American Economic Review*, **82**, 493–507.

Huang, K.X.D., L. Zheng and L. Phaneuf (2004), 'Why does the cyclical behavior of real wages change over time?', *American Economic Review*, **94**, 836–57.

Ireland, P.N. (2003), 'Endogenous money or sticky prices?', *Journal of Monetary Economics*, **50**, 1623–48.

Jackson, A.L. (2005), 'Disinflationary boom reversion', *Macroeconomic Dynamics*, **9**, 489–575.

Jensen, H. (2002), 'Targeting nominal income growth or inflation', *American Economic Review*, **94**, 928–56.

Jensen, S. and S. Nielsen (1993), 'Aging, intergenerational distribution and public pension systems', *Public Finance*, **48**, 29–42.

Jones, C.I. (1995), 'Time series tests of endogenous growth models', *Quarterly Journal of Economics*, **91**, 495–525.

Jones, C.I. (2002), *Introduction to Economic Growth*, 2nd edn, New York: W.W. Norton.

Jones, C.I. (2003), 'Population and ideas: a theory of endogenous growth', in P. Aghion, R. Frydman, J. Stiglitz and M. Woodford (eds), *Knowledge, Information, and Expectations in Modern Macroeconomics*, Princeton, N.J.: Princeton University Press.

Judd, K.L. (2002), 'Capital income taxation with imperfect competition', *American Economic Review Papers and Proceedings*, **92**, 417–21.

Keynes, J.M. (1936), *The General Theory of Employment, Interest and Money*, London: Macmillan.

Kim, J. and D.W. Henderson (2005), 'Inflation targeting and nominal-income-growth targeting: when and why are they sub-optimal?', *Journal of Monetary Economics*, **52**, 1463–95.

King, R.G. (1993), 'Will the New Keynesian macroeconomics resurrect the IS–LM model?', *Journal of Economic Perspectives*, **7**, 67–82.

King, R.G. (2000), 'The New IS–LM model: language, logic, and limits', *Federal Reserve Bank of Richmond Economic Quarterly*, **86**, 45–103.

King, R.G. (2006), 'Discretionary policy and multiple equilibria', *Federal Reserve Bank of Richmond Economic Quarterly*, **92**, 1–15.

Kirman, A.P. (1992), 'Whom or what does the representative individual represent?', *Journal of Economic Perspectives*, **6**, 117–36.

Kirsanova, T., C. Leith and S. Wren-Lewis (2006), 'Should central banks target consumer prices or the exchange rate?', *Economic Journal*, **116**, F208–31.

Knight, F.H. (1921), *Risk, Uncertainty and Profit*, London: London School of Economics.

Koskela, E. and R. Schöb (2002), 'Why governments should tax mobile capital in the presence of unemployment', *Contributions to Economic Analysis and Policy*, **1**.

Kremer, M. (1993a), 'The O-ring theory of economic development', *Quarterly Journal of Economics*, **108**, 551–75.

Kremer, M. (1993b), 'Population growth and technical change: One Million B.C. to 1990', *Quarterly Journal of Economics*, **108**, 681–716.

Krugman, P. (2011), 'The profession and the crisis', *Eastern Economic Journal*, **37**, 307–12.

Kydland, F.E. and E.C. Prescott (1977), 'Rules rather than discretion: the inconsistency of optimal plans', *Journal of Political Economy*, **85**, 473–92.

Kydland, F.E. and E.C. Prescott (1982), 'Time to build and aggregate fluctuations', *Econometrica*, **50**, 1345–70.

Lam, J.-P. and W. Scarth (2006), 'Balanced budgets vs. Keynesian built-in stabilizers', mimeo.

Leijonhufvud, A. (1973), 'Effective demand failures', *Swedish Economic Journal*, **75**, 27–48.

Leijonhufvud, A. (2009), 'Macroeconomics and the crisis: a personal appraisal', Centre for Economic Policy Research Policy Insight No. 41.

Levinson, A. (1998), 'Balanced-budgets and business cycles: evidence from the States', *National Tax Journal*, **51**, 715–32.

Lipsey, R.G. (1960), 'The relationship between unemployment and the rate of change of money wage rates in the U.K. 1862–1957: a further analysis', *Economica*, **28**, 1–31.

Lipsey, R. and K. Lancaster (1956), 'The general theory of the second best', *Review of Economic Studies*, **24**, 11–32.

Loh, S. (2002), 'A cold-turkey versus a gradualist approach in a menu cost model', *Topics in Macroeconomics*, **2**.

Lucas, R.E., Jr (1976), 'Econometric policy evaluations: a critique', in K. Brunner and A.H. Meltzer (eds), *The Phillips Curve and the Labor Market*, Amsterdam: North Holland.

Lucas, R.E., Jr (1987), *Models of Business Cycles*, Oxford: Blackwell.

Lucas, R.E., Jr (1988), 'On the mechanics of development planning', *Journal of Monetary Economics*, **22**, 3–42.

Lucas, R.E., Jr and T.J. Sargent (1979), 'After Keynesian macroeconomics', *Federal Reserve Bank of Minneapolis Quarterly Review*, **3**, 1–16.

McCallum, B. (1980), 'Rational expectations and macroeconomic stabilization policy: an overview', *Journal of Money, Credit and Banking*, **12**, 716–46.

McCallum, B.T. (1983), 'On non-uniqueness in rational expectations models: an attempt at perspective', *Journal of Monetary Economics*, **11**, 139–68.

McCallum, B.T. (1984), 'Are bond-financed deficits inflationary? A Ricardian analysis', *Journal of Political Economy*, **92**, 123–35.

McCallum, B.T. (1986), 'On "real" and "sticky-price" theories of the business cycle', *Journal of Money, Credit and Banking*, **18**, 397–414.

McCallum, B.T. (1995), 'Two fallacies concerning central-bank independence', *American Economic Review Proceedings*, **85**, 207–11.

McCallum, B.T. (2001), 'Monetary policy analysis in models without money', *Federal Reserve Bank of St. Louis Review*, **83**, 145–60.

McCallum, B.T. (2003), 'Multiple-solution indeterminacies in monetary policy analysis', *Journal of Monetary Economics*, **50**, 1153–75.

McCallum, B. and E. Nelson (1999), 'An optimizing IS–LM specification for monetary policy and business cycle analysis', *Journal of Money, Credit and Banking*, **27**, 296–316.

McDonald, I. and R.M. Solow (1981), 'Wage bargaining and employment', *American Economic Review*, **71**, 896–908.

McGrattan, E.R. (1994), 'A progress report on business cycle models', *Federal Reserve Bank of Minneapolis Quarterly Review*, **18**, 2–16.

Majundar, S. and S.W. Mukand (2004), 'Policy gambles', *American Economic Review*, **94**, 1207–23.

Malik, H.A. (2004), 'Four essays on the theory of monetary policy', Ph.D. dissertation in economics, McMaster University.

Malinvaud, E. (1977), *The Theory of Unemployment Reconsidered*, Oxford: Blackwell.

Mankiw, N.G. (1985), 'Small menu costs and large business cycles: a macroeconomic model of monopoly', *Quarterly Journal of Economics*, **100**, 529–37.

Mankiw, N.G. (1992), 'The reincarnation of Keynesian economics', *European Economic Review*, **36**, 559–65.

Mankiw, N.G. (2000), 'The savers–spenders theory of fiscal policy', *American Economic Review Papers and Proceedings*, **90**, 120–25.

Mankiw, N.G. and R. Reis (2002), 'Sticky information versus sticky prices: a proposal to replace the New Keynesian Phillips curve', *Quarterly Journal of Economics*, **17**, 1295–1328.

Mankiw, N.G. and W. Scarth (2011), *Macroeconomics*, Canadian edn, 4th edn, New York: Worth Publishers.

Mankiw, N.G. and M. Weinzierl (2006), 'Dynamic scoring: a back-of-the-envelope guide', *Journal of Public Economics*, **90**, 1415–33.

Mankiw, N.G. and M. Weinzierl (2011), 'An exploration of optimal stabilization policy', *Brookings Papers on Economic Activity*, **2011** (Spring), 209–72.

Mankiw, N.G., D. Romer and D.N. Weil (1992), 'A contribution to the empirics of economic growth', *Quarterly Journal of Economics*, **88**, 407–37.

Manning, A. (1990), 'Imperfect competition, multiple equilibria, and unemployment policy', *Economic Journal Supplement*, **100**, 151–62.

Mansoorian, A. and M. Mohsin (2004), 'Monetary policy in a cash-in-advance economy: employment, capital accumulation, and the term structure of interest rates', *Canadian Journal of Economics*, **37**, 336–52.

Marrero, G. and A. Novales (2005), 'Growth and welfare: distorting versus non-distorting taxes', *Journal of Macroeconomics*, **27**, 403–33.

Meadows, D. (1972), *Limits to Growth*, New York: Signet.

Mehra, Y.P. (2004), 'The output gap, expected future inflation and inflation dynamics: another look', *Topics in Macroeconomics*, **4**.

Metzler, L.A. (1941), 'The nature and stability of inventory cycles', *Review of Economics and Statistics*, **23**, 113–29.

Milbourne, R.D., D.D. Purvis and D. Scoones (1991), 'Unemployment insurance and unemployment dynamics', *Canadian Journal of Economics*, **24**, 804–26.

Minford, P. and D. Peel (2002), *Advanced Macroeconomics: A Primer*, Cheltenham, UK and Northampton, MA, USA: Edward Elgar Publishing.

Moseley, F. (2010), 'Criticisms of aggregate demand and aggregate supply and Mankiw's presentation', *Review of Radical Political Economics*, **42** (September), 308–14.

Moutos, T. (2000), 'Neutral technological change and the skill premium', *Economics Letters*, **69**, 365–70.

Moutos, T. and W. Scarth (2004), 'Some macroeconomic consequences of basic income and employment subsidies', in J. Agell, M. Keen and A. Weichenrieder (eds), *Labor Market Institutions and Public Regulation*, Cambridge, Mass.: MIT Press.

Mulligan, C. (2010), 'Aggregate implications of labor market distortions: the recession of 2008–9 and beyond', NBER Working Paper No. 15681.

Mullineux, A. and W. Peng (1993), 'Nonlinear business cycle modelling', *Journal of Economic Surveys*, **7**, 41–83.

Mundell, R.A. (1963), 'Capital mobility and stabilization policy under fixed and flexible exchange rates', *Canadian Journal of Economics and Political Science*, **29**, 475–85.

Mussa, M. (1981), 'Sticky prices and disequilibrium adjustment in a rational model of the inflationary process', *American Economic Review*, **71**, 1020–27.

Nelson, E. (2003), 'The future of monetary aggregates in monetary policy analysis', *Journal of Monetary Economics*, **50**, 1029–59.

Nielsen, S. (1994), 'Social security and foreign indebtedness in a small open economy', *Open Economies Review*, **5**, 47–63.

Nordhaus, W.D. (1992), 'Lethal Model 2: The Limits to Growth revisited', *Brookings Papers on Economic Activity*, **2**, 1–43.

OECD (2009), 'The effectiveness and scope of fiscal stimulus', OECD Economic Outlook Interim Report, March, pp. 105–50, available at: http://www.oecd.org/oecdEconomicOutlook (accessed May 2009).

Oh, S. and M. Waldman (1994), 'Strategic complementarity slows macroeconomic adjustment to temporary shocks', *Economic Inquiry*, **32**, 318–29.

Ohanian, L. (2009), 'The economic crisis from a neoclassical perspective', *Journal of Economic Perspectives*, **24**, 45–66.

Okun, A.M. (1962), 'Potential GNP: its measurement and significance', in *Proceedings of the Business and Economic Statistics Section of the American Statistical Association*, Alexandria, Va.: American Statistical Association, pp. 98–104.

Okun, A.M. (1975), *Equity and Efficiency: The Big Trade-Off*, Washington: Brookings Institution.

Pemberton, J. (1995), 'Trends versus cycles: asymmetric preferences and heterogeneous individual responses', *Journal of Macroeconomics*, **17**, 241–56.

Persson, T. and G. Tabellini (1994), *Monetary and Fiscal Policy*, Cambridge, Mass.: MIT Press.

Pesaran, M.H. (1982), 'A critique of the proposed tests of the natural rate–rational expectations hypothesis', *Economic Journal*, **92**, 529–54.

Pesaran, M.H. (1987), *The Limits to Rational Expectations*, Oxford: Blackwell.

Phelps, E. (1997), *Rewarding Work*, Boston: Harvard University Press.

Pigou, A. (1943), 'The classical stationary state', *Economic Journal*, **53**, 343–51.

Pissarides, C.A. (1998), 'The impact of employment tax cuts on unemployment and wages: the role of unemployment benefits and tax structure', *European Economic Review*, **42**, 155–83.

Ploeg, F. van der (1996), 'Budgetary policies, foreign indebtedness, the stock market and economic growth', *Oxford Economic Papers*, **48**, 382–96.

President's Advisory Panel on Federal Tax Reform (2005), *Final Report*, November 1, available at: http://govinfo.library.unt.edu/taxreformpanel/final-report/.

Ramsey, F.P. (1928), 'A mathematical theory of saving', *Economic Journal*, **38**, 543–59.

Ravenna, F. and C.E. Walsh (2006), 'Optimal monetary policy with the cost channel', *Journal of Monetary Economics*, **53**, 199–216.

Ravenna, F. and C.E. Walsh (2008), 'Vacancies, unemployment, and the Phillips curve', *European Economic Review*, **52**, 1494–1521.

Rebelo, S. (2005), 'Real business cycle models: past, present and future', *Scandinavian Journal of Economics*, **107**, 217–38.

Roberts, J.M. (2006), 'How well does the New Keynesian sticky-price model fit the data?', *Contributions to Macroeconomics*, **6**.

Rogerson, R.D. (1988), 'Indivisible labor, lotteries and equilibrium', *Journal of Monetary Economics*, **21**, 3–16.

Romer, C. (1986), 'Is the stabilization of the postwar economy a figment of the data?', *American Economic Review*, **76**, 314–34.

Romer, C.D. and D. Romer (1989), 'Does monetary policy matter? A new test in the spirit of Friedman and Schwartz', *NBER Macroeconomics Annual*, **4**, 121–70.

Romer, C.D. and D.H. Romer (2004), 'New measure of monetary shocks: derivation and implications', *American Economic Review*, **94**, 1055–85.

Romer, D. (1993), 'The New Keynesian Synthesis', *Journal of Economic Perspectives*, **7**, 5–22.

Romer, D. (2001), *Advanced Macroeconomics*, 2nd edn, New York: McGraw-Hill.

Romer, P. (1990), 'Endogenous technical change', *Journal of Political Economy*, **98**, S71–102.

Rosser, J.B., Jr (1990), 'Chaos theory and the New Keynesian economics', *Manchester School of Economic and Social Studies*, **58**, 265–91.

Rowe, N. (1987), 'An extreme Keynesian macro-economic model with formal micro-economic foundations', *Canadian Journal of Economics*, **20**, 306–20.

Rudd, J. and K. Whelan (2005), 'New tests of the New-Keynesian Phillips curve', *Journal of Monetary Economics*, **52**, 1167–81.

Rudd, J. and K. Whelan (2006), 'Can rational expectation sticky-price models explain inflation dynamics?', *American Economic Review*, **96**, 303.

Rudebusch, G.D. (2005), 'Assessing the Lucas critique in monetary policy models', *Journal of Money, Credit and Banking*, **37**, 245–72.

Saint-Paul, G. (2006), 'Distribution and growth in an economy with limited needs: variable markups and the end of work', *Economic Journal*, **116**, 382–407.

Samuelson, P. (1947), *Foundations of Economic Analysis*, Cambridge, Mass.: Harvard University Press.

Samuelson, P.A. (1955), *Economics*, 3rd edn, New York: McGraw-Hill.

Sargent, T.J. (1978), 'Rational expectations, econometric exogeneity, and consumption', *Journal of Political Economy*, **86**, 673–700.

Sargent, T.J. (1982), 'Beyond demand and supply curves in macro-economics', *American Economic Review Papers and Proceedings*, **72**, 382–9.

Sargent, T.J. and N. Wallace (1981), 'Some unpleasant monetarist arithmetic', *Federal Reserve Bank of Minneapolis Quarterly Review*, **5**, 1–17.

Scarth, W. (2004), 'What should we do about the debt?', in C. Ragan and W. Watson (eds), *Is the Debt War Over?*, Montreal: Institute for Research on Public Policy.

Scarth, W. (2005), 'Fiscal policy can raise both employment and productivity', *International Productivity Monitor*, **11**, 39–46.

Scarth, W. (2007), *Macroeconomics: An Introduction to Advanced Methods*, 3rd edn, Toronto: Thomson.

Scarth, W. (2010a), 'Aggregate demand–supply analysis and its critics: an evaluation of the controversy', *Review of Radical Political Economics*, **42**, 321–6.

Scarth, W. (2010b), 'Stabilization policy debates: assessing the case for fiscal stimulus', in C. Beach, B. Dahlby and P. Hobson (eds), *The 2009 Federal Budget: Challenge, Response and Retrospect*, Kingston, ON: John Deutsch Institute for the Study of Economic Policy, pp. 59–80.

Scarth, W. (2012), 'Employment insurance: a macroeconomic comparison with other income-support initiatives', in K. Banting and J. Medow (eds), *Making EI Work: Research from the Mowat Centre Employment Insurance Task Force*, Montreal: McGill-Queen's University Press, pp. 213–30.

Scarth, W. and M. Souare (2002), 'Baby-boom aging and average living standards', SEDAP Research Paper No. 68.

Schumpeter, J.A. (1942), *Capitalism, Socialism, and Democracy*, 3rd edn, New York: Harper & Brothers.

Shiller, R. (2010), 'How should the financial crisis change how we teach economics?', *Journal of Economic Education*, **41**, 403–09.

Smets, F. and R. Wouters (2003), 'An estimated stochastic dynamic general equilibrium model of the euro area', *Journal of the European Economic Association*, **1**, 1123–75.

Smyth, D.J. (1974), 'Built-in flexibility of taxation and stability in a simple dynamic IS–LM model', *Public Finance*, **29**, 111–13.

Soderstrom, U. (2002), 'Targeting inflation with a role for money', *Contributions to Macroeconomics*, **2**.

Solon, G., R. Barsky and J.A. Parker (1994), 'Measuring the cyclicality of real wages: how important is composition bias?', *Quarterly Journal of Economics*, **109**, 1–25.

Solow, R.M. (1956), 'A contribution to the theory of economic growth', *Quarterly Journal of Economics*, **70**, 65–94.

Solow, R. (1957), 'Technical change and the aggregate production function', *Review of Economics and Statistics*, **39**, 312–20.

Solow, R.M. (1979), 'Another possible source of wage stickiness', *Journal of Macroeconomics*, **1**, 79–82.

Solow, R.M. (1998), *Monopolistic Competition and Macroeconomic Theory*, Cambridge: Cambridge University Press.

Solow, R.M. (2003), 'General comments on Part IV', in P. Aghion, R. Frydman, J. Stiglitz and M. Woodford (eds), *Knowledge, Information, and Expectations in Modern Macroeconomics*, Princeton, N.J.: Princeton University Press.

Solow, R.M. and J.-P. Touffut (2012), 'Introduction: passing the smell test', in R.M. Solow and J.-P. Touffut (eds), *What's Right with Macroeconomics?*, Cheltenham, UK and Northampton, MA, USA: Edward Elgar Publishing.

Stiglitz, J.E. (1979), 'Equilibrium in product markets with imperfect information', *American Economic Review Papers and Proceedings*, **69**, 339–46.

Stiglitz, J.E. (1992), 'Capital markets and economic fluctuations in capitalist economies', *European Economic Review*, **36**, 269–306.

Stone, R. (1954), 'Linear expenditure systems and demand analysis: an application to the pattern of British demand', *Economic Journal*, **64**, 511–27.

Stoneman, P. (1979), 'A simple diagrammatic apparatus for the investigation of a macroeconomic model of temporary equilibria', *Economica*, **46**, 61–6.

Summers, L.H. (1986), 'Some skeptical observations on real business cycle theory', *Federal Reserve Bank of Minneapolis Quarterly Review*, **10**, 23–7.

Summers, L.H. (1988), 'Relative wages, efficiency wages and Keynesian unemployment', *American Economic Review Papers and Proceedings*, **78**, 383–8.

Svensson, L. (1999), 'Price level targeting vs. inflation targeting', *Journal of Money, Credit and Banking*, **31**, 277–95.

Svensson, L. (2003), 'Escaping from a liquidity trap and deflation: the foolproof way and others', *Journal of Economic Perspectives*, **17**, 145–66.

Swan, T.W. (1956), 'Economic growth and capital accumulation', *Economic Record*, **32**, 334–61.

Taylor, J.B. (1977), 'Conditions for unique solutions in stochastic macroeconomic models with rational expectations', *Econometrica*, **45**, 1377–85.

Taylor, J.B. (1979a), 'Estimation and control of a macroeconomic model with rational expectations', *Econometrica*, **47**, 1267–86.

Taylor, J.B. (1979b), 'Staggered wage setting in a macro model', *American Economic Review*, **69**, 108–13.

Taylor, J. (1993), 'Discretion versus policy rules in practice', *Carnegie-Rochester Conference Series on Public Policy*, **39**, 195–214.

Tobin, J. (1969), 'A general equilibrium approach to monetary theory', *Journal of Money, Credit and Banking*, **1**, 15–29.

Tobin, J. (1975), 'Keynesian models of recession and depression', *American Economic Review Proceedings*, **65**, 195–202.

Tobin, J. (1977), 'How dead is Keynes?', *Economic Inquiry*, **15**, 459–68.

Turnovsky, S.J. (2002), 'Knife-edge conditions and the macro-economics of small open economies', *Macroeconomic Dynamics*, **6**, 307–35.

Van Parijs, P. (2000), 'A basic income for all', *Boston Review*, **25** (October/November).

Walsh, C. (2003a), *Monetary Theory and Policy*, 2nd edn, Cambridge, Mass.: MIT Press.

Walsh, C. (2003b), 'Speed limit policies: the output gap and optimal monetary policy', *American Economic Review*, **93**, 265–78.

Wieland, V. (2006), 'Monetary policy and uncertainty about the natural unemployment rate: Brainard-style conservatism versus experimental activism', *Advances in Macroeconomics*, **6**.

Woglom, G. (1982), 'Under-employment equilibrium with rational expectations', *Quarterly Journal of Economics*, **96**, 89–107.

Wolfson, P. (1994), 'A simple Keynesian model with flexible wages: a succinct synthesis', *Journal of Macroeconomics*, **16**, 129–56.

Woodford, M. (1991), 'Self-fulfilling expectations and fluctuations in aggregate demand', in N.G. Mankiw and D. Romer (eds), *New Keynesian Economics*, Cambridge, Mass.: MIT Press.

Woodford, M. (2003a), 'Inflation stabilization and welfare', *Contributions to Macroeconomics*, **3**.

Woodford, M. (2003b), 'Comment on: "Multiple-solution indeterminacies in monetary policy analysis"', *Journal of Monetary Economics*, **50**, 1177–88.

Woodford, M. (2009), 'Convergence in macroeconomics: elements of a new synthesis', *American Economic Journal: Macroeconomics*, **1**, 267–79.

Index